THE GREAT MERCHANTS

Books by Tom Mahoney:

THE GREAT MERCHANTS

PUBLIC RELATIONS FOR RETAILERS
(with Rita Hession)

GEMS AND JEWELRY TODAY
(with Marcus Baerwald)

THE
GREAT MERCHANTS

The Stories of Twenty Famous Retail
Operations and the People Who Made
Them Great

By TOM MAHONEY

HARPER & BROTHERS   PUBLISHERS   NEW YORK

CONTENTS

v

FOREWORD

THIS work presents for the first time in one volume accounts of the history and workings of twenty remarkable retail institutions and the merchants who built them. Any such selection from the biggest field of business has to be somewhat arbitrary but the enterprises reported are both representative of the wide range of modern retailing and of unquestioned importance themselves.

Included in the chronological order of their start are the world's largest department stores, the largest specialty shop, the largest mail-order house, the largest food chain, the largest apparel chain, the largest drugstore and a dozen others that dominate their sections or their special fields. The smallest of them is a million-dollar business. Three have sales of more than a billion dollars a year and one is at the four-billion-dollar mark.

All have distinctions other than size and, though widely diverse in their operations, all have many qualities in common which will interest any student of retailing or business in general. All have definite personalities. Several have pioneered important innovations in retailing and their founders are in the retailing "Hall of Fame" at the Chicago Merchandise Mart. All are persistent and, in most cases, large advertisers. All have made important contributions to the communities in which they operate and some to the nation as well. All have adapted themselves to change and have survived wars, panics, population shifts, and the rivalry of countless competitors.

Each is worthy of a lengthy volume but accounts of many appear here in detail for the first time. There are books in print on only seven of the institutions covered. Professor Ralph M. Hower's *History of Macy's of New York 1858–1919* (Harvard University Press, 1946) is a work of great scholarship on the store for this period. Any account of Sears, Roebuck and Company is indebted to *Catalogues and Counters,* the huge work of Boris Emmet and John E. Jeuck

(The University of Chicago Press, 1950). Professor Henry Givens Baker's *Rich's of Atlanta* (University of Georgia, School of Business Administration, 1953) details the history of that institution.

An entertaining centennial history of Marshall Field & Company is *Give the Lady What She Wants!* by Lloyd Wendt and Herman Kogan (Rand McNally & Company, 1952). Emily Kimbrough's *Through Charley's Door* (Harper & Brothers, 1952) and John Tebbel's *The Marshall Fields* (Dutton, 1947) also are valuable sources on this store. Frank X. Tolbert's *Neiman-Marcus, Texas* (Henry Holt, 1953) records the history of that store. Norman Beasley has recounted the rise of J. C. Penney in *Main Street Merchant* (Whittlesey House, 1948) and J. C. Penney has told his own story in *Fifty Years with the Golden Rule* (Harper & Brothers, 1950). Douglas MacKay's *The Honorable Company* (McClelland & Stewart, revised 1949) is a readable history of the Hudson's Bay Company.

Some of the chapters in this work have appeared in shorter form in *The Reader's Digest, Saturday Evening Post,* and *Coronet,* and the material is used here with the permission of these publications. The writer is under special obligation to Ralph McGill, Atlanta editor, and Mort Weisinger, New York magazine writer, for collaboration on the original magazine accounts of Rich's and Tiffany's. Help on the manuscript also came from Jack Lenhart, Kendall L. Tolle, Caroline Bird, Mary Holbrook, Louise Levitas, Grace Mahoney, Margaret Martin, Mary Ellen Murphy, Jean Rogers, Anita Singer, Septima Snowden, Alberta Thomas and Jean Potts.

Among many others, the author is indebted for information to James Alberts, Douglas Alexander, Marcus Baerwald, Roger Barton, L. L. Bean, Helen Brennan, Ralph Brown, P. A. Chester, Hibbard Christian, Ruth Cole, Hazel Conway, Philip Corrin, Elisa Daggs, J. Gordon Dakins, Richard Gauen, Nixon Griffis, Albert E. Haase, Pat Harden, S. J. Harrington, Dickson Hartwell, Rita Hession, H. D. Hodgkinson, Paul M. Hollister, Harold Horton, William Howard, Ray Josephs, Mark Klauser, Jerome Klein, Alexander Kroll.

Also Agnes Rogers Allen, Irene Bender, Hobart S. Bird, Donald Cooley, John Crone, Stacy Holmes, Clive Howard, Hobart Lewis, Milton Lightner, Carol Menuez, Edna O'Brien, Vee O'Brien, Frank

Rice, Emma Rich, Shirley Rucks, Milton Samuels, Paul Sheldon, Irvin Taubkin, Susan Thompson, Patricia Lochridge.

Also Chess Lagomarsino, Fred Lazarus, Jr., Godfrey M. Lebhar, Maude Lennox, Joseph Liebman, Stanley Marcus, Sam McCool, Marihelen McDuff, Lee Newcomb, Jerome and Nathan Ohrbach, David Parry, John Payne, J. D. Ratcliff, Richard Rich, Barbara Robinson, Carl Ruff, Wheeler Sammons, Joyce Scarborough, Gilda Lewis, Dick Schroeter, Leonard Schwartz, Marie Sheets, Myron S. Silbert, Ed Smith, Wilbur C. Smith, Bee Strawway, Bogart Thompson, Donald C. Vaughan, George Vidal, Frank B. Walker, E. B. Ward, E. B. Weiss, Henry Woods, Thomas Yutzy and Elizabeth T. Zwart.

If this work goes into additional editions, the author hopes to include detailed accounts of several institutions now covered only briefly.

TOM MAHONEY

THE GREAT MERCHANTS

I. Peddlers to Palaces
The Evolution of American Retailing

RETAILING is a business of infinite variety that has been growing in importance ever since primitive men began to produce or snare goods for trade to others for articles that they did not have but needed or desired. As civilization developed, it became easier to do this through merchants, who often traveled from country to country, than by face-to-face exchange. From the shops of early craftsmen, who sold their own wares, and from the stalls of itinerant merchants at medieval fairs, modern stores and modern retailing have evolved.

Every nation can boast at least a few notable stores. In some places, the oldest and newest forms of retailing exist side by side. In Baghdad, the modern Orosi-Back department store sells goods from everywhere at fixed prices while native traders a few yards away haggle with their customers exactly as in the days of Caliph Harun Al-Rashid of the *Arabian Nights.*

Moscow took pride in Muir & Mirrieless, a fine department store run by Scotsmen until the Revolution, and now boasts G.U.M. (State Department Store), an enormous government-owned gray baroque establishment facing the Kremlin on Red Square. Its goods are serviceable and it offers fashion shows five afternoons a week with new styles in overalls for factory girls among the garments modeled. The place attracts as many as 150,000 Russians a day.

France has contributed the great Bon Marché, La Ville de Paris, the original Maison Blanche, and more recently the Galeries Lafayette, whose stores are visited regularly by retailers from all over the world in search of ideas. Its big Paris department store and its five branches do an annual business of $60,000,000 and its chain of 153

I

smaller stores around $150,000,000 additional. A distinction of the Paris store is a day nursery for the care of children of employees.

Harrods, Ltd., of London, founded in 1849 by a grocer named Henry Charles Harrod and managed for many years by Sir Richard Burbidge, is the greatest store in the British Isles and has a branch in Buenos Aires. Harrods business is largely food and clothing but it also arranges funerals, sells real estate, insurance and theater tickets, hires out servants and provides entertainment.

The Mitsukoshi store in Tokyo, the largest department store east of Suez, is even more remarkable. It dates from 1673 and was the foundation of the fortune of the famous Mitsui merchant family. It introduced cash down, *Gen-Gin,* and fixed price, *Kakene-Nashi,* in Japan when few but Quakers practiced the latter in the Western world. From a dry-goods store selling silks and brocades, it gradually became a full-line department store. In addition to supplying complete wedding outfits, it has since 1944 also been furnishing brides and grooms.

There is a government marriage bureau on the first floor. Men and women seeking mates leave their photographs, vital statistics and a list of qualifications they seek in a spouse. Marriage ceremonies are performed in a chapel in the basement. Mitsukoshi offers couples a bargain in services for 700 yen, about $14. This borrows trousseau for the bride, maid service to dress her, rent of an adjoining banquet hall, and tea and cakes for guests. Many Japanese literally owe everything to Mitsukoshi and would never dream of shopping elsewhere.

But nowhere has retailing become so important as in the United States. On its success in distributing the fruits of mass production, the prosperity of our entire economy very largely depends. Retailing is literally the biggest business in the country. Nearly half of all American enterprises are retail businesses. It is a hard, competitive field, with one out of three new ventures failing within the first year, but in no other country have so many stores become vast enterprises.

Why have American retailing institutions grown so hugely? One obvious reason is that never before have there been such quantities of goods and so many customers able to afford them. American stores also have led the world in advertising, the use of electric lights, plate glass, air conditioning, self service, credit, parking lots and other devices for painlessly bringing together buyers and sellers, and causing yesterday's luxuries to become regarded as today's necessities. Nowhere else have competing retailers of every kind gone to such lengths to guarantee satisfaction to every customer. When an American consults his doctor or his lawyer, he must pay regardless of whether he likes the outcome of his case but, in virtually any store, he is assured of happiness or his money back.

Also important is the wide freedom that the retailer enjoys as to what and how he sells in the United States and the consumer's equally glorious freedom as to how and where he will spend his money. In medieval Europe, a man risked his soul as well as his capital when he attempted to sell at a profit goods that he had not made; "The man who buys it in order that he may gain by selling it again unchanged and as he bought it, that man is of the buyers and sellers who are cast forth from God's temple," warned St. Thomas Aquinas. American retailing has never had any such restrictions.

By custom and sometimes by law, for tobacco is often a state monopoly, cigarettes are purchased in Europe from the tobacconist. In the United States, you can buy cigarettes from the American equivalent of the tobacconist. You can also buy them at the drugstore, delicatessen, restaurant, gasoline filling station, and perhaps from a vending machine where you work. Sears, Roebuck and Company will be delighted to sell you a machine for making your own cigarettes.

A consumer may live in a community with but one store but even this does not necessarily mean that he is a captive customer of that store. If he has an automobile, as more and more Americans have, he can get into it and shop a hundred miles away if he likes. Or he may shop by telephone or by mail and what he wants will come to him even though his post office may be in the local store which he is not patronizing.

New forms and variations of retailing are emerging constantly despite the obstacles and harassments thrown in their way by adherents of older forms. The new usually proves neither as problem-solving as its adherents predict nor as destructive as its foes fear. The same fears that are now being voiced about discount houses and robot selling in the past have been shouted about department stores, mail-order houses, trading stamps, chain stores, supermarkets and shopping centers.

The first retail selling in most of America was done by peddlers. Just starting they walked. Those of more stature rode horseback and the even more prosperous rode in wagons or carriages. The father of John D. Rockefeller was a carriage peddler of patent medicines. If the peddler did not plan to return to the community, there was no limit to his chicanery but many of them were responsible men who sold New England wares of good quality repeatedly to the same customers. The espionage of a peddler named Enoch Crosby in behalf of General Washington during the Revolution was the basis of *The Spy*, James Fenimore Cooper's first successful novel.

A peddler's life was strenuous, lonely, and hazardous. When the opportunity developed or "when they found the right place or the right girl," many were happy to settle down as storekeepers. Many dry-goods stores (so called to distinguish them from those which sold liquor or "wet" goods) were started in this way. As soon as he was established as a storekeeper, a peddler began to take a dim view of his former vocation and, as often as not, would contrive to have laws passed requiring exorbitant license fees from peddlers or even banning them entirely.

The many antipeddler efforts culminated in a Green Bay, Wyoming, ordinance making it a misdemeanor for a salesman to call at a home without having been previously "invited" to do so by the occupant. This was upheld by the United States Supreme Court in 1951. But despite all the obstacles, house-to-house selling endures and more than three thousand companies were engaged in it in 1954. Three of them, the Fuller Brush Company, Avon Cosmetics and Stanley Home Products, have sales of more than $46,000,000 a year each.

As money was scarce in rural America early in the nineteenth century, the country general store of nostalgic memory did a lot of its business by barter. Phineas T. Barnum, the great circus man, in his youth learned about human nature while clerking in such a store at Bethel, Connecticut.

Like many greenhorns before me [he wrote later in his autobiography], this was the height of my ambition. Ours was a cash, credit and barter store; and I drove many a sharp trade with old women who paid for their purchases in butter, eggs, beeswax, feathers, and rags, and with men who exchanged for our commodities, hats, axe-helves, oats, corn, buckwheat, hickory-nuts, and other commodities. It was something of a drawback upon my dignity that I was compelled to sweep the store, take down the window-shutters, and make the fire; nevertheless the thought of being a "merchant" fully compensated me for all such menial duties.

There is something to be learned even in a country store. We are apt to believe that sharp trades, especially dishonest tricks and unprincipled deceptions, are confined entirely to the city, and that the unsophisticated men and women of the country do everything on the square. I believe this to be measurably true, but know that there are many exceptions to this rule. Many is the time I cut open bundles of rags, brought to the store by country women in exchange for goods, and declared to be all linen and cotton, that contained quantities of worthless trash in the interior, and sometimes stones, gravel, ashes, etc. . . .

Craftsmen of various kinds, also importers, tailors and apothecaries, as well as peddlers, were among America's earliest merchants and store founders. The oldest business in the United States seems to be the Perot Malting Co., founded in Philadelphia in 1687 and now in Buffalo, New York. What is now A. F. Brombacher & Company, the New York hardware firm, was founded as a cutlery and mechanics' tool business in 1760. Caswell-Massey, America's oldest chemists and perfumers, was begun in Newport, Rhode Island, in 1780 and later moved to New York. Captain Kidd, the pirate, bought perfume there. One of its employees became Sir Henry Wellcome, a founder of Burroughs & Wellcome, the British pharmaceutical firm. Schieffelin & Co., the New York drug house, dates from 1794.

R. C. Williams & Co., Inc., the wholesale grocers identified with the Royal Scarlet brand, began with a fleet of packet ships in 1811. J. H. Thorp & Co., Inc., the New York fabric house, started in 1819. The Gunther Jaeckel, Inc., fur business, began in 1820. John Jacob Astor was once associated with it. Hager & Bro., Inc., was founded as a general store at Lancaster, Pennsylvania, in 1821. It is now a department store run by the fifth generation of the Hager family. William Mills & Son, Inc., New York dealers in fine fishing tackle, and Browning, King & Company, clothiers, date from 1822.

Jacob Reed's Sons, Philadelphia clothiers famous for their uniforms, began in 1825.

Arnold Constable, the oldest New York specialty shop, was founded as a dry-goods store in that year by Aaron Arnold, an immigrant from the Isle of Wight. A century later it was joined with Stewart & Co., and Isaac Liberman, head of the latter, became president. Only a few months junior is Lord & Taylor founded in 1826 by Samuel Lord and George Washington Taylor. It led fashion stores to Fifth Avenue and in recent years has been headed by a woman, Dorothy Shaver, America's first lady of retailing. Another man from the Isle of Wight, George Arnold Hearn, founded Hearn's, the New York department store, in 1827. The S. S. Pierce Co., Boston's fancy grocers, began in 1831. McKesson & Robbins, the wholesale drug firm, dates from 1833.

Gimbel Brothers, Inc., was founded in 1842 in the then frontier town of Vincennes, Indiana, by Adam Gimbel, an immigrant peddler from Bavaria. He inaugurated the one-price policy in the area and advertised: "Fairness and Equality of All Patrons, whether they be Residents of the City, Plainsmen, Traders or Indians." First of the modern Gimbel stores opened in Milwaukee in 1887. A Philadelphia store, since grown to many acres of space, was opened in 1894. New York was invaded in 1909. The Saks Company was absorbed in 1923, Saks Fifth Avenue was opened the next year and the Kaufmann and Baer Company of Pittsburgh purchased in 1925. Under dynamic Bernard F. Gimbel, one of the founder's grandsons who became president in 1927 and board chairman in 1953, the firm developed unusually forceful advertising and promotion. Expansions carried it into Chicago, Detroit, Beverly Hills, Miami Beach, San Francisco and elsewhere. Bruce Alva Gimbel of the fourth generation succeeded his father as president.

Thalhimer Brothers, Inc., began in Richmond, Virginia, and D. H. Holmes in New Orleans in 1842. The former now provides free shower baths for women shoppers. The latter was the first big store in the South to hire women and one of the first to provide free delivery service for customers. Free delivery but by wheelbarrow was the boast also of the store founded by Gershon Fox in 1847 at Hartford, Connecticut. It is now a great department store owned and directed by his granddaughter, Beatrice Fox Auerbach, and boasts a theater for community events. Cartier, Inc., the jewelry firm, was founded in Paris the same year. W. & J. Sloane, the famous home-furnishings firm, started in New York in 1843. The Joseph Horne Co. of Pittsburgh and Famous Barr of St. Louis began in 1849 and what became Scruggs-Vandervoort-Barney, Inc., of the latter city, the following year.

At this time a French silk-stocking manufacturer, dissatisfied with the turn of politics in his country and hearing of gold in California, sold his business and sailed for San Francisco with a shipload of merchandise. He was Felix Verdier, who arrived in May, 1850, and set up a waterfront store which he called The City of Paris, after his ship and also the big French store of that name, and gave it the motto of the French capital, "Fluctuat nec mergitur—It floats, and never sinks." The gold-mad Californians bought his luxurious merchandise almost as fast as he could unload it. From this beginning, the establishment grew into a great and distinctive store guided for generations by the Verdier family.

Eben Jordan, a ribbon clerk from Maine, started Jordan Marsh in Boston in 1851. It is now biggest of the seventy-eight units of the Allied Stores Corporation, which under B. Earl Puckett has become the largest department-store chain. The Rike-Kumler Co. began in Dayton, Ohio, in 1853. Carson Pirie Scott & Co., the great Chicago store, was founded by Scotch-Irish immigrants at LaSalle, Illinois, in 1854. John T. Pirie, a grandson of one of the founders, is now president of the company. The store that became the White House of San Francisco began the same year. Mandel Bros., Inc., was started in Chicago and James A. McCutcheon & Co., "The Linen Store," began in New York in 1855. Younker's, the biggest store in Iowa, was founded by Samuel Younker at Keokuk in 1856 and later removed to Des Moines. Headed now by Morey Sostrin, it has branches throughout the state and also in Omaha, Nebraska, and Wichita, Kansas. Meir & Frank of Portland, Oregon, traces its history to 1857. Julius L. Meier, of the firm, served as Governor of Oregon and organized its state police. Aaron M. Frank, grandson of the founder, is president. The store boasts one of the highest per capita sales records. The Higbee Co. began in Cleveland in 1860. The Daniels & Fisher Stores Co. started in Denver in 1864.

Many of the stores established originally by peddlers, as their communities gained in population, grew into great specialty shops and, in some cases, famous department stores with buildings like palaces. The distinction between specialty shop and department store should be understood.

A specialty shop is a store which, regardless of size, limits its merchandise to certain specialties and appeals to its customers on the basis of fashion or price rather than completeness of stocks. The limitation may simply be the broad classification of merchandise termed "soft goods." It may be as limited as clothing and accessories for brides, expectant mothers, or even tall girls.

A department store, on the other hand, is a large store, organized by departments, selling under one management a wide variety of merchandise, including at least ready-to-wear, dry goods and home furnishings. The U.S. Census considers only stores of this type with sales of $100,000 or more as department stores.

It is difficult to determine at what stage of their history many stores met these qualifications and the identity of the "first" department store is a matter of controversy. Macy's, Wanamaker's and Stewart's all have their partisans, and Joseph Kane, the author of *Famous First Facts,* thinks the distinction belongs to Zion's Co-operative Mercantile Institution founded at Salt Lake City in 1868 by Brigham Young, the Mormon leader.

In any case, America's leading merchant in the middle of the nineteenth century was Alexander Turney Stewart, a self-made millionaire. Born at Lisburn, near Belfast, Ireland, and educated at Trinity College, Dublin, he emigrated at twenty to New York. Two years later in 1823, he opened a small dry-goods store. He moved to a larger one and in 1862 opened the biggest store in the world at Broadway and Tenth Street. He was a single-price pioneer, hired handsome and courteous clerks to charm his woman customers and sold quality merchandise, much of it imported from Europe. "I got it at Stewart's" was a phrase denoting value and satisfaction. Mrs. Abraham Lincoln redecorated the White House with goods from his store.

Stewart sent shiploads of food to famine-stricken Ireland and generously aided sufferers in the Franco-Prussian as well as the American Civil War. He was appointed Secretary of the Treasury by President Grant but was kept from the post by a law forbidding importers to hold the post. He died in 1876. In one of the most bizarre crimes of the century, his body was stolen and recovered to be buried in the Episcopal Cathedral which he gave to Garden City, Long Island, a community which he founded as a model city for workingmen.

A Philadelphia merchant named John Wanamaker replaced Stewart in the American scene and in 1896 acquired his New York store. A son of a bricklayer, he became a partner in 1861 of a brother-in-law in the Oak Hall Clothing Bazaar, a Philadelphia men's clothing store. On the latter's death, Wanamaker, buying usually direct from manufacturers, expanded the business into a great department store. He was the first merchant to buy a full-page newspaper advertisement and personally wrote much of his copy which appeared in national magazines as well as the Philadelphia and New York newspapers.

As early as the Civil War, he had his famous "money back" guarantee in print. He advertised in 1865,

Any article that does not fit well, is not the proper color or quality, does not please the folks at home, or for any reason is not perfectly satisfactory, should be brought back at once, and if it is returned as purchased within ten days, we will refund the money. It is our intention always to give value for value in every sale we make, and those who are not pleased with what they buy do us a positive favor to return the goods and get the money back.

In 1878, he moved his store into a vast unused Philadelphia freight depot, made it the first store completely lighted by incandescent lamps, and advertised that his ground floor of nearly three acres was "the largest space in the world devoted to retail selling on a single floor." The Wanamaker stores sold nearly everything. Their book departments were among the largest. For a time they sold airplanes and Ford automobiles.

Wanamaker, termed "Pious John" by cynical rivals, had many other interests, especially Sunday schools, the Young Men's Christian Association and the Republican party. President Harrison appointed him Postmaster General and possibly the highest point of his life was in 1911 when President William Howard Taft dedicated a new Wanamaker store building in Philadelphia. Though he turned many affairs over to his son, Rodman, John Wanamaker was an alert merchant as long as he lived.

In 1920, when nearly eighty-two years old, he foresaw a postwar downturn in business. Though prices were at a peak, he ordered storewide 30 per cent discount sales. On Saturday, May 8, more than $1,000,000 worth of merchandise was sold, a world record it is believed up until that time. In addition to his advertising contributions, John Wanamaker was a pioneer in employee training and the relations of a store to its customers. One of the last lines that he wrote before his death in 1922 was this: "You have got to run a store that people will feel at home in!"

The Wanamaker stores had some adverse years during the depression. They again became profitable under John E. Raasch, a notable management consultant, who was made executive vice president in 1935, president in 1947 and chairman in 1952. Employee relations were excellent with Local 9 of the Retail Clerks International, American Federation of Labor, which at times spent union funds to advertise Wanamaker's. The firm adapted to changing conditions by opening branches in both the Philadelphia and New York areas but in Manhattan clung too long to its lower Broadway location. One of its two bridge-connected buildings with marble and gold décor was vacated in 1952 and the spacious old store closed entirely the week before Christmas in 1954 as uptown department stores enjoyed a record holiday business.

Mail-order or catalog selling and chain stores became important in the latter half of the nineteenth century. A lowering of postage rates and expansion of postal service made possible the former. It was government policy to aid the farmer and end his isolation. Even today it is possible to mail larger parcels to rural addresses than to those served by first-class post offices.

Young Montgomery Ward, previously a $23-a-week salesman at Marshall Field's, was the first to grasp the opportunity. In 1872, he and a friend, George R. Thorne, started business in Chicago with $2,400 capital. They began in one room with a catalog of one page. "Our business," Ward recalled later, "was looked upon with suspicion by those whom we wished as customers. It was ridiculed by retail merchants, doubted by manufacturers and predicted a short life by all." The results were just the opposite. Sears, Roebuck and Company has been even more successful. Aldens, Inc. (formerly Chicago

Mail Order Company), Spiegel's and National Bellas Hess also have become great enterprises.

The idea of one merchant or one company owning and operating many stores is an old one. The Fuggers of Augsburg had branches in a score of European cities as early as the fifteenth century. It remained for George Huntington Hartford's Great Atlantic & Pacific Tea Company and Frank W. Woolworth to develop the low-cost merchandising possibilities of chain operation and to create chain-store empires.

After experimenting with a "5-cent" table in another store during county fair week in Watertown, New York, Woolworth, a farm boy, established $350 credit and opened his first "5 and 10" on a Utica, New York, side street on February 22, 1879. Receipts were as low as $2.50 some days and the store was a failure. Undaunted, he moved it to Lancaster, Pennsylvania, where it became a success. Seven years later, he had a store in New York where he later built the Woolworth Building, tallest in the world for a time. His company, first of the low-priced chains, grew rapidly, and at his death in 1919, Woolworth left an estate of $27,000,000. When James T. Leftwich became the company's sixth president in 1954 it had 1,981 stores in the United States, Canada and Cuba; 819 in a British affiliate and 50 more in a German company.

Notable successes in the variety and drug chain fields have been attained by J. G. McCrory, S. S. Kresge, S. H. Kress, W. T. Grant, G. C. Murphy, J. J. Newberry, H. L. Green, L. K. Liggett, Charles R. Walgreen and numerous others. There are also highly successful clothing chains like Robert Hall, Bond's, John David and the Lerner Stores Corporation. Joseph J. Lerner, founder of the last, left an estate of more than $3,500,000 when he died in 1953.

With the development of self-service, the super market, the suburban shopping center, and a constant expansion of the variety of goods on their shelves, the grocery chains have steadily increased their gigantic volume. An idea of the extent of the last was conveyed in the plaintive suit of a variety-store owner in 1953. He contended that he took space in one of the 1800 new shopping centers with the assurance that he would have no competition only to find the center's supermarket competing with him in the sale of razor blades, machine oil, fuses, cosmetics, candles, shelf paper, sanitary napkins, brushes, stationery, auto wax and plants.

Super-market methods, of course, can be employed by individual store owners as well as chain operators and items other than food can be sold. An outstanding example is Packard's in Hackensack, New Jersey. Frank William Packard, a Yale graduate with some store experience, acquired the place in the depression. By low prices, advertising, parking space for a thousand automobiles, merchandise of many kinds, and a constant carnival atmosphere, he built it into a $12,000,000 a year business. Sixty per cent of this is in groceries and and it has been described as the "largest retail food operation under one roof," as well as "the world's greatest general store." Packard's also sells liquor, home appliances, books, women's apparel, records, cut flowers, drugs, gasoline and boasts its own barbershop and post office substation.

Still another retailing development is the so-called discount house. Enactment in the thirties of "fair trade" laws encouraging manufacturers of branded goods to set retail prices at levels to insure profits for small retailers proved an invitation to others to flout the rules and, by trimming expenses, sell the articles at a discount. Masters, Inc., the big New York establishment of Steve Masters, began business in 1937.

Operations of Masters, Inc., E. J. Korvette Co. of New York and other discounters did not become huge until appliances, television sets and other hard goods became freely available some years after World War II. Discounters were encouraged also by confusion over the legality of fair trade and the apathy of manufacturers, except General Electric, Sunbeam, Simmons and a few others, in enforcing prices. To make the customer feel a privileged "insider," and in some cases to avoid charges of selling to the general public, most discount houses issue identification cards. These are distributed by the thousand to members of organizations and employees of industrial companies.

A Los Angeles discount house, the Wm. E. Phillips Co., sends catalogs to its card holders at their places of employment. In 1954, a mail-order house, Chicago's National Procurement and Distributing Corporation, was offering six thousand items, including new automobiles, at an average discount of 17 per cent off list. It claimed sales of $26,000,000 the previous year.

A notable discounter in the phonograph record field is Sam

Goody of New York. Selling long-playing records at a markup of about 9 per cent against the usual 38 per cent, he had sales of $125,-000 in 1948, his first year of business. Six years later, his sales were running $3,000,000 a year, and he had catalog customers in every state. His average over-the-counter sale was $13 and mail order $17. With each $30 purchase, he gave away a long-playing attachment. Some of his employee benefits attracted attention. When the wife of an employee became pregnant, Goody gave him a ten cent an hour increase in wages with another five cents when the baby was born.

These new trends have affected but not eliminated other forms of retailing. Because of the success of self-service, goods are displayed more openly everywhere. Many conventional department and specialty stores have grown great during the same decades as the big chain development.

But to go back to post-Civil War retailing. L. Hart & Son Co., Inc. began in San Diego in 1866. Stern Bros., now an important Allied unit, was founded in New York in 1867. Strawbridge & Clothier was started by Philadelphia Quakers in 1868. The Herpolsheimer Co. began in Grand Rapids, Michigan, in 1870.

A "Trade Palace" started in 1872 by a former wagon peddler grew into the great L. S. Ayres store in Indianapolis. The Joske Brothers Co. of San Antonio, Texas, was formed in 1873. Forbes and Wallace, Inc., of Springfield, Massachusetts, dates from the next year, as does Rogers Peet Co., New York and Boston men's clothiers. The Hecht Co., with big stores now in Washington, D.C., and a dozen other cities, also began in 1874. The Fair of Chicago started in 1875 and what is now Namm-Loeser's, Inc., of Brooklyn was born in 1876. Two famous jewelry stores, Lambert Brothers of New York and Linz Brothers of Dallas, started in 1877. Best & Co., headed in recent years by the colorful Philip LeBoutillier, was founded in New York in 1879.

David May in Leadville, Colorado, that same year abandoned mining to open a clothing store. He moved it to Denver in 1888. The enterprise, now headed by his grandson, Morton J. May, has grown into the May Department Stores Co. with twenty-four great stores, many of them with branches, located from Baltimore to Los Angeles. Besides stores under the May name, the company owns the Famous Barr Co. of St. Louis, founded in 1849; Kaufmann's, the big Pittsburgh store; the M. O'Neil Co. of Akron, Ohio; and others.

Miller & Rhoads of Richmond began as a partnership in 1885. The Bon Marche of Seattle started in 1890. The Halle Bros. Co. began in Cleveland in 1891. Stix, Baer & Fuller started in St. Louis and Abercrombie & Fitch Co. in New York in 1892 and the W. C. Stripling Co. at Fort Worth in 1893. The Emporium began in San Francisco in 1896. Burdine's, Inc., was founded at Miami in 1898. Ed Schuster & Co., Inc., of Milwaukee started in 1901. New York's Bergdorf Goodman store was born the same year when Herman Bergdorf, an Alsatian tailor, sold first half and then all of his Fifth Avenue business to Edwin Goodman, a designer and tailor from Rochester, New York. This fabulous store once employed Grand Duchess Marie of Russia as a saleslady. In 1902, Franklin Simon opened his Fifth Avenue specialty shop and Titche-Goettinger Co. got under way in Dallas. Marvin and Obadiah Leonard, two energetic Texas farm boys, started a high-volume low-price food and general merchandise business in Fort Worth at the end of World War I. It grew to be the city's biggest advertiser. Leonard's clerks some days cash more checks than local banks. In 1925, Bert Gamble and Phil Skogmo opened at St. Cloud, Minnesota, the first of many Gamble Skogmo, Inc., one-stop shopping centers.

The depression thirties proved an opportunity for many merchants. Max Hess took over Hess Brothers, the Allentown, Pennsylvania, store founded by his father and uncle back in 1897. When he took charge in 1932, its sales were around a million dollars. By a series of dramatic innovations, the best known of which is a "Fashion Caravan" of specially designed International trucks providing traveling fashion shows, he has increased the volume twenty times. The caravan has been the subject of a motion picture. The store has a children's barbershop, which gives the customer a diploma and a lock of his hair on the occasion of his first haircut. The store offers free interior decorating and home-furnishing advice, a club program service and a free art school. It draws trade from a wide area and boasts the largest sales volume of any department store in a city of less than 200,000 population.

Gertz of Jamaica, Long Island, expanded from a stationery and phonograph shop to a full department store in the depression. It built a new building, added parking lots, clubs for kids and a Consumer Advisory Board of forty women's club leaders. Sales increased from less than a million to $30,000,000 a year and by 1950 the store was boasting one of the highest sales per square foot of any department store.

Fred Harvey, a former basement merchandise manager at Marshall Field's, found an opportunity at the same time in Nashville, Tennessee. In 1943, he took over a moribund department store there with sales of $560,000. He remodeled, introduced night openings and advertised with blimps. In a decade, he raised sales to $11,000,-000 and made Harvey's Nashville's leading store.

As the population has increased, and become more urban and less rural, both the sales volumes and costs of big retailers have soared. Harvard University's Graduate School of Business Administration makes an annual study, under the supervision of Malcolm P. McNair, Lincoln Filene Professor of Retailing, of the operations of big department stores. In 1939, this study revealed, it cost 67 cents for the average big department store to make an average sale, then $2.10. By 1954, this had risen to $1.37½. At that time the average gross sale in department stores was $5.15. The profit per sales dollar has dropped since 1950 but for the leaders this has been more than offset by increased volume.

Earnings of retail executives, whether owners or not, have increased with the growth of the enterprises. Securities and Exchange Commission records show scores of retail executives earning salaries of more than $100,000 a year.

There have been increases in many of these salaries in recent years but percentagewise the advances, in most cases, have been much less than the increases for rank-and-file workers. Wages have increased 300 per cent in most stores in less than twenty years. Between 1946 and 1954, average earnings of Sears, Roebuck and Company workers, for example, were increased 43 per cent. Retail wage increases in general have run ahead of increases in the cost of living. In addition, most retail workers enjoy discounts and other benefits of definite value.

Why do shoppers prefer one store to another? The answers are as varied and as mysterious as the ways of love. If a merchant is fortunate enough to be the only one with essential goods, he may not need to be overly concerned with service or price. If he is just one of a swarm of competitors, he must be concerned with everything and must decide what he can offer that will appeal most to his community.

On the basis of 296,752 answers to questions asked customers in 1949, Professor N. H. Comish of the University of Oregon listed efficient salespeople as the first reason for shoppers' preferring one store to another. Of all queried, 34.4 per cent put this factor first. In descending order were these: high quality of goods, wide choice of merchandise, convenient store location, prompt services, low prices of goods, dependable store, nationally advertised goods, attractiveness of store, good store layout. Less frequently mentioned were friendships in store, fair adjustments and liberal credit.

A 1954 survey by the New York University School of Retailing on Thirty-fourth Street and lower Fifth Avenue found that of shoppers who did not buy, 63 per cent blamed an inadequate selection of merchandise. Only 8 per cent said prices were too high and only 3 per cent blamed poor service.

What is necessary for success as a merchant? In the case of "Lord" Timothy Dexter of Newburyport, Massachusetts, in the eighteenth century, luck was enough. He sent eight shiploads of bed warming pans to the tropical West Indies. While the beds of the islanders were warm enough, they found the long-handled articles ideal for frying fish and yams over open fires and for skimming the scum off boiling cane syrup in sugar refining. He reaped a 79 per cent profit.

"A successful merchant," said John Wanamaker, "must be a scientist, a reformer, a custodian of social interests and an arbiter of industrial problems. He must be big enough, broad enough, far seeing enough to survey the whole field and then stand as a bulwark amid the confusions, heresies and fears of his times." The late Ralph E. Gould, famous Maine storekeeper, put it more simply, saying that a shopkeeper needs the determination of Grant, the resourcefulness of Napoleon and the patience of Job.

Today's merchant, according to Harold D. Hodgkinson, general manager of Filene's, must have "a feel for goods," an "instinct for pricing," must be willing to work long hours and perhaps keep his store open at night, must be willing to contribute time and money and assume some responsibility for the welfare of the community in which he operates. Finally he must develop a "personality" for his store.

II. The Hudson's Bay Company

A Venerable Enterprise Reborn

FOUNDED in 1670 to develop the fur trade of then largely un-explored Canada, the Hudson's Bay Company today is the oldest trading company in the world. It is older than the Bank of England. In the past, it has issued its own money and maintained forts. Over its ships, stores and trading posts, it still flies its own officially authorized flag, a British merchant ship ensign initialed "HBC."

The Hudson's Bay Company is the most outstanding example of a commercial enterprise successfully adapting its operations to tre-mendous economic, social and political changes. It might easily have vanished into the mists of history along with the East India Com-pany, the Muscovy Company and all the other great companies chartered by the British Crown in the century of the first Queen Elizabeth. Instead, the venerable company, largely due to shrewd and courageous British leaders, many of them Scottish, developed a vitality that enabled it to survive Arctic cold, wars, disasters, and rivalries of all kinds, to become one of modern Canada's most in-teresting and important enterprises.

Under Sir Patrick Ashley Cooper, its thirtieth governor, who served from 1931 to 1951, and Philip Alfred Chester, who became general manager in 1930 and managing director in 1952, the com-pany has enjoyed a remarkable rejuvenation. In 1952, it paid a 100 per cent stock dividend. In the next few years, accounts "laid before the proprietors" at their annual "general court" in London's Beaver Hall revealed almost doubled earnings and sales volume soaring past $197,000,000, the highest in the company's long history.

Airplanes and radio have now replaced the canoes and dog teams in supplying and communicating with the company's fur-trading posts in the Arctic. The company's 120 privately owned radio stations talk constantly with headquarters at Winnipeg and with each other. Many of these stations also serve as meteorological posts and are a vital part of North America's aircraft warning system.

Oil has been added to the retail, wholesale, land and fur activities of the company. It owns a 25 per cent interest in Hudson's Bay Oil and Gas Company Limited, a new company organized with the Continental Oil Company of Delaware to develop the oil and gas in western Canada. While 160 producing wells had been brought in by mid 1954, exploration costs had been greater than the revenue up until that time. But the oil company has oil and gas rights to 11,646,000 acres, of which 4,460,000 are Hudson's Bay property.

So bright is the oil outlook that a group of speculators attempted to buy stock control of the company with a view toward exploiting the oil and possibly liquidating its other activities. But the management was alert to the threat and the company's twelve thousand proprietors, three-fourths of whom live in the United Kingdom, cold shouldered the idea. The agreement with the Continental Oil Company was extended to 1999.

The big and little Hudson's Bay retail stores have been enlarged and expanded to keep pace with Canada's quickening economy. While it still trails Eaton's and Simpson's in this field, retail sales of "the Bay," as shoppers know it, have increased at a greater rate than for Canadian retailers generally. Let a new uranium mine open or a new hydroelectric development start and the company is likely to have a new store adjoining. A new Hudson's Bay store, for example, serves Kitimat, British Columbia, site of the recently completed world's largest aluminum smelter. Workers building the new railroad from Seven Islands to the new iron development in Labrador were supplied by rolling Hudson's Bay stores in box cars.

Sales of the retail stores department increased from $73,000,000 in the year ended January 31, 1951, the first time such figures were announced, to $95,721,000 for the year ending the same date in 1954. This increase of over 31 per cent compared with an increase of only 18 per cent in Canadian department store sales. This division now accounts for 65 per cent of the company's net profits.

It is possible to buy a marriage license or a ton of coal in the great Hudson's Bay department store in Winnipeg. As the mercury drops as far as forty degrees below zero, the coal business is important. The company also has big department stores, in some places where it once had fur-trading posts, in Vancouver, Calgary, Edmonton, Victoria, and Saskatoon. All carry a complete line of ready-to-wear apparel for men, women and children; house furnishings and floor coverings, appliances, smallwares, sporting goods, china, furs, diamonds, drugs and other types of merchandise.

The company also operates a chain of twenty-two "interior" stores in small cities or towns, usually built around primary industries, and scattered from British Columbia to Quebec. There were only four of these in 1931. In addition, the company sells merchandise at its 196 fur-trading posts, fourteen of which are north of the Arctic Circle. Transportation expense in some places is many times the initial cost of the goods. It is the company policy, however, to maintain low prices on the necessities of life, but profits on merchandise in some years have offset drastic declines in the values of furs.

A wholesale department, which accounts for 10 to 15 per cent of the profits, had sales of $39,000,000 in 1954. This division supplies the famous Hudson's Bay "Point" blankets, its "Best Procurable" Scotch whisky, and other products bearing company brands like "Fort Garry" not only to its outlets but to many others, some of them outside of Canada. The wonderful woolen blankets, which have warmed Antarctic explorers and the climbers of Mt. Everest, indicate how conditions have changed for the company. A four-point blanket once meant that it could be exchanged for four first-grade beaver skins. It now means that it fits a double bed. Incidentally, the company gives every woman employee who has worked five years in a Hudson's Bay store a four-point blanket as a wedding present when she marries. The wholesale department has twenty-six branches and packages tea and coffee. A new coffee plant was opened in Vancouver in 1953.

Though a smaller proportion of company business than in the past, the Hudson's Bay fur business of around $60,000,000 a year is much larger than when this was the company's only activity. It is subject to the vagaries of price and fashion but sometimes accounts for 10 per cent of the earnings. Only the fur operations of Soviet

Russia are larger. It has beaver and muskrat reserves in Quebec, Ontario, Manitoba, Saskatchewan and the Northwest Territories. The company's traders buy furs in Iran and Tibet. Prior to World World II, it sold only its own furs through auctions in London. It now sells also in Montreal and New York and handles furs of others as well as its own, including all of the karakul skins from South Africa.

The story of the fabulous company began with two Indianized Frenchmen, Pierre Esprit Radisson and his brother-in-law, Médart Chouart, Sieur des Groseilliers, of Three Rivers, Quebec. "A more daring pair of international promoters cannot be found in the history of commerce," wrote one historian of them. "Glib, plausible, ambitious, supported by unquestionable physical courage, they were completely equipped fortune hunters."

Less than fifty years after Henry Hudson sailed into the bay while seeking the Northwest Passage, Groseilliers and Radisson made their way there overland from the French settlements and returned in 1660 to Quebec with Indians carrying beaver skins worth $300,000. Of this, the colonial authorities took in taxes and fines for illicit trading all except $20,000. Unable to obtain redress in France, Groseilliers and Radisson turned to England.

They met rebuffs. It was the period in English history depicted for Americans by Kathleen Winsor's best-selling novel, *Forever Amber*. London was ravaged by the bubonic plague and in 1666 was destroyed by the great fire. There was war with Holland. At last in 1668, they talked Prince Rupert, a cousin of King Charles II, and others into outfitting two ships for Hudson's Bay. One was damaged in a storm and turned back.

The other, the *Nonsuch*, a fifty-ton ketch in which Groseilliers sailed, won through to Hudson's Bay and after 118 days anchored in what was christened Rupert's River. The Hudson's Bay Company still has a fur-trading post at the spot. After a winter of trade with the Indians, the *Nonsuch* returned to England with a fortune in beaver skins, then highly valued for men's hats. Thus encouraged, the adventurers and Prince Rupert, their first governor, on May 2, 1670, obtained from King Charles their celebrated charter with privileges greater than any ever granted before or since.

This assured "The Governor and Company of Adventurers of

England trading into Hudson's Bay . . . the sole trade and commerce" and absolute control of all lands they should discover
through Hudson Strait. It was later interpreted to mean the water-
shed of Hudson's Bay. This was a territory equivalent to European
Russia and roughly a third of North America. The Company was
given "the fishing of all sorts of fish . . . and all Mines Royal, as
well discovered as not discovered, of gold, silver, gems and precious
stones. . . ."

Obligations of the company included a promise to seek the Northwest Passage. Two of its ships eventually made this voyage and its
Fort James sailed almost entirely around North America. King
Charles also required the company "to yield and pay" two elks and
two black beavers "whensoever and as often as we our heirs and
successors shall happen to enter into . . . the regions hereby
granted." This curious tribute, compromised to elk heads and beaver
skins, was paid at Winnipeg with ceremony in 1927 to the Prince
of Wales and in 1939 to King George VI.

The company adopted as a coat-of-arms a design of elks and
beaver with the motto "Pro Pelle Cutem," meaning "a man risks
his own skin for the skin of an animal." This represented accurately
its activity for almost two centuries. Ships took out guns, knives,
hatchets, glass beads, brass kettles, blankets and other items and
brought back furs. Hudson's Bay men early established a reputation
for integrity and fair dealing in their trading with the Indians. The
company's affairs prospered. In 1684, the company paid its first
dividend, 50 per cent on the original capital of 10,500 pounds.

Prince Rupert died and was succeeded as governor by James,
Duke of York, an early shareholder. When he became King James
II in 1685, he yielded the position to Lord Churchill, the future
Duke of Marlborough, an ancestor of Winston Churchill, the
twentieth-century premier. Dividends were paid to British rulers
until 1813.

The early struggles of the Hudson's Bay Company with the
French and other rival traders in North America have supplied material for many novels and motion pictures. A young Scot, R. M.
Ballantyne, a nephew of Sir Walter Scott's publisher, was one who
found romance in the fur trade. He joined the company as a clerk in
1841. After six years at York Factory, Norway House and other

posts, he quit and wrote eighty books, most of them novels for boys, based on his adventures. Some are still in print and many a later Hudson's Bay man has confessed that he joined the company after reading Ballantyne's *The Young Fur Traders* or *Hudson's Bay*. The Hudson's Bay Record Society has published thirteen scholarly vol- umes of papers prior to 1846 and the company's magazine, *The Beaver,* is devoted half to history.

French attacks by land and sea reduced the enterprise to a single trading post toward the end of the seventeenth century. In 1697, the company's ships and the French fought the greatest naval action in Arctic history, with the latter victorious. The Treaty of Ryswick that year confirmed the French in their conquests. The Duke of Marl- borough, the company's former governor, however, led the British to victory in the War of the Spanish Succession that followed. In 1713, the Treaty of Utrecht gave all of Hudson's Bay back to the British. From 1690 to 1718, the company paid no dividends. Wolfe's capture of Quebec in 1759 and surrender of Montreal the next year ended French authority in Canada, but in 1782, during the American revolution, La Pérouse, the French admiral, led a final raid into the bay, capturing and burning the company's forts.

As trading moved inland, Hudson's Bay men came into conflict with other fur traders as shrewd and as tough as themselves, who ignored the Royal Charter. These were Scottish-Canadians from Montreal who moved west and in 1784 formed the North West Company, Alexander Mackenzie, who explored the great river which bears his name, was employed by the North West Company. By 1818, this was powerful enough to buy the Pacific Fur Company of John Jacob Astor which had sent traders from the United States into what is now Oregon.

Meanwhile, rivalry of the traders from Hudson's Bay and Mon- treal reached a blood peak in 1816. In that year, Northwesters en- couraged half breeds to massacre settlers established in the Winnipeg area by Lord Selkirk, a Hudson's Bay Company stockholder. Twenty men, including the local governor, were killed. Merger of the companies in 1821 ended this struggle.

From this struggle, Sir George Simpson, one of the most forceful figures in the company's history, rose to head its operations in Canada. Being better managed and free of debt, the Hudson's Bay

Company was dominant in the merger but adopted were a number of North West activities, notably the sharing of 40 per cent of the profits among the chief factors and chief traders. The merged company began to use the St. Lawrence River as well as the bay of its name for its shipping.

An illegitimate son, Simpson, was born in Ross-shire, Scotland, in 1787. At thirty-three, he was a clerk in a London office when he was noticed and sent to Canada by Andrew Colvile, a member of the Hudson's Bay Company's governing London committee. Though bland in manner and short in stature, Simpson proved a man of iron will in the fur trade and advanced rapidly. Some contemporaries called Simpson the "Little Emperor" and one historian described him as "a composite of fur trader, merchant prince, Machiavelli and statesman." With the companies merged, he eliminated duplicating operations and found new sources of revenue.

One of these was the shipment of ice from Alaska, then in Russian hands, to what is now San Francisco. This added "the first ice man of the Pacific" to his distinctions. Under Simpson, the company added posts in San Francisco, Honolulu, Okhotsk, Siberia; and Point Barrow, Alaska. Hudson's Bay furs were sold profitably to the Russian American Fur Company and two thousand skins a year were paid for rent of Alaskan territory. When British and Russians fought in the Crimea, and the Light Brigade charged at Balaklava, the companies by one of the most curious agreements of history preserved neutrality in North America.

Simpson's firm rule was abhorrent to some of his subordinates, notably Dr. John McLoughlin, the "father of Oregon," who resigned, but the company prospered. Dividends were paid every year and additional stock was issued in 1825, 1850, 1852 and 1854 to bring the capital to 500,000 pounds. Simpson made incredible journeys and in 1841 crossed Siberia by land in a trip entirely around the world, to be knighted by Queen Victoria in recognition of the Hudson's Bay Company's exploration in the Arctic. John Henry Pelly, governor of the company, was made a baronet at the time. Sir George entertained the Prince of Wales lavishly on his Canadian tour in 1860 and died of apoplexy a few months later. He was mourned not only by Lady Simpson's four children but by at least seven others from extramarital unions of his lusty early years.

By this time it was obvious that the Canadian West would be opened to settlers and that the Hudson's Bay Company would have to surrender some of its unique privileges. Its charter had been assailed at intervals through the years and had been the subject of a Parliamentary inquiry in 1857. Sensing the chance for a bold financial coup, Thomas Baring of the famous banking family and others in 1863 bought control of the company, paying stockholders 300 pounds for shares previously valued at less than 200 pounds. As soon as control was gained, Baring and his friends named a new London committee and increased the stock to 2,000,000 pounds, most of which was sold to the public.

In 1867, the Dominion of Canada was proclaimed by authority of the British North America Act, a clause of which provided for admission of the company's territory into the new confederation. The details were worked out in a Deed of Surrender. Under this, the Hudson's Bay Company gave up its governmental powers and most of its vast lands. In exchange, the Canadian government paid Hudson's Bay Company 300,000 pounds. The company retained five to three thousand acres around each of its 120 forts or trading posts and, in addition, was allowed to claim one-twentieth of the fertile plain area, a matter of seven million acres, for sale to settlers.

This led to a new crisis. Some of the Indians who had depended all their lives on the paternalistic company for food, shelter and government feared the coming of hordes of settlers and Dominion authority. Under Louis Riel, a persuasive half breed, the métis rose in rebellion and for a time held Fort Garry, the forerunner of modern Winnipeg. As troops approached, Riel, a tragic figure, fled to the United States but later returned, led a new uprising, was captured and hanged.

From this turmoil Donald A. Smith, later Baron Strathcona and Mount Royal, emerged as a powerful Hudson's Bay figure. He was born in the Scotch village of Forres, grim scene of Shakespeare's *Macbeth,* and joined the company as a boy apprentice. A man of thirty years' company experience, he dashed six hundred miles by sleigh to prevent serious bloodshed in the rebellion. He also induced the new management of the company to distribute 107,000 pounds from its Oregon indemnity to the traders hitherto entitled to share in the company profits.

Lord Strathcona speculated successfully in the building of the Canadian Pacific Railroad and many other ventures and became such a large stockholder in the Hudson's Bay Company that he was made deputy governor and, in 1889, governor of the company, becoming the first man from Canada ever to rise through the organization to the top post. He was then sixty-nine years old and divided his energies among many projects. He believed the fur trade doomed and was interested only in sale of the company's seven million acres of land. Oil was undreamed of but coal was a possibility and mineral rights were reserved as the acreage was sold to settlers who poured west.

As the population grew and gold seekers rushed to the Klondike, the western trading posts became stores, but aged Lord Strathcona was more interested in other matters, including a regiment of Canadian cavalry which he sent to the Boer War. He let Timothy Eaton and James Simpson launch and spread their great retail enterprises in the Canadian cities without challenge. He was still governor of the Hudson's Bay Company when he died at ninety-three on January 21, 1914, leaving an estate of $25,000,000 to numerous beneficiaries, including some Eskimo friends of his youth.

His successors took charge vigorously. With outbreak of World War I, the Hudson's Bay Company became purchasing agent for the French government on a 2½ per cent commission basis and also undertook to deliver supplies to Russia via the Arctic port of Archangel. A subsidiary shipping company was formed and it amassed a fleet of 275 vessels for transport. Of these, 110 were lost, principally to submarines.

Five of the company's vessels were frozen in the ice in the winter of 1915–16. An explosion at Bakaritsa gravely damaged five other vessels. In 1917, the icebreaker *Iceland* blew up at Economia, wrecking a steamer alongside, damaging three more and setting munitions on shore afire to start a blaze which lasted for days in weather eighteen degrees below zero. To replace cranes destroyed at the time, the company located a floating one, capable of lifting 125 tons, at the Spanish port of Cadiz and one even larger in Holland and towed them safely to the Arctic port.

Despite mishaps such as these, the company procured and delivered safely some eighteen million tons of cargo. In addition to munitions, this included breadstuffs secured from Algeria, Australia, the Argentine and Canada; sugar from Cuba, Java and Martinique; timber and wood pulp from Canada; coal from England, Canada and the United States; groundnuts, palm kernels and other produce from West Africa and Morocco. During 1918, the company delivered one thousand tons of freight daily in French ports.

One of the most exciting war episodes involved the tug *Vigilant*. Caught in a heavy gale 480 miles out of Queenstown, the eighty-six-ton vessel seemed doomed. Her captain and most of the crew abandoned her and were picked up by a passing steamer. The second mate, a fireman and a greaser, however, refused to quit the ship and brought her safely to Ireland. The company gave them 5,000 pounds as a reward for their heroic work.

The S. S. *Nascopie,* an icebreaker named for a tribe of Indians in Labrador and in time of peace the summer supply ship for the company's Arctic posts, made many wartime voyages to Murmansk and Archangel. In June, 1917, shortly after sailing from Archangel for Montreal, she was attacked by a large enemy submarine. The *Nascopie* shot back. Her fourth shell was a direct hit. The submarine exploded and disappeared. The captain and crew received the thanks of the Admiralty. With peace the *Nascopie* returned to her supply ship duties and was the best-known ship of the Arctic until her thirty-five years of service ended in July, 1947, when she sank after striking a reef at the entrance to Dorset Harbour.

In 1920, Sir Robert Kindersley, the twenty-eighth governor of the company, visited Canada for celebration with some pageantry of the 250th anniversary of the old company. With the war profits, the company built a new London headquarters, Beaver House, on Great Trinity Lane. This contained the finest facilities for the storage and sale of pelts from all over the world. It also provided a magnificent board room on the walls of which were hung portraits of Prince Rupert, King James II and other great figures of its long history.

Under the leadership of Charles Vincent Sale, Deputy Governor from 1916 to 1925 and Governor from then until 1931, the company belatedly spent lavishly on new store buildings in Canada. Before amassing a fortune as a trader in Japan, Sale had married a Canadian girl and was deeply interested in the Dominion. He created the company's Canadian committee for on-the-spot direction. He was the first to interest the company in fur farming and also the first to throw open the company's early archives to historians.

There had been some store building earlier. In Edmonton, for example, a store building completed in 1905 had been one of the first in the area to have elevators. These and also mirrors were a source of wonder to the Indians. On seeing his reflection for the first time, a chief once said: "Now I can see into the Spirit World."

Employing some of the experts who had built Harrod's great store in London, the Hudson's Bay Company in the twenties erected new and magnificent store buildings in Winnipeg, Vancouver and several other cities. These were no sooner completed than the depression struck in the fall of 1929. The company began to lose money in all departments and was soon in arrears on dividends on preferred stock which had been issued in 1912 and later. Even in the land department, sales failed to cover salaries and taxes. The London committee resigned and a committee of stockholders chose a new Governor in 1931.

Major and later Sir Patrick Ashley Cooper, who had been born in Aberdeen, Scotland, in 1887 and had studied law there and in Cambridge, was their choice. He had also seen Army service in World War I. He at once made a tour of the company's Canadian properties and, something that no previous governor had done, began to make annual visits to Canada.

"On arriving in Canada on my first visit," he reported later, "I was dismayed at what I found—a very extravagant administration and, worse still, a disheartened staff." Fur prices in 1931 were only 17 per cent of what they had been ten years earlier. Major Cooper found such heavy losses in the wholesale department that closing it down was considered. He found the magnificent retail store buildings "filled with merchandise instead of customers, with staff despondent and with little faith in the future. This unhappy situation was partly the result of the economic conditions then prevailing in Canada but also due to too rapid expansion, bringing with it overcostly administration and lack of coordination. The absence of a strong guiding hand was only too obvious."

In Philip Alfred Chester, a six-foot astute former accountant, Major Cooper found the executive to lead the company's rehabilitation. Born in Long Eaton, Derbyshire, March 14, 1896, Chester had run away from home to serve with the King's Rifle Corps in World War I. He then earned his articles as an accountant and joined this department of the Hudson's Bay Company in London in 1923. He was transferred to Winnipeg the next year and became chief accountant in 1925. He was promoted to general manager in 1930.

At the 1932 annual meeting, Major Cooper read a letter from a Canadian farmer setting forth the plight of many of the company's customers. "I got your letter about what I owe," wrote the man. "Now be pachant. I ain't forgot you. Please wait. When I have the money I will pay you. If this was the Judgment Day and you was no more prepared to meet your maker than I am to meet your account you sure would go to hell. Trusting you will do this."

Major Cooper was convinced that much of the company's trouble stemmed from the remote control which the London committee had attempted to exercise over its operations. He turned to the Canadian committee, which had been given real power only in 1930, and it began to function as a frequently meeting board of directors. Under the chairmanship of C. S. Riley and later John E. Woods, the committee has included Charles A. Dunning, Joseph Harris, Stewart A. Searle, C. Gordon Smith and other notable Canadian business leaders. Manager Chester was elected to it in 1941.

Drastic economies were instituted to meet the depression. Many positions were abolished. New executives took charge in all departments. The organization was strengthened by new attention to the selection, training and welfare of the company's employees. Under executives such as K. A. Wallick and Robert H. Chesshire, the wholesale and fur trade departments again became profitable.

No employer looks after his workers with greater care than the Hudson's Bay Company expends on its fur-trade post managers and their families. All the resources of science are employed to mitigate the hardships of the Arctic. Each manager and his family have a completely furnished rent-free six-room home especially designed for the climate. The company looks after the household needs, supplying and replacing some twenty-seven hundred different items as required.

There are books for adults and children, toys and textbooks for the latter. There are free government-approved correspondence courses for children up to ten years old. The company will pay the fare of those between ten and seventeen to the nearest urban school and $350 a year toward the tuition.

For a flat fee of $50 a month for adults and $4 to $25 for children, depending on age, the family can order almost anything it wants in the way of food from the company's nearest supply depot. The company supplies its employees with a wealth of booklets with titles like *Your Food and Health in the North, How to Grow Gardens at HBC Posts* and *Prenatal Care.* The last explains how to use dried milk instead of fresh, and the importance of vitamins. Each post has a company-supplied medicine chest, full of sulfa drugs, vitamins, and first-aid supplies, but the seriously ill and mothers expecting babies are taken to city hospitals, often by airplane.

"A striking feature of life in the far north," noted the company's 285th Annual Report in 1954, "is the very close cooperation, both official and personal, which exists between representatives of the Federal and Provincial Governments, the Royal Canadian Mounted Police, the Missions, and the Company's personnel." Each fur-trade post usually consists of a store, warehouse, and the residence of the manager, all immaculate white buildings with red roofs. Electric power for these, and sometimes for neighboring missions and police stations, is generated by a company-developed gasoline-powered unit. There are stoves which operate on electricity as well as wood or coal.

Each post has two-way radio equipment, often radio-telephone facilities which do not require a knowledge of code. During World War II these became weather-observing posts and in many cases sent out hourly observations for the guidance of airplane pilots. The company's three airplanes and dozen or so ships travel more than a quarter of a million miles a year, taking supplies and personnel to these posts and bringing out furs.

But the company's greatest rejuvenation has come in its retail stores department. One of the new executives employed in the 1931 search for fresh talent was Frank F. Martin, a six-foot New Englander who for some years had done an outstanding job as controller of The Wm. Taylor Son & Co. department store in Cleveland, Ohio. As a boy in Lynn, Massachusetts, Martin had worked briefly for the famous Lydia Pinkham patent-medicine company and also in General Electric's personnel department. During World War I, he served with the Quartermaster Department in Washington. He joined the Hudson's Bay Company as controller of its Vancouver store. He later became assistant general manager and in 1935 was promoted to general manager of the department. He is a member of the Canadian committee.

Merchandise lines were expanded and improved. The company became the exclusive Canadian outlet for products developed by the Associated Merchandising Corporation buying organization. Advertising was increased. The big stores gave more attention to lower-priced merchandise and basement operations. Food departments, which account for half the business of some of the small stores, were enlarged. This is usually self-service and the company pioneered the self-service sale of meats in Western Canada. The average sales ticket in Canadian department stores is only about half that in United States stores but with food stocked the customers come in oftener.

Almost anything is obtainable in the great Winnipeg store. It once sold in one day six thousand dozen cut daffodils flown in by airplane. It regularly does a big business in diamond rings, television sets, pianos, fine chinaware, boats, canoes, hardware, food and drugs. It has one of the largest book departments in Canada. This also sells magazines and daily newspapers. There are parking facilities for customers, and an arrangement for delivering their parcels to their cars. The store has a museum of early company relics. An auditorium called Beaver Hall is available in the store as a meeting place for organizations. Shopping mothers can leave their children in a store playroom or wheel them about on red strollers supplied by the store. There is no adjustment bureau. Clerks are empowered to accept returns and make refunds.

Executive salaries were increased. Prior to 1931, no Hudson's Bay buyer earned as much as $15,000 a year. Systematic training and profit-sharing programs were introduced. Store buyers have the title of department manager and are responsible for the expenses of their department as well as the merchandise. The company expects to earn at least 2 per cent on food sales and 3 per cent on sales in general.

The profit sharing is calculated by deducting the required 3 per cent from the earnings of a store before taxes and then taking 15 per cent of the difference for distribution to the executive group. This includes assistant department managers, also non-selling executives, and all with head-office contracts. Since instituted, this has amounted to from 5 to 28 per cent of an executive's basic salary, which is supposed to be the equal of what other Canadian retailers pay for the same work. Except in unusual circumstances, an executive whose department is unprofitable does not share.

While reports are frequent, the managers of the widely scattered Hudson's Bay stores are largely on their own in a decentralized operation. "Our men are expected to be self-reliant," explains Manager Martin. "They're supposed to adjust their operations to local conditions and take care of the profit and loss." He sees most of them twice a year.

In addition to the usual employee benefits of discounts and vacations, the company pays its employees interest on their savings, 5 per cent up to $500 and 4 per cent from $500 to $5,000. At sixty-five, those employed for twenty years are eligible for pensions. Cash awards and extra holidays with pay are given veterans. Any Hudson's Bay employee who is discharged is told the reason why. An employee with fifteen years' service can be discharged only with the approval of the Canadian committee.

All of this plus Canada's improved economy made the retail stores department profitable. One of the Winnipeg store's credit men, J. Gordon Dakins, later executive vice president of the National Retail Dry Goods Association, found that a great many charge customers whose accounts had been written off wanted to pay them anyway and did so as soon as they had the money, in some cases many years later. In 1936, the company resumed payments of dividends on its preferred stock and retired all of this stock by 1945. Dividends were resumed on the common stock in 1938 and since then have been paid continuously.

Sir Patrick Ashley Cooper, who also had held important British government posts including Director General of Finance while guiding the Hudson's Bay Company, retired in 1952 after twenty-one years of service as governor. Eric O. Faulkner was appointed deputy governor and William Johnston Keswick, one of the most famous figures of trade in the Orient and who had been deputy governor since 1946, became the thirty-first governor of the "Honorable Company."

To the post, Governor Keswick, a graduate of Trinity and Cambridge, brought years of experience in international affairs. He was Managing Director of Jardine, Matheson, Ltd., Far Eastern trade company. He had helped organize the Anglo-Iranian Oil Company. He had served as chairman of the Municipal Council of the Shanghai International Settlement. He had flown out of Singapore in the last airplane to leave before the Japanese occupation. He had helped Field Marshal Montgomery plan the Normandy invasion. After nearly three centuries, the Hudson's Bay Company is still directed by adventurers.

III. Brooks Brothers

America's Oldest Clothing Store

WHAT in common have these illustrious persons? Abraham Lincoln, Theodore Roosevelt, Franklin D. Roosevelt, John Foster Dulles, Charles Lindbergh, Gene Tunney, the Duchess of Windsor and Marlene Dietrich? If you were asked this question on a television quiz program, the answer would be easy. All have been customers of Brooks Brothers, the New York firm whose unparalleled existence since 1818 gives it the distinction of being America's oldest clothing store.

Theodore Roosevelt, Ulysses S. Grant and Woodrow Wilson all were clad in Brooks Brothers suits when they took their oaths as Presidents of the United States. President Franklin D. Roosevelt wore a Navy cape made by the firm to the Yalta Conference and it is immortalized in a statue of him in London's Grosvenor Square. President Lincoln was wearing a Prince Albert coat, a waistcoat and trousers from Brooks Brothers when he was assassinated and a number of statues reproduce these in bronze.

Secretary of State Dulles, like his predecessor Dean Acheson, is a Brooks customer. This predilection of the diplomatic set for the store led Lindbergh to it. When the airman landed in Paris without luggage after his historic flight alone across the Atlantic, Ambassador Myron T. Herrick loaned him a Brooks Brothers suit. Lindbergh liked it and became a customer.

To wear clothing made by Brooks Brothers is the equivalent of membership in an exclusive club and identification as a Brooks Brothers customer is inescapable. A novelist has only to write that one of his characters is wearing a shirt, suit, coat or even a night-

33

shirt made by Brooks Brothers, and the reader knows instantly what type of citizen is being described. He is always outstanding, an executive or would-be executive, well born and well schooled, invariably well behaved. In his appearance he follows the advice of Lord Chesterfield to "take great care to be dressed like the reasonable people of your own age, in the place where you are; whose dress is never spoken of one way or another."

The conservatism that characterizes clothing made by Brooks Brothers is one of the factors that has made the firm such an American phenomenon. In a nation dedicated to speed, change and the shouting headline, Brooks Brothers has endured under the founder's original policies of good taste, fine quality and expert workmanship in everything made and sold. There is no high-pressure salesmanship. Superlatives and comparisons never appear in advertising.

Customers feared this might come to an end when the old firm was purchased in 1946 by Julius Garfinckel & Co. of Washington. Even by way of experiment, the new management attempted few changes. There seemed no reason for a button behind the collar of a button-down shirt when men no longer buttoned down collars in back, nor any need for shirttails to reach all the way to the knee. But when they were cut, customers complained. The long shirttail was at once restored and anybody who wants it can have a button sewed behind his collar and a buttonhole added.

The store's dignity continued. The new owners merely introduced more efficiency in the production of Brooks' fine merchandise and brought it to the attention of more people. Six-foot John C. Wood, who had just taken off a lieutenant colonel's uniform, was installed as president. A graduate of Dartmouth, he had been prior to army service an executive for many years of B. Altman & Co., a store also known for dignity and taste.

Wood opened a Brooks store in Chicago and greatly increased Brooks' distinctive and restrained advertising. The sales volume increased. In 1954 this soared to $13,000,000, almost double the most that it had been in the best year of the old regime. The average Brooks sales ticket is $22, more than four times the average for big department stores.

Suits are piled neatly on table tops as was customary in the early days. "It's the most inefficient way in the world to handle suits," says President Wood. "But we continue to do it because we've learned that you don't change the brand of oats on a winning horse."

But Brooks Brothers has never been averse to changes of the right sort in clothing and has pioneered dozens of innovations that rival clothiers have adopted. These include the button-down-collar shirt, the foulard tie, the four-button suit, the Brooks sweater, and the famous No. 1 sack suit. The last, three-buttoned and single-breasted, with natural shoulders and straight hang, has been for six decades the "uniform" that stamps a man as being "correctly dressed." The firm was first in modern times to sponsor linen crash, shantung silk and other cooler summer suits for men, jackets with odd trousers, and any number of styles in the boys' clothing field. They have reintroduced such items as the Norfolk jacket, the Tattersall vest, the "deerstalker" cap, and were in great measure responsible for the once overwhelming vogue of the box-cloth spat. More recently they have launched new man-made materials and were the first in the world to offer shirts made of Dacron and cotton oxford, called Brooksweave, and Dacron and cotton broadcloth, copyrighted as Brookscloth.

Possibly the most important feature of the Brooks tradition is the personal service given regular customers. Brooks salesmen refer to these people as "see-you" customers. Because of a policy of "open book" selling, whereby one clerk may serve all the needs of a customer, strong relationships are established. These customers are frequently reluctant to be served by any other than their favorite salesman, and should he be on vacation, the customer waits until his return. "Mr. So-and-So wants to see you," goes the word. Many customers never bother to learn their own measurements but rely wholly on the little black book of their favorite salesman.

So unswerving in their loyalty to the store are these "see-you" customers that four or five generations from one family is not uncommon. One salesman, the late Frederick Webb, served five generations of Morgans, calling them by their first names. It is doubtful if any store in the world can equal such continuous patronage as that given Brooks Brothers by the late John R. Voorhis, one-time Grand Sachem of Tammany Hall and noted for his immaculate dress. When he was 10, his mother bought him his first long pants at Brooks Brothers and, until his death at 102, he never bought a suit elsewhere.

Other long-term customers include notables in every walk of life —Presidents, bankers, diplomats, prize fighters, military officers, Hollywood stars and European royalty. Seven hundred elite European customers order by mail when necessary and embassies abroad keep extra Brooks Brothers suits on hand in case of emergencies. John Stahl, the former California postal clerk known as "Old Iron Legs" because he walked thirteen thousand miles *after* retiring, once while on a walking tour landed in Madrid, his clothes shabby and unpressed. He appealed to the American Embassy there for a change and was loaned a custom-made Brooks suit that had the name Nicholas Duke Biddle sewed in it. Stahl wore the suit for an audience with Pope Pius XII.

That consideration of customer whims pays off is evinced by the fact that today the firm has, in addition to two New York stores, major branches in Chicago and Boston, and shops in San Francisco and Los Angeles. Customers in thirty-one other large cities are served seven or eight times a year by traveling salesmen who, with some six hundred swatches of materials and a variety of samples, set up temporary shop in the leading hotels. The firm has its own clothing factory in Brooklyn and its shirt factory in Paterson, New Jersey. On the tenth floor of the Madison Avenue store in New York a customer can still see the vestigial remains of a fast-disappearing craft— tailors sitting cross-legged, sewing by hand on custom-made suits. On the ninth floor is a fine neckwear factory.

As the oldest clothing store in America, Brooks Brothers' history parallels both the growth of New York and the nation. The founder of the business, Henry Sands Brooks, son of a Connecticut physician, opened his shop on the northwest corner of Catherine and Cherry Streets on April 7, 1817, a month after James Monroe was inaugurated as President of the United States. New York, with less than 125,000 inhabitants, was then a seafaring city. Four months after the shop was opened, the *Savannah,* first American ocean-going steamship, was launched a few blocks away.

Henry Sands Brooks was noted for his fine taste in clothes. He was forty-six years old when he opened his shop and prior to this had been a successful provisioner. He was a dapper gentleman who

made frequent trips to Europe on sailing ships from which he returned with new items for his wardrobe. Each time he sailed some
friend invariably said: "Henry, bring me back a waistcoat like
yours." Or, "Henry, have your London tailor make me a coat like
yours."

Just when the idea struck him to pioneer in ready-made clothing
nobody knows, but Henry Sands Brooks was among the first, if not
the first to offer such clothing anywhere in the world. His sea captain friends often couldn't wait for something to be made. He also
tailored clothes "to measure" as did clothiers everywhere, but his
shop, offering the dual service, was unique in those days.

The site selected for the shop was in the center of New York's
busiest mercantile district, and within a block or two of the most
fashionable residences. Henry Sands Brooks bought the ground and
a frame building for a little over $17,000, and his first entry on
opening day is significant. It wasn't for a sale but for a loan of $25
to a friend. Then and there was established the Brooks dictum to
make friends of all customers. He also treated seafaring customers
to a drink of Medford rum and often wrapped packages in black
silk kerchiefs for which he did not charge.

Henry Sands Brooks guided the first store for fifteen years until
his death in 1833. By then he had initiated his two older sons,
Henry and Daniel H., into the business, firmly implanting in them
his "only" principles: "To make and deal *only* in merchandise of
the best quality, to sell it at a fair profit *only,* and to deal *only* with
people who seek and are capable of appreciating such merchandise."
In 1850, the firm name was changed from H. & D. H. Brooks & Co.,
to Brooks Brothers.

By this time, the familiar Golden Fleece trademark of the firm
was in use. A sheep suspended in a ribbon, this had long been a
symbol of British woolen merchants. Dating from the fifteenth century, it had been the emblem of the Knights of the Golden Fleece,
founded by Philip the Good, Duke of Burgundy. Worn suspended
over each knight's heart, it symbolized the Lamb of God.

As New York City grew and moved northward, the firm followed.
While the original store was occupied until 1874, a second and
larger store was opened in 1858 in "elaborate" new quarters at
Broadway and Grand Street. Henry Brooks, the eldest son of the

founder, was dead by then and control passed to the four younger brothers, Daniel H., already initiated, and John, Elisha and Edward S. Brooks.

How elaborate the new premises were at Broadway and Grand is indicated by an entry in Mrs. George Shepard's diary of 1861, now in the Burton Historical Collection of the Detroit Public Library. Mrs. Shepard, a cousin of Ralph Waldo Emerson, was spending the winter with her husband at the Astor House in New York. On December 9, 1861, she wrote:

Fair warm like the spring of the year. . . . Smith came with his carriage we drove to Brooks Brothers Clothing House corner of Broadway & Grand Street where Mr. Shepard changes his Scotch wool Drawers for 2 pair English Merinos we went upstairs and looked over this large establishment where all kinds of Garments for Men were cutting out & making . . . they employ 400 persons cutting and sewing. . . . Columns & pillars bronze colour, with large looking glasses: were well worth seeing.

Mrs. Shepard did not mention the unique pagoda in the store, a structure fifteen feet in diameter by thirty feet in height, which was occupied by the desks of the "measurers" for all clothing made to order. Another feature of the store was an enormous four-dialed globe clock, illuminated from the inside by gaslight.

A store advertisement of the time stated that

Our Custom Department will at all times be found complete in stock and variety of piece goods, imported expressly for our trade, consisting of French, English and German Cloths, Cassimere, Doeskins, rich Velvet, Silk, Satin and every new style of cloths, etc. of the finest quality, which will be made to order in the best manner and most fashionable mode.

During the Civil War, many of the Union Army notables patronized this five-story establishment, then probably the largest of its kind in the world. Generals Grant, Sheridan, Sherman and Hooker, and thousands of the men they led, were all outfitted in uniforms made by Brooks Brothers. The contract for these came from Governor E. D. Morgan of New York.

Most illustrious of all Civil War customers was President Abraham Lincoln. He bought the overcoat for his Second Inaugural and many other articles at the Grand Street store. One of Brooks Brothers' present-day customers is Raymond Massey, the actor whose portrayal of Lincoln has been so masterful as to make him seem a reincarnation of the President. One of the store clerks tells of the eerie feeling he had on a Lincoln's birthday when the first customer was Raymond Massey.

Times were perilous during the issue over slavery and the Cherry Street store was sacked from top to bottom by a rowdy mob during the draft riots of 1863. *Valentine's Manual,* a publication of the time, has probably given the best description ever made of the character of the Brooks Brothers and their associates in its account of the sacking. Their reporter stated, "We can find no reason for the looting, for the Messrs. Brooks are fair, upright gentlemen, of mild manners and such simplicity of deportment as to allay and conciliate rather than excite ill feeling in any with whom they come into intercourse."

In 1868, store spokesmen mentioned "having the most fastidious among our regular customers," and said, "the one-price system is always observed." The firm valued its property at $750,000 and stated that "half of the sales of this house are for cash, yet the firm carries from 3,000 to 4,000 accounts which are extended to approved credit." In 1869, Brooks Brothers became a neighbor of the Singer Company on Union Square and began to use Singer sewing machines. Garments, however, continued to be finished by hand, as they still are today.

During migrations farther north, two of Henry Brooks' grandsons entered a partnership with six of the oldest employees. In 1889, two more grandsons came into the business. This made a total of four grandsons and six old employees, and in 1903 the group incorporated. The presidency went to one of the old employees, then senior partner, Francis Guerin Lloyd, with the first vice presidency going to Frederick Brooks, one of the grandsons of Henry Sands Brooks. Eugene Mapes, an employee since 1880, became secretary. Lloyd had been with the firm for forty-one years when he became president. He stayed at the helm until his death in 1920, making in all fifty-eight years of service to the store.

There were many reasons for the group's selecting Lloyd for President, but certainly one was his appearance. A man addicted to bow ties and a goatee, he was as fastidious in dress as any member of the Brooks clan. He had an exceptionally fine color sense and many of the East Indian and British design blocks still used for printing Brooks' exclusive ties were selected by Lloyd in England. During his regime, a branch was opened in fashionable Newport at 220 Bellevue Avenue. It was more of a club than a store and some of society's most colorful notables dropped in daily. Charley Sands stopped in every morning to buy just one polo shirt, and Joe Harrison would flip coins with friends for $50 polo coats.

In 1915, Lloyd supervised the move to the firm's present ten-story walnut-paneled building as 346 Madison Avenue. Although the building was modern in every respect, Lloyd persisted in a few antiquated business methods. Since he was able to add up columns of four-digit figures faster than the first adding machines could, he saw no reason why everyone else couldn't do the same, so the store had no adding machines until after his death.

Lloyd, who had a fine Spencerian style, continued to write the firm's direct-mail advertising by hand just as he had previously for years. Lithographed, this was mailed as a personal letter to customers and called their attention to new imports, new styles or new patterns.

Under Lloyd's guidance, the store weathered World War I, outfitting General John J. Pershing and many lesser officers, some of them the store's own employees.

When the war made it increasingly difficult to import woolens, Frederick Brooks, then chairman of the board, exhibited the same paternalistic attitude toward customers that has always characterized the store. Outsiders who had never been in the place before started flocking in, particularly on Saturdays, buying up as many woolen items as their budgets permitted. One Saturday morning in May, 1917, Vice President Brooks came down to the main floor and, for the first time, saw them.

"Who are all these people?" he wanted to know.

When told who they were and why they were there he said firmly: "Close the store on Saturdays. We must save this merchandise for our regular customers."

And every Saturday thereafter during that summer, the store remained closed, the first time in its history to have Saturday closings in any month other than August.

After Lloyd died in 1920, Eugene Mapes, who had then been with the store for forty-three years, became president. He had started to work for Brooks Brothers at the age of fifteen and progressed to the top through the uniform and livery department. The store's collection of livery buttons, incidentally, dates back to the 1870's and is a museum record of the Goulds, Vanderbilts, Morgans, Rockefellers and other families prominent in American society.

Mapes held the post of president until 1935, during which time the firm continued to expand, opening branch stores in Boston and in Palm Beach. The latter had a distinguished but short-lived history.

The firm had started wooing college and prep school trade back in the 1900's and by the twenties to look "Brooksy" was practically a requirement for entering any of the Eastern schools. F. Scott Fitzgerald, who chronicled American life of this era, alluded to Brooks Brothers so often in his novels that quotations from *This Side of Paradise* helped the firm obtain an injunction against a California company using the Brooks name. Characters also wore Brooks Brothers clothing in novels by Ernest Hemingway, Somerset Maugham, and John P. Marquand. A woman writer, Mary McCarthy, called a short story about a romance aboard a transcontinental train "The Man in the Brooks Brothers Shirt."

Mapes increased the store's display advertising and Donald C. Vaughan, advertising manager, wrote most of the copy. It helped increase the sales volume to over $6,500,000 in 1929, the highest figure for the firm for any year until that time. Vaughan, a slight bookish man who is now retired, describes the Brooks Brothers advertising policy of those days as "no policy at all," adding that the store's real advertising was "done by loving friends." One of these friends was another literary man, the late Frederick Lewis Allen, long editor of *Harper's Magazine,* and a Brooks customer and Vaughan friend for thirty years. Vaughan translated and adapted Honoré de Balzac's *Art of Tying the Cravat* for the firm in 1921, and the booklet proved as useful to customers as had an earlier one compiled called *On Going Away,* a handbook for travelers.

Age forced Mapes to resign in 1935, and the presidency was then taken by Winthrop Holley Brooks, a great-grandson of the founder, and a son of Frederick Brooks. Winthrop H. entered the store several years after graduating from Yale in 1915. Although professing to dislike the clothing business, he headed the store for eleven years.

Douglas Fairbanks and other motion-picture stars had been hounding the store management for years to open a branch in or near Hollywood, and finally, in 1939, Winthrop H. Brooks reluctantly consented to opening small shops in San Francisco and Los Angeles. There the stars could at least examine samples of clothing and buy furnishings. However, if they wanted a real Brooks wardrobe they still had to visit the New York store. Today it is not at all unusual to see the sartorially correct movie stars shopping leisurely there—among them Fred Astaire, Burt Lancaster, Robert Montgomery, Tyrone Power, Chester Morris and Clark Gable—and the clerks are instructed to pay no more attention to them than to less celebrated individuals.

Occasionally a customer recognizes one of the movie greats with unmistakable delight. One Christmas, for example, an elderly little woman was buying a cashmere muffler as a present for her husband when she recognized a tall, lanky figure beside her.

"Why, you're Gary Cooper, aren't you?" she said. With characteristic aplomb, Cooper raised his hat, bowed, said, "Howdy, ma'am," and went on with his shopping.

No one could much blame Winthrop H. Brooks if he found the clothing business a pretty big task when he took over. He had the responsibility of directing the store through World War II and of seeing many of its employees march off to fight, including his own son, Frederick. It was an honor to outfit General Wainwright and Jimmy Doolittle and other illustrious military figures, but the employees experienced real grief when customers like Theodore Roosevelt, Jr., failed to come back. Roosevelts both from Oyster Bay and Hyde Park have always been among the favorite Brooks Brothers customers.

Brooks Brothers lost money several years during the depression, and because the firm depends so heavily on materials from abroad for its merchandise World War II was a great hardship. The 1946 sale followed. This did not end the Brooks blood in the business. Winthrop H. Brooks continued as chairman of the board and as a director for several years, and his nephew, Ashbel T. Wall, a fifth-generation representative of the famous family, became a vice president under the new management.

While no change will be made in the original Brooks policy of quality merchandise for quality customers—President Wood describes Brooks Brothers as "not a business but a world standard for men's good taste"—there have been some changes made, and for the better. Advertising remains understated and underwritten but the lineage in the leading newspapers has been upped considerably. More clothing in a greater variety of styles is being stocked and customers can "get what they want when they want it." Formerly when a customer came in, say for the ever-popular gray flannel suit, he might have to wait weeks for delivery.

"Now you can order anything," says President Wood, "even an African bush coat if you have it custom made. You can get it *when* you need it, it will be the *best* of its kind, and it will be correct for the *locale* where it is to be worn."

More emphasis is also being placed on the rapidly growing boys department. A young man of four can be completely outfitted by Brooks Brothers, the idea being that in order to have long-time customers they should be caught young.

Not that all small fry want to be little gentlemen. Abe Burrows, of radio and television fame, once took his young son into the New York store for an outfit. Master Burrows shied from a suit with coat and trousers that matched until reassured by a diplomatic salesman that such an outfit was really being worn. It was then suggested that some new shirts be purchased to go with the suit.

"I want the kind with writin'," announced young Burrows.

"You mean shirts with your monogram?" asked the clerk.

"I mean with writin'—like the Dodgers and Giants."

President Wood, a deep-voiced executive, growls about women invading a store run for men. Nonetheless, it's quite a tribute when some of the nation's best-dressed and most glamorous women adopt a man's store for their very own. The Duchess of Windsor, Marlene Dietrich, Elizabeth Taylor, Katharine Hepburn, Billie Burke, Katharine Cornell and Audrey Hepburn are among the women who insist upon wearing Brooks dressing gowns, slacks, pajamas, sweaters and shirts. In fact, it was the pink shirt Brooks Brothers made in the nineties to stir up color consciousness in men that caused the first big invasion of the store by women, when they finally "discovered" it. Women bought thousands of these shirts at $8 each in 1950.

The little-boy look, popular with women since 1953, has caused Brooks Brothers to "allow" women to buy Bermuda shorts and English raincoats originally designed for boys. And since business has boomed these last few years the store has one tiny corner on the first floor *just for women*.

Brooks Brothers, however, has no intention of sacrificing its men's business or changing the character of its merchandise to cater to women.

"If colors or styles change, and if, for example, women's sweaters become longer or shorter, we will be out of the women's business," says Vice President Wall. "Women's styles just aren't our dish of tea. We believe in the maxim, 'Shoemaker, stick to your last.' "

The new regime takes pride in the store's old-time employees. Twenty-five years of service makes an employee eligible for membership in the Quarter Century Club, an organization that meets once each year in September. The club has 152 members, well over ten per cent of the 1,025 employees. Many of these have worked for the firm much longer than twenty-five years. Twenty-nine can claim between forty and fifty years of service, fourteen between fifty and sixty years, and one member, D. W. Guiry, now honorary manager of the Boston store, has been with Brooks Brothers for sixty-two years. The record for continuous service, however, is that of the late Horatio Kiernan, who served the firm sixty-seven years.

Many of the Brooks employees speak foreign languages, and the United Nations in 1954 sent a letter to the store asking how many languages were spoken, in case some of the foreign delegates wanted to shop there. Miss Anne Duncan, head of personnel, counted up and sent back a letter enumerating twenty-five languages.

Miss Duncan, the only woman executive of the firm, has been with Brooks Brothers for twenty-five years. She has charge of a special training course that Brooks salesmen must take before they start work. In addition to thorough knowledge of woolens—manufacture, cutting, etc.—there must be the mastering of selling etiquette, with dignity, courtesy and imperturbability high in the technique.

Miss Duncan herself possesses these qualities to an outstanding degree, particularly imperturbability, as she demonstrated in 1950 when she was sent to Chicago to hire employees for the new branch opening there.

The Chicago store was scheduled to open on a Tuesday. On the Friday afternoon before, so much still had to be done that meeting the deadline seemed an impossibility. Everyone was working under great tension when suddenly a big crash sounded.

Miss Duncan looked down from a second-floor office and saw that a big Cadillac had run up on the sidewalk in front of the store. It had crashed through the plate-glass show windows. A passerby remarked to her companion: "Well, *they* were certainly anxious to get into Brooks Brothers. The doors aren't even open yet!"

Calmly picking up the telephone, Miss Duncan asked to be connected with the store's general superintendent, who would have to have the damage repaired. "Mr. Sheffield," she said, "our first customers have arrived."

Her coolness was matched a few months later by the wife of an elderly Boston Brooks customer who announced that he intended to do away with himself. "I'm seventy-two years old," he complained. "And I'm no use to you or anybody else. I'm going out and drown myself."

He took a coat from a clothes rack and started for the door.

His wife, weary of the oft-repeated threat, looked up briefly from her knitting.

"No need to wear your new Brooks coat," she told him calmly. "Not if you're going to drown yourself. Leave it for John. He's being proposed for membership in the Somerset Club this week."

What is the psychology back of Brooks Brothers' unique success? What makes the store tick? Why has it survived since 1818? How has it become one of the household words in America?

There are numerous reasons, but the chief one is probably that a lot of people find comfort in reliability. There's a feeling of security when a shopper knows he can depend upon a store to carry the same quality merchandise year in and year out. And there's a feeling of importance when particular whims are catered to, and when a salesman remembers everything about a customer.

If asked, Brooks Brothers has a lot of good advice about care of a man's clothes. The most important point is that a man should have at least eight or nine suits. These should be rotated and worn only one day at a time. Each added suit makes the others wear longer and cuts down the need for pressing and dry cleaning. Body heat and cleaning dry out wool suits. A suit that is worn constantly develops a "tired" look. If allowed to hang two or three days, it recuperates. Only the best cleaners and laundries should be patronized.

Do clothes make the man? How much is behavior influenced by dress? No one could blame the current juvenile crime wave on the sloppy-joe clothes so favored by kid gangs, but it is quite indisputable that most people who take pride in their appearance also take pride in behaving well. Brooks Brothers stand as a bulwark against this particular rising tide.

IV. Tiffany's

The Most Famous Jewelry Store in the World

GLOBAL fame in business usually results from vast operations, low-priced products and wide advertising, but Tiffany & Company, the New York jewelry firm founded in 1837, has reversed the process. Most of its products are costly, its advertising is persistent rather than large; and for a stretch of thirty years in its long existence, it didn't even bother to put its name over the door.

Yet Tiffany's, by adherence to self-imposed standards, has become a world-wide synonym for quality, integrity and exclusiveness. It is a classic example of a store "trading up" in its merchandise and also of the wisdom of a store shifting its location to keep abreast of the vagaries of shoppers. It has moved five times.

Its seven-story marble and limestone building at Fifth Avenue and Fifty-seventh Street, in the heart of Manhattan's fashionable shopping district, is a storehouse for twinkling diamonds, rubies, emeralds, platinum, gold and silver—a private palace bulging with some of the most fabulous riches ever collected outside of the *Arabian Nights*. On display are millions in diamonds and other precious stones. For aloof or shy customers, there are private elevators and private rooms.

Tiffany's is not the oldest jewelry store in America. Bixler's of Easton, Pennsylvania, dates from 1785. Kennard & Co., Inc., a fifth-generation Boston firm, began in Portsmouth, New Hampshire, in 1800. Galt & Bro. of Washington, D.C., whose widowed owner married President Woodrow Wilson, dates from 1802. Black, Starr & Gorham, Inc., of New York has a history extending back to 1810.

C. D. Peacock started in Chicago in 1837, the year Tiffany's opened in New York.

To appreciate Tiffany's and these firms, it is necessary only to review the difficulties of the jewelry business. Jewelry is a romantic luxury, not a necessity. Many persons live and die without buying or wearing a diamond, a ring or a brooch. There are even religious denominations which regard such display as sinful. Jewelry sales are the first to drop when general business declines and are among the first to be taxed when governments need extra revenues. The levy has been as high as 100 per cent in England, and firms as venerable as the House of Garrard, crown jewelers for two hundred years, have closed their doors.

There are also merchandising problems. Selling fine jewelry demands not only probity but expertness, technical knowledge and taste. It is difficult to find individuals with all these qualities. The jeweler selling precious stones competes not only with department stores and mail-order houses selling them but with countless outlets offering synthetic and imitation stones in costume jewelry.

While the Jewelry Industry Council has achieved some success in promoting jeweled gifts for anniversaries and birthdays, it continues to be largely a seasonal business. Thirty per cent of the year's volume comes in December and about 8 per cent in the graduation and wedding month of June. Expenses continue all year. To operate profitably, Dun & Bradstreet figures reveal, a jeweler must have a markup of around 100 per cent and can hope to turn his inventory only about 1.2 times a year, about the same as the merchant who sells tombstones instead of precious stones. If the inventory is too low, impulse sales will be lost. If it is too high, some of it may go out of style, and costs of insuring and safeguarding it will increase.

Tiffany's serenely survives such difficulties and, if a fine stone doesn't immediately find a purchaser, the store will keep it until somebody with the proper discernment comes along. It thus held for several years a fine emerald from the belt buckle of Abdul-Hamid, the last Sultan of Turkey.

As many surprised persons have learned, Tiffany's would sooner lose a customer than waive a rule. For example, laboratory magic enabled an important industrial company to make star sapphires not only as beautiful as the natural gemstone but exactly duplicating its composition. An executive of the firm proudly took one of these man-made beauties to Tiffany's to be set into a ring.

A clerk received the stone with the reverent respect that all Tiffany clerks bestow on all articles that receive their attention. Remarking that the star was the clearest he had ever seen, he took it to a department head who studied it through a loupe. After a whispered consultation, the clerk returned.

"I'm sorry," he said, shaking his head, "this is synthetic."

"But it's worth $600!" protested the executive. "My firm made it and I want a nice setting. I've been one of your customers for years."

It was not a question of value, explained the clerk. Tiffany's simply made it a rule to set only natural stones and of these usually only stones that had been purchased at Tiffany's. The clerk remained politely adamant and the amazed customer took his man-made sapphire to a rival establishment a few blocks away which was happy to set it in gold and diamonds for $1,250.

This cost Tiffany's a profit and a customer but such standards have enabled the firm to sell millions of dollars' worth of jewelry and silverware, largely of its own manufacture, and to become the most famous jewelry store in the world.

"Tiffany's isn't just a place of business," the head of a neighboring store once remarked. "It's part showplace, part museum, part institution and part legend." This is no overstatement. No other store has so impressed itself on the business world, and the greatest accolade that any company can earn is to be called the "Tiffany" of its industry.

The store's reputation for integrity and fair dealing extends far beyond Fifth Avenue. Poor pensioners have been customers. There was the farm girl who turned up an unusual stone while helping her father "chop cotton" at Searcy, Arkansas. She cherished it until she grew up and, in 1946, mailed it to Tiffany's. The stone proved to be a 27.21-carat diamond, the third largest found in North America.

Man or nature somehow had moved the single stone to Searcy from a little-worked diamond mine 140 miles to the southwest. Tiffany's bought the stone. Today it is displayed in the store, not far from the celebrated Tiffany Diamond.

This is a 128.51-carat yellow gem as big as a bird's egg, the largest and finest canary-colored diamond in the world. It was purchased by Tiffany's soon after it was found as a 287-carat rough in a De Beers mine at Kimberley in 1878. It is a showpiece, not for sale. The name of the store also was given to the Tiffany Queen Pearl, an 83-grain pink freshwater pearl found only seventeen miles away at Notch Brook, New Jersey. Tiffany's paid the carpenter who found it $2,500 cash and $250 in trade. It was sold to the Empress Eugénie, then to a German industrialist and later to the King of Saxony.

Tiffany's has also enriched the vocabulary of the jewelers' world with its creation of the Tiffany catch and the Tiffany setting. The first is a device for the safe locking of a brooch. The latter is the almost universally used six-prong setting for engagement rings created years ago by the firm. It holds and protects a stone and at the same time makes it appear a little larger.

The fame of the Tiffany setting is attested by a straight-faced account in a Johannesburg, South Africa, newspaper of the attempted theft by a native of a large diamond from a mine. A sharp-eyed inspector detected the gem and reported: "The inspector noted that the accused had allowed his left large toenail to grow two-thirds of an inch and had cut from the inner surface six swaths of nail, which he bent to encase the stone in a Tiffany setting."

At the Fifth Avenue edifice, you can usually find a $250,000 diamond necklace. However, if you are not in a hurry, the sky is the limit. The store's Christmas catalog offers diamond solitaires as high as $25,000 and bracelets at $20,000 some years. But there are many items under $100 and a few as low as $5, such as silver thimbles, baby spoons and letter openers. You can purchase a champagne swizzle stick of solid gold or have your door key set with diamonds.

On the upper floors are Tiffany's famed wedding gifts, silver, china and glassware. Brides cherish even the boxes in which they are sent. In addition to American products, Tiffany's has big stocks of Swiss watches and English chinaware. At one time, it owned a watch factory in Geneva, Switzerland. The firm's metalsmiths fashion its own jewelry and set its own gems in the building. Its silversmiths create Tiffany silverware in a factory at Newark, New Jersey. The store also sells antique silver.

Surprising as it may sound to the uninitiated, Tiffany prices on fairly standard items, like men's gold cuff links, where the principal cost is the weight of pure metal, are sometimes less than the prices at which other stores sell comparable items. This is simply the result of manufacturer-to-user operation. The store's repair department often pleasantly surprises customers by doing jobs at less than the estimated cost and most items are initialed or inscribed gratis.

Tiffany executives would sooner commit hara-kiri than reveal the names of their customers, but the identity of many is well known. Mrs. Cornelius Vanderbilt, queen for many years of New York's Four Hundred, has been one. The elder J. P. Morgan bought whole collections of Tiffany jewels. The late Payne Whitney is reputed to have spent $1,000,000 at the store in a single year. Jewels were a sizable part of his estate, the largest ever probated in America. Charles M. Schwab once strolled into the store, wrote a check for $91,000 and walked out with a sixty-carat diamond pendant for his wife.

Shirley Booth, the actress, and perhaps half a million other women, have been given Tiffany wedding rings which sell for $7.75 to $450 and higher. Tom Girdler, the industrialist, had Tiffany's make for him a solid-gold miniature of an airplane that one of his firms produced. William Durant, the dynamic founder of General Motors, regularly ordered golden small-scale duplicates of his latest car models. A Texas millionaire once sauntered into the store and had made a golden model of an oil well which was the source of his fortune. A judge had Tiffany's make him a jeweled weathervane in the likeness of his favorite horse.

When friends of the late Al Smith wanted to honor his successful completion of the Empire State Building, they could think of nothing more appropriate than a fourteen-carat Tiffany model of the world's tallest skyscraper. Smith later gave it to Pope Pius XI. James W. Gerard bought many jewelry items and had Tiffany bind for presentation to President Wilson a historic letter written to him in Kaiser Wilhelm's own hand. Probably the most expensive paperweight of all time is the Tiffany all-gold replica of the S.S. *Nieuw Amsterdam* which a shipping official ordered for his desk at a price of $5,000. The late Crosby Gaige, when running a Broadway theater, had Tiffany's make permanent sterling silver tickets for dramatic critics of the New York newspapers, each engraved with the recipient's name and the location of his opening-night seats.

Scores of noted trophies have come from the Tiffany workrooms, among them the Vanderbilt Cup, the Horse Show Military Trophy and the International Polo Cup. The rifle prizes, pigeon-shooting cups, racing cups and other coveted sportsmen's prizes which have been made by Tiffany's have filled several showcases at famous expositions. The firm also has struck medals for military heroes throughout the world.

By Royal Appointment, Tiffany's has served kings, queens and princes. Its rare gems have sparkled through the years in the palaces of the rulers of England, the czars of Russia, the kings of Belgium, Italy, Greece, Spain, Denmark and Portugal. Tiffany's glitter has also brightened the thrones of the Khedive of Egypt, the Shah of Persia and the Emperor of Brazil. Kings and nobility are few these days but Tiffany's has on an upper floor a file of all the peerages and almanacs of blue blood. With no more than normal delay, its craftsmen can turn out articles authentically marked with any current or past coat of arms. Nor will the firm knowingly make such items for persons not entitled to display the arms.

The famous firm is named for Charles Lewis Tiffany, who was born February 15, 1812, at Killingly, Connecticut. At fifteen, he ran a general store started by his father, a small cotton manufacturer. In September of the depression year of 1837, when Charles was twenty-five, he borrowed $1,000 from his father and came to New York. He went into partnership with a schoolmate, John D. Young, who had preceded him by six months and had been working in a stationery store. They rented half of a lower floor of a dwelling on lower Broadway. A dressmaker had the other half. From the beginning they stocked unusual items; Chinese goods, Japanese papier-mâché and terra-cotta ware, umbrellas, walking sticks, cabinets, fans, fine stationery, pottery and all manner of novel bric-a-brac.

Receipts for the first three days totaled only $4.98. But on Christmas Eve their sales reached $236 and on the last day of the year $675. In 1839, burglars carried away $4,000 worth of merchandise, virtually the whole stock of the fledgling establishment. But it continued to grow.

Tiffany further united the business by marrying Young's sister in 1841. This was an eventful year. Young made the first of many trips to Europe to buy French and Dresden porcelain, cutlery and clocks and Parisian jewelry. A third partner, J. L. Ellis, joined the firm and the store expanded into adjoining quarters.

But until 1848 Tiffany jewelry was of the sort that is not now allowed in the store. In that year the partners decided to go into precious gems and to manufacture as well as sell gold jewelry. This was a year of revolution in Europe. Prices of diamonds declined 50 per cent in Paris, and Tiffany, Young and Ellis, as the firm was then known, bought all that they could, including a necklace once owned by Marie Antoinette. They opened a Paris branch for both buying and selling.

When gold from California began to arrive in New York the next year, Tiffany and his partners had merchandise for which the newly rich were glad to trade their wealth. In 1850, when P. T. Barnum brought Jenny Lind to America, one of the first shops she visited was Tiffany's. She ordered a costly silver tankard as a gift for the captain of the vessel which had brought her over. Barnum was so impressed with the tankard that when his two famous midgets, General Tom Thumb and Lavinia Warren, were married, he gave them a silver chariot from Tiffany's almost big enough to carry the tiny couple.

Young Tiffany had no special training for the jewelry business, but brought to it qualities valuable in any business. These included old-fashioned New England integrity, energy and courtesy, love for the genuine and scorn for the spurious, a belief that bills should be paid and debts collected promptly. This became store policy. Anybody who doesn't pay Tiffany's is likely to be sued and the store has obtained judgments against some notable heiresses, playboys and at least one diplomat's wife.

Tiffany's early introduced the sterling silver standard from England and advertised "every silver article we sell is guaranteed English sterling (925/1000)." In 1851 the firm also advertised that "every article is marked in plain figures, upon which there will not be the slightest variation." The one-price system was then far from general.

Tiffany's unique advertising began at this time and has continued ever since. The partners advertised "their magnificent stock, believing it to exceed in extent, variety and richness, any other in the country." This was modest in comparison with the flamboyant claims of the day and soon their copy became so restrained that for many years all adjectives were eliminated. But when an authority on the subject chose the "One Hundred Greatest Advertisements in History," he picked one just saying: "Tiffany & Co., Pearls, Pearl Necklaces."

Completion of the Atlantic cable gave the firm the opportunity for the nearest thing to a publicity stunt in its long history. The store bought cable fragments and fashioned them into paper weights, cane and umbrella handles. A jeweled inkstand for President Lincoln and a fabulous sword for General U. S. Grant were among the Civil War products made by Tiffany's. The hilt of the latter was encrusted with precious stones. The scabbard was of gold and richly studded with rubies, diamonds and sapphires to represent the national colors. The firm made lockets which girls wore to carry hair of a favorite soldier. Medals and flags, the latter priced as high as $500 each, also were produced. But the firm's factory soon was converted to the actual making of military supplies. This set a pattern for World War I when Tiffany's made surgical instruments and World War II when precision airplane engine parts were made.

Tiffany & Company, the present firm, was incorporated in 1868 coincident with the merger of the partnership, from which Ellis and Young had retired, with John C. Moore's Silverware Company, which had been supplying its American-made silverware. Tiffany was the first president. Members of the Tiffany family, courtly, mustached gentlemen of short stature, and members of the Moore family, taller versions of the same, have been running Tiffany's ever since.

Louis de Bebian Moore, the debonair Harvard graduate who became president of the firm on retirement of his father in 1940, is a great-grandson of the original Moore. He has been at Tiffany's more than forty years. Long listed in the New York *Social Register* but only since 1952 in *Who's Who in America,* he pursues Tiffany's traditional anonymity and speaks to the public only through the luster of Tiffany's gems, most of which he personally inspects and approves.

Tiffany's five vice presidents, all veterans of more than a quarter of a century, include William T. Lusk, a great-grandson of the founding Tiffany. Also a social registerite, Lusk has been a Tiffany man since graduation from Yale in 1924. The other vice presidents are Robert S. Douglas, S. Hinman Bird, A. L. Barney and James B. Dickey.

Of the intervening Tiffanys, the founder's son, Louis Comfort Tiffany, was the most famous. He was a vice president of the store, but spent most of his long life in art. He developed a remarkable iridescent glass, Tiffany Favrile, used for vases and bowls sold in the store and also for stained-glass windows. A perfectionist, Louis Comfort inspected every product before it left the factory, stalking down the aisles carrying a long stick and breaking faulty pieces. He redecorated the White House for President Chester A. Arthur, putting in some glass screens, and supplied a $100,000 curtain made of small crystals, for the National Theater in Mexico City. A noted oil and water-color painter himself, he established with $1,000,000 the Louis Comfort Tiffany Foundation which gives annual cash grants to promising painters and sculptors. His glass company went bankrupt in 1932 but many of its creations are exhibited in museums and survive in the Cathedral of St. John the Divine and other churches.

Tiffany's won medals at countless expositions and opened an office in London. When the French Republic sold the French crown jewels, Tiffany's was the largest purchaser, buying a third of them. The store also bought heavily at the sale of diamonds of Prince Esterhazy of Hungary. A Tiffany-made silver centerpiece, reproducing the Statue of Liberty, was presented by grateful New Yorkers to Frédéric Auguste Bartholdi, the French sculptor, on completion of this famous symbol of freedom. Mrs. Finley J. Shephard, daughter of Jay Gould, also had Tiffany's make a five-pound sterling silver copy of the statue's torch for New York University academic processions.

After three locations on lower Broadway, the store moved in 1870 to Union Square and in 1905 to Fifth Avenue and Thirty-seventh Street. This was near the first Waldorf-Astoria Hotel, where John W. "Bet-a-Million" Gates and some other Tiffany customers resided. There the firm erected its own seven-story building modeled on the Palazzo Grimani on the Grand Canal in Venice.

A remarkable feature of this building was the fact that for thirty years it bore no sign of any kind. It was not until 1935 that a modest "Tiffany & Co." went up over the doors. Five years later, the store moved to its present site. In this move, an old whistle that had long sent Tiffany craftsmen to lunch was discarded, but taken along was the old Tiffany clock, supported by a carved wood figure of Atlas, which dates from 1853. The store's Union Square building was one of the first to boast burglar-proof vaults and the present store has a protective system of visible guards and secret alarms that probably rivals Fort Knox.

Men outside the Tiffany and Moore families, of course, contributed to the success of the store. One of these was Charles Cook, a Tiffany man for fifty-nine years. He was president from the death at ninety-four in 1902 of the first Tiffany, who left an estate of $35,000,000, to the accession of John Chandler Moore in 1907.

Of greater renown was Dr. George Frederick Kunz, dean of the world's gem experts. As a New York boy of ten, he began to collect colored stones from excavations. He sold a tourmaline to Charles Lewis Tiffany, who like other leading jewelers until then had been interested only in diamonds, emeralds, rubies, sapphires and pearls. Educated at Cooper Union, Kunz went to work at twenty-three as Tiffany's gem expert and continued there until his death fifty-three years later. In a score of books and countless lectures, he championed the beauty of gemstones. One of his chance remarks about their abrasive qualities led an admirer, Dr. Edward G. Acheson, to invent the valuable abrasive, Carborundum.

Dr. Kunz was the confidant of the elder J. P. Morgan and sold him collection after collection of rare gems. The greatest of these, representing twenty years of searching by Kunz, is now at the American Museum of Natural History. Kunz could sell Morgan any gem except an opal. The financier was among the superstitious who considered this gem one of ill omen.

Dr. Kunz named a newly discovered pink beryl gem morganite in honor of Tiffany's great customer and also dedicated his best-known book, *The Curious Lore of Precious Stones,* to him. In this work, the gem expert reviewed all of history's superstitions about jewels. These he did not accept, but wrote: "Nevertheless, the possession of a necklace or a ring adorned with brilliant diamonds, fair pearls, warm, glowing rubies, or celestial-hued sapphires, will today make a woman's heart beat faster and bring a blush of pleasure to her cheek."

A rare milky blue Brazilian diamond, which Dr. Kunz noticed glowing in his wife's ring when she hung a gown in a dark closet, he named tiffanyite in honor of the store founder. This gem has a phosphorescent inclusion. In addition to receiving decorations from France, Norway, Japan and other nations, Kunz was honored by one of his admirers giving the name kunzite to a lilac-colored variety of spodumene discovered in California which the expert had identified. It has since also been found in Madagascar.

Only once did the astute Dr. Kunz nod in identifying gems. Some unusually large rubies arrived in a shipment supposedly from India and he bought them. It was later discovered that these were "reconstructed rubies," made by French scientists electrically fusing powdered fragments of natural Burma rubies.

While the stones were of ruby material, they did not meet Tiffany's idea of ethics and quality. All that had been sold were recalled and the purchasers given back their money. In consequence of this, the firm bought an X-ray machine and other equipment for the scientific study of gemstones and precious metals. The government, incidentally, adopted the firm's standards for platinum alloys.

Tiffany's present scientific laboratory, the most elaborate of any store, includes specially constructed X-ray and camera equipment. Every important stone is photographically "fingerprinted." There is a density balance for the separation of jadeite and nephrite, the two varieties of jade. There are five different instruments for the testing of pearls and the staff includes a scientist, Dr. A. E. Alexander, often introduced as the world's greatest authority on pearls.

In most cases, the instruments merely confirm the judgment of Tiffany men. Only the store's senior officers buy stones. The staff includes many specialists. A dozen designers, some of them graduates of art schools, are available to sketch the possible settings for a gem or to show visually how an old piece can be modernized. There are fashions in the design of jewelry just as in the design of dresses.

Two women string pearls. Dowagers who don't want their pearls out of their sight, make appointments and watch the job done in private rooms. The cost is according to the length of the strand. Some million-dollar necklaces, mostly the property of Indian Maharajas, have been in and out of Tiffany's. The store, of course, will have nothing to do with artificial pearls or even with cultured pearls. When the Japanese began to make the latter by inserting beads of foreign particles into pearl-making oysters, the firm sought to prevent their being called pearls. "No artificial or cultured pearl has ever been produced," contends a Tiffany expert, "that can compare with the warm, rose-colored natural pearls from the Persian Gulf."

One of the few people ever to out-expert Tiffany's was Louis Marks, famous dealer in rubies and star sapphires. He found a fine star sapphire underpriced at Tiffany's in London, bought it and brought it to America and sold it to Tiffany's in New York at a much higher price. Marks never tired of telling the story.

Tiffany's employees are a devoted group. Legend has it that one of them made his way through the German lines into besieged Paris in 1870 to safeguard the Tiffany branch there. More than half of the slightly more than six hundred store and factory employees belong to the firm's Twenty-five Year Club, thirty-five have been employed for more than fifty years. The late George F. Heydt, who began as secretary to the founder and rose to advertising manager, served the firm sixty-eight years before retiring.

Only rarely has Tiffany's faith in its employees been betrayed. One embezzled $10,000 long ago by payroll padding. From an inside caged-off enclosure on the repair and manufacturing floor, three pear-shaped diamonds, weighing twelve carats each and valued at $80,000, later disappeared and were never located. These stones, cut from the famed Excelsior diamond, once the largest in the world, were Tiffany's most spectacular loss.

More recently a Tiffany man was victimized by one of the oldest swindles in the confidence man's book. An attractive blonde entered the store and with the bored nonchalance of the rich, said her fiancé had asked her to select some rings. She chose two, a solitaire and a diamond wedding band, valued at $6,300, then told the clerk she would like her mother's approval before buying. She demurely asked the clerk to deliver the rings at her Riverside Drive apartment.

When the clerk arrived, she took the kid-covered box and walked through a door, calling, "Mother, the Tiffany man is here with the rings." When she failed to reappear after fifteen minutes, the clerk became alarmed. He knocked on the door, got no answer and turned the knob. The door was another exit into the hall. Tiffany's never saw the blonde or the rings again.

Tiffany's is concerned with its dignity. The firm obtained a permanent injunction, for example, against a motion-picture company which adopted the name Tiffany, used a sparkling diamond as an emblem and referred to its productions as gems and pearls. In the course of this litigation, Tiffany's in 1932 revealed some sales figures for the first time but only to the extent of saying that it had done a gross business of more than $350,000,000 in the previous forty years and had spent $3,500,000 for advertising in the previous twenty-three years.

During the depression, the store reduced its capital and adjusted its operations to a much lower volume than during the lush twenties and earlier years. World War II closed the Paris and London branches and they were not reopened. The New York City sales tax, increased to 3 per cent, and the 20 per cent federal excise tax, not reduced until 1954, hardly encouraged profligate buying.

Nevertheless, Tiffany's dividends continued. The shares were split five for one in 1920 and again sixteen for one in 1949 and a few investors outside the Moore and Tiffany families became stockholders. The firm began to publish a brief balance sheet and profit statement. Earnings fell to $14,787 in 1952 and were but $24,906 in 1953 despite a reduction in operating expenses from $2,516,960 to $2,482,869. But the firm still had a surplus from previous years of $4,544,395 after paying $2 in 1952 and $1 in 1953 on its 132,451 outstanding shares. For the jewelry industry as a whole, Department of Commerce figures showed larger sales in 1952 and 1953 than in 1951.

President Moore announced in 1954 that the firm had earned an average of $323,530 a year or $2.44 a present share, for the eleven complete calendar years since the store moved to its Fifty-seventh Street location. Of these profits, totaling $4,205,889, dividends amounting to $3,360,814 had been paid.

Back in 1916, court appraisal of the estate of Charles M. Moore, for many years manager of the Paris branch of the firm, revealed that in the seven years prior to 1914, when he died, Tiffany & Company earned a total of $7,544,319, or an average of $1,077,759 a year.

Whether these days will return is doubtful but there are people outside as well as inside the firm who believe in Tiffany's. The reduction in the federal excise tax has affected the business for the better. In recent years, the advertising, handled as formerly by Milton Towne of Alley & Richards, has shown specific items with prices. There are price tags too on items in the show windows, something unthinkable in past years. Most important, Tiffany's now allows leading jewelers in a score of other cities to sell its silverware.

Investors seem eager to buy Tiffany stock. Even the smallest shareholder regularly receives offers to buy his shares without commission. A change such as has taken place at Brooks Brothers, the New York Central and the Statler Hotels may be coming for Tiffany's. But whoever owns the institution is certain to preserve its most valuable asset, the world-famous name and its good will. This, incidentally, is not valued at even the traditional $1 on the balance sheet, but the frequency with which the name figures in song and anecdote attests its great value.

When Mrs. Stuyvesant Fish, the famous Newport hostess, coughed in the night air, her husband considerately asked: "Can I get you something for your throat, my dear?"

"Yes, you can," she replied. "That diamond necklace I saw today at Tiffany's."

Eartha Kitt has entertained Broadway audiences more recently with a song demanding that somebody trim her Christmas tree "with ornaments from Tiffany."

V. The Singer Sewing Machine Company

World-wide Pioneer of Installment Selling

Penniless and beset by law suits, a forty-year-old sewing-machine inventor named Isaac Merritt Singer turned for help in 1851 to a New York attorney named Edward Clark. They became partners in I. M. Singer and Company. From this modest beginning grew The Singer Manufacturing Company, with great factories in seven countries, and the world-wide Singer Sewing Machine Company and other sales affiliates which now sell direct to user some $350,000,000 worth of sewing machines and related items a year.

In addition to making sewing machines of a mechanical excellence that is the standard of the world, the Singer organization has facilitated their sale by everywhere pioneering installment selling, a development that has affected the economy of mankind almost as much as the sewing machine itself. This innovation has helped the organization, under statesmanlike management, to sell more than 100 million Singer machines and enabled the parent company to pay dividends continually since incorporation in 1863.

The Singer Sewing Machine Company is the foremost exponent of manufacturer-to-consumer selling and its family sewing machine is the most widely used product in the world.

Mahatma Gandhi, the late Indian leader, while in jail learned to sew on a Singer and exempted the sewing machine in his ban on Western machinery. "It," he said, "is one of the few useful things ever invented." Singer is better known and occupies bigger buildings than the United States government in parts of India. A native-language letter, for example, was delivered addressed: "Exalted Holiness of the Consul General of the United States of America by the backside of the Singer Sewing Machine Company, Calcutta."

The company prints directions for using Singers in fifty-four languages. South Pacific islanders rate a Singer high among the necessities of life. First comes food, then shelter, and next the sewing machine. The only reason shelter comes ahead of the Singer is to protect it from the rain.

It might be an exaggeration to say that Japanese dress was Westernized to provide a market for Singer machines but the company had a great deal to do with the process. With the encouragement of Marquis Okuma, one of the last elder statesmen, Singer opened the first sewing school in Japan. Its graduates taught the nation machine sewing.

Singers are popular throughout Europe. A shop in Norway is above the Arctic Circle. Africa had Singers before Stanley went searching for Livingstone and there is a Singer-equipped shirt factory in the heart of the Belgian Congo. In the Americas, Singer Sewing Centers marked with the big red "S" extend from Anchorage, Alaska, to Magallanes, Chile.

In the United States, there are more sewing machines than telephones in homes and most of the machines are Singers. In addition, more complex Singers are the heart of the four-billion-dollar-a-year apparel industry. They also fabricate millions of shoes, furs, hats, gloves, full-fashioned hosiery, belts, mattresses, automobile upholstery and thousands of other articles of everyday life.

Singer machines are exactly the same whether purchased in New York's forty-seven-story Singer Building, the tallest structure in the world when built; in London's City Road; in Patriot Street of Addis Ababa or anywhere else. Only its catalog number differentiates a Singer made in Elizabethport, New Jersey, or Bridgeport, Connecticut, from the same type when produced by Singer factories in Canada, Scotland, France, Italy or Brazil.

Singer executives smilingly describe the workings of the organization in a deceptively modest sentence. "All we do," they explain, "is make a machine, take it out and sell it, collect the money and then send it back to make another machine."

As most sewing machines are sold on the installment plan, this may require two or three years. Singer fathered installment selling and is possibly its foremost exponent. Singers are made in dollar, sterling, franc and lira nations and sold not only in those currencies but also elsewhere for pesos, pesetas, yen, krone, rupees, guilders and other moneys. In consequence Singer probably does business in more currencies than any other company. It is usual for Treasurer John Morton's department to be owed many millions in foreign currencies which may fluctuate upward or downward.

Isaac Merritt Singer, for whom the companies are named, was a restless Yankee machinist. When thirty-nine years old, he borrowed $40 for capital and made his first sewing machine in Boston in 1850. When completed, it would not work. He was about to give up in despair when he recalled a neglected thread adjustment. He returned to the shop after midnight, made the change and the machine functioned. It was the first device with which it was possible to sew continuously. He was granted patents and began to make machines, first in Boston and then in New York.

As a relic in the Smithsonian Institution shows, the Singer was the first practical sewing machine and the first to resemble modern models. It was far from being the first sewing machine. As early as 1790, Thomas Saint, "cabinetmaker of Greenhill Rents, Parish of St. Sepulchre," obtained an English patent on a forgotten machine for chain-stitching leather. In 1814, Josef Madersperger, a master tailor of Kufstein whose portrait later graced an Austrian postage stamp, received an Imperial privilege, the equivalent of a patent, for a sewing machine using an eye-pointed needle but died in a Vienna poorhouse without developing the device. In America, sewing devices were made in 1819 by John Knowles of Monkton, Vermont, and in 1826 by Henry Lye of Philadelphia.

The first sewing machine of any tangible success was made by Barthélemy Thimmonier, a French provincial tailor, and patented in 1830. Eighty of his machines, which employed a single thread to make a chain stitch, were put to work making French army uniforms only to be smashed by a mob of jealous tailors. Walter Hunt, an American Quaker genius who invented the safety pin and paper collar, made a machine in 1834 but abandoned it when his daughter told him it would throw seamstresses out of work. In 1843, Dr.

Frank Goulding, a Presbyterian clergyman of Macon, Georgia, made a machine. Neither he nor Hunt patented their machines.

Elias Howe, Jr., a Cambridge, Massachusetts, machinist with much more forethought, in 1846 won the recognition of history with a patent on a sewing machine employing an eye-pointed needle with a shuttle. When Singer and two other makers appeared with their improved machines, Howe sued them. After a few lawsuits, in one of which Rufus Choate, the greatest attorney of the day, represented Howe, it was apparent that the new machines could not be made without the needle and shuttle idea. At the same time, it was obvious that Howe's machine, which sewed only straight seams a few inches at a time, could be sold only with the new improvements.

Soon each of four manufacturers was suing all of the others. Each maker also denounced his rivals in scathing newspaper advertisements and what the public called "the sewing machine war" was under way.

For help on the legal front, Singer turned to the New York law firm of Jordan & Clark. As Ambrose Jordan, the senior partner of the firm, was state attorney general, Singer saw Jordan's junior partner and son-in-law, Edward Clark. For a third interest in the company, he agreed to fight the legal battles. The man who had advanced the original $40 a little later fell ill and for $6,000 sold his third to Clark and Singer. They became equal partners in I. M. Singer and Company in 1851. Singer remained in charge of manufacturing. Clark took charge of finances and sales as well as legal matters.

Two more different men than Clark and Singer would be difficult to imagine. Born of poor German immigrant parents, Singer had little education and left his Oswego, New York, home when twelve years old. He grew up to be a truculent man of lusty appetites. He was without success a farmer, a machinist, an actor in a Shakespearean troupe, and an inventor of machines for excavating rock and carving wood. He employed the vertical action and horizontal work platform of the latter device in his sewing machine.

By contrast, Clark, a man of the same age, was a well-educated, quiet-spoken lawyer from upstate New York. He was a graduate of Williams College and a building there later was named for him. As his father was a pottery manufacturer, Clark grew up with some knowledge of business and as Singer's partner proved extremely successful in it.

He and other lawyers ended the "sewing machine war" by organizing the Sewing Machine Combination, America's first patent pool. Manufacture was licensed at $15 a machine. Because of the greater importance of their patents, the Howe and Singer interests received $5 each and the others less. Twenty-four companies were licensed and machine making greatly increased. Though he made few machines himself, Howe received at least $1,185,000 in royalties before his death in 1867. The Combination continued until 1877 when the last of the patents involved expired.

The earliest sewing machines were heavy devices for tailors and harness makers but by 1856 all the leading companies were making lighter models for home use. A machine enabled a housewife to do in one hour what took ten to fourteen hours by hand. The great obstacle was the fact that the average family income was less than $500 a year and the price of a sewing machine was $125 or more. Edward Clark attacked this problem with a trade-in allowance for old machines, the barter of machines for advertising, discounts to schools, and, most important and enduring of all, the development of installment selling.

As early as September 30, 1856, a Margaret Hellmuth of 47 Centre Street, New York, paid $50 in cash and signed a special agreement to pay $100 more in six monthly installments of $16 or $17 each. Thus was born the hire-purchase plan. The nearest approach to it at the time was the sale on credit of reapers by Cyrus McCormick, founder of the International Harvester Company. He collected a down payment and the remainder plus interest the following December 1. Clark's systematic monthly payment plan seems to have been the first in all business.

Installment sales kept the Singer business going when the panic of 1857 struck the next summer with the failure of many banks, railroads and insurance companies. Only $5 was needed now to place a new Singer sewing machine in a home. The remainder was paid in small monthly payments. If the purchaser failed to make payments, the machine was repossessed.

The idea became popular so rapidly that Clark was apprehensive about the results. "It appears," he wrote a Milwaukee agent, "that

$955.50 worth of machines were sold, of which you received $76 in cash. This is too small a proportion . . . leave the doubtful customers to your competitors." The firm's *Gazette,* one of the first house organs in American business, published a warning against the pawning or selling of machines on which payments had not been completed.

But losses were slight. Various special printed forms were worked out for this form of sale. Sometimes stamp receipts were given for payments and these were affixed to the contract until the full amount was paid. If a customer could make a larger payment than $5, he, of course, was encouraged to do so.

Installment selling became a bulwark of Singer sales in the United States and soon was instituted in Great Britain and many overseas countries under the original term of "hire-purchase." Nearly all machine purchasers everywhere were found to be honest. All Singer records in Manila, for example, were destroyed during World War II but with peace fifty thousand persons owing money on machines voluntarily paid up their accounts. A small army of collector-agents was long employed to collect the installments but most payments are now made by mail.

Clark managed so well that Singer was happy to leave everything to his partner or others while he pursued pleasures he could not afford in his youth. After incorporation of the business as The Singer Manufacturing Company in 1863, the inventor spent nearly all of his time in Europe. He was completing a great house, called "The Wigwam," at Paignton, England, when he died there in 1875, leaving $13,000,000, mostly in Singer stock, to a numerous progeny. Clark, who then became president of the company, left an even larger estate when he died in 1882 at Cooperstown, the beautiful upstate New York community to which his family was devoted. One of his grandsons, Stephen C. Clark, is now a director of the company. The Civil War, meantime, demonstrated the advantages to the Singer Company of foreign trade, when the dollar was depreciated temporarily, and of integration. With establishment of its own cabinet factory in 1867, Singer became virtually a maker-to-user manufacturer and has remained so. Wood for cabinets is grown in the company's own forests in Canada, Arkansas and South Carolina. This is sawed in its own mills and moves to main lines over three small Singer-owned railroads. Starting from pig iron, rough forgings or wire, Singer makes its own machines in four thousand varieties and its own needles in ten thousand sizes. It makes its own electric motors. Equally important, nearly all of its machines have been sold direct to the user through the company's own salesmen and shops.

Some extraordinary salesmen introduced Singer machines to the world. It was a difficult business at first. James Bolton, an early agent in New Haven, recalled in his memoirs that as he started for his post Isaac Singer slapped him on the shoulder and said: "Jim, we'll send you all the machines you want but not one cent of money." Singer men had to be mechanics, collection agents, sewing teachers and versatile adventurers. They traveled mostly in well-marked buggies but also by dugout canoe and every other form of conveyance.

A Singer agent who penetrated the Everglades greatly improved the dress of the Seminole Indians, until then drably and scantily clad. Women of the tribe adopted the machine enthusiastically and Seminole costumes soon became elaborate and colorful with hundreds of pieces of bright materials being sewed together in striking designs. It is not unusual to find a Seminole skirt with forty-four bands of color between the hem and waistline.

Some Singer machines moved abroad early. One took a grand prize at a world's fair in Paris in 1855. Singers were advertised the next year in Rio de Janeiro. Despite great growth in domestic business, the company by 1861 was selling more sewing machines abroad than in the United States.

First manufacture of Singers overseas began in 1867 in Glasgow, Scotland. Fifteen years later, Clark's successor as head of the company, George Ross McKenzie, who left Scotland as a barefoot immigrant boy, returned there and built the biggest of all Singer plants at nearby Clydebank. It is so important in the community that a Singer machine is now part of the city's coat of arms. Assembly of Singers began in Montreal, Canada, in 1873, the same year that the big Elizabethport, New Jersey, plant was completed and United States manufacturing shifted there from New York. Other plants are of later construction.

When Singer salesmen found people lacking the co-ordination to operate the usual treadle machine, they were sold hand machines.

When one African tribe, believing "good iron makes good noise," demanded noisy machines, a Singer man obligingly loosened up his machines until they achieved the required clatter. Agents even sold Singers to customers who thought the machine witchcraft.

As the native Japanese kimono was sewed with a few long stitches, which allowed it to be taken apart for washing and drying, the first Singers introduced there were adjusted to make such stitches. The company then taught thousands of Japanese how to make Westernized garments by machine. In later years, sewing lessons were broadcast by radio with thousands at times listening in the Tokyo and Yokohama municipal halls.

A Singer model introduced into the old Turkish Empire at the time a constitution was being demanded with the slogan, "Freedom, Justice, Equality and Brotherhood," was christened "Hurriya," the Arabic translation of freedom. Though superseded by later models, many of these "Hurriya" machines are still in service.

One of the most amazing Singer pioneers was George Neidlinger, first employed as a factory waterboy in New York. At twenty-two, he went to Hamburg as a European agent. Against heavy competition, including that of machines sold under imitation Singer labels, he introduced the Singer into Germany, Denmark, Sweden, Norway, the Balkans and eventually into Russia. As a step in the last, he had 250,000 tents for the Czar's army made on Singer machines.

Singer sales organizations employ where possible the citizens of the countries in which they function. "A Frenchman," a Singer executive once remarked, "knows better than anybody else how to sell a sewing machine to another Frenchman." Natives head the Singer organizations in every European country. The Australian and South African Singer organizations are 100 per cent national.

The Singer Manufacturing Company has had only three presidents since the retirement in 1889 of George Ross McKenzie. They have been Commodore Frederick G. Bourne, Sir Douglas Alexander and Milton C. Lightner, all of them world-traveling forceful executives.

Under Commodore Bourne (the title was from the New York Yacht Club), Singer made its first electrically-powered machines, separated the family and factory business in the United States, and began to organize overseas subsidiaries. Sales of machines passed the million-a-year mark.

Sir Douglas, a Canadian subject, rose from a clerical job to head the company for forty-four years. These saw erection of the Singer Building in New York and world-wide expansion. This included construction of a great Singer plant at Podolsk, near Moscow, and the opening of Singer shops across Russia to Vladivostok. In recognition of his and the company's services in World War I, he was made a baronet by King George V.

Mr. Lightner became head of both the manufacturing and sales companies on the death of Sir Douglas in 1949 after several years as vice president. He directed the rehabilitation of the company's European properties after World War II, built new plants at Anderson, South Carolina, and Campinas, Brazil; guided a big expansion of Singer Sewing Centers in the United States; and for the first time published annual reports showing consolidated sales and earning figures on the company's world-wide operations.

Nearly all Singer executives have come from the ranks. Vice President Max L. Waterman, in charge of research, and Vice President Robert W. Stewart, in charge of manufacturing, began as factory engineers. Otto Myslik, vice president in charge of Europe, North Africa and the Middle East, was born near Prague and joined Singer as a clerk in Odessa, Russia. He headed Singer affairs in Russia at the time of the Bolshevik Revolution and barely escaped with his life. In addition to his native Czech, he speaks a dozen languages and continues to study others. "A new language," he says, "is a new life."

Another linguist, Alvin K. Aurell, vice president in charge of the Orient, began similarly in Japan where his father, a Baptist minister, represented the American Bible Society. He was a prisoner in the Philippines during the war. W. M. Miller, vice president for Latin America, joined Singer as a clerk in Buenos Aires. Percy W. Bullock, head of Singer in Great Britain, began as a mail boy in London.

World War I saw the end of the vast Russian development. All of the Singer property, representing an investment estimated at $115,000,000, was seized by the Soviet government. After World War II Russians also stripped the machinery from a Singer plant in Wittenberge, Germany, and took it to Podolsk.

Singer suffered other serious World War II losses while winning acclaim with record production of intricate fire controls, airplane parts and other military items. Thirty-nine Singer workers were killed in the vicinity when the great Clydebank Singer plant was blitzed by high explosives and incendiary bombs. The fire burned for days. Bombs also hit two hundred Singer shops in Great Britain and many on the Continent. Some Singer workers were killed in the French factory at Bonnières which was both bombed and sabotaged. Singer men also died in the Far East while several executives and their families suffered in the Santo Tomas prison camp and other concentration camps.

Two Singer men, one Japanese and one American, helped effect the surrender of the Korean port of Inchon in 1945. The latter, George Jones, who had traveled for Singer in the Orient, served with Army Intelligence and was with the fleet that steamed in to accept the surrender. Because of his knowledge of English, one Tani, who had been a Singer agent in Seoul under the Japanese, headed the Korean party that came out in a small boat.

"Why, it's our Mr. Jones!" shouted Tani as he saw the American.

Singers are found in all sorts of places. Nearly every ship carries at least one. They are used in prison, leper colonies and mental institutions where the satisfaction of creating something is an important factor in rehabilitation. The Wright brothers stitched the wings of the first airplane on a Singer, preserved in Dayton, Ohio. Admiral Richard Byrd took six Singers with him to the Antarctic.

Both the gowns and shoes of Queen Elizabeth of England are made on Singers and Westminster Abbey has a Singer for repair of the ceremonial robes of the British Royal Family. The Empress of Ethiopia visited the Singer shop in Addis Ababa and enrolled two of her ladies-in-waiting for a sewing course.

In Indonesia, a Singer man critically hurt in an accident took advantage of his stay in the hospital to sell eight machines to his doctors and nurses. The first business establishment to reopen in Managua, Nicaragua, after the great earthquake was Singer. Greek monks in ancient St. Catherine's Monastery on Mt. Sinai sew their robes with a Singer.

Long before the basic sewing machine patents expired, the Singer management shifted emphasis to quality, service, advertising and trademarks. As maker of the first article sold all over the world, Singer pioneered the use of trademarks in many lands. Singer machines were marked with the name from the first and the stands of many spelled "Singer" in metal. By 1870, the company had an oval trademark. It included a large "S," crossed needles and a shuttle.

Early in the seventies, the famous red "S" with a woman at a sewing machine also began to be used. Since then it has become the world's best-known trademark. The woman has been drawn in appropriate costume as the native of many lands. Her machine is always up-to-date and every few years the woman herself is given a new hairdress and has her skirt lengthened or shortened to keep her modern. As this is written the woman pictured is Susann Shaw, a television actress who in private life is a Connecticut housewife who sews for herself and two daughters.

There had been surreptitious counterfeiting of Singer trademarks earlier but with expiration of the last basic patent in 1877, many imitators came into the open. They imitated the Singer design. They also called their machines Singers and imitated the Singer trademarks. The Singer Manufacturing Company filed suits.

Hardest-fought was one against Frank T. June, head of the June Manufacturing Company of Chicago, and George P. Bent, a Chicago and Kansas City sewing machine dealer. Stationery of the June firm described it as "manufacturers of the new and greatly improved Singer Sewing Machine." Metal stands of its machines embodied the word Singer and a monogram, "S. M. Co.," which was explained as standing for Standard Machine Co., an earlier name of the June enterprise. Bent sold the June-made machine as the "Improved Singer," "June Singer," "New York Singer" and "Philadelphia Singer," though he had offices neither in New York nor Philadelphia.

Litigation lasted nineteen years. The defendants contended that the name Singer had reverted to the public with the Singer patents as in the case of the harmonica, the macintosh coat and linoleum, all names of once patent-protected articles that had become generic. Singer attorneys put forth the trademarks, introduced the full line of Singer machines, and argued that the name meant "the source of manufacture" rather than a type.

In a decision by Justice Edward D. White, the Supreme Court ruled finally against June and Bent, saying each manufacturer should indicate who made his machine and "unmistakably" inform the public. Justice White termed June's imitation of the Singer marks "an injury to private rights and a deceit upon the public." The deceptive practices of the defendants were "perpetually enjoined."

Since then Singer has consistently succeeded in protecting its famous trademarks against efforts at imitation and deception in many lands.

The Singer sales organization, headed by Vice President J. L. Ray and later Vice President Charles Bruder, naturally has had a leading role in the great revival of home sewing in the United States. Ready-to-wear dresses and the movement of women out of the home had combined to reduce interest in the domestic art. A large section of the "flapper" generation of American women grew up without learning to handle a needle. In 1922, a study revealed that schools, always supplied with Singers at a discount, had no up-to-date sewing textbooks and had almost ceased to teach the subject.

Singer attacked the problem by working more closely with schools. A new textbook, *Machine Sewing,* was prepared for home economics teachers, with a condensed version for students. Half a million copies of the first and three million copies of the latter have since been distributed. Wall charts and instructional motion pictures were produced.

When the depression gave American women more leisure and less money for clothes, home sewing began to boom. Introduction of a new portable electric aluminum machine weighing only eleven pounds gave Singer sales new impetus. Works Progress Administration projects, work of the Department of Agriculture's Extension Service, reduced electric rates and extensions of electric lines, pattern promotion and home economics activities in the schools, 4-H Clubs and Girl Scouts, all helped increase home sewing.

After World War II, Singer Sewing Centers were modernized and new ones were opened in well chosen retailing locations. In the new sites, the company started systematic sewing courses for adults, similar to the instruction which had proved successful in Argentina,

Japan and other countries. Courses were free to buyers of machines and open for a small fee to others. For increased volume, the new centers also were stocked with sewing notions, dress forms and every imaginable sewing aid; also with vacuum cleaners, electric fans, electric irons and similar articles.

End of World War II found Singer, because of complete conversion of its plants to military work, 500,000 orders behind and foreign sewing machines gained a foothold in the American market for the first time.

As production increased, competition became unscrupulous. One development of this was "the bait and switch" racket. Practitioners of this advertised secondhand Singer machines at bargain prices but, when the prospect reached the store or a salesman entered the prospect's home, the Singer was ancient or broken and every effort was made to switch the prospect to a new foreign machine. Some who accepted one for a trial found the "receipt" they signed was a sizable installment contract. The source of some foreign machines also was concealed by mounting an American-made motor over the label of origin.

The Federal Trade Commission and Better Business Bureaus took action in many cases and Singer obtained a number of injunctions against violators of its trademarks.

Singer also met the new competition with a series of new machines, developed by its Research Division under Vice President Waterman, increased promotional activities and additional sewing centers. There are now 1750 in the United States and Canada. In these, 400,000 women and teen-age girls learn to make dresses, draperies and slipcovers each year. There are several thousand Singer centers abroad.

Singer advertising, sometimes unconventional, helped sell machines. In India, the first Singer agent popularized the name by printing it in four languages on thousands of yards of white cotton cloth. He sold this at slightly below cost for loin cloths and Singer had hundreds of walking advertisements. Singer advertising included millions of picture cards, pocket mirrors, tape measures, thimbles, face powder tissues, fans and calendars. At one time the company gave away a song about its product, titled "The Merry Singer." In more recent years, under Advertising Director Harold Horton, evening network television programs as well as much newspaper and magazine space have been used. Advertising agencies, first G. Lynn Sumner and then Young & Rubicam, Inc., have been employed.

A development was a new *Singer Sewing Book* by Mary Brook Pickens. Published in 1949 and revised in 1954, this became an offering of the Book-of-the-Month Club and more than half a million copies were sold.

Singer machines and needles have increased so greatly in number and complexity that a catalog of them weighs a dozen pounds. While some competitors clung to a single type of machine, Singer engineers from the start offered a variety of sturdy, trouble-free machines and, at the same time, arranged a world-wide system of service and replacement. Even a simple type of sewing head, as the machine mechanism is called, requires 157 parts, some of which are finished to a few ten-thousandths of an inch.

The most popular type of machine is the two-thread lock-stitch which locks an upper and lower thread in the fabric. But Singer also makes chain-stitch machines, and on the industrial side, machines with as many as fifty needles. While most machines are now electrical, treadle and hand models are still made. Some hand machines are made with special raised controls for the blind.

Smallest of Singers is a child's machine weighing three pounds. This is tiny enough to hold in the hand but sews a seam. The biggest Singer is a 2,526-pound device for stitching heavy conveyor belts an inch and a half thick, for mining and heavy industry. The most expensive Singer is a $3,000 machine for the zigzag lock-stitching of camel's hair fabrics used in extracting oil from cottonseed.

A Singer for binding books has a drill that precedes the needle and bores a hole for it. There are Singers for sewing up bags after they have been filled. There is even a Singer made partly of phosphor bronze to eliminate static electric sparks in sewing up bags of gunpowder.

Electricity and improved bearings have greatly speeded up sewing. A household machine can now do fifteen hundred stitches a minute while many manufacturing models work as fast as five thousand stitches a minute. The miracle is that they can be stopped safely in a split second. A Singer that looks like a black, foot-high streamlined toadstool seams hosiery at forty-five hundred stitches a minute.

Some of the fastest machines are now self-lubricated and have the needles cooled by a blast of compressed air. Different types of work, as well as different thicknesses of the same work, require needles of different design and size. This and new textiles account for the ever-increasing types of needles. Singer needles range from .017 to .180 of an inch in diameter. Each needle, incidentally, goes through a score of swaging, straightening, punching, tempering, sharpening and polishing processes.

One of the newest Singer machines uses neither needle nor thread. Instead, it employs the stabbing heat of high-frequency electric current to bond plastic film materials into raincoats, shower curtains, balloons and similar articles.

For garment-trade customers, Singer has a factory layout service. A customer has only to submit samples and say what production he wants. From this information, Vice President J. P. Baiter's manufacturing trade department plans everything. The layout will place units for scientific straight-line production and will permit their rearrangement overnight to make different garments. Many big clothing factories built in the United States and abroad in recent years have been thus laid out.

Possibly the greatest tribute to Singer was voiced by a man in a sidewalk café in Spain. He and a friend were debating the possibility of the moon being inhabited.

"There is a simple way of settling the matter," he said. "Across the street is a Singer shop. Go into it and ask the manager. For assuredly if there is anyone on the moon, the Singer Sewing Machine Company will have a shop there."

VI. Filene's

The World's Largest Specialty Store

BOSTON has been famous for the excellence and enterprise of its stores for generations. More than one hopeful retailer opening for business far from New England has paid tribute to this reputation by calling his establishment "The Boston Store" in an effort to give it character and distinction. In some places the effort was successful. Milwaukee's Boston Store, for example, grew into a great institution, and in Rochester, New York, a Boston store prospered as the Sibley, Lindsay & Curr Co.

Biggest store volume-wise in Boston long has been that of the Jordan Marsh Company. It is a complete department store and the principal unit of the Allied Stores Corporation. Its magnitude is epitomized in its boast "New England's Greatest Store." Richard Mansfield, the actor, once worked there. Eben Jordan, one of its founders, gave Boston an opera house. Other notable Boston stores, some of them more than a century old, include those of the R. H. White Corp., Chandler & Co., Gilchrist Co., R. H. Stearns Co., and the E. T. Slattery Co. In Raymond's, Inc., the city has a remarkable helter-skelter bargain spot. The Shreve, Crump & Low jewelry store and Goodspeed's bookshop are nationally known in their fields.

It is Filene's, short for the William Filene's Sons Company, however, that is the Boston store that has been oftenest in the headlines. This is the world's largest specialty store. Its main building, a full city block in width, was one of the last structures designed by the late Daniel H. Burnham. It stands at Washington and Summer Streets and the spot is brass plaqued as "the hub of the universe" of which Oliver Wendell Holmes spoke. Thanks to this location, with access to two subways, and its fame as a store with a successfully split personality, high fashion upstairs and low prices downstairs in a unique basement, its dollar sales volume per square foot, more than $1,000 a year in some departments, is one of the highest in the world.

Filene's contributions to retailing include important advances in employee selection and training, sustained showmanship and community service, and merchandising innovations which have been adopted widely. Cycle billing, which changed a frantic end-of-the-month operation to an orderly procedure, was born at Filene's. The need of the store for a simple identification device for charge customers spurred invention of the Charga-Plate and Filene's was the first to use it. Since then it has been adopted by more than 650 stores and carried by at least twenty-five million shoppers. Branch-store operation was pioneered by Filene's and, as many branches were in college towns, led the store to develop first college and then high school student advisory fashion boards.

The William Filene of the firm name was born in 1830 in the Polish city of Posen, when it was within the borders of Prussia, where the name was sometimes spelled Filehne. There his father sold ribbons, then an important part of fashionable dress, profitably enough to send William and another son to Berlin to study law. The latter died there and William, discouraged, abandoned the law. It was 1848, a year of revolt in Europe which brought a bloody uprising in Posen. Instead of returning home, William renounced the religion of his Jewish fathers and emigrated first to England and then to the United States.

At eighteen, William went to work as a tailor in Boston. Three years later in 1851, he was able to open a tiny shop, stocking some dry goods, on Hanover Street. This lasted only a short time and 1856 found him with a small store on Essex Street in nearby Salem. There in 1856, he married Clara Ballin, an immigrant from Bavaria who proved a remarkable wife and mother. To them were born four sons and a daughter.

Of these, only the second son, Edward Albert, born in 1860 in Salem and named for the Prince of Wales who had just visited America, and the youngest son, Abraham Lincoln, born April 5, 1865, in Boston, figure importantly in the history of Filene's. The latter shortened his name to A. Lincoln Filene and eventually legally dropped the first name.

During the Civil War, William Filene left retailing for an unsuccessful manufacturing venture in New York, moving there in 1863 and losing all of his money in the metal trade by 1870. He then moved his family back to Lynn, Massachusetts. Despite the business troubles which culminated in the panic of 1873, he launched two small stores at Lynn, one at Salem and one at Bath, Maine.

The older boys had a year at the Handels Institut, a famous boys' school in Segnitz, Bavaria, their mother's birthplace, before collapse of the New York venture. They then continued in the Lynn High School. After classes, they ran errands, washed floors and cleaned the windows of their father's two Lynn stores, one of which was devoted to women's wear and the other to men's and boys' clothing.

These prospered and college was planned for Edward. But he had no sooner passed the Harvard University entrance examinations in 1879 than the father fell ill. As the eldest son Rudolph had no aptitude for or interest in the work, Edward had to abandon his college plans and at nineteen go to work full time. He cherished his Harvard entrance certificate, "No. 276," all of his life, however, and became a benefactor of the Harvard Business School. Young Lincoln soon followed his brother into the stores. In fact, it was William Filene's hope that each of his sons would take over one of the four stores, and the store at Bath, Maine, eventually was given to Bertram Filene, the brother born between Edward and Lincoln.

In 1881, the father and sons opened a store at 10 Winter Street in Boston and soon afterward sold the Lynn and Salem properties. The Boston store was only twenty-four feet square but was described as "one of the most modern of the day with its genuine white marble floor and most artistic windows." Bearded William Filene respectfully advertised that "purchasers can save a large percentage on esmeralda and embroidered sleeves from 25 cents to $3 a pair . . . dress trimmings in the latest patterns . . . French, chantilly, barege and tissue veils . . . lisle thread and silk gloves and mitts . . . and cotton stockings." A glove shop was added the next year also on Winter Street.

With the sons gradually relieving their ailing father of responsibilities, the business grew. The brothers lived on a small allowance and came in on Sunday to clean the store. Father and sons did all of the buying and employees were few enough for all to discuss their plans and problems every Friday evening at William Filene's home. In 1890, much larger quarters were leased in a five-story-and-basement building at 445–447 Washington Street, and the business was moved there. The space was the largest in Boston at that time devoted exclusively to women's wear and accessories.

The father, who suffered from a heart ailment, turned the management over to Edward and Lincoln in 1891 and they inherited the store at his death in 1901. The company was organized briefly as William Filene, Sons and Company and then as William Filene's Sons Company. Edward proved a wizard at merchandising, and Lincoln a genius at managing a store staff. They owned equal shares of the business, took turns using the title of general manager, and became one of the most famous brother teams in retailing.

They were among the first to recognize the value of good employee relations and systematic employee training. They went on record against absentee ownership and nepotism. As Edward remained a bachelor and Lincoln, who married in 1895, fathered only daughters, the latter, of course, was no personal hardship but it helped establish a remarkable spirit among the workers.

"If we were to create contentment in front of the counter," once explained Lincoln Filene, "we had first to create contentment behind it. Many employees learn their manner of serving the public from the manner in which they are served by their managers."

Without offending its carriage trade in piece goods, the store stocked machine-made dresses and lingerie as they became available. Its sales passed the half-million-dollar mark in 1900. The exact figure was $554,424. The next year the store trebled its space by moving to the buildings numbered 453 to 463 on Washington Street. In 1902 sales exceeded a million dollars for the first time with a volume of $1,165,183. The next year the previous quarters were leased again and designated as a "Baby-to-Miss" annex. In 1904, the intervening structure, Oliver Ditson's music shop, was occupied and the two Filene stores became one. But more and less awkward space still was needed.

Burnham, the famous architect and city planner, was employed to design a great store building to include eight floors above ground and a basement, sub-basement and cellar beneath it. The greater space would enable the store to enter the men's wear field. Plans provided for underground access to the new Boston subway to permit customers to arrive in comfort regardless of the weather.

"Make no little plans," Burnham had said in an address. "They have no magic to stir men's blood and probably themselves will not be realized. Make big plans. Aim high in hope and work, remembering that a noble, logical diagram once recorded will never die, but long after we are gone will be a living thing, asserting itself with ever growing insistency. Remember that our sons and grandsons are going to do things that will stagger us. Let your watchword be order and your beacon beauty."

When the new building was completed, this quotation was posted in the general manager's office and became a store motto. So great was the interest in the new structure that 235,000 persons visited it when it opened, decorated with American Beauty roses, on September 3, 1912. Within a week, 715,000 persons went through the doors. So well planned and constructed was the building that, with only slight changes, it was still in service more than forty years later.

To obtain the well-known Hart Schaffner & Marx line of clothing for its men's department, Filene's bought two Boston stores of the Continental Clothing House. One was resold and the other, a nearby structure, was absorbed into Filene's when the store spread over the entire block. A public-address system and air conditioning were added later with the Filene basement becoming the first large-scale application of air conditioning in retailing.

Outlying branches began to be established immediately after World War I. Taxation rather than traffic was the initial impetus. Many places undertook to collect a year's taxes from any store that presented a fashion show or otherwise showed merchandise there. Some of the early branches at Providence, Rhode Island, Falmouth, Massachusetts, and Portland, Maine, did not survive. Those at Northampton, Wellesley, Hyannis, Winchester, Belmont, South Hadley and Worcester proved more profitable. The B. Peck Co., second largest store in Lewiston, Maine, was added as a branch in 1945. A large Raymond Loewy-designed branch was opened at Chestnut Hill, a Boston suburb, in 1950.

As Wellesley, Smith, Mount Holyoke and other famous colleges for women were served by these branches, out of them grew the store's college board which helps it select and test fashion apparel for college girls. At times members have been rewarded with trips to Europe and South America. As an extension of this activity, Filene's also has a high-school fashion board selected annually on a competitive basis from several hundred eager applicants. Many board members have graduated to the store staff.

As the store became a great business, sales leaped from $4,810,899 in 1912 to $8,466,467 in 1913. With completion of the new building the Filenes pioneered a four-pyramid organization for their business modeled somewhat on the branches of the national government. Under the top authority, originally the Filene brothers, were four executives. One headed merchandising, another all publicity, another managed the store's services, and a fourth was the controller, in charge of accounts and money. These divisions successfully checked and balanced each other and this form of organization was adopted by many big stores as a result of its use at Filene's.

"I always believed that the store would grow if it had the right people," said Lincoln Filene, "and that if it didn't have the right people, it wouldn't grow." Booklets outlining opportunities in retailing and containing an application blank for employment at Filene's were distributed to graduating high school and college students in the area.

Promising young men and women were hired, systematically trained, their progress recorded and evaluated long before such personal methods were general in industry. Among those employed in the work were the late Professor Frank Parsons of Boston University, "the father of vocational guidance," Robert G. Valentine, one of the first industrial counselors, and Frank B. Gilbreth, noted motion study specialist and exponent of scientific management. In recognition of his own contributions to vocational training, Lincoln Filene, whose formal education like that of his brother stopped with high school, was awarded an honorary Master of Arts degree by Dartmouth College in 1916 and elected to honorary membership in Phi Beta Kappa by the parent William and Mary College chapter of the scholarship fraternity in 1922.

Filene training ranges from instruction in how a waitress shall place silver in the store restaurant, in which tipping is forbidden, to courses in the Harvard Graduate School. Job specifications are mimeographed. Workers are told how to perform their duties, how these fit into the store operations, why they are important. Workers are encouraged to make suggestions. An employee suggestion system, something which many businesses discovered only in World War II, was in effect as early as 1899 and $25,000 was once distributed in a single contest.

Humorous drawings by Francis Dahl, famous cartoonist of the Boston *Herald,* have enlivened Filene's instructions to salespeople. These are taught not that the customer is always right but that she is a guest and must be treated with consideration and tact. Even small details are given attention.

Clerks are not to ask: "About how much do you want to pay?" They are instructed to show the medium-priced article or, if there are only two prices, the one of better quality. Nor are Filene clerks permitted to ask, "What size?" They are supposed to estimate the customer's size, erring if necessary on the small side. If the customer's feet are not mates, the clerk is not to say, "One of your feet is larger than the other," but, "One of your feet is smaller than the other."

Clerks are told not to greet a shopper with "May I help you?" If the customer says "No," the clerk is defeated at the start. If the customer is looking at merchandise, the Filene approach is to describe its merits. If the shopper isn't looking, it is simply: "Good morning." Filene clerks are asked not to call customers "Dearie" nor to say that merchandise is "sweet," "cute" or "lovely."

In line with their oft-expressed belief that it is possible to attain more by co-operation than by conflict, the Filenes encouraged formation in 1898 of a remarkable employee organization called the Filene Cooperative Association. The complaint of a cashier whose pay had been docked for a shortage was responsible for the start of a liberal and unique system of settling employee grievance through this organization.

"If I'm short in my accounts," said the girl, "it's supposed that I've stolen the money. If I happen to be over, it's a 'clerical error,' and you pocket the money. It isn't fair."

Three arbiters decided for the girl. As a consequence an elected

Board of Arbitration was made part of the Filene Cooperative Association. It was given power to settle, without interference from management, any matter regarded as an injustice to an employee, or group of employees, resulting from a store rule, a discharge or a question of wages. The rules were drawn by the great Louis D. Brandeis, attorney for Filene's who later became a Justice of the United States Supreme Court. As they gave the employees on the board greater power over management than was later possessed by any labor union, some business leaders predicted dire consequences.

These did not develop, nor did the leaders of the F.C.A. evince any ambition to assume responsibilities of the management. This was a sad disappointment for Edward Filene. He had hoped that the organization might be the means eventually of turning over ownership of the store, in whole or in part, to its employees. The workers proved more interested in immediate problems of hours, wages and various disputes and the management met them more than halfway.

The store was one of the first to establish a minimum wage for women and girls. In 1913, the store inaugurated Saturday closing during the summer months and was the first in Boston to do so. In 1924, winter vacations were instituted in addition to the usual summer holiday.

In its thirty years of existence, the Board of Arbitration handled nearly a thousand disputes. In 308 cases studied by Russell Sage Foundation investigators, the board ruled for employees in 55 per cent of its decisions, for the management in 42 per cent, while 3 per cent were compromises.

With passage of the Wagner Act, the Filene Cooperative Association became the Independent Union of Retail Store Employees and conventional bargaining replaced the Board of Arbitration. But relations between Filene's and its thirty-five hundred to forty-two hundred workers continued smooth. For its personnel who served in World War II, the store made up any difference between the service pay and regular earnings and sent checks to families each month. The store became the first in Boston to establish a year-round forty-hour five-day work week. Filene's and the union shared the expense of a job evaluation study. Filene workers have group insurance, their own weekly magazine, *The Echo,* a library, a card room, restaurants and cafeterias, a twenty-five-bed clinic with two doctors and three nurses in attendance, and the services of a woman counselor for personal problems. Any employee ill more than three days receives a personal letter and a gift of fruit or flowers from the general manager.

New employees meet executives at a monthly breakfast in the store. At a ceremony every few months, employees who have worked fifteen years for the store are given "F" pins; those who have been employees twenty-five years, gold watches; and those who have been with Filene's forty years, engraved silver trays. An annual dinner, usually in the spring at the Hotel Statler, honors the more than six hundred workers who have been with the store more than a quarter of a century. At intervals, employees also receive scrolls and other awards for performance "beyond the call of duty."

The Filene employees' Credit Union, which has loaned more than $5,000,000 for the purchase of homes, payment of doctors' bills and similar purposes, is the prototype of credit unions throughout the country. While on a trip around the world, Edward Filene in 1907 found credit unions functioning successfully in Bombay, India. As a result, an informal loan fund which the store maintained to keep its employees out of the hands of loan sharks eventually was changed with legislative sanction into a credit union operated by employees with their own money.

So enthusiastic was Edward Filene about the economic value of credit unions that he personally employed Roy Frederick Bergengren, a lawyer who had been an outstanding finance commissioner for Lynn, to lead a national credit-union movement. A Credit Union National Extension Bureau was formed and later reorganized as the Credit Union National Association. State and then national legislation was obtained authorizing credit unions. There are now thousands of credit unions lending millions of dollars to workers who might not be able to borrow otherwise. Filene and Bergengren quarreled over the tactics to be pursued and the views of the latter prevailed, but the "shopkeeper from Boston," as Edward Filene often called himself, is entitled to a sizable share of credit for the success of the credit unions. This was acknowledged when the Credit Union National Association's headquarters building at Madison, Wisconsin, was dedicated formally by President Truman as "Filene House."

It was also from his restless brain that came Filene's most unique contribution to retailing. This is the world-famous Automatic Bargain Basement started in 1909. There was nothing remarkable about a basement store. Many firms had them, often as an outlet for the mistakes of buyers on the upper floors. But a basement in which prices were plainly marked and automatically reduced by a definite per cent on a definite day, if the goods remained unsold, was unique in 1909 and after nearly half a century still is unique.

Under the Filene system, basement goods are automatically reduced 25 per cent after twelve selling days, another 25 per cent if still unsold at the end of eighteen selling days, a third 25 per cent if remaining after twenty-four selling days. If still on hand after thirty days, items are given away to organized Boston charities.

The business world predicted failure for the scheme, but by faithfully adhering to these rules, candid advertising, and paying cash for distress stocks, the Automatic Basement became a spectacular success. In the depths of the depression of the thirties, the earnings of the basement were great enough to keep the store profitable when every upstairs floor was operating at a loss. Items as costly as mink coats and diamond jewelry have been handled. New York's finest Fifth Avenue shops regularly use it as an outlet for odd lots and remainders.

Buyers for the basement, which has a staff entirely separate from the rest of the store, have scoured the world for bargains. As the Germans approached Paris in 1940, buyers for Filene's basement picked up four hundred of the latest dresses by Schiaparelli, Lelong, Chanel and other famous modistes and shipped them out through Spain. A week after Paris fell, the basement announced a sale of the dresses, normally priced at several hundred dollars each for $11 to $49 each.

Fifteen thousand women were on hand when the doors opened. Several had come from New York, and the wife of a famous radio executive and the wife of a great manufacturer had flown together from Chicago. Within sixty seconds, every dress was off the racks. Fifteen minutes later all had been sold.

Another wartime coup was the Austin Reed of London haberdashery from the R.M.S.S. *Queen Mary*. Buyers laid out the inventory in the liner's swimming pool and, after intricate negotiations involving international exchange and British and American officialdom, acquired it for Filene's basement. Included were cashmere sweaters, lounging robes, pajamas and ties of the highest English quality. Among the ties were 412 of an identical design, yellow, royal purple and red stripes against a dark blue background, made for the *Queen Mary*. These were marked down to $1 each and, along with everything else, sold out in two and a half hours. For years afterward, strangers wearing the ties would greet each other on Boston streets as loyal fellow members of Filene's *Queen Mary* club.

As many as 150,000 bargain hunters have swarmed through the basement in an eight and a half hour day. This mark was hit during a 1947 sale of $1,400,000 worth of smoke-damaged luxury goods from Neiman-Marcus, the famous Dallas store. An imported $190 black lace brassiere then went for $8.95. Women also stormed the basement two years later to buy $514,000 worth of coats and dresses from Saks Fifth Avenue at 50 to 60 per cent less than the original price. That same year the two-million-dollar surplus inventory of the famous Waltham Watch Company was sold upstairs at half price. Many men bought three and four each, and the $200 watches were the first to go.

An annual basement event is a sale of men's suits and overcoats at $11 each. As many as seven thousand have been sold in one day. Only the coat hangs on the rack. The pants and vest, if any, are in a box. The customer puts on the coat and if he likes it grabs the box with the corresponding number and pays a clerk. Men are sometimes in line before dawn for these sales. John Barry, a Boston newspaper man, wore one of the $11 suits when the press met King George and Queen Elizabeth on their American tour and wrote about it.

Probably the biggest crowd of expectant mothers ever assembled in Boston showed up for the sale of two thousand baby carriages from a Gardner, Massachusetts, factory. There wasn't room for these in the basement and they were sold in a single morning from the store's Charles River warehouse. Mourning handkerchiefs from Ireland were once sold at three cents each. At the end of one Folies-Bergère season, a Paris buyer sent to Filene's a lot of hip-length silk stockings made especially for the chorus. They went fast at 59 cents a pair.

Charity gets less than 1 per cent of the basement merchandise but the basement has had some long-remembered mistakes. One involved two thousand woolen overcoats bought to sell at $12. The sample was all right but when the whole lot arrived the coats literally stank. They still stank at $9 and $6 but most moved at $3. Another involved a whole carload of 50-cent "hard" collars, some 1,100,000 in number, from Van Heusen. These were seconds and Filene's offered them at 25 cents each. That day neighboring stores offered first-quality Van Heusen collars at 15 cents each. In addition, the lot contained many size eighteen and thirteen collars which even the Salvation Army refused as they had no necks that big or small to collar. Filene's finally made a bonfire of the remaining collars.

The Automatic Basement has had both famous customers and noted help. John Roosevelt began his business career in the basement at $18.50 a week while his father was President of the United States. The youth's job was to keep the bins filled. He worked faithfully and modestly but for a time attracted so much attention that he had to be hidden in the stockrooms. Failing to find him, one portly lady unrolled and gave to the manager a big scroll bearing an ode starting, "Oh thou youth of sterling character."

Show-business notables regularly visit the basement when in Boston. Joe E. Brown has boasted in the Hollywood Brown Derby of shirts from Filene's basement. The famous Joseph Kennedy family of Boston like the place. The entire population of remote Pitcairn Island, descendants of the Bounty mutineers, buy their shoes in the basement by sending a sailor there once a year with pencil tracings of all the feet in the colony.

Why haven't other stores been able to establish similar operations? Attempts have been made in Boston, Philadelphia and a few other places but without success. The principal reason seems to be that there is only a limited amount of worthwhile distress merchandise available and the fame of Filene's is likely to give it first call. Some rivals have been unable to bring themselves to follow through on the automatic reductions when sizable quantities of goods failed to sell, and customers were quick to detect this. None has promoted its efforts as faithfully and as forcefully as Filene's. The first motion picture ever made in a store, a silent called *One Flight Down,* was filmed in the basement. It has used large newspaper space, radio and television personalities and even illuminated blimps to advertise anniversary sales.

While the basement was winning its fame, Filene's upstairs also had the benefit of some of the most notable talents in retailing. One of these was Louis E. Kirstein of Rochester, New York. He was induced to leave the Stein-Bloch Company, men's clothing manufacturers there, and join Filene's in 1911 as a vice president when the store entered the men's wear field. After a slow start, the store became successful in this in the face of fierce competition. He later was given charge of all upstairs merchandising and publicity as well. He made great contributions to the store for thirty-one years until his death in 1942.

A colorful and forceful figure, his aphorisms on management were still being quoted in retail publications more than a decade after his death. Some of the best known are:

"The expense rate cannot be lowered by worrying about it."

"Overnight we have all become accountants rather than merchants."

"Retailing needs less figuring; more fingering."

"One thing wrong with business is that business men do not attend to it."

"We need more individuality and less foolish straining to be all things to all men."

"No industry can rise higher than the caliber of men in it."

"Advertising pays when it is believed."

Expenditures for advertising, he believed, should be increased and not curtailed when business became sluggish. He argued that it was a waste to use huge newspaper space at Christmastime, for example, when without persuasion customers were struggling to get into the store.

A major contribution to merchandising initiated by Lincoln Filene enabled the company to exchange information hitherto regarded as confidential with important stores in other cities. After some preliminary discussion, he invited the principals of eighteen stores to lunch on September 6, 1916, at the Aldine Club in New York. Stores represented included L. S. Ayres & Company of Indianapolis, The Dayton Company of Minneapolis, The Emporium of

San Francisco, B. Forman Company of Rochester, Joseph Horne Company of Pittsburgh, The J. L. Hudson Company of Detroit, F. & R. Lazarus & Company of Columbus, The Rike-Kumler Company of Dayton, and the William Taylor Son & Company of Cleveland.

Lincoln Filene suggested that an organization be formed for the scientific study of the problems of merchandising and store operation. He contended that this would enable all to operate more efficiently, cut expenses and reduce distribution costs. Two months later the Retail Research Association was organized and opened a modest office in New York with Alvin E. Dodd, previously secretary of the Society for Vocational Education, as director. When he joined the U.S. Chamber of Commerce five years later, he was succeeded by Dr. Paul H. Nystrom, Columbia University professor of marketing.

One of the first projects of the association was the working out of a uniform system of records so figures of the co-operating stores could be compared. Some of these later were telegraphed to permit the prompt detection of any new trend. Detailed studies also have been made of every store activity and members often have helped each other on special problems without going through the association office. Of the many reports supplied its members, the most important are the annual and semiannual general manager's reports. These are as large as an atlas and present a complete operating picture of every department of every store.

As an outgrowth of this activity, the same stores beginning in 1918 formed a twin organization, the Associated Merchandising Corporation, and recently the A.M.C. Wholesale Corporation, for the co-operative mass buying of many of the items which all sold. In 1920, a committee chairmaned by Vice President Kirstein of Filene's toured Europe and opened A.M.C. buying offices in London, Paris, Brussels, Berlin and Milan, the last later removed to Florence. Buying offices subsequently were opened in the Orient.

At the same time, A.M.C. began to buy in the American markets for important foreign stores as well as its members. Firms thus represented included Harrods Ltd., of London and Buenos Aires, The Myer Emporium, Ltd., of Melbourne, Farmer & Co. of Sydney, and the Panama Railroad Co. which operates stores in the Canal Zone.

As A.M.C. buying became a multi-million dollar activity more famous stores joined. Bullock's of Los Angeles became a member in 1919; Strawbridge & Clothier of Philadelphia, in 1921; Abraham & Straus of Brooklyn, in 1923; Hutzler Brothers Company of Baltimore, in 1925; Stix, Baer & Fuller Company, St. Louis, in 1926; the H. C. Capwell Company, Oakland, California, in 1927 and others later.

Lincoln Filene served as president and chairman of the executive committee of the R.R.A. from its organization until 1943 and of the A.M.C. from 1921 until that date when he retired with a notable collection of gavels as souvenirs of his long service. A few years later, A.M.C. buying became more than a billion dollars a year. It had long been the largest central buying organization outside the chain and mail-order fields.

At Filene's, top management, meanwhile, went through a grave crisis. On March 1, 1913, in a reorganization after completion of the store building, control of the company was vested in six executives, the Filene brothers and the heads of the four pyramids in the store's organization chart. Each brother had 26 per cent of the stock. Each of the other four had 12 per cent. These were Vice President Kirstein, merchandising; John R. Simpson, publicity; Thomas K. Cory, the store manager; and Edward J. Frost, the comptroller. The Filenes pledged that they or their heirs by the same date in 1928 would transfer 4 per cent of their holdings to the others and yield them control of the store. These six men and five other employees composed the company's board of directors.

All went smoothly for a time but tension and antipathy developed between Edward A. Filene, who under the reorganization had the title of president of the company, and Vice President Kirstein. Both were intense, ambitious, driving personalities. As both were merchandising men, collision possibly was inevitable. They differed in appearance. Kirstein was a big kindly bear of a man. "Little Eddie," as some old employees termed him, was a small dapper fashion plate with a close-cropped bristling mustache. They differed more in ideas.

Kirstein was a man of family, interested in the Boy Scouts, headed the Boston Jewish charities for a time, and was a conventional and understandable executive. Sigmund Freud would have been greatly

interested in Edward A. Filene. From a shy youth who suffered from
eczema, he grew into an aggressive, complicated, tactless, restless,
brilliant and dictatorial man.* In his thirties, he became engaged to
a young woman but, as he explained later, the engagement came to
an end one evening on a streetcar when he neglected her to conclude
a business deal with a man he had been seeking who chanced to be
on the car. He had little use for conventional charities. With no
family interests, he flung himself intensely into all manner of causes.
He was the leading spirit in the organization of the Boston Chamber
of Commerce, the U.S. Chamber of Commerce and finally the International Chamber of Commerce.

He made an annual trip to Europe at first to buy merchandise
but soon to visit leaders of all sorts and pursue his causes. Outbreak
of World War I found him in Paris helping Ambassador Myron
Herrick mark American property and care for stranded Americans.
During the war, Filene was a dollar-a-year organizer of procurement. After the war, he resumed his European trips, even studying
retail stores in Soviet Russia. With writers as notable as Lincoln
Steffens polishing his sentences, he spoke in favor of the League of
Nations, the Dawes Plan, daylight saving time, sickness insurance
which evolved into the Blue Cross plan, tourist rates on steamships,
and low-cost housing.

Invention also interested him. A footstool of his design came to
nothing but, with an engineer, he worked out the Filene-Finlay si-
multaneous translator for the proceedings of the League of Nations.
With this, earphone-equipped listeners hear in their own tongues
addresses as they are made. Produced by International Business
Machines, the equipment later was adopted for the Nuremberg war
criminal trials and the sessions of the United Nations. All of these
interests, of course, took Edward A. Filene away from Boston for
long periods and responsibility fell increasingly on his associates.

The cleavage with Vice President Kirstein became evident in
1918 when Vice President Simpson enlisted for war service and resigned. His associates could not agree on a successor. His stock was
purchased and placed in trust and his duties were assumed by Vice
President Kirstein. In 1925, Vice President Cory died. With Ed-

* Gerald W. Johnson, *Liberal's Progress*, Coward-McCann, Inc., New York,
1948, pages 21–35.

ward A. Filene dissenting, the directors allowed Cory's stock to be purchased and divided by Vice Presidents Kirstein and Frost and the latter assumed the late executive's duties.

Events came to a head in 1928. A further reorganization of the store's financial structure that year and a compromise division between Edward A. Filene and the others of what had been Simpson's share of the business left the original 100 units of common stock divided this way: Edward A. Filene 30; Lincoln Filene 24; Frost 19.5; Kirstein 19.5 and the last three together 7. In that year, it was proposed that the store join Abraham & Straus of Brooklyn and The F. & R. Lazarus & Co. of Columbus, Ohio, with whose principals the Filene executives had worked successfully for a decade in the Associated Merchandising Corporation, in formation of a holding company to be known as Federated Department Stores, Inc. One aim was the stabilizing of earnings through a geographical distribution of risk. Edward A. Filene opposed the idea. All his associates favored it.

Weary of the quarreling and fearful of the future of the store, Lincoln Filene then voted his stock with the others and deposed his brother as head of the company, but not without conditions. No loser in a store struggle was ever treated more generously. The elder brother for life was to continue to have the title of president, occupy the president's office and draw a salary of $100,000 a year, the same as the younger brother, Frost and Kirstein (all these salaries came down in the depression). He could make suggestions to the operating committee of the store but was not to interfere in its management. He could not start a business in competition with Filene's but he was free to do anything else he liked.

For the next nine years, the man derided by some "as a cross between a pack peddler and the prophet Isaiah" did exactly this. He spoke and traveled more than ever. He offered but never awarded a $25,000 prize for an essay on world peace. He became a well-known figure of the New Deal, serving as Massachusetts administrator for the National Recovery Administration, and campaigning for President Roosevelt. The night before the 1936 national election, the President, Senator Robert Wagner, National Chairman James A. Farley and Edward A. Filene spoke over the combined networks of the National Broadcasting and Columbia Broadcasting System.

The next day his candidate swept every state except Maine and Vermont. It was the happiest day of Edward A. Filene's restless, lonely and ambitious life.

Death in the form of pneumonia overtook him less than a year later on September 25, 1937, in Paris. In accordance with his wishes, his ashes were returned to Boston and cast into the Charles River Basin, which his apartment at 12 Otis Place overlooked. His will left the bulk of his $2,000,000 estate to two foundations which he had founded and to which he had given larger sums earlier. These were the Twentieth Century Fund, Inc., and an organization that after his death was renamed the Edward A. Filene Good Will Fund, Inc.

One of the obligations of the latter was to advance $1,000,000 to the Consumer Distribution Corporation, founded earlier to start co-operative department stores as part of the donor's hope of finding ways to cut distribution costs. This action by a merchant who had made a fortune in private enterprise gave critics an excuse to call him a traitor to his class. It was not until 1948 that the first co-operative department store backed by $550,000 of Filene's money was opened in Shirlington, Virginia, a suburb of Washington, D.C. Five years later its assets were sold for $260,000. A similar experiment failed, not necessarily because of the form of operation in Providence, Rhode Island.

The Twentieth Century Fund proved more fortunate. Since 1919 when E. A. Filene founded it with $5,000,000 in securities, by grants to others and through its own operations the Fund has conducted economic research on timely subjects of public importance and disseminated the results by pamphlets, books, motion pictures, radio and, in recent years, television. Though expenditures have been more than $600,000 a year, the Twentieth Century Fund has been so well managed that the endowment in 1954 had increased to more than $11,000,000.

In large part this was due to the dividends of Filene's and Federated Department Stores, Inc., of which Filene's became a unit by a share-for-share exchange of common stock in 1929. Net sales of Filene's for the year ending January 31, 1929, were $34,173,186. Sales reached $47,422,264 the next year as the depression hit the nation. "The honeymoon is over," Vice President Kirstein then told the store staff. "Now the labor pains begin."

Thanks to the remarkable basement, Filene's sales during the depression thirties were never less than the $30,620,089 for the fiscal year ending January 31, 1934. On this figure there was a profit of 3.35 per cent though only 1.90 per cent had been earned on sales of $32,593,795 the previous year. Filene's sales reached $52,320,951 during World War II and a few years afterward passed $70,000,-000. The store's earning record, broken only by expansion expense in 1913, continued with profits of 1.3 to 8.6 per cent on sales.

Lincoln Filene, a serene and courtly gentleman, adored by an increasing number of grandchildren, outlived all of the men he and his brother had picked in 1913 as their possible successors. After his brother's departure, he became president of the firm, relinquished the title for a time to Vice President Frost, who died in 1944, and again resumed it. Vice President Kirstein died in 1942. His successor in charge of publicity, Vice President William McLeod, died in 1946. The store survived these deaths just as it had the loss of Edward A. Filene. A new generation of executives came from its training system.

Chief of these was Harold Daniel Hodgkinson, a six-foot-three executive of boundless energy. He was born May 8, 1890, in Wallingford, Connecticut, where his father, Samuel Hodgkinson, was a small silverware manufacturer, and attended Yale. There he studied engineering and earned his first money by breaking in pipes for his less robust classmates at ten cents a pipe. Work as a campus correspondent for the Associated Press shifted his interest to journalism but the AP had no job for him when he received a degree in 1912 from Yale's Sheffield Scientific School.

"Why don't you try Filene's in Boston?" suggested the New Haven correspondent of the news service. "They are expanding into a new building and I hear it's a good place for college men."

Hodgkinson obediently went to Filene's and was hired by Ernest Martin Hopkins, a personnel man who later became president of Dartmouth College. Like most initial jobs in the store, Hodgkinson's was far from romantic. He first addressed envelopes and then sorted overshoes in a sub-basement. Meanwhile, he studied at the Harvard Graduate School, a bit of application that later gave him the distinction of being the first Yale man ever to become a governor of the Harvard Club of Boston. He married Laura White Cabot, descendant of two old Back Bay families.

After Navy service in World War I, he became copywriter, advertising manager, buyer and merchandiser and then, in 1931, manager of the Automatic Basement. Hodgkinson traveled widely for the basement, buying linen in Ireland, rugs in Africa and even the wardrobes of movie stars in Hollywood. In 1942, he became top executive for the whole store as vice president and general manager.

To next in rank rose Samuel Seegal, a statistician with a notable talent for merchandising, who modernized E. A. Filene's "model stock plan." A graduate of both the Massachusetts Institute of Technology and Harvard, he joined Filene's after work as an aide to Secretary of Commerce Herbert Hoover. Jack Goldberg took charge of the basement; John Perkins, acquired from Boston University, operations; California-born Alvah Kindall, personnel; William Lee, the branches; and Francis B. Gummere, planning and research.

The store was rebuilt and remodeled at a cost of $5,000,000. Its showmanship continued. Some World War II war bond promotions earned congratulatory advertisements from rival Jordan Marsh. Ackley Slee, an assistant store superintendent at Filene's, singlehandedly sold $4,824,525 in bonds to lead individual sales in the Seventh War Loan. He was honored in a ceremony on the battleship *Missouri*. A liberty ship launched during the war was named the *S. S. Edward A. Filene*. The day the atom bomb was announced, the store assembled, with the aid of Harvard scientists, a window display explaining fission of the uranium atom. When President Truman announced an end to price ceilings at 10 P.M. one Saturday, many stores took pride in pledging to hold the line on prices in Monday advertisements. Filene's had one in the Sunday newspapers that went to press Saturday night. A Filene's window display modeled President Eisenhower's inauguration and won an award as the best retail-store institutional window of the year.

A series of postwar promotions, many of them planned by a notable woman executive, Harriet Wilinsky, fashion director and later sales manager, attracted wide attention. She flew to France on the first Boston-to-Paris plane and conducted a fashion show there for French war brides awaiting passage to the United States. After showing clothes suitable for various sections of America, she answered questions like, "How do I get along with an American mother-in-law?" and "Is it true that American men go out at night without their wives?" Back in Paris later, she was hostess at a party at which French friends of Bostonians heard recordings of messages from them and posed for movies which she took back to Boston. Goods from Ireland, Italy and other foreign lands were the subject of promotions, sometimes in co-operation with *Life, Vogue* or other national publication. The maiden voyage of the American Export Liner *Constitution* featured a Filene fashion show and the French liner *Ile de France* made a special stop in Boston for a similar Filene event.

An annual promotion of New England products called the "New England Revelation," was started with a special New Haven train carrying designers, manufacturers and editors from New York to Boston for the initial affair. A fashion show was presented en route to the tune of a specially composed musical number titled "New England—It's Grand."

A cartoon-illustrated 1947 advertisement in the *New York Times* headed, "One doesn't wear Jones Beach fashions on Cape Cod," urged vacationing New Yorkers to take empty suitcases to New England and let Filene's or one of its branches outfit them. This made New York merchants seethe but drew business and a favorable reaction for Filene's. "You are helping all New England," wrote a hosiery mill president. "This is a conspicuous example of regional promotion at its best," commented a recreation leader. "It was a superb bit of showmanship and caused a great deal of eyebrow raising around here," reported a Philadelphia manufacturer.

Boston's initial helicopter flights were sponsored by Filene's. One landed merchandise in a baseball park. Another to Wellesley took mail and an evening gown, to be worn that night by a selectman's wife. Four hundred workmen, members of fourteen building trades unions, who completed the Raymond Loewy-designed Chestnut Hill branch store ahead of schedule were entertained by Filene's. When forest fires swept much of Maine, the store's trucks and drivers labored there for four days rescuing residents and their belongings, an act of civic helpfulness that was repeated in the city of Worcester when it was devastated by a tornado.

All innovations of Filene's, of course, have not proved successful. Those that failed to justify expectations have been abandoned and usually without delay. In an effort to reduce and equate distribution costs among different classes of customers, the store during World War I undertook to collect a fee of fifty cents a month from customers who maintained charge accounts. It also began to collect a ten-cent fee for each parcel delivered. Both ideas were abandoned when customers complained and rival stores continued to provide the services without special charges.

In 1929, Filene's acquired R. H. White's, an important Boston store dating from 1859. It was the first store to have an electric stairway and to use pneumatic cash tubes. The purchase was made with the idea of shifting some non-fashion departments out of Filene's and operating the stores as complementary institutions. This was not realized and in 1944 White's was sold to the City Stores Company.

An interesting experiment in the automatic vending of merchandise was undertaken by Filene's in 1950. Twenty-five vending machines were installed in what was called a "U-Serv-U" center in a new Greyhound bus depot in the Back Bay section. Later twenty-four similar units were placed in service at the Logan International Airport. For the first time, specialty store merchandise other than nylon stockings was offered via coin-in-the-slot sale.

Women's hosiery and gloves, men's T-shirts and Hopalong Cassidy wallets for children sold well at first but volume proved disappointing. Customers did not want to buy style goods and items costing more than $1 via vending machine at least in these two locations. Small toys, key chains, puzzles, tools and costume jewelry sold better. After two years the experiment was abandoned but Filene's continues to be open to new ideas.

To help keep alert to these and its civic duties, Filene's board includes three notable "outside" directors. These are President Margaret Clapp of Wellesley College; Michael T. Kelleher, philanthropist; and Jacob Kaplan, noted attorney.

Few civic enterprises are launched in Boston without somebody from the store having a part. "I always tell people," Lincoln Filene once remarked, "that just making money out of a city and its inhabitants isn't the only thing to do." He became the leading spirit of the

New England Industrial Development Corporation, a non-profit organization aiding small business. Among many other activities, Vice President Hodgkinson has been a leader of the Greater Boston Development Committee, which has made progress toward solving Boston's intolerable traffic tangle; director of the Federal Reserve Bank of Boston; and a member of the Massachusetts Committee of Catholics, Protestants and Jews.

A Lincoln Filene Professorship of Retailing in the Harvard Graduate School of Business Administration was established with $300,-000 given by Federated Department Stores, Inc., and the Lincoln and Therese Filene Foundation. Coincident with Lincoln Filene's eighty-fifth birthday, Professor Malcolm P. McNair was chosen as the first to fill the chair. In announcing the professorship the Dean of the Harvard Business School said:

"Lincoln Filene helped build retailing from mere shopkeeping into the finest type of business administration. The progressive management which he developed made him a leader in department and specialty store operation, and all retailing has benefited from the high standards which his example has fostered."

A $600,000 educational television station, WGBH, was built in 1954 as a memorial to the Filene brothers. The Ford Foundation joined the Twentieth Century Fund and other Filene foundations in paying for the transmitter at Blue Hill adjoining the Harvard Observatory. It is operated by the Lowell Institute Cooperative Broadcasting Council, which includes the Boston Symphony Orchestra, Boston University, Harvard University, Lowell Institute, M.I.T., Museum of Fine Arts, New England Conservatory of Music, Northeastern University and Tufts College.

In 1954, Edward A. Filene was elected to the retailing Hall of Fame at the Chicago Merchandise Mart.

In the retail world a man trained at Filene's has something of the prestige of a hotel man who worked for E. M. Statler or of a surgeon who interned at the Mayo Clinic. At least sixty great stores, at one time nine in New York alone, have been headed by alumni of Filene's.

The long roll has included William O. Riordan, president of Stern Brothers, New York; Harold Lane, head of Lerner Stores; the late Clarence G. Sheffield, president of Garfinckel's, Washington,

D.C.; Max Levine, president of Foley Brothers, Houston; P. A. O'Connell, president of E. T. Slattery Co., Boston; Harold Brightman, president of Lit Bros., Philadelphia; Charles Whipple, president of Parke-Snow stores in New England; Sidney Reisman, president, D. M. Read Co., Bridgeport, Conn.; Arthur Madison, executive vice president, Garfinckel's, Washington, D.C.; Sidney Solomon, executive vice president, Abraham & Straus, Brooklyn; Sargent Eaton, head of Howland Dry Goods Co., Bridgeport.

Graduates of Filene's also have won fame in other fields. Ernest Martin Hopkins, a Filene employment manager, as mentioned earlier, left the store to become president of Dartmouth College. Donald David was named Dean of the Graduate School of Business Administration at Harvard. Paul Mazur became a partner of Lehman Brothers. Muriel Cox became director of the Chamberlain School of Retailing. Owen Stoner became president of Prince Matchabelli, Inc. Glenn Frank, who helped E. A. Filene with his writing, later was president of the University of Wisconsin. Wheeler Sammons and Charles Merz, who did the same, became respectively publisher of *Who's Who in America* and editor of the *New York Times*. Robert L. Moore became a co-founder of the Sheraton hotel chain.

VII. F. & R. Lazarus & Company

Ohio's Famous Department Store Dynasty

A SHOPPER is like a baby who wants milk. When he cries for milk, he doesn't want a meal ticket. He doesn't want an argument or an excuse. He wants warm milk that is right for him—and he wants it at once.

Providing this sort of service is all there is to success in retailing, says Fred Lazarus, Jr., head of the Ohio family which has built the extraordinary Lazarus and Shillito department-store businesses in Columbus and Cincinnati. Since 1945, he also has been president of Federated Department Stores, Inc., of which these big Ohio stores are model units.

Under the adventurous leadership of Mr. Fred, as the short Napoleonic-appearing gentleman is called to distinguish him from his numerous relatives in the business, Federated in less than a decade doubled in size and increased its sales to half a billion dollars a year. By 1954, it had big stores in nine cities. Through branches of these and a growing chain of independent Fedway stores, located mainly in the Southwest and West, Federated units operate in twenty-four smaller communities from Lewiston, Maine, to Westwood Village in Los Angeles.

All the stores reflect Mr. Fred's restless ideas. These also have found expression in the Ohio State Council of Retail Merchants, formed in 1922 at his instance to represent Ohio retailers of all kinds, and the American Retail Federation, similarly organized in 1935 to speak for many retail groups in Washington. At least one of his ideas affected everybody in the country.

This was the matter of the date of Thanksgiving which tradi-

tionally starts the Christmas shopping season. In 1939, a year when
business was not too good, the last Thursday of November, on which
the holiday was then observed, fell on the very last day of the month.
At a dinner in Cincinnati on June 14, Mr. Fred remarked to George
V. Sheridan, executive director of the Ohio State Council of Retail
Merchants, that there would be six more days of Christmas business
if Thanksgiving could be advanced a week.

Next day Sheridan visited a library and found no legal bar to
changing the date; in fact, it had been observed on many different
dates in American history. The late William F. Wiley, then publisher
of the Cincinnati *Enquirer,* endorsed the idea. Sheridan and Ed
Martin, secretary of the Ohio Newspaper Association, took the pro-
posal to Washington and through Lowell Mellett presented it to the
White House, where President Roosevelt gave it a warm welcome.
He promised to proclaim the earlier date and to give Lazarus and
Wiley advance notice of his proclamation.

"But he forgot that part," recalls Lazarus. "The announcement
came just as I was sitting down to the first company dinner of the
bride of my son Ralph. She had broken her back over it but I spent
the evening on the long-distance telephone talking to retailers. Wiley
did the same with publishers. But it was too late. Everybody knows
about the big squabble that broke out and continued for three years.
We hadn't thought of the long-planned football schedules, school
holidays, almanacs and calendars, railroad timetables and other
things. Even my brothers who were interested in Ohio State's football team were annoyed."

Eventually everybody conceded the value of the change and Congress on December 29, 1941, legalized the fourth Thursday in November as Thanksgiving. This can fall no later than November 28,
and may be as early as November 22. Manufacturers, shoppers and
workers as well as retailers benefit.

Some less spectacular Lazarus ideas have been the conversion of
store buyers into department managers, making them responsible for
operating costs, including selling, warehousing and delivery, as well
as the selection and sale of merchandise; the display of merchandise
by "size selection"; the use of perimeter stockrooms adjacent to selling departments; and the adaptation to a store of the latest industrial material-handling techniques and devices. He believes that the

costs of a store should be analyzed operation by operation and that great savings can be effected by the elimination of waste motion and antiquated methods.

But Mr. Fred's favorite idea, perhaps, is the strongly held view that a store's success is almost in direct ratio to its hippodrome qualities and that older customers as well as children like to shop in a lively, animated atmosphere. As a department store usually provides this on a bigger scale than one of its smaller competitors, he does not regard the big stores as doomed dinosaurs. He has even enlivened Federated stockholders' meetings with fashion shows.

"A good store is like a big circus," he explains. "You can have one ring, or five or twenty. That is why a department store has it all over others in attracting people to come in and look around." He also believes a store should be exciting to those who run it. "Retailing is our life," he once said. "We enjoy its excitements. It is a life in itself full of challenge."

Showmanship combined with good merchandising helped the Lazarus store in Columbus grow to 156 departments sprawling over 32 acres of floor space and to do a business of more than $52,000,-000 a year in Columbus, a city of 400,000. This monumental institution sometimes attracts ninety thousand shoppers a day, does 60 per cent of the local department-store business and for thirty years has been the largest store in central Ohio. Its chief local competitor is its own three-level basement, "upstairs" from some entrances because of the sloping site. The store's garages park 1,500 customer automobiles and many shoppers come from 150 miles away. Two of its delivery routes are so long that the drivers make overnight stops.

A live alligator, brought back from Florida by an uncle of Fred, Jr., was part of the equipment of the Lazarus store until the reptile died after eighteen years of exhibition. For years the store had a raucous whistle that tooted a weather forecast at 3 p.m. daily. Santa Claus early became a Lazarus property with the store bringing the old gentleman into town with a parade. Every year thousands of Ohio letters to Santa Claus are addressed to him in care of Lazarus. The store sometimes marks Arbor Day by giving a tree to every Columbus schoolchild. When an early electric automobile crashed into a show window, instantly up went a sign reading "Everything Comes to Lazarus." Once a year the store entertains several hundred customers more than eighty years old at a tea. The store auditorium is constantly in use for hobby shows, club meetings, photography exhibitions and similar gatherings and a sizable electrically lighted blimp was employed by Lazarus to announce a change in store hours.

Dramatic exploits also turned Shillito's in Cincinnati from a moribund fifth-place store doing $4,000,000 business when the Lazarus family bought it in 1928 to the biggest department store in southern Ohio with sales of more than $40,000,000. Cincinnatians still talk of the service of Shillito's in the record 1937 Ohio flood. Food, blankets, gasoline and other merchandise, as well as drinking water, went from the store to refugees, and its staff fumigated, sorted and distributed thousands of garments donated for flood sufferers.

Telephone for the time of day in Cincinnati and you will be connected with a Shillito number where it will be supplied along with a suggestion that you support the local opera or some other civic enterprise. Shillito's sponsors a Junior Town Hall at which selected students from high schools of the area argue questions like: "Should parents be held responsible for the delinquency of children?" or "Should eighteen-year-olds be allowed to vote?" The store gives space to a Craft Shop of the Handicapped, all the profits of which go to the local blind or crippled.

Behind the dramatics are several generations of solid merchandising. The original Lazarus store was opened as a tiny men's clothing store in Columbus in 1851, the same year that William Filene became a storekeeper in Boston. Fred, Jr.'s sidewhiskered grandfather, Simon Lazarus, an immigrant from Prussia, founded the store. He also served as the first rabbi of Temple Israel, the oldest Jewish congregation in Columbus. Temple Israel, in which his descendants are still active, incidentally has on its walls two bronze plaques, one expressing the thanks of members of the First Methodist Church, who worshiped there when fire destroyed their nearby building, and the other from members of the Broad Street Presbyterian Church, who used the Temple while their structure was remodeled.

Simon Lazarus started with a capital of $3,000. His store was twenty by fifty feet and on South High Street. There was but one clerk. The founder had four daughters and two sons, Fred and

Ralph. When not in school, they helped in the store, sometimes breaking ice in the Scioto River for water to mop the floor.

First of many expansions came in the early sixties when an adjoining boot and shoe store was purchased for $3,500. In 1870, the Lazarus store, then one of sixteen local retail clothiers, became the first Columbus store to operate a delivery wagon. In 1877, the founder died and his two sons took charge.

Store advertising then emphasized "One Lowest Price" or "Strictly One-Price Store" and "Every Article Marked in Plain Figures." In 1887, the store added men's, women's and children's shoes to the men's and boys' clothing and furnishings previously carried. In 1888, on the occasion of the state fair and centennial celebration, the store closed at 10:30 A.M. and all the employees, numbering between thirty and forty, went to the fair in a body. Led by Fred and Ralph Lazarus and a brass band, they marched to Union Station and entrained for the fair grounds.

Ralph Lazarus wrote most of the store advertising in the nineties. "He would just sit down," a veteran employee once recalled, "and write an ad out, with pencil, on a piece of wrapping paper." The store at this period consisted of eleven ground-floor rooms with connecting doors. "Uncle Ralph" Lazarus, as he was known, had an office in an elevated cubbyhole in the center of the eleven rooms. This was equipped with a system of mirrors so arranged that by their chain reflection he could see every part of the store.

In 1891, the store expanded vertically with the moving of the tailor shop to the second floor and connecting it with the main store by a circular stairway. In another expansion the space between the store and the southwest corner of Town and High Streets was acquired and a clock tower, a landmark for many years, was constructed atop the structure.

Merchandising at the turn of the century involved presents and premiums. A baseball and bat usually went with the purchase of a suit of boy's clothing. A man received a pair of suspenders with each suit. A purchaser of a pair of shoes expected to receive a strip of tickets entitling him to free shines. Complaints were loud when the practice was stopped in 1903.

All employees, called associates then as now, wore nickel lapel buttons bearing their number. These buttons were required to be polished and in evidence at all times. Even floorwalkers wore large badges saying "Lazarus Floor Walker."

In 1903, Ralph Lazarus died. He had never married and was even such a misogynist that he shuddered at the thought of a woman secretary. The business continued under the direction of his brother Fred with the latter's four sons, Simon, Fred, Jr., Robert and Jeffrey, all assuming responsibilities in the store as they grew up.

All of founder Simon's sons, grandsons and great-grandsons have gone into the business. A great-grandson, Simon Lazarus, Jr., studied law but only to become a full-time executive of Federated as company counsel. All have been competent and successful merchants but the most kinetic and peripatetic of them is Fred Lazarus, Jr.

Until he and his three brothers began to take charge, the Lazarus store was little more than a men's clothing store. Simon, the eldest brother, developed a flair for employee relations and headed the store for thirty years. The younger brothers, Robert and Jeffrey, became notable merchandise and sales-promotion executives and then respectively heads of the stores in Columbus and Cincinnati. To Fred, Jr., was left finance and the freedom to consider bold innovations.

Soon after he cut short his education in his freshman year at Ohio State to take the place of his dying uncle in the store, Fred, Jr., induced his family to construct a new building and expand into the department-store field. He personally supervised the building of a five-story structure that is part of the present Lazarus store and termed its opening in 1909 as the happiest day of his business career. He was then twenty-four years old. Since then he has supervised so many expansions in Columbus, Cincinnati and elsewhere that he can talk to architects and engineers in their own language.

Sales surpassed $1,000,000 for the first time in 1914 with a gross for the year of $1,109,811. Several new departments were added then and later, one a notable book department under the late Mrs. Lulu S. Teeter which became a center for Ohio literary affairs.

Though Lazarus sales mounted to $4,000,000 a year during World War I, its business still was exceeded by one Columbus store and equaled by another in 1920. That summer, Fred, Jr., visited New York and became convinced that the war inflation had run its course. Markdowns, greater than the profits of the previous year, were taken, especially on items like silk shirts, but the overpriced goods were cleared out. The store's 1921 gross of $5,773,000 was the largest in Columbus.

Fred, Jr., early developed a liking for travel and out of his trips have come many ideas. While visiting Europe, he once wandered into the Printemps store in Paris and noticed that all the dresses of one size, regardless of price, were grouped in single alcoves. The simplicity of it impressed him immediately. Why should stores scatter garments of the same size all over a floor, perhaps even on different floors, simply because they are of a different price or a different make? After all, the customer had to determine one fact before all else—would the garment fit? With all dresses of one size grouped, customers often buy an item of better quality than they planned. Size selling is now used widely.

Out of Mr. Fred's interest in construction has come adoption of horizontal warehousing, the practice wherever possible of storing merchandise, except bulky furniture, on the same floor level that it is sold. It places salespeople close to the stock and enables them to do work in slack hours that might otherwise require a separate staff in a warehouse. Errors in handling are greatly reduced.

One of the Lazarus family's most successful ventures was the purchase in 1928 for $2,500,000 of the John Shillito store in Cincinnati. Founded in 1830, this had the distinction of being the oldest store west of the Alleghenies. Mrs. Fred Lazarus, Sr., a native of Cincinnati, bought her wedding dress there and the family knew the store well. It had been the city's biggest store but after the death in 1925 of Stewart Shillito, a son of the founder, it was no better than fourth among Cincinnati stores. Many departments were leased, the merchandise was cheap and the building was fifty years old.

Shillito's was rehabilitated with startling speed under Fred Lazarus, Jr., president for some years, and his brother, Jeffrey Lazarus, first general manager and then president. Leonard R. Minster, from another Cincinnati store, improved service and personnel. The store was cleaned up, rearranged, refixtured and, department by department, stocked with better merchandise.

In the first year of Lazarus management sales increased to $5,700,000 and in 1929 reached $6,500,000. While other large

Cincinnati stores lost as much as half of their volume during the depression, Shillito's dropped only to $4,500,000 in 1932 and then began to rise steadily. For 1935, the volume was $7,300,000, more than it had ever been at the peak of the Shillito family's operation. The building was expanded and air conditioned and a customers' garage built. In 1939, sales passed $10,700,000 and Shillito's was definitely the No. 1 store in Cincinnati. At the end of World War II, they were nearly $30,000,000 and were accounting for 33 to 35 per cent of the Federal Reserve department-store figures for Cincinnati. By 1954, Shillito's volume was estimated at $47,000,000.

Federated Department Stores, Inc., was born on a yacht in Long Island Sound one week end in the summer of 1929. The craft belonged to Walter Rothschild, president of Abraham & Straus, the big Brooklyn store. Guests were Fred Lazarus, Jr., and Louis Kirstein, general manager of Filene's in Boston. All three firms had been associated since 1916 in the Retail Research Association and the Associated Merchandising corporation. They returned from the cruise with a plan to share the risks of the three businesses through a holding company to be set up by an exchange of stock.

The new company was incorporated in November and a majority of the stock of each company exchanged. Holders of each Lazarus share received nineteen-thirty-sevenths of a Federated share, an A. & S. share received two-thirds of a Federated share and Filene shares were traded evenly. Lehman Brothers, the investment bankers, were interested in the venture and first Arthur Lehman and then Paul Mazur of the firm, the latter a former Filene man, served as directors.

Bloomingdale's, the big New York store, joined the group the next year on the basis of a share of Bloomingdale stock for three-fourths of a Federated share. Bloomingdale's and Abraham & Straus are curiously intwined in department-store history. Just before the Civil War, the small and now forgotten Bettlebeck & Co., dry-goods store of Newark, New Jersey, employed three clerks. They were Benjamin Altman, Abraham Abraham and Lyman Gustave Bloomingdale. Within a few years each founded great stores, the first B. Altman & Co. in New York, the second Abraham & Straus in Brooklyn and the last Bloomingdale Bros., Inc.

The depression struck just as Federated was organized and it was

October 31, 1931, before the first dividend was paid. They have continued unbrokenly since then. Until World War II, Federated continued to be simply a holding company, without authority, headquarters offices or formal work. Between 1933 and 1945, the number of stockholders increased only from 1,173 to 2,861.

With the advent of Fred Lazarus, Jr., as president in the latter year, Federated abruptly changed character. All existing stores were enlarged and rehabilitated. The transformation at Bloomingdale's, under James S. Schoff and J. Edward Davidson, made it one of the most profitable Federated units. A Federated headquarters was established in Cincinnati with operations, finance, research and acquisitions divisions. Owen C. Frost, son of the Filene executive, headed the last. Research was headed by Myron S. Silbert, co-author with Paul Mazur of *Principles of Organization Applied to Modern Retailing*. This division began to make studies of all kinds for the store managements. As treasurer, John Lebor took over financial and tax problems. Within a few years, stockholders increased to more than ten thousand.

A trip of Fred Lazarus, Jr., in 1941 to visit his son, Ralph, then an Air Force lieutenant at Ellington Field, led to Federated starting its expansion in Houston, Texas. While waiting for his son to come off duty, Fred, Jr., visited the local stores and discovered the largest to be Foley Brothers. This was founded in 1900 by Pat C. and James A. Foley with $2,000 borrowed from an Irish immigrant uncle. Since 1917, the store had been owned by the George S. Cohen family.

When Fred, Jr., found Foley's doing only a fourth of the business of Shillito's in a city as big as Cincinnati, he decided Federated should build in Houston. While sites were being purchased and plans for a new store were being made, the owners of Foley's decided to sell. After several highly involved discussions, one of which lasted eighteen hours, Fred, Jr., worked out a plan which in 1945 gave Federated both the Foley business and real estate in exchange for $3,250,000 in securities. As the real estate included a surplus store site, this gave Fred, Jr., the chance to turn real-estate salesman. He did this with such success that he sold the extra site, which had been optioned at $1,250,000, for $3,055,000, a matter of $2,000 a front inch, a record price even for busy Houston.

This profit helped pay for a new $13,000,000 store completed in 1947 and embodying all of the Lazarus ideas of perimeter stockrooms, movable walls, size station selling, and scientific operation. A tunnel under Travis Street connected the six-story and basement store with a garage and service building. Packages of shopping customers reached their cars by a system of chutes and conveyor belts. Kenneth Franzheim was the architect and Raymond Loewy designed the interiors including a luxurious Crystal Room.

Even before the new store was completed, the Federated management increased Foley's sales from $6,500,000, the year before it was purchased, to $16,000,000. By 1950, Foley's sales passed $29,000,000. President is Max Levine, a Harvard graduate trained at Filene's, Abraham & Straus and Lazarus. Vice President is Maurice Lazarus, a son of Fred, Jr. His son, Fred III, became a vice president of Shillito's. Ralph and his cousin, Charles, became vice presidents under their uncle, Robert Lazarus, at Columbus and Ralph is now executive vice president of Federated.

Federated bought fifty-year-old Halliburton's, the third-largest store in Oklahoma City, in 1947 and attempted to buy the John Taylor Dry Goods Store in Kansas City but was outbid by Macy's. Federated bought the well-publicized Milwaukee Boston Store, one of the largest retail stores in Wisconsin, in 1948. With it were acquired units in Oshkosh and Manitowoc, Wisconsin, and a branch in West Allis, a Milwaukee suburb. Pat Maher, a Lazarus-trained executive, became head of the Boston Store.

Sanger Brothers, pioneer Dallas store, was purchased in 1951. It was founded in 1872 by Isaac, Lehman and Philip Sanger, immigrant brothers from Bavaria who previously had a succession of stores at the rail head of the Houston and Texas Central Railroad as it was built northward from Houston. The store was the first in the area to hire women as clerks and the first to expand to department-store status. It was long the biggest store in Dallas but, after passing from Sanger ownership, suffered from the competition of Neiman-Marcus in fashion and from Sears, Roebuck in hard lines. Under Henry X. Salzberger, formerly of Bloomingdale's, Federated began its revival of Sanger's with an expansion of apparel departments.

The first of the smaller tightly-engineered Fedway stores was opened at Wichita Falls, Texas, in the fall of 1952. Others followed rapidly in Corpus Christi, Longview and Amarillo, Texas; Albuquerque, New Mexico; also Bakersfield, Pomona and Westwood Village, California. Each was constructed at a cost of around $2,000,000 and provides full department-store stocks, charge accounts, parking and usual Federated services.

Federated's first decade of expansion was financed largely by earnings, the sale of installment accounts to banks, and the sale of real estate occupied by many stores to insurance companies and foundations with subsequent lease-back arrangements. Only $10,-000,000 in additional stock was issued.

Fred Lazarus, Jr., is the first to point out that many others have contributed greatly to the growth of the Ohio stores and to emphasize that the Federated group is more of a family than a chain of stores, that the big units have great autonomy. The late Simon Lazarus was a remarkable developer of executive personnel in the Columbus store. For years, he personally recruited promising beginners, planned training programs for them, and encouraged them with promotions. As a result, 99 per cent of the executives in the store came from its own staff.

Robert Lazarus, the present head of the Columbus store, is a Phi Beta Kappa with a great understanding of merchandising trends. He has been active in countless civic affairs. Of the younger group, Ralph Lazarus, who joined the store in 1935 after graduation from Dartmouth, and Charles Y. Lazarus, a Yale graduate, made important contributions to success of the big store. Ralph became executive vice president of Federated in 1951. Charles, now with the same title in the Columbus store, improved the merchandising of sportswear and, after military service, turned to operations. He applied wartime developments in goods handling in a new bulk service building and was one of the first to experiment with electronic machines in department store record keeping.

Because Federated was made up of a group of long-established stores, each with its own traditions, background and management set-up, individual identity has been preserved and emphasized. Few executives are less a dominant business tycoon than Fred Lazarus, Jr. At meetings, he listens carefully, encourages by questions, urges each man to have his say. Frequently, he may have one idea, others an opposing one. If several oppose, he does not insist.

Each store carries on its operations with considerable independence. The central office in Cincinnati correlates information from the stores, from the government, from trade associations and other sources and gives each store the benefit of it. The head of any individual unit can see how he stands in relation to the others in the organization and with the field. Rather than trying to mold all of the units into a standardized pattern, the effort is to exchange information, to let all benefit from the experience of others, without headquarters telling them what must be done or how it should be done.

The Federated stores are in a constant competition to find new, faster and more economical ways of performing retail operations. Wrapping costs have been cut in many departments, for example, by having the same clerk who sells an item wrap it by placing it in a paper "sleeve" and simply staple the ends. Men's suits, once invariably folded and boxed, now are delivered in better shape on hangers at considerable saving in costs. Stick-on labels have replaced tie-on labels, with a saving of a cent each, on numerous items. Some items have been found not to need a label.

Fred Lazarus, Jr., continues, however, to be Federated's most ardent researcher despite a wide variety of activities. Among other honors, these have earned him an honorary degree of Doctor of Laws at Ohio State, which he left as a freshman; the first gold medal of the National Conference of Christians and Jews, and a Tobé retailing award. He is a versatile and constant reader, often devouring a volume in an evening. He interrupts trips to tour any kind of store that looks like it might contain new ideas. He is open to these personally as well as professionally. He learned to dance the samba at sixty-two.

VIII. Marshall Field & Company

Elegance for the Middle West

Every great store is a showplace in its community but Marshall Field's with its elegance and its clocks has achieved and retained an attraction value for visitors to Chicago that probably is unmatched in any other city. Out-of-towners go to Field's before visiting the Art Institute, the Union Stockyards or the great museums. This is true of the famous as well as the ordinary traveler. The store's tooled-leather guest book includes the autographs of Queen Marie of Roumania, Prime Minister Winston Churchill, President William Howard Taft, Crown Princess Martha of Norway, Eleanor Roosevelt and many others.

It is a sentimental store, where Hughston M. McBain, Chairman of the Board, keeps five red roses on his desk in memory of his five illustrious predecessors. It is also a resilient enterprise which survived the Great Chicago Fire and since has surmounted difficulties that would have defeated a store of less stamina. It has doubled its sales in recent years by divesting itself of wholesale and manufacturing interests and investing its money in purely retail expansion. It owns one of the finest stores in the West in Frederick & Nelson of Seattle and has half a dozen modern branches built or building in the Midwest. Its Cloud Room at the Chicago Airport is the first and last restaurant encountered by the air traveler to the city.

When first built in 1907, the huge store at State, Washington, Wabash and Randolph Streets, was the "largest store in the world." With over 450 departments in 73 acres of space on 13 floors, Field's today still is one of the three physically largest stores in the world. Macy's of New York and Hudson's of Detroit boast only a few more square feet. The longest selling aisle in the world is in Field's basement; on the Wabash Avenue side it extends six hundred feet under Washington Boulevard into the Field's Store for Men across the street. Each December Field's displays "the largest indoor Christmas tree in the world."

Field's boasts more show windows than any other store and each is numbered to enable a shopper to be specific when asking for something displayed. As of 1954, it claimed the largest department-store restaurant operation in the world; the largest retail shoe operation under one roof; the largest china department, the largest year-around toy department, the largest book department, in the United States; the largest imports of linen and one of the largest imports of women's fashions. Historically, Field's was the first to establish an underprice basement and to use the basement for selling. It was the first to offer a personal shopping service and was among the first to exchange goods and offer a delivery service.

What the Biltmore Hotel clock is to rendezvousing New Yorkers, the two Field clocks are to Chicagoans. Big enough to be visible for blocks, they have marked the State and Washington and State and Randolph corners since the turn of the century. Each is twelve feet six inches high, has minute hands more than two feet long, and weighs seven and three-quarter tons.

The store traces its history to 1852 when a young Quaker named Potter Palmer, later famous for his hotels and other enterprises, arrived in Chicago from Lockport, New York, where he had operated a small dry-goods store. He started a similarly modest store in Chicago on Lake Street. Palmer was a careful student of *Godey's Lady's Book* and from the beginning saw the importance of the ladies as customers. Everything about his establishment was calculated to attract and please them. His store had no whiskey barrel and pot-bellied stove. Instead there was an atmosphere of refinement and gentility. There was a tempting array of stylish shawls, laces and cloaks. There were price tags on them. Above all, there was acceptance, something new, even cordial acceptance, of the fact that women sometimes change their minds.

Four years later, Marshall Field, a twenty-one-year-old Presbyterian youth, also arrived in Chicago from Pittsfield, Massachuetts, lured by the West. One of nine children, he had started life as a farm boy but had become a $4-a-week clerk in the store of Henry G. "Deacon" Davis at Pittsfield. There for nearly five years the shy, serious-minded, conscientious youth put in ten hours a day, six days a week. He swept the floor, dusted the counters and shelves, arranged the goods, and waited on the shrewd New England customers. The women in particular liked him as a clerk. He was polite and painstaking, with a good memory for names and faces—bolstered by a little book in which he made notes about the customers, their families and their special preferences.

In Chicago, through the help of his brother Joseph, Marshall found a job with Cooley, Wadsworth and Company, the largest dry-goods firm in the city. He managed to save half of his $400-a-year salary by sleeping in the store and buying nothing for himself except some overalls. Hard-working and single-minded as always, he rose to the position of traveling salesman for the company, to a junior partnership and finally to a full partnership with Cooley and Farwell. The firm of Farwell, Field and Company—the first in which Marshall Field's name appeared as a partner—was formed in 1864, when Cooley stepped out of the picture. The next step came the next year, when Potter Palmer decided to retire from active work in his store. He sold an interest to Field and one to Levi Leiter, Field's junior partner, and the firm of Field, Palmer and Leiter was launched.

Their first advertisement made it clear that they were "Successors to P. Palmer." This was indeed true. The pioneer merchandising ideas which had made Palmer's so popular formed a solid foundation for the new company and for the development of Field's own far-sighted convictions about successful storekeeping. "The best way to show a lady that the merchandise she purchased is worth the dollar she paid for it," said Field, "is to give her the dollar in return." He laid down as one of the company's rules: "What we write and what we say about our merchandise or service must be strictly, scrupulously, unfailingly the truth." Low prices, Field believed, could not do the trick alone. Nor could goods of the highest quality. There must be the personal touch—that atmosphere of honest, pleasant service that makes customers feel they are *special* customers and brings them back faithfully, year after year.

It worked then, as it does today. The ladies liked the courteous attention they received, no matter how small their purchases. They liked the three female clerks who were hired as an experiment to make them feel more at ease when buying the elaborate lingerie of the period. They appreciated the distinction lent to the store's front entrance by the two men who were hired to sweep the street three times a day. And there was no doubt about it, they loved the goods-on-approval policy. Through the years some of them, of course, have taken advantage of it. There was the society woman who returned a cape on the day after a ball, maintaining that she had not worn it. It was such an expensive cape that the matter was brought to the attention of Field himself. He took her word for it—and found, after she had left with her refund, a lace handkerchief tucked into one of the folds of the cape. His comment was characteristic: "If she said she didn't wear it, she didn't wear it. But I guess we'd better send her handkerchief back to her." However, the percentage of cheaters has always been surprisingly low; honesty seems to beget honesty.

Business was so good that by 1868 Field and Leiter decided to take Palmer up on his offer to rent them his palatial marble store building on State Street. The $50,000-a-year rental was breathtaking. So was the grand opening, which Chicago newspapers described as "A Dazzling Assemblage of Wealth, Beauty and Fashion." The main attraction was the first floor, the retail floor, with its walnut counters, frescoed walls, and—lit by splendid gas fixtures—its rich display of silks and satins, sable-trimmed cloaks, black and white astrakhans, Persian cashmere and point-lace shawls.

While the wholesale trade was an important part of the firm's business, he noted that it was the retail floor which drew the most ecstatic Ohs and Ahs from the ladies who swarmed into the store on opening night. They continued to swarm, and more often than not Marshall Field was there to greet them, unobtrusively polite, his youthful shyness ripened now into dignity. A quiet-mannered, handsome man, he made his presence felt among customers and clerks alike. He was unswerving in his determination to attract new customers and keep them happy.

Striding through the store one day, Field encountered one of his assistants arguing with a woman customer.

"What are you doing here?" demanded Field.

"I am settling a complaint," the man explained.

"No, you're not," ordered Field. "Give the lady what she wants."

This was done and the phrase became a motto for the store and the title years later of a book on its history.

Representatives of Field and Leiter ranged far afield, visiting the fashion centers of Europe to study the latest trends, and buying the highest-quality mill products on the spot in England. The firm's advertisements could now boast of its "unparalleled foreign imports." The one fly in the ointment was that New York importers could still be first in offering new foreign goods because Chicago was not a federal port of entry. Finally, Congress passed a bill establishing in Chicago a federal customhouse, warehouse, and a corps of appraisers, and in 1871 the first direct importation, for Field and Leiter, arrived in the city. It was a triumphant occasion. Before any of the fabulous foreign merchandise could be displayed, however, disaster struck not only the marble palace on State Street but the whole city.

News of the fire which was sweeping Chicago roused both partners out of their beds that night and brought them racing to the store. Field organized a brigade to hang wet blankets in the windows while Leiter supervised the job of moving the most valuable merchandise to safety—to the lake front first, later to Leiter's home and a nearby schoolhouse. Luckily, somebody thought to hurry to the basement and fire up the furnace so the steam elevators would run, thus speeding the task of removing goods from the doomed store. For it was doomed, in spite of all the partners and their faithful employees could do. By morning nothing was left but smoking ruins and twisted steel. A significant notice was posted on a pole stuck in the rubble: "Cash Boys & Work Girls will be Paid what is due them Monday 9 A.M. Oct. 16th at 60 Calumet Ave. Field, Leiter & Co."

In two days Field found a new business site—a brick barn at State and Twentieth Streets which had been built by the Chicago City Railway Company as quarters for its horses. Here the merchandise salvaged from the fire was arranged on pine counters hastily set up in the horse stalls. New orders arrived from New York in such quantity that bobtail horsecars were needed to help haul the goods from the railroad depot. In Field's opinion speed was vital. The big store that opened first after the fire would not only make money but would be doing an important service for the stricken Chicagoans. All but $750,000 of the firm's $2,500,000 loss was covered by insurance. Less than two weeks after the catastrophe the partners announced their new location, adding, "We sincerely thank our friends for their many kind expressions of sympathy and hope soon to renew our former pleasant business relations."

In the spring Field and Leiter moved to Market and Madison Streets. It soon became clear that the ladies did not care to travel so far west to shop, even for the tempting array of stylish goods the firm had to offer. State Street, rebuilt after the fire, was again Chicago's logical shopping center, and back to State Street Field and Leiter moved their retail store. Business continued to be excellent. Even the panic of 1873 and the subsequent depression failed to hurt the firm. Soon they were expanding their delivery system, which before had hardly existed, except when an errand boy occasionally carried packages to waiting carriages. Now, for $2 a week, boys were hired specifically for the purpose of making deliveries to residences within a few miles of the store. At first the youngsters went on foot, later on the cable cars. As the store and the city grew, the delivery boys were replaced by horse-drawn delivery carts. When an epidemic of distemper hit Chicago horses in 1872, the store used oxen for deliveries.

Today Field's corps of delivery men, more than four hundred strong and making about twenty-five thousand deliveries a day from International trucks painted a special green, are trained to be goodwill ambassadors. A Field deliveryman wouldn't think of barging right up a customer's steps with a Christmas sled or bicycle. He reconnoiters first, empty-handed. If the coast is clear he goes back to his truck for the gift; often he is requested to leave it with a neighbor. He knows which of the customers on his route have a new baby that may wake up screaming if he leans on the doorbell at nap time. He is a regular Boy Scout when it comes to good deeds. Maybe he'll be called upon to climb up a house and open the window for a customer who has forgotten her key, or pack down snow in a driveway with his big truck tires to clear the way for the owner's car. Frequently he returns small children or pets who have strayed. One Field driver, seeing an elderly lady slip and fall on an icy street, promptly stopped his big furniture truck and rushed to her rescue. By the time an ambulance reached the scene the lady, wrapped in quilted furniture pads, was resting comfortably on the cushions the driver had pulled from chairs and sofas in his truck. Field's deliverymen are proud of their ten-million-mile no-accident record. Some of them have been on the same route for forty years.

In 1877 fire once more ravaged the Field and Leiter store on State Street. The Italian-style building which the Singer sewing machine people had put up for Field was destroyed, and with it $750,-000 worth of merchandise covered by insurance. The Chicago *Tribune* reported: "The destruction of St. Peter's at Rome could hardly have aroused an apparently deeper interest than the destruction of this palatial dry goods establishment." Again the partners salvaged what they could and moved temporarily to a vacant hall on the lake front. An offer from the Singer people to sell Field what was left of the store, plus the corner lot, was declined. Singer put up a new building on the site and offered to rent it to Field; this offer too was declined and James Bolton, the alert Singer agent in Chicago, leased the structure to Carson, Pirie and Company. But Field changed his mind and wound up paying the Singer company $700,000 for it and giving Carson, Pirie $100,000 to relinquish their lease.

Field and Leiter took possession of their new store in 1879. The atmosphere was one of homecoming, on a grand and dignified scale. There was a uniformed official greeter at the entrance. Clerks no longer shouted "Cash! Come Cash!" The cash boys, scrubbed and brushed until they shone, now had numbers. Tense in their tight-fitting uniforms, they waited on a bench for their numbers to flash on a nearby board. They were paid $2 for a six-day week and considered themselves lucky. There were still only two elevators, but they were fancy ones, and a splendid staircase led to the second floor. An impressive stock of carpets and upholstery occupied the entire third floor, while on the fifth three hundred women worked at making dresses.

Field and Leiter parted in 1881. Leiter, never an easy man to get along with, did not share Field's enthusiasm for the retail end of the business. Field proposed a figure at which either of the partners might buy or sell the business. He named $2,500,000, low for a business with sales of more than $24,000,000 the previous year. Leiter made up his mind to buy, only to discover what Field had already made sure of—that none of the key executives of the store would stay with Leiter in case Field left. Leiter was cornered, and he knew it. "You win, Marshall," he said. "I'll sell."

At forty-seven, Marshall Field was one of the richest men in America. The country boy had made good in true Horatio Alger style. Spare and erect in carriage, with cold blue-gray eyes, prematurely gray hair and ruddy complexion, he was a dignified, aloof figure who wore white gloves even in summer. Although he and his ailing wife lived with their two children in a mansion on Prairie Avenue, Chicago's "street of the stately few," Field never cared for the lavish ostentation which typified the social life of the period. His tastes were simple, his friends few, his life—outside of the store— lonely and pathetically lacking in satisfactions that his wealth should have brought him. His wife Nannie spent more and more of her time abroad, trying to regain her health; she died in France in 1896. Sometimes Field and their son and daughter accompanied her, but Field's trips to Europe were more often on business than on pleasure. Nearly all his time and energy went into the smoothly running, vast machinery of his store.

The standards for even the humblest of Field's employees were high. Wages and praise were skimpy, but the prestige of working for Field's made up for these lacks. Field's had "tone," a quality which was recognized even in shoplifting circles. One shoplifter, an oldtimer who was nabbed repeatedly by the store detectives, was asked why she didn't sometimes work the other side of the street instead of concentrating so faithfully on Field's. The lady explained why. "I'm no jitney thief boosting cheap stuff," she said. "I work your store because you got all the best stuff in the city!"

Though Field's usual attitude toward his employees was one of awe-inspiring reserve, he could on occasion be surprisingly indulgent. Once two clerks who were playing with a heavy basket on wheels in the wholesale department managed to send it careening down the aisle just in time to catch Field and throw him. The clerks were struck dumb with horror. But Field's only comment was: "Boys, don't forget to be gentlemen." Again, when he happened on four clerks who had organized an impromptu quartet during working hours, he remarked: "Sing it again, boys, but this time just a little softer." It was his custom to arrive at the store every morning at nine o'clock. He rode only part of the way in his carriage; the last few blocks he covered on foot. No morning passed without his making a tour of the store, during which his sharp eye noted mistakes and commendable performances alike. After conferences with his department managers he repaired to the wholesale store, where a similar routine was repeated. This system enabled Field to spot talented executive material among his employees.

The career of John G. Shedd is a case in point. As a clerk in the women's neckwear section, Shedd attracted Field's attention and approval through a method he worked out for keeping track of sales by sizes so that the store's buyers would have an accurate basis for their purchases. The method, when tried out, was a success, and Shedd was put in charge of the lace and neckwear departments. From then on he advanced rapidly.

A man who worked his way up from office boy at Field's was Harry Gordon Selfridge, who later became a merchant prince in his own right in London. Selfridge, known as "Mile-a-Minute Harry," was a fountain of spectacular and imaginative ideas. As general manager of the retail store, he hired a window-display genius named Arthur Frazer away from a store in Creston, Iowa, and Field's show windows became world famous. Selfridge lit up the merchandise displays with more and more electric globes. He tripled the number of telephones in the store, which until 1883 had consisted of only five, and today the store handles more than a million telephone orders a year. He ripped out counters and piled up assortments of piece goods on tables in the middle of the first floor so that customers could paw through them. At his urging Field increased the newspaper advertising budget in 1885 to $28,000, a boost of almost $15,000 over several preceding years, but advertising in Sunday newspapers was forbidden. Selfridge himself wrote a good share of the advertising copy; it was exuberant and eye-catching but also completely honest. Basement merchandise was described as "trustworthy" and "less expensive but reliable," out of deference to the store's more conservative partners, who shuddered at such words as "cheap" or "lower priced." Field's sold in the basement as early as 1868 but Selfridge made it a bargain center. Eventually the basement, which grew to be the largest single salesroom in the world, was known as the "Budget Floor."

It was Selfridge, too, who persuaded Field to open a tearoom on the third floor, arguing that many women cut short their shopping to go home or elsewhere for lunch. There were only fifteen tables to begin with, and on the first day the patrons numbered a mere fifty-six. But customers were quick to appreciate this new convenience. In a year the tearoom was serving as many as fifteen hundred each day. Today Field's entire seventh floor is devoted to five restaurants—the Walnut Room, the Narcissus Room, the English Room, a cafeteria called the Crystal Buffet, and the Veranda (a dollar in advance, limited menu, no tipping). Field's menus still include such specialties as the chicken pot pie which was featured on the first opening day, back in 1890.

Selfridge took advantage of the Chicago World's Fair of 1893 to lure the Infanta Eulalia of Spain and other visitors from all over the world into Field's. At this time an admirer wrote a poem in honor of Field's, calling it "Cathedral of All the Stores." A Wabash Avenue addition to the store was completed that year. Later a new twelve-story building was erected north of the original store and spread over the remainder of the block to Randolph Street. This was advertised as "everybody's store," with low- as well as high-priced items available.

In 1904, Selfridge left Field's to run another store briefly in Chicago and to make and lose two fortunes in London before his death there in 1947. An earlier alumnus of Field's, a $23.08 a fortnight salesman named Montgomery Ward, by this time had founded the great mail-order house bearing his name and earned a great fortune. More recently, Fred Harvey, once a Field's basement merchandiser, has built the biggest store in Nashville, Tennessee, while Hector Escobosa and Egil E. Krogh, executives of a Field's subsidiary, have become respectively president of I. Magnin & Co. in California and Sibley, Lindsay & Curr in Rochester, New York. The influence of Field's has been felt throughout retailing.

Marshall Field, the founder, outlived most of his early associates.

Golf was his only recreation. On New Year's Day of 1906, he played golf in the snow, using red balls, with his nephew, Stanley Field; his employee, James Simpson; and Robert Todd Lincoln, the Pullman executive who was the son of the Civil War President. The seventy-year-old merchant caught cold but insisted on making a trip to New York as planned. He developed pneumonia and died there on January 16, disposing of an estate of $120,000,000 in a shrewdly drawn will. The last months of his life had been brightened by a second marriage and shadowed by the mysterious fatal shooting of his son, Marshall Field II, officially termed an accident but later generally believed suicide. The merchant's funeral was attended by three thousand store employees. One of these, Pierre Funck, veteran of forty-three years who had been left a pension, was so affected that he made a daily pilgrimage to the Field grave, regardless of the weather, and died himself apparently of grief.

The store remained as Marshall Field's monument. His grandson and great-grandson served on its board of directors but no member of the family has ever run it and the estate's interest has shrunk through the years. John Shedd, stepping into Field's shoes as president, went ahead with the project of tearing down the original store at State and Washington Streets and building a new one which would consolidate all units into one grand whole. The thirty-five acres of selling space in the main store of the new building were divided into more than 150 retail sections; a fabulous dome of multicolored Favrile glass, the biggest glass mosaic in existence, was designed by Louis Comfort Tiffany for the light well; foreign buyers beat the bushes far and wide for rare items; a famous Belgian sculptor was commissioned to develop the central theme of the opening, the contribution of merchants to civilization. Once more Chicago was treated to the full dress of a Field opening. A few years later Field's leased the one remaining corner of the square block, that at Randolph and Wabash, and constructed there a twelve-story building to match the rest of the block. And in 1914, the firm, spreading across the street, put up a twenty-one-story structure to house its famous Store for Men.

Two extraordinary doormen, first Eddie Anderson and then Charles Pritzlaff, the latter a former coachman, greeted Field's carriage-trade customers by name at the Washington Street entrance for many years. Charley in particular made a point of jotting down names and other pertinent details in a little notebook. Among the famous names in Charley's book were those of Mrs. Potter Palmer, leader of Chicago society, Grover Cleveland and Theodore Roosevelt, Prince Henry of Prussia, Mrs. William McKinley, who came to Field's for her inaugural gown, Isadora Duncan, at that time an unknown who was looking for a job as a dancer, and Hetty Green, the richest woman in the world.

Out of the services of these doormen developed Field's personal shopping service and the personal information service desk on the third floor where courteous experts answer questions about Field's and Chicago, translate for those speaking foreign tongues, find hotel rooms, arrange sight-seeing tours, or just take messages.

It is practically impossible either to surprise or stump Mrs. Elizabeth Skinner, head of this service. Somebody in Winnipeg, Canada, called up requesting a Willkie campaign button (two years after the campaign) by next noon. The caller had bet he could find a Willkie button within twenty-four hours, and with Mrs. Skinner at the helm, he won his bet. When a woman customer's pet canary got rattled and flew up under Field's big metal canopy—the bird was a nervous type who didn't like cages, so the lady had been carrying him on her finger—it was Mrs. Skinner who rose to the occasion. She called for a butterfly net and a small, agile porter, and in ten minutes the rescue was accomplished. Every day she and her staff are bombarded with questions, not only about where to find what at Field's, but on such historical points as who was mayor of Chicago during the 1871 fire. People often leave money at the Personal Information Service Desk to be passed on to some particular charity, and one man used to leave his alimony check there every week.

The shopping service started one morning when the doorman found a note on the Washington Street door, placed there before opening time and ordering a pair of baby shoes and a spool of thread. A LaSalle Street broker had thought up this effortless method of carrying out the shopping errands assigned to him by his wife. The doorman took care of the order himself, and when the broker's coach turned up again in the afternoon the package was ready and waiting. Evidently the broker spread the glad tidings among the other husbands of his acquaintance, because from then on similar notes appeared with increasing frequency. The result was the development of today's large and busy department.

The personal shopping service, with a staff of from 80 to 150 shoppers, averages more than three thousand purchases a day for customers with problems. Often they are complicated problems. There was the Milwaukee woman, for instance, who was going to spend Christmas in Europe and thought it would be nice to take a present for each member of her husband's family. The list of relatives turned out to be forty-seven names long and time was alarmingly short. Then the woman thought of Field's. She turned the list over to the personal shopping service, with a description of each of the forty-seven relatives, and when she boarded her ship in New York there were the forty-seven gifts, each labeled and ready for presentation.

Another lady, wife of a candidate for governor in a southwestern state, appealed to Field's for advice about her wardrobe in case her husband was elected. He was; Field's whisked off a $2,000 outfit to her by air express; and the lady was so pleased that she invited a store representative to the inaugural.

All executives have made a great point of the public-service idea at Field's. During World War I the store was the headquarters for Red Cross and Liberty Loan drives; and when the steamer *Eastland* sank, with a death toll of 812 lives, the survivors were supplied with clothes and other necessities by Field's, and the store's employees worked all night making stretchers to carry the victims on Field trucks to a temporary morgue.

When Shedd retired in 1923, his place was taken by James Simpson, who had started out as an office boy at Field's. In an effort to pump new life into the wholesale part of the business, Simpson built the huge $28,000,000 Merchandise Mart. It was the largest commercial building in the world. Half the space was to be occupied by Field's wholesale and manufacturing divisions, and the rest was to be leased out to jobbers' representatives and manufacturers' agents. But depression was gripping the entire country, there was a dearth of tenants for the Mart, and the wholesale division kept on sinking. Even the retail store, for the only time in its history, lost money in 1932.

A. T. Stewart, John Wanamaker and Macy's years earlier had

built up big manufacturing and wholesale operations only to abandon or reduce them. "Manufacturing is quite another business," explained Wanamaker once, "and a man had better attend to the business he knows. If you have a factory you must keep it going all the time; and you must keep the people employed; you must keep your machinery going. If you sell at less than cost, you are losing your own money." But because Field's wholesale trade had once been highly profitable, Simpson, by then the principal stockholder, and others clung to the idea of integration.

His successor, John McKinlay, who rose from cash boy to president of the store, struggled with the growing losses. Simpson, who was board chairman, could help but little. Chicago banks had given him the even greater task of salvaging something from the wreckage of the Insull utility empire. Year after year, retail earnings were almost wiped out by wholesale losses.

In 1935, James O. McKinsey, a noted management consultant, was called in by the directors. Once professor of accounting and marketing at the University of Chicago, and a founder of the management-consulting firm bearing his name, he had improved the workings of several industrial companies. Pointing out that wholesale had lost $12,000,000 in five years, he recommended that the losing operations be lopped off. He was put in as chairman of the company, the first time an outsider had such a job at Field's, and McKinlay resigned.

In what came to be called "McKinsey's purge," domestic jobbing and eight hundred wholesale employees were dropped. Manufacturing operations were streamlined. But McKinsey was unfamiliar with retailing and Field traditions. When cotton and wool went down instead of up after he had made heavy purchases for the manufacturing division, he found himself in hot water with the directors. He died late in 1937, a victim of worry and work as well as pneumonia. While it took more than a decade, virtually all of his recommendations were carried out to the store's great profit, and employees who once derided McKinsey came to speak of him with respect. Frederick D. Corley, the president, became executive officer and continued in charge until retirement in 1943.

Hughston M. McBain, once an office boy for John Shedd and a Field's man since 1922, then became president. He was only forty but had experience in every part of the business. At the same time, James L. Palmer, a native of Maine and a graduate of Brown University, became first vice president and second in command. Palmer had come to Field's in 1937 from the University of Chicago, where he was professor of marketing. He also had been an adviser to Sears, Roebuck and Company and a number of other firms. The two worked as a team to regain Field's profits and prestige.

One step was the opening of the "28 Shop," so called because of the 28 Washington Street address, the old carriage entrance of the store. Reached by a private elevator, each of the twenty-eight luxurious fitting rooms has a telephone, and there are facilities for serving lunch or tea in the shop. Here, in a luxurious setting of carpeting, hand-woven draperies, and subtle lights, today's equivalent of the carriage trade views and buys clothes ranging from simple daytime clothes and accessories to fabulous imports.

The 28 Shop was followed by a Tip to Toe Shop, where a lady can get one costume or a complete wardrobe. If the customer happens to be from a foreign country, she doesn't even have to appear in person; Tip to Toe will outfit her from photographs and measurements. The shop also gives advice for the right clothes for travel anywhere in the world. The shop keeps a climate file on such farflung spots as Alaska, Turkey, South Africa and Burma.

McBain and Palmer redecorated notable old departments, such as the Store for Men and the book department. Built by Marcella Hahner and Rose Oller Harbaugh, the latter pioneered book fairs and autographing parties in the department stores and has assured the success of many a book. Though its volume is not as great as the Doubleday or Brentano stores, its sales often have run more than a million dollars a year and it disputes Macy's for the honor of being the biggest in the department-store world.

McBain and Palmer modernized employee training. The store's girl elevator operators, who once numbered Dorothy Lamour, later of the movies, were sent to charm school, beginning in 1947. Instruction manuals, little changed since the days of the founder and John Shedd, were revised. A film on employee courtesy, titled *By Jupiter,* proved so successful that prints were sold to other schools. A pension plan paid for by the company was devised. It soon had assets of $26,000,000. With Social Security, this assures many retirees 60 per cent of their salaries.

Public relations also received attention. A research firm was employed to determine what the customers thoughts of the store. Advertising and promotion, under Vice President Lawrence B. Sizer, were expanded. The store became the first to purchase a double-page color spread in *Life*. In local newspapers, a new "newspaper within a newspaper," called *Pace,* proved an effective vehicle for institutional advertising. In 1952, Field's centennial was publicized nationally. A match book promoting the 28 Shop received a 1953 award as the most distinguished example of that form of advertising in the department-store field.

All of the innovations combined to achieve an operation more profitable than many larger companies in the department-store field and enabled the store to solve long-standing financial problems. Rent was reduced by the purchase of the store site from the Field estate. Half of the preferred stock was retired. Finally in 1946, the Merchandise Mart, a white elephant for most of its existence, was sold to Joseph P. Kennedy for $18,000,000. It was a good deal for both parties. He acquired the great structure at less than its cost. The loss that Field's took materially cut the taxes that otherwise would have been paid in that prosperous year. In 1949, McBain and Palmer became respectively chairman and president. In 1953, the Fieldcrest Mills, last of the firm's textile manufacturing interests, were sold and McBain that year received the Tobé Award in recognition of his contributions to retailing.

These transactions made available millions of dollars for expansion. Field's established suburban branches at Lake Forest and Evanston in 1928 and another at Oak Park in 1929. These were modernized and enlarged following World War II. In 1950, land was acquired for more suburban expansion.

In 1952, the store purchased a 192-acre farm, thirty miles out of Chicago, and transformed it into an artificial hunters' paradise, with clay pigeons popping from every kind of natural cover. Here sportsmen—beginners or otherwise—have a chance to practice. Known as Fieldale, there is a branch of the store's huge gun shop on the farm, for the sale and repair of shotguns and rifles, but those who bring their own firearms are welcome too. Rates for targets are the same as at city-operated skeet clubs in Chicago.

Field's executives toyed with the notion of such a farm for a long time, but it took a survey of sporting habits of Chicagoans to clinch the matter. The survey showed that, while golfers and bowlers had plenty of places to practice, the 650,000 licensed hunters in the area had none.

In 1954, construction was started on new branch stores at Park Forest, Illinois; at the Mayfair Shopping Center in the Milwaukee suburb of Wauwatosa, Wisconsin; and at the great Old Orchard Shopping Center in Skokie, Illinois, the last a great hundred-acre development to be constructed and managed by American Community Builders, Inc.

One of the most important ventures in the history of Field's was the purchase for about $6,000,000 of Frederick & Nelson, Seattle's largest department store. This was founded in 1890 by D. E. Frederick, son of a Georgia farmer, and Nels Nelson, a Swedish immigrant. The store prospered during the gold rush to Alaska and a new store modeled somewhat on Field's was built in 1918. Nels Nelson died at sea and by 1929 Frederick, then seventy, was ready to retire.

As he admired Field's, which he often visited with his daughter, Frederick called at President Simpson's office. Finding him absent, the Seattle merchant picked up an envelope and wrote on the flap: "I will sell my business to Marshall Field & Company and to them only." After some negotiations, which at one point almost collapsed, the purchase was concluded July 25, 1929. The staff was almost undisturbed, only treasurer Thomas Lewis going out from Chicago.

William H. St. Clair, a Frederick & Nelson man, became president, and was succeeded by Charles C. Bunker and then William S. Street, a native Californian who for some years was general manager at Field's. Sales which had been $12,000,000 in 1929 and dropped to half that in the depression rose to more than $30,000,000 after World War II. A shopping center was opened in suburban Bellevue. In 1949, it was decided to add five additional floors to the main store at a cost of $6,250,000, increasing the space 50 per cent. Later, an adjoining parking garage costing $3,250,000 was constructed. The expansion, completed in 1953, finally totaled $9,000,000.

Frederick & Nelson's multitudinous civic activities and promotions of the Northwest were recognized by the Seattle Chamber of Commerce with a Paul Bunyan Award of Merit in 1947. The store was then advertising in ten national magazines.

How well the big Seattle store follows the customer-wooing traditions of Field's is illustrated by the handling of the complaint of Mrs. Kathryn Kavanaugh in 1949. She made a trip to Eire and photographed her Irish relatives and a number of Irish scenes in color. On her return to Seattle, she left the films at Frederick & Nelson to be developed. The store lost them.

When Mrs. Kavanaugh's complaint came to the attention of President Street of Frederick & Nelson, he had her list and describe the lost pictures. This list was sent to the office which Field's has maintained in London for many years. Joseph Hollander, the London photographer for the Fairchild News Service, was commissioned to retrace Mrs. Kavanaugh's journey through County Limerick, County Kerry and County Leix and to duplicate the pictures she had made.

IX. Brentano's

"Booksellers to the World"

AMERICA'S biggest book retailer independent of publishing con-
nections and one of the greatest sellers of books in the world is
Brentano's. The name identifies the main Fifth Avenue store in New
York and fifteen branches scattered from Paris, France, to a book
department in the City of Paris, the San Francisco department
store.

The firm owes its success to a combination of nostalgic friendliness, reminiscent of the tiny bookshop, and shrewd operation. New
books cost less in quantity, the difference between 40 and 45 per
cent, or more, a margin which may mean profit or loss to a store.
Hard-headed Brentano buyers disregard pressures of all kinds from
publishers to order the quantity their intuition tells them is the
optimum. Their intuition is sound and, by correctly estimated
original orders, Brentano's usually enjoys maximum discounts. At
the same time, clerks and branch managers, some of them women,
know the tastes of many customers so well that books are sent them
unordered and returns are few.

The main store stocks some forty thousand titles and around half
a million volumes in many languages but will supply any book in
print, regardless of where published. The store basement stocks a
great array of U.S. and foreign magazines, many of them on the
scholarly side and probably the biggest selection of twenty-five-cent
books in America. Upstairs, the rare-book department sometimes
sells an old volume in a fine binding at a price in five figures and a
few years ago offered but did not sell a hand-illuminated jeweled
Lives of the Popes at $50,000.

Leading writers of the day, visitors such as the King of Greece and notable as varied as Eleanor Roosevelt and Greta Garbo are among Brentano's shoppers. Through the years, it has managed to create about itself a blend of the romance and knowledge that its customers seek in the books it sells. It has maintained this unique fame and prestige despite fire, book clubs, bankruptcy and inroads on the time of the human race by motion pictures, automobiles, radio and now television.

The business was founded by an enterprising immigrant news vendor shrewd enough to supply sporting news ahead of his competitors. August Brentano was young, ambitious, and newly arrived from Austria in 1853 when he set up a newsstand in front of the New York Hotel. Newspapers and magazines at that time usually were peddled from door to door; but the hotelkeeper allowed Brentano this desirable space because he was handicapped by a withered arm.

Discovering that the hotel guests, who included visitors from abroad, were betting on the great English horse races, Brentano ordered newspapers from England and met the clipper ships bringing them at the dockside. The Atlantic cable was still in the future and Brentano's newspapers made him first with the racing news. He prospered and moved his stand to a hallway of the old Revere House, at Broadway and Houston Street. Above the table which offered some books as well as papers, he had an imposing sign reading "Brentano's Literary Emporium."

The John Heenan-Tom Sayers prizefight in England, in which an American and an Englishman fought a bloody thirty-five-round draw for the heavyweight championship, aroused so much interest that young Brentano sold great bundles of papers at $1 apiece, and became rich enough to open a real emporium in 1860. His store was a basement at first; seven years later it took up half the building at 708 Broadway. The other half was occupied by the Frohmans' tobacco business, conducted by the fathers of Charles and Daniel Frohman, famous theater managers.

Brentano's, because it catered to a cosmopolitan patronage and offered foreign books and periodicals unobtainable elsewhere, became a rendezvous for the fashionable hotel guests from across the street, and for "the carriage trade" from all over the city. By 1870, when August moved his store to an even better residential neighborhood, at 33 Union Square, next door to the Goelet mansion and just down the block from Tiffany's, Brentano's was already one of New York's landmarks. In the next two decades, the Union Square store acquired a reputation throughout the country. Sightseers came to gape at the browsers, who included Ralph Waldo Emerson, Lillian Russell, John Drew, Charles Dickens, James Russell Lowell, General U. S. Grant, and other socially important or wealthy customers.

August, by his enterprise and resourcefulness, created a successful business. His nephew, Arthur, who started in the store in 1873 and sold books from the floor for seventy-one years, made Brentano's an institution. He was fifteen years old at the time he first set foot in the store. A cholera epidemic in Cincinnati had killed his father, a sister and brother. His mother moved with the remaining six children to Evansville, where she had two brothers, and soon thereafter Arthur was sent to his uncle in New York to earn his fortune.

His first job was a paper route for the store, from Broadway to the East River. Later, because he did so well at it, he was rewarded with a route that reached to Central Park. He delivered papers morning and evening; during the day he sorted books and also delivered them, becoming so familiar with the stock that he was consulted by the customers in preference to the senior salesmen. The best sellers with which he dealt in those days were by such authors as Louisa May Alcott, T. B. Aldrich, Lew Wallace, Bret Harte, Mark Twain, and William Dean Howells.

A few years after Arthur's arrival at the store, his younger brothers, Simon and August Brentano, came from Evansville and were taken into the business. The store was open seven days a week, 9 A.M. to 8 P.M. All worked hard. In 1882, the three brothers bought out their uncle. August, Sr., by then an elderly man, wanted to retire and make a tour of the world. After extensive farewells, he got as far as Montreal when nostalgia brought him back to the Union Square store. Until his death in 1886, he remained there, working at the cashier's desk.

Meanwhile, in 1884 Brentano's opened a Washington branch; and in 1887 Arthur went to Paris to open another branch. Three years later, in Paris, he married a California girl, Maria Louise Sepulveda Lan Franco. His best man was Robert Chambers, the novelist, and another friend at the ceremony was Whitelaw Reid, publisher of the New York *Tribune* and American Ambassador to the Court of St. James.

Financial difficulties first afflicted Brentano's after the great business depression of 1893. Another disaster occurred in 1898. The Union Square establishment and all its stock was destroyed by a fire that started in the house next door, and the store had to be rebuilt. To straighten out their finances at this crisis, Simon Brentano sued his two brothers for dissolution of the partnership, and in 1899 the firm was reorganized. Simon became president. Charles E. Butler, president of the American Booksellers Association, who represented the publishers' interests in working out credit, became secretary; and Clive Mecklim, a veteran employee, was made treasurer.

Arthur, who hated office work, fled from financial statements, and wanted to stay with his books, was named vice president. Arthur had never been to high school, a fact which embarrassed him all through his life. "I don't know a scrap of Latin or Greek," he once explained, "and for more than sixty years I have been in perpetual fear of being exposed." He learned French and German fluently, however, and through the books he handled gave himself a remarkable education. His courtly manners, his impeccable appearance— he always wore a navy-blue suit, starched collar, dark tie, and pince-nez—and his considerable knowledge made him a great favorite with the customers; indeed, in the store he became the good friend of many eminent men and women in art, politics and society.

He inaugurated the old and rare department, which became his special pride. As well as collecting fine old books of great value, the store was also offering a service at that time unique among bookstores—scouring the market to locate any publication requested, no matter when and where published, including privately printed pamphlets, books and periodicals in foreign languages, first editions, out of print, and other rare items. This service brought Brentano's orders from all over the world and gave it international importance in the book world.

Arthur Brentano once listed the two things that he liked most about his business: "Getting a nice library . . . good, solid, useable, permanent books," and "Making a good sale—getting those

good, solid, useable, permanent books into the hands of an apprecia-
tive buyer." Arthur's idea of hospitality—that each customer should
be greeted at the door and made welcome—was followed as long as
he was alive.

A reporter for *Publishers' Weekly*, who interviewed this gentleman
when he was eighty, remarked that Arthur Brentano was always at
the door. For years the reporter had been visiting the store and talking to him without realizing it. "Brentano," he wrote, "had been as
gracious, as friendly, as urbane, as kindly, as communicative when
I bought nothing as if I were negotiating for the four Shakespeare
folios."

Sales clerks hired by Arthur Brentano were carefully selected and
instructed by him to maintain the store's tradition of boundless eru-
dition and limitless, unhurried service. Laurence Gomme, long head
of the old and rare department, recalled that, when he arrived from
England in 1907 and applied for a job, Arthur subjected him to a
lengthy test of his knowledge, manners, and grooming, then hired
him at $12 a week. It was considered a distinction and rare privilege
just to work for Brentano's.

In 1907, Brentano's, keeping up with the fashionable trend,
moved again, this time to Twenty-seventh Street and Fifth Avenue.
In this new headquarters, a great deal of literary history was made.
"I can remember the wonderful store they had down there," recalled
Bennett Cerf, the publisher, years later in the *Saturday Review of
Literature*. "There were originals of all the magazine covers in the
side-street windows and the huge pile of periodicals from all over
the world in the basement! Theodore Roosevelt came in one day
and ordered the pigskin library that he took with him to Africa.
The store had an indescribable glamour; the staff harbored some
rare and congenial personalities." Mayor William Jay Gaynor of
New York, Andrew Carnegie, J. P. Morgan, Henry Clay Frick,
George Ade, Oliver Herford and other celebrities of the period con-
gregated at the Twenty-seventh Street store. There an autographing
party for Gertrude Stein was mobbed by her readers and non-
readers. The firm discontinued the sale of sheet music, newspapers
and theater tickets but there were more books and magazines. Displays of art work for the covers of these by Charles Dana Gibson,

Montgomery Flagg, Maxfield Parrish and others attracted a daily crowd.

When Simon Brentano died in 1914, Arthur became president. The sons of these brothers—Lowell and Arthur Brentano, Jr., joined the business. Since the elder Brentano continued to avoid administrative details and devoted himself to rare books, his son worked at retailing, store management and the development of branches. It was a period of expansion for the firm. Additional New York branches were established, and stores followed in Pittsburgh, Cleveland and Philadelphia.

An author and playwright himself, Lowell Brentano in 1918 took charge of the firm's publishing department after his graduation from Harvard, where he attained Phi Beta Kappa despite a serious congenital hearing defect. This part of the business previously had been directed by Volney Streamer and the late Temple Scott. From 1879 to 1881, Brentano's published a magazine of field and water sports; from 1881 to 1882 it issued a chess monthly. In place of catalogs, announcements, and a monthly bulletin previously supplied to its customers, the store in 1907 started *Book Chat,* advertised as "a periodical which should be chained to the desk of every man in search of literary information." Subscription was first 25 cents, then $1 a year. *Book Chat* offered news about books and authors, notes written by prominent authors, answers to queries, scholarly information about old and rare books and manuscripts offered for sale at Brentano's; and, of course, announcements of the new books—including those in Spanish, Italian, German and French—which Brentano's stocked. South American literature and foreign Christmas cards also were advertised.

At the same time Brentano's published noteworthy books. It was the first to print the plays of George Bernard Shaw in America and the letters in the company's files attest to the fact that, even then, Shaw was a vigorous and unorthodox correspondent. Other Brentano authors included George Moore, Margaret Sanger, whose books on birth control were the subject of violent controversy; David Loth, Robert Briffault, Eugène Brieux, Ronald Firbank and Channing Pollock.

The Brentano family once went to meet the unpredictable Shaw when he landed in New York. An elaborate program was planned but the great dramatist remained only a few hours and sailed home the next day. Later in London, Arthur Brentano one day rushed in to his daughter, Rowena, and said, "Come, Lambie, it's time for lunch with Mr. Shaw." Rowena replied, "Papa, I'd rather stay here and knit if I may."

All Brentano departments were profitable as the main store moved northward again in 1926 to its present L-shaped quarters with entrances on both Forty-seventh Street and Fifth Avenue. The new store, a journalist noted, had the "same admirable features" as the old with "The varied and enormous stock, the easily accessible galleries, comprehensive foreign department administered by clerks who understand the languages of the literature to which they are accredited, and the fascinating display of periodicals on the tables of the basement." The Bible, a steady seller at Brentano's, was stocked in several versions and a dozen languages. There were thousands of technical books.

Books of its own authors sold well and those by Sinclair Lewis, F. Scott Fitzgerald and Anita Loos went by thousands to the customers. American tourists going to Europe read books from Brentano's in New York on the way over and from Brentano's store in Paris on the way back. In 1928, Arthur Brentano, Jr., told the convention of the American Booksellers' Association that the store had delivered as many as twenty thousand books to one liner. The firm's sales were more than $3,000,000 a year.

The stock market crashed the next year just as the first novel of a writer named Thomas Wolfe appeared. The book business was hit hard. With a huge inventory of expensive books, several new branches, and a big new main store, Brentano's was in serious financial trouble. Because it was one of the largest retail outlets for books in the world, publishers could not afford to see it go out of business. A publishers' committee took over the management.

Salaries were cut drastically, in some cases to as low as $7 and $12 a week, but employees continued loyally at their jobs. The American rights to the plays of George Bernard Shaw were sold to Dodd, Mead & Company. The remainder of the Brentano book publishing department went to Coward-McCann. At this point, Lowell Brentano left the firm, except for an interest in the Paris Branch, and devoted himself successfully to his own writing. He lived until 1950, turning out plays, novels, motion-picture scenarios, anthologies and a final book, *Ways to Better Hearing,* inspired by his own lifelong struggle against deafness.

As the depression deepened and competition for the remaining book business increased, the business shrank further. All outlets except the main store in New York and the branches in Washington, Chicago and Paris, were discontinued. But even these economies were not enough. After the "bank holiday" in 1933, Brentano's was bankrupt. The Irving Trust Company was named receiver.

A savior appeared in the person of an urbane Brentano customer, Stanton Griffis, a partner in the investment banking firm of Hemphill, Noyes & Co. and a man of many other interests. He was chairman of the executive committee of Paramount Pictures and the Lee Tire & Rubber Co., and a director of Madison Square Garden. He had backed some Katharine Cornell stage productions and reorganized many corporations. He heard of the plight of Brentano's in the course of a bridge game on his yacht and promised to help. "I thought it would be amusing," he explained later, "to see what a hard-headed businessman could do in such a situation with a famous name like Brentano's as an asset."

On June 4, 1933, Griffis paid $150,000, only $72,000 of it in cash, for nearly all of the firm's assets. It had grossed $1,500,000 the previous year, listed assets at $745,983 and liabilities at $511,-445. Three-year notes were signed for the remainder and book publishers assured Griffis liberal credit. He was joined in the purchase by Adolph Kroch, a leading Chicago bookseller, who acquired a 20 per cent interest. After three years, Kroch was given the Chicago branch and bought out. Merged later in larger quarters on South Wabash Street, Kroch's & Brentano's advertises as "the world's largest bookstore."

Griffis became chairman of the board of Brentano's, Inc., as the new firm eventually was titled. The courtly Arthur Brentano continued as president until his death in 1944 and his son, Arthur, Jr., remained as vice president and general manager. Some of Griffis' bookish Wall Street friends, Amos Tuck French, Winky Thomas and Bruce Ryan among them, came to work in the store for a time but Griffis himself remained so much in the background that fifteen years later a noted Broadway columnist breathlessly printed: "Has Stanton Griffis purchased the Brentano bookstores?"

While Griffis had counseled his friend, Arthur Brentano, Sr., against expanding earlier, the financier, when he took charge, believed on the basis of business trends that a chain of bookstores could be run something like the A & P, or even Woolworth's, and book-selling could profit from an application of similar large-scale merchandising. This seemed valid for a time. Under his regime, the business quickly began to improve. Thousands bought *Anthony Adverse* and *Gone with the Wind,* the heavyweight historical romances that were the best sellers of the depression. "Best sellers are the vitamins of the book business," explained Joseph Margolies, formerly Washington manager who then became vice president and chief buyer. "They bring in the customers who buy not only the new best seller but a classic like *David Copperfield* for a niece or nephew."

Griffis amazed his publisher creditors by paying their notes after only six months, giving them a 35 per cent return on their claims against the old company. The firm earned profits in 1937, operated at a deficit of $16,918 in 1938, and from the next year onward had profits through World War II.

A branch was reopened in Philadelphia. More branches were opened in the Washington area, including one on the concourse of the Pentagon Building. Under the management of Mrs. Virginia Ward it soon numbered the highest military brass as customers. A leased department established in the City of Paris store in San Francisco under Sybil Bardshar became the largest bookstore west of Denver. Lillian Friedman was promoted from there to be chief buyer for the firm. Several other branches were opened, including one at Waikiki Beach, Hawaii, to which Horace Hutchins was dispatched as manager after a hilarious hula-hula party.

World War II caused a boom in the book business. With gasoline rationed and television still in the future, some bought and read books to forget their worries. Brentano's sold twenty-eight thousand copies of Kathleen Winsor's *Forever Amber.* More bought books to help them qualify for commissions or to obtain jobs in war industry. Soaring taxes created a demand for the works of J. K. Lasser, Brentano's own tax adviser. Hundreds of copies of Professor Smyth's

Atomic Energy for Military Purposes were sold. Governments bought books in quantity for instructional and propaganda purposes.

At the request of the Free French government, Brentano's returned profitably to publishing during the struggle. With French publishing plants in the hands of the enemy and the sale of their books banned in occupied countries, Brentano's produced paperbacked editions in French of the works of writers like André Maurois, Pierre Lazareff and André Girard. These were shipped by the thousands to North Africa, the French colonies and via the underground into occupied France.

The Brentano branch in Paris, at 37 Avenue de l'Opéra and extending through to Rue des Petits Champs, felt the tramp of Nazi soldiery. As the Wehrmacht marched into the city in June of 1940, the store executives, who were British subjects, fled by motorcycle and bicycle to the coast. The French employees remained until the Nazis took over. But first an official of a German library walked in and placed an order for 6,000 books, including 349 assorted titles in Everyman's Library, a variety of art books, the unexpurgated *Lady Chatterley's Lover* and some expensive erotica. He paid 755,-000 francs for his order and sent trucks to carry the books away.

After that the Nazis confiscated without payment all leather goods, stationery, fountain pens, guidebooks, dictionaries, encyclopedias, maps and atlases; and converted the premises into the official film and camera supply center for the Wehrmacht in Paris. The firm name on the windows was covered over with black paint, the fixtures and remaining stock were moved to the rear of the store and to the basement. In a period of almost five years, the converted photo shop, which was also a place where German soldiers could have their pictures taken or developed, made a profit of a million francs ($20,000). Deposited in a Paris agency, and left behind when the Nazis departed hurriedly, that money was turned over to Brentano's by the French government after the liberation.

When Arthur Brentano, Jr., who became president of the firm at his father's death, reached Paris on March 15, 1945, he found that, along with hundreds of pictures of German soldiers, in the cluttered up basement and rear of the store approximately one-third of the previous stock remained—about 12,000 books. The concierge and his wife, who had lived in the concierge apartment on the premises all through the occupation and had tried to protect what they could of Brentano's property, and the office secretary were also waiting for him. While they were all digging through the debris to clean up and refurbish the place, a truck arrived with a shipment of five hundred books; these had been ordered from London early in 1940, had been stored in a Paris warehouse during the German occupation, and were now being delivered per order.

To determine prices in the new inflated currency Brentano simply marked up each item 500 per cent of its prewar price. That was in line with the inflated prices existing in other Parisian bookstores and also permitted the firm to buy books in France, where they were expensive, to restock the depleted shelves. It was the only Paris bookstore with stock to sell.

By great effort and much slashing of red tape, he managed to reopen the store on April 19, giving it the distinction of being the first American retail establishment in the city to resume business. The first customer on the day of reopening was an American sergeant who bought two Penguin books—*Walden* and *City of Beautiful Nonsense*. This Parisian shop, which since its beginning in the eighties has been a favorite meeting place for Americans traveling abroad, began to do a thriving business with European customers, too, filling the great demand for American technical books useful in rebuilding war-devastated areas.

Sales volume of Brentano's passed $4,000,000 in the years following the war but profits dropped and some branches failed to develop enough volume to sustain themselves under changed conditions. Noted prelates admired the $50,000 *Lives of the Popes* offered in 1946 but nobody would buy it for them. There were signs of trouble in 1947. Beginning in 1948 the firm operated at a loss for three years. By this time the versatile Stanton Griffis was far away. During the war, he had embraced a chance to make history as well as sell books about it. He headed government missions to England, Finland, Spain, Portugal and Sweden, in the last stopping the export of vital ball bearings to Germany. He served as Red Cross Commissioner in the Pacific. He then became successively ambassador to Poland, Egypt, Argentina and Spain.

He wrote of Brentano's and bookselling as well as diplomacy, in an autobiographical volume, *Lying in State,* published on his return from Spain in 1952. Among difficulties besetting a book-seller, he listed: the book clubs, which sell some current books at lower prices than the wholesaler can buy them; and the depart-ment store "loss leader," a method of attracting customers into the department store by selling items such as books at lower than cost. These practices, Griffis charged, have been promoted by publishers. "In no other industry," he said, "does the manufac-turer go to such lengths and use such vicious means to destroy his outlets." Finally, in this list of forces that cut profits in the bookselling business, he mentioned unions. In the old days, he re-lated, bright young intellectuals found the satisfaction of working in a bookstore to be payment enough, and so they worked for very little. At present, the unions "tell us what we should pay everyone in the business from the shipping clerk to the buyer." Years earlier, incidentally, Arthur Brentano and some other booksellers had pro-tested the book clubs by refusing to sell the early selections of the Literary Guild. The gesture was abandoned when it was found that its only effect was to deprive the stores of more sales.

His investment in Brentano's, Griffis said, had brought him fun rather than cash. "I would spend sleepless nights of horror if I heard that any customer of Brentano's felt that we had made a profit on his purchase," he wrote. "We are in trade only for dignity, atmos-phere and service." And to make this point even more emphatic, he added, "I am happy to have had the experience of high hopes and failure in the retail bookselling business."

But even as the diplomat wrote, his son, Nixon Griffis, was making the century-old enterprise again a profitable one. Like his father Nixon was a graduate of Cornell University, where he studied as-tronomy and became a boxing champion. After Army service and work at Hemphill, Noyes, he joined Brentano's in 1947 as secretary of the firm. In 1949, he became president and the next year on the retirement of Arthur Brentano, Jr., became chairman of the board as well. Young Griffis was then thirty-two. Leonard Schwartz, who had been with the firm since 1937, except for war service, became vice president.

Changes involved both expenditures and economies. The Paris branch was modernized. At a cost of $100,000, the main New York store was refurbished and rearranged to do the same business in less space. The Waikiki Beach branch was sold and Horace Hutchins returned to take charge in Philadelphia. Several branches were closed. Machine bookkeeping replaced a hand ledger system with a reduction in cost and a gain in efficiency. Modern window displays were introduced.

Clerks were asked to quit spending hours looking up the answers to obscure questions and to refer such queries, which as often as not were from a contestant in a puzzle contest, to the New York Public Library. The first time this was done, the questioner replied: "But I called there first. They said to telephone Brentano's." Some of the library staff apparently had been diverting baffling requests to the store for many years. The New York store ended its out-of-print service but this was continued in Washington where it is profitable.

Branches established for a time on the *Independence* and *Constitution,* new liners of the American Export Line sailing to the Mediterranean, proved reasonably profitable from a business standpoint and tremendously successful from a Brentano's morale point of view. The floating branches and libraries were managed each cruise by a manager or employee who had done an outstanding job in New York or Washington. Many cruise passengers, however, felt that their passage should include free library service, as it does on many liners, and the free voyages to Naples, Capri, Sorrento, Genoa and the Riviera came to an end.

Efforts were made to find merchandise that could be sold along with the books, magazines and stationery that are the backbone of the business. Sophisticated greeting cards by artists like Rosalind Welcher proved successful. So did games like Scrabble, which Brentano's discovered early; many purchasers were found for a $15 toy planetarium. Seashells, records, 16-millimeter films and rare postage stamps did not work out at the main store though stamp albums continued to be sold. More successful were reproductions of museum statuary which, in most cases, had been available previously only in the museums owning the Aphrodites, Han Dynasty horses and Egyptian Sacred Cats.

In 1953, Brentano's centennial year which passed without any special celebration, it all added up to give the venerable enterprise a modest profit on sales of $2,823,326. This was roughly a million dollars more than the volume from many more outlets a decade earlier. The unique commerce between Brentano's far-flung customers and its erudite employees seemed assured for some years to come.

Much of Brentano's durability is due to its employees, remarkable both for their learning and their loyalty to the enterprise. Scholarly George W. Stair, who formerly ran his own bookstore in Rockefeller Center, came out of retirement to head the rare-book and fine-binding department. May Ryan, a remarkable woman, went to work in 1918 and thirty-six years later still presided expertly over the Fifth Avenue store's information desk, knowing by heart most of the twelve thousand new titles published each year and able to identify any other from fragmentary or inaccurate information. Florence Wimer went to work in the store as a young girl and has become treasurer and comptroller.

Arthur Baxter has been buyer and manager of the Paris branch for forty years. Einar Thompson, Pauline Mazie, Sylvia Saul, Rose Hoff and many others have long worked devotedly. Alexander Malitsky developed the art department, which offers unusual books and prints from all countries, and George Sinks was one of its assets for many years. Employees like Jean Lawlor, George Colgan, Charles E. Butler and Thomas Cadigan served Brentano's until their deaths.

Customers of Brentano's include the famous, the learned and the eccentric. Most notable of all, perhaps, was twenty-three-year-old Dorothy Arnold, daughter of a millionaire. On December 12, 1910, she bought a novel from Ernest Dell, a salesman in the New York Brentano store. She then stepped out into the Fifth Avenue traffic and was never heard from again. Her family exhausted their fortune seeking her and the case remains New York's leading unsolved mystery.

Many of the names on Brentano's charge accounts have been the subject of books. They include the country's artistic, social, political and financial leaders, as well as scientists and specialists in every field. The firm's mail-order business is even more remarkable. It has a mailing list of seventy-five thousand persons living in every corner of the globe. To customers from Allahabad to Zomba, Brentano's importance rests not only on the forty thousand titles it keeps in stock, and on its long-standing ability to obtain others, but also on the fact that the United States for years after World War II was the only country where so many books were freely obtainable. The war's destruction of great libraries abroad, paper shortages, political and economic restrictions in other countries enhanced the value of American books. Also in many underdeveloped countries and those rebuilding after the war, there was a great curiosity about this country, especially about our technical skills. Brentano's, as the best-known American bookseller, became a kind of literary UN and has retained this position.

The Brazilian government, for example, ordered $8,000 worth of books to be sent to their embassies all over the world. One of the books listed in the order was out of print, and Brazil wanted a thousand copies. So Macmillan, the publisher, printed a special edition at Brentano's request.

There is also the story of the Bibliothèque de l'Université de Caen. This library was completely destroyed during the war, but a group of Americans raised $12,000 to help the university start a new library. The French officials deposited the entire sum with Brentano's, sending in orders from time to time. One of its orders: the complete bound set of the *Journal of Geology,* priced at $1,190.

From the countries of Asia have come orders for books on American history, American economic organization, American political thought, American industrial development, American jokes, and American movies. Mail comes from the forty-eight states, too. A mother orders "the very best book which you have on learning to be a good chess player" for her son, an ensign in the Navy. "I would like you to write his name in it and put an Easter card in for me." A minister in Arkansas asks for advice: he wants to build a library on the whole range of human knowledge, which he feels should be in his ken. A woman who wants Brentano's to pick out a book on reducing explains how much she weighs and where the fat is distributed. A customer in Auburn Prison sends for a French-English dictionary. A grateful patron in Sault Sainte Marie, Michigan, advises, "I have been buying books from you for 25 years, and I have just been elected mayor, largely due to those books."

It can be seen from this sampling that to these distant customers Brentano's is more than just a bookseller; the store seems to take on a personality—that of a wise old gentleman with a fatherly interest in the welfare of his customers. That was undoubtedly the gentleman pictured by a certain American engineer in Colombia, who wrote for fifteen or twenty books to be read to and by his nine-year-old daughter. "I will trust you to choose."

Brentano's did not disappoint him. Accompanying a package which included *Rip Van Winkle, King Arthur and the Knights of the Round Table,* Lamb's *Tales from Shakespeare* went a letter which said, "We hope the books selected will meet with your approval and also that of the little girl. However, intelligent children and adults reading to them seldom agree on book selections. If our taste and yours do not coincide, you may return those books which you do not wish to keep."

Unless asked to do so, Brentano's does not attempt to guide or improve a customer's taste. An order for "60 feet of white books" to fit the decorative scheme of a customer's new apartment was filled without comment largely with volumes from Italy where publishers favor such bindings. Attempts of pressure groups to censor or prevent the sale of books usually are ignored by Brentano's though titles likely to incite any important segment to riot are not displayed prominently.

Early in his career as a bookseller, Stanton Griffis refused to stock *The Truman Merry-Go-Round* by Robert Allen and W. V. Shannon because it was critical of Griffis as an ambassador. Drew Pearson reported the fact and the book received more notice than it would have otherwise. Since then the Griffis policy has been: "Brentano's believes that the condemnation of any given book should be determined by the courts and the publishers themselves, and not by the booksellers." Friends of Senator Joseph McCarthy were ignored when they attempted to stop Brentano's selling copies of a Senate report on his financial affairs; so were his foes when they protested display of an admiring biography of him.

When the store gave a window to *The Frenchman* by Philippe Halsman, a French committee protested that the book was in bad taste and would give Americans "the wrong impression of Frenchmen." The author-photographer solved this problem by obtaining a letter from the French Ambassador certifying that he found "the book delightful, in excellent taste, and fine for promoting good relations between the two countries." In the next printing, Simon & Schuster left out one of the more sexy photographs in the volume to be on the safe side.

While selling more copies of Rachel Carson's masterpiece on the sea than were initially printed, as well as hundreds of volumes of T. S. Eliot's plays, Brentano's also sold nine thousand copies of Dr. Alfred C. Kinsey's *Sexual Behavior in the Human Male.* Its female sequel, skimmed by countless magazine articles, was much less popular. Mention of this subject at Brentano's recalls two women customers. One with an accent asked a salesman to direct her to "Sex." He took her to the man in charge of the store's array of Havelock Ellis and similar volumes. Everybody was embarrassed. It seemed she wanted directions to the store across the street, Saks Fifth Avenue. At another time, woman shopper stopped a Brentano employee and asked: "Do you have *Fun in Bed?*" As he was the store detective and unfamiliar with the writings of Frank Scully, he politely replied: "I manage to get along."

Authentic royalty have visited Brentano's a number of times. The King of Siam was a daily visitor while in the country for treatment of an eye malady. A visiting Japanese prince expressed a wish to visit the store. His bodyguard came in advance with elaborate instructions. Nobody was supposed to stand within ten feet of His Highness. All conversation was to be through an aide. This was forgotten when the prince and his retinue arrived.

"How do you do, sir, I am Mr. Brentano," said Arthur Brentano, Sr., advancing with an outstretched hand. The prince took the hand and they chatted while the retinue vanished. In fact, after the prince found his book, the retinue was found gazing with fascination at a young woman changing a lingerie display in a show window across the street. They had to be reminded that their noble charge was ready to leave.

Brentano's customers also have included Herbert Hoover, General Pershing, Charles Lindbergh, Alice Longworth, Eva Le Gallienne and Evelyn Nesbit. The principal store in Washington, D.C., at 1322 F Street, is known as "the book shop of the Presidents" and since its opening has been patronized by occupants of the White House, as well as most government bureaus. Managers there have included Sydney Avery, Joseph Margolies, Margaret Specht and Stephen Platou.

The F Street store and its branches are on extremely friendly terms with many customers. The manager of the Spring Valley store, for example, once held a book for a small boy until he earned its price by licking stamps for his father at the rate of five stamps for a penny.

Without waiting for orders, Barbara Robinson, a young lady of beauty and taste in the F Street store, regularly sends to a number of customers books which she thinks will interest them. These include the head of a labor union, who reads prodigiously and is interested in serious books, and a Virginia gentleman who is collecting a library on the War Between the States. This store's out-of-print service sometimes fills orders for the Library of Congress. It also does considerable overseas business. By error, a customer in Iceland was once sent three instead of one Icelandic grammar. Instead of complaining she sold the extras to her neighbors and paid Brentano's for all three books.

Sometimes the courtesy of the Washington staff costs it a sale. One day the embassy of a new and rather backward country telephoned frantically for a book of etiquette to be delivered within a matter of minutes. The distance was too great for this and the clerk asked discreetly what was the problem.

"Somebody left cards for the ambassador with P.P.C. written in the corner," said a desperate diplomatic voice.

"Oh," explained the all-knowing clerk, "that just stands for *pour prendre congé,* French for good-by."

"Thanks," gasped the relieved diplomat, "never mind the book."

Manager Platou and some of his staff were guests at a 1954 Washington party launching the *Captains and the Kings,* the memoirs of Edith Helm, White House social secretary to a succession of First Ladies. The Brentano's manager and former President Harry Truman met in the course of the festivity.

"You are one of Stanton Griffis' men, aren't you?" asked the latter. Platou confirmed this.

"He wrote a book a while back and I remember you had the store window filled with it," continued Truman. "Yes," said the bookman.

"Well," said the former chief executive, "you know I'm writing a book too!"

"We will do the same for your book," promised Platou. Just then handsome Dean Acheson, the former Secretary of State, came through the throng.

"Hey, Dean," shouted Truman. "Brentano's is going to give me a window!"

X. Macy's New York

The Biggest Store in the World

M ACY'S is the store Manhattan built. To New York alone belong
the polyglot of its tolerant crowds, its competitive nervousness,
its din, its reflex response to the customer. New Yorkers are always
mildly surprised to learn their city holds more Italians than Rome,
more Jews than Israel, more Poles than Warsaw. Through the years
millions of these shoppers have become convinced that whatever they
want, they usually find it at Macy's.

Macy's is fabulous the way New York is fabulous. Everything and
everybody arrive there sometime, and everything there is bigger and
better and there is more of it and anything can happen. The store's
Thanksgiving parade has been the subject of a Hollywood motion
picture. Babies have been born on the premises and a young lady
named Ann Macy Hettrich is growing up with a middle name to
remind her of where she came into the world.

"The World's Largest Store" has been a Macy slogan since it
moved to Herald Square at Thirty-fourth Street in 1902. This boast
was challenged by big Wanamaker, Marshall Field and J. L. Hudson store buildings erected in later years but Macy's added twenty-
story additions in 1924, 1928 and 1931 to bring its space to 2,157,-
330 square feet, conceded by all to be the most of any store under
one roof.

Until Macy's began to open suburban branches, the Herald
Square store also was definitely the world's biggest in sales volume
under one roof. Its more than $150,000,000 a year is now neck and
neck with that of J. L. Hudson of Detroit, which has been slower to
open branches. When the automobile business is booming that store

is first in sales. At other times, thanks in part to a big liquor department which Hudson's doesn't have, Macy's main store is out in front. Neither discloses exact figures.

Every solvent American now pays his income tax on the pay-as-you-go plan devised by Beardsley Ruml, long treasurer and later board chairman of Macy's. James P. Mitchell, who learned about labor as Macy's director of personnel and industrial relations, was appointed Secretary of Labor by President Eisenhower. Jesse Isidor Straus, whose son Jack now heads the Macy corporation, served as Ambassador to France.

The impact of Macy's is everywhere. "Macy's basement" has passed into the language for any mob scene; "Macy's window" is well understood as the ultimate in public exposure. Traffic engineers say there is statistical truth as well as poetry in these slang expressions. With as many as 165,000 shoppers a day, the human population per square foot has rivaled the pack of Hindu worshipers along the Ganges, and Macy's windows look out on the intersection of more transportation facilities than any other store enjoys.

Macy's security force of young men and women chosen for their resemblance to customers is deputized by the New York City police force. Macy's zealously protects their anonymity, even from the store's own sales staff. They patrol a different beat every day, are not permitted to eat in the regular company lunchroom, and had to be photographed from the back when *Life* wanted a picture of them. Four Doberman pinschers (Mom, Red Star, Cash and Suzy) help watchmen guard the Macy treasure house at night.

Macy's bigness creates a number of small problems as tragicomic as the inability of the fat woman in the circus to tie her own shoelaces. Macy executives have had to use all their wit to cope with the unnaturally large size of the operation. Here is how some problems have been solved:

Problem: How to keep fifty thousand purchases a day moving smoothly to the basement for delivery or shipment?

Solution: Once every hour, a clerk slips a numbered block of wood down each of the nine main tubes and times their appearance on the conveyor belt in the basement. If they don't show up promptly, or he detects a tell-tale thud, he calls for a professional akin to a chimney sweep who dons protective clothing and slides through the chute to the site of the trouble like a youngster going down the enclosed spiral slide of the fun house at Coney Island.

Problem: How to get over a million dollars in small cash to the bank every day?

Solution: An honest and infallible robot sorts, counts, and wraps the change in an elaborately guarded cashier's room mined with secret alarm devices.

Problem: How to convince 200,000 child visitors that the one and only Santa is at Macy's?

Solution: Seven Santas are strategically spotted through the store so that special traffic guards can route the youngsters in such a way that none need encounter more than one of the seven.

Problem: How to maintain the personal touch with hundreds of thousands of customers?

Solution: Customer letters are answered in the same style in which they are written. If Macy's receives a poem, Macy sends a poem back. Equally adaptable are the complaint adjusters. A woman who bet she could duplicate a $369 antique lamp for practically nothing if she had a picture of it was supplied a photograph. When a newlywed couple didn't get their bedroom set, Macy's sent a bed by special truck to the rescue. In fact, this particular emergency is so painful that the complaint department keeps a special bed in readiness for victims of misdelivered furniture. When the right bed is retrieved, the emergency bed is returned and sterilized for the next time.

Macy's 168 selling departments carry over 400,000 items, without counting sizes or colors, and customers simply take it for granted that Macy's has everything. A battery of correspondents cope with letters like the one from the woman who wanted a sort of love seat "something in which two could snuggle and have the luxurious feeling of being crowded yet not uncomfortable . . . strong and tasteful" or the one from the man who wanted a dead horse for eel bait. The Governor of Liberia ordered new decorations for his mansion from Macy's. Sailors of the U.S.S. *Argonne* once sent the store their 104-page Christmas list, an $8,730 order.

Hard-working multilingual girls at the information booths on the main floor direct shoppers looking for a pony, a prefabricated house, an antique chess set, a left-handed pair of scissors, or an elephant hunting rifle. When Macy's advertised Bob Froman's book *One Million Islands for Sale* the girls had to explain that Macy's was selling a book about islands, not the islands themselves. Macy's huge and largely self-service book department, incidentally, offers fine bindings and limited editions along with standard works. Its dress shops offer high-style French and Italian originals but the emphasis is on Macy copies of them and most advertising is directed at the thrifty.

To live up to its title as biggest competitor, the biggest store in the world has become one of New York's biggest retail customers. Scores of scouts disguised as shoppers spend as much as $250,000 a year in competing stores. If any identical item is less than at Macy's, the Macy price comes down in twenty minutes flat. Competitive price reductions are posted on a big blackboard and in ordinary times there are some six hundred a week. In a battle such as the one following release of many items from fair-trade pricing in 1951, prices may tumble several times a day, or as fast as Macy shoppers can phone from their posts in other stores. During that field day for consumers, aspirin tablets fell to 4 cents a hundred. A similar bout in 1945 dropped the ball-point pen to a new and permanent 98-cent price level. Macy's may buy up the entire stock of a competitor running a limited-quantity loss-leader sale, but store policy forbids a wounded buyer from withdrawing a competitive item from the fray.

Competing goods are bought at retail instead of simply window-shopped for price in order to make sure that they are of the same quality as the Macy article. Macy's is a sharper customer than any it serves. Its Bureau of Standards puts its own and competing products through relentless laboratory tests. Golf balls are subjected to a guillotine which hooks and slices them a thousand times. A shoe-testing machine nicknamed "Rocky Road to Dublin" is designed to outpound a growing boy. "Iron Man McGinnity" rides bicycles and "Fannie the Folding Fool" manipulates leather to the breaking point.

This, then, is Macy's. How did it become the biggest store in the lushest and toughest retail market in the world? To find out, Professor Ralph M. Hower of the Harvard Business School spent several years digging through the archives of Macy's. He concluded that the secret of Macy's success is the continuity with which the store has maintained four basic policies for nearly a century: (1) selling at definite prices (now taken for granted); (2) selling for less; (3) buying and selling for cash; (4) advertising vigorously.*

Founder Rowland H. Macy did not invent any of these policies, although all of them were radical when he adopted them. What he did do was to stick with them as articles of faith through thick and thin and pass them on to successors who stuck to them too. As we shall see, the result of this persistence was not only a fabulously profitable business, but in no small measure a new way of retailing which was to have many followers. Whether Macy's, Zion's Co-operative Mercantile Institution or Wanamaker's was the first real department store is an academic point. Professor Hower asserts that John Wanamaker, before he became "historically minded," once said Macy's was first.

No such institution existed in 1858 when Rowland Hussey Macy scraped together the resources to start a small fancy dry-goods store with an eleven-foot front on Sixth Avenue near Fourteenth Street, New York. Nor did Rowland Macy himself, then all of thirty-six years old, seem likely to create such an institution. A Nantucketer, he had spent what should have been his high-school years on a four-year whaling trip around the world in the good ship *Emily Morgan*. In 1844, he had started a little thread and needle shop on Hanover Street in Boston. It promptly failed, and so did another store in Boston. He made a profitable trading venture in Marysville, California, during gold-rush days. Then, he had another store in Haverhill, Massachusetts, which did not prosper. Yet through all these ups and downs, Macy was developing the philosophy of retailing which later made his big New York store a revolutionary influence.

What we know of Rowland Macy hardly adds up to the stereotype of a merchant prince. A stocky, bearded veteran of hard times, we know he was frugal (he refused to shade the lamps in the store because he was paying for the light) and we know his temper was hot (he once broke all the umbrellas in stock because a customer complained of a weak handle). Professor Hower finds him "more of a human being than cold, calculating A. T. Stewart, less narrowly righteous than John Wanamaker." We glimpse him flirting with the

* Ralph M. Hower, *History of Macy's of New York 1858–1919* (Harvard University Press, 1946, page 48).

girls on buying trips to Europe, lunching long at Delmonico's, playing billiards, getting religion all over again at a Moody and Sankey revival meeting.

A surviving advertisement for the "Haverhill Cheap Store" would spell Macy's to any modern New Yorker. Headed by the Macy rooster, the very style of the ad itself is a radical departure from the tombstone formality of trade notices in 1852. It reads, in part:

Macy!!!

Haverhill Cheap Store!

Ever Onward!! Ever Upward!!

English, French and American

DRY GOODS

1. We buy exclusively FOR CASH!!!

2. We sell exclusively FOR CASH!!!

3. We have but one price, and that is named first! No deviation except for imperfection!

These are the three great principles upon which we base our business. Buying *exclusively* for cash, we keep our stock in constant motion and are having new goods from New York, Philadelphia and Boston *every day*. It also enables us to procure many of our goods under the market price, and our customers have the advantage of these bargains for this reason, viz: selling exclusively for cash, we have no bad debts on our books, consequently our good customers do not have to pay them in the shape of extra profits.

By adopting one price and never deviating, a child can trade with us as cheap as the shrewdest buyer in the county.

Perhaps because of these modern-sounding principles, the Haverhill Cheap Store failed. In spite of its failure, Rowland Macy carried its three principles to his New York store. There obscure changes in distribution were unwittingly creating more favorable conditions for them.

Pre-industrial retail channels were already cracking under the rising volume and diversity of goods pouring from factories—much of it merchandise which had formerly never been sold because it was made and consumed at home. The peddler and the general store-keeper could no longer supply the more sophisticated wants of the growing number of city wage earners. The first response of merchants was to follow production into specialization. A mid-nineteenth century observer of the fragmentation of trade jokingly predicted that someone would start a store confining itself to the sale of pocket handkerchiefs. But there were other pressures affecting both merchants and customers which favored a horizontal organization of specialized lines under one roof. The merchant needed a broader financial base to weather cycles and seasons and he could get it only by diversifying (in the early years, Macy stocked parasols in summer and furs in winter). By offering many kinds of goods, he could create demand and make impulse sales to customers eager to learn new ways of living. As more everyday necessities had to be bought, shopping became a recurrent chore for customers and they were ready to have it made easier. One store for everything with standard pricing and selling methods could draw patrons from a widening urban area.

Rowland Macy's bid for this dynamic market was unpretentious even by its standards. On October 28, 1858, he offered ribbons, laces, embroideries, artificial flowers, feathers, handkerchiefs, cambric flouncings, hosiery and gloves on two long counters at 204–206 Sixth Avenue. His first-day sales were $11.06. His was a specialized shop confined as many others were to "fancy goods," an offshoot of the general dry-goods store. It had the luck to occupy a central crossroads of the growing city. But the most important influence on its spectacular future was the character of Rowland Macy himself.

The most important thing about Rowland Macy, historically speaking, is that he was brought up a Quaker. In all his retailing ventures he adhered, as a matter of religious principle, to the one-price policy originated by George Fox in 1653. Many other merchants in the new world as well as in Europe had recognized the good business sense of the Quakers, but few merchants before the Civil War were proof against the temptation to deviate from it. Implicit in the Quaker thinking were further Macy policies of "true value"—policies which were later to flower in the Bureau of Standards and the fight to sell for less in spite of restricting laws.

Rowland Macy had furthermore experienced the seamy side of the credit system which was the biggest hazard to retailing in his time. Some say that his credit was so badly dented by his previous business failures that his cash policy was sheer necessity. It is characteristic of him, however, that he saw in his early misfortunes with credit the competitive advantage of dealing in cash. This was a saving grace during the period of rapid changes and alarms in which he lived.

There was also a fortunate bit of P. T. Barnum in this Nantucket Quaker. We know that he wrote much of that modern-sounding advertising at Haverhill and that its promotional flavor in New York was his own personality. By temperament he was fitted to reach out to the new middle-class customers and draw them to his store with informally written messages quoting actual prices to prove his claim of bargains. We know, too, that he was one of the first to use typographic devices to gain attention and that he was willing to spend 3 per cent of sales on advertising at a time when well-established competitors like Lord & Taylor and Arnold Constable's were spending only 1 per cent.

But the most dramatic aspect of the rise of Rowland Macy was the way in which he turned to good account the very restlessness and impatience which had early marked him a ne'er-do-well by New England standards of storekeeping. As a young man he had gone whaling, gold hunting in California, and he had disappeared from sight on several occasions to engage in nonretailing ventures. Settled down in the New York store he was to express his need for new fields by taking on new lines of merchandise.

In his very first year he took a flyer into gloves and hosiery for men, the nucleus of a men's furnishing business. He tried a small stock of towels and sheets and found himself in house furnishings. In 1860 he added a miscellany of "French and German fancy goods" including pocketbooks, tea sets, photograph frames, games, dolls, and toys. In 1861 came fancy soaps, the birth of the drug department; in 1864 costume jewelry, in 1868 clocks and silver, in 1869 baby carriages and kitchen utensils. By 1872 he was scandalizing more conservative competitors by selling books, rocking chairs, garden tools, even fancy groceries for picnics. If books for children, why not books for adults? If books, why not stationery and magazines? Soon came velocipedes, bathing suits, barometers, and even a short-lived experiment with potted plants. Every year saw wider assortments of each line. The Macy pattern of providing everything a consumer needs and responding daringly to her wants was a direct expression of Rowland Macy himself. It is no accident that he was in Paris hunting for new lines when he died in 1877, leaving an estate of $300,000 to $500,000.

It's difficult to fix the precise year in which Macy's became a department store, but it certainly was one at Rowland Macy's death.

1. Its volume was large. From $90,000 during his first thirteen months, sales rose to $1,612,788 for the year 1876. Operating expense was 14.33 per cent and profits were 6.32 per cent.

2. It sold a wide diversity of merchandise in twenty-two departments: white goods, linens, curtains, laces and embroideries, corsets, ladies' underclothing, small wares and notions, ribbons, silverware, hosiery and furnishings, ladies' ties, furs and parasols, fancy goods, jewelry, toiletries, boys' and youths' clothing, house furnishings, toys and dolls, books, stationery, albums, worsteds and worsted embroidery, china, glass and crockery, soda fountain and candy, kid gloves, millinery, flowers and feathers, ladies' and children's shoes, cloaks and suits, black dress goods and silks.

3. It was organized by departments with a buyer completely responsible for each as to selection of merchandise, amount of stock and profits. Meanwhile, bookkeeping, cash handling, marking, and personnel matters were centralized.

4. It was directed to the woman customer.

5. It was drawing customers from faraway Brooklyn and enticing others by mail order.

6. It offered delivery service, had planned the first store lunchroom in America, opened in 1878 a writing room with the daily papers, a ventilating system and "bell calls" for the service of customers were under consideration. The privilege of returning goods was not yet institutionalized, but the liberal attitude toward the customer and a concern for making shopping convenient presaged further developments in the direction of the "free" services.

In addition to the policy of selling low for cash, the department store Rowland Macy left behind him was already committed to most of the policies for which Macy's is known today. In addition to competitive, low and fixed prices, aggressive advertising, and a strict cash basis, he left a lasting aversion for extravagant quarters. Quaker

and Nantucket simplicity ruled against the marble palaces competing storekeepers were building. Macy's at Fourteenth Street expanded into a labyrinth of nearby buildings which were not
primarily designed for retailing. The big store on Thirty-fourth
Street is efficient and spacious, but it seems designed to give the
shopper the impression that overhead is not adding unnecessarily to
prices.

Rowland Macy was the first great merchant to employ a woman
to run what has since aptly been called "a woman's business." In
1860 he engaged Margaret Getchell, a pretty and bright schoolteacher from Nantucket, to preside over his cash drawer. She rose to
bookkeeper and in 1866 became the store's first general superintendent. Macy not only relied on her aptitude for figures to keep his store
books, but generously attributed a large part of his success to her
accounting and administrative talent. And he did even more. When
he learned that she had lost her heart to a good-looking young salesman she had seen visiting the store he connived to bring them together at parties. The upshot was that Abiel T. La Forge took a
job in the store to be near its cashier, married her, and wound up as
a partner in the business. Appropriately enough, the La Forges lived
over the store and Margaret continued to lend a hand when she
could spare time from her growing family. Abiel La Forge's pride in
Margaret's ability and his respect for her opinion were all a career
wife could wish. "She is the Superintendent, having full charge of
the entire business," he boasted in a letter to his sister. "As we sell
a million dollars' worth of goods a year and have nearly 200 employees, her position is a very responsible one."

Finally, Macy planned for his own succession so well that his
store survived the biggest hazard of a one-man business. Realizing
that his son, Rowland, Jr., was unfit for business, Macy shifted increasing responsibility to two junior partners, La Forge and Robert
Macy Valentine, the son of Macy's youngest sister. They bought
out his estate at his death but the well-loved La Forge succumbed
to tuberculosis. Valentine survived La Forge just long enough to
buy out his share and bring in a Macy relative and employee,
Charles B. Webster. Webster had neither extensive funds nor retail
experience, but he solved the first problem by marrying Valentine's
widow and the second by bringing in a brother-in-law, Jerome B.

Wheeler. Webster then proceeded to interest himself in a lady employee whom he insisted on promoting to positions for which she was unqualified. Wheeler objected to this breach of store discipline, and Webster objected to Wheeler's growing interests outside of the store. Thanks to its solid foundation, however, Macy's continued for the next ten years to grow with the times and hold its own although it did not break new retailing ground.

When Webster finally broke with Wheeler and bought him out in 1887, he was able to turn for new blood to a great merchant family whose unique association with Macy's made them close enough to the store to provide unbroken succession without involving them in the personal deadlock of its owners. The story of that association illustrates a cardinal feature of the Straus character, a character providentially designed to build on Rowland Macy's foundations.

In 1874, Nathan Straus was torn between his love of home and his family duty to continue the sales trips which were building wide Midwestern outlets for L. Straus & Co., china, glassware and crockery. Nathan Straus's creative solution was a partnership with customer stores under which they would sell Straus-selected and Straus-owned merchandise, and it was only natural that he should try the arrangement out on home ground. His resulting contract with R. H. Macy & Co., biggest Straus customer in New York, led to similar deals with out-of-town stores. It also determined the future both of Macy's and the Strauses.

Founder Macy's son had been a disappointment. He himself was a hot-tempered unstable adventurer favored by his times. He was intuitive and resilient to failure. His credit was so bad that when he arrived in New York he had to deal for cash. In dramatic contrast, the Strauses have succeeded for five generations in passing on a tradition of prudent risk-taking which has steadily added to the family jackpot. They are cool, almost scholarly analysts of business situations. They have never put all their eggs in one basket and lost. To this day, the Straus family tie has held firm against the pressures of an outsize family business.

Lazarus Straus, the head of this remarkable line, was a well-to-do cultured Jewish grain merchant of liberal principles who left his farmlands in Bavaria following the uprisings of 1848. Unlike most immigrants, he by-passed the melting-pot cities to start a modest store in little Talbotton, Georgia. It wasn't until 1866, when Lazarus and his son Isidor had required a larger nest egg than could reasonably be employed in the bankrupt South, that they essayed New York.

Their entrance to the country's financial capital was as characteristic as that of Rowland Macy. The first move of Lazarus Straus was to visit every firm to whom he had owed money at the outbreak of the Civil War and offer full payment in cash. Hower reports that some were so astonished that they actually refused to take the money. Straus credit has been unassailable ever since. In fact, Macy's Bank founded for deposit accounts of customers has had to refuse the large sums frightened New Yorkers have wanted to leave with the Strauses for safekeeping.

Under the Strauses, Macy's china and crockery departments grew until in 1888 they accounted for nearly 13 per cent of sales and returned the highest profit in the store. It was the first to feature bargain sales and public exhibitions. To the china department, too, goes the credit for introducing Macy's famous odd prices "psychologically" set to make the customer feel she is getting a bargain. Psychological prices exploit the difference between $3.98 and $4.00. An unflattering explanation of the origin of this practice is that it encouraged honesty by forcing clerks to get change from the cash register. Another theory holds that the prices were the arithmetic results of a percentage markon added to round wholesale prices. There is no question, however, that Rowland Macy avidly adopted the price slimming for his other departments.

Webster offered the Strauses a partnership in 1888, joined with them in 1893 in acquiring a half interest in the Brooklyn store thereafter called Abraham & Straus, and seems to have deferred to their superior merchandising judgment until he finally sold his remaining half interest in Macy's to them in 1896 for $1,200,000. Temperamentally, the Straus boys were far better suited to preserving Macy's through a protracted period of competition and hard times than Rowland Macy himself would have been.

Isidor Straus, the oldest son of Lazarus Straus, was a typical patriarch: confident, dignified, reliable, he watched the store's finances and developed the operating systems required to keep a growing business under control. His hobby was foreign exchange and his idea of recreation was advising his friend, President Grover Cleveland, on currency reforms. Younger brother Nathan was enthusiastic, gregarious and popular. He endeared himself to employees by wandering around the store whistling "There'll Be a Hot Time in the Old Town Tonight" and thought up most of the stunts and promotions which kept Macy's before the public. A natty dresser, he loved horses and amused himself with Tammany politics and spectacular philanthropies like the free milk fund. Nathan was so visible, in fact, that most New Yorkers thought he ran the store singlehandedly.

Under this well-balanced team, Macy sales inched slowly upward from about $5,000,000 in 1888 to $10,800,000 in 1902, the year of the move uptown. There were no radical departures, but assortments and lines grew steadily as the middle classes filled their gaudy parlors with the first luxuriant fruits of mechanization. Selections from the long lists of products the Strauses saw fit to add every year afford a provocative backward glimpse into the days of bloomer girls and bicycles built for two: 1889, oriental rugs, engraved stationery, buggy whips; 1890, brass beds, rowing machines; 1891, bicycles; 1892, diamonds, Tokay wines; 1893, oil paintings, fancy groceries; 1895, amateur photographers' supplies, sleighs; 1897, firearms; 1898, wallpaper, pianos, talking machines; 1899, cocktail shakers.

Progress was slow because Macy's was not the only big store in New York. During this period, Lord & Taylor's, Hearn's, Arnold Constable's, Stern's, and B. Altman's—to mention only stores still in existence—were vying with Macy's for the privilege of supplying almost all of madam's wants. While none of them equalled Macy's assortments, and few of them even tried to compete with Macy's low cash prices, their success proved that customers were willing to buy convenience and service as well as goods.

Macy's competed on service as well as it could. Like other stores, it was adopting the "satisfaction guaranteed or your money back" principle, as a steadily rising rate of returns testified. At the close of the century the store was teaching purchasers of bicycles how to ride, installing stoves and ranges, packing the provisions the wealthy bought for their yacht trips. In order to dramatize a delivery service that required hundreds of horses to serve customers lured into

Macy's from faraway Jersey and Long Island, Macy's imported two Mercedes horseless carriages, the first European automobiles to come to America. They attracted a great deal of attention but did little to lighten the delivery burden. One of them finished third in the Chicago *Times Herald* race of 1895 from Jackson Park, Illinois, to Evanston and back.

But it was increasingly clear that a great store could no longer do with the makeshift quarters which were now spread on both sides of Sixth Avenue to the confusion of shoppers and the profit of at least one merchant who encouraged the public to think he was part of Macy's. Furthermore, trade was on its historic march uptown and Macy's would have to downgrade its merchandise or upgrade its address. Isidor's sons, Jesse and Percy, who were already in the business, campaigned successfully for a new building uptown.

The choice of Macy's present location on Thirty-fourth Street and Broadway, a crossroads which the years have improved, was at the time a radical leapfrog over the competition in the historical northward movement of New York retailing. It was particularly alarming to Henry Siegel, a Chicago merchant who had just pushed the center of shopping gravity northward by building Siegel Cooper New York on Eighteenth Street. Through agents, Siegel bought up a little over a thousand square feet of the strategic Thirty-fourth Street and Broadway corner, paying $375,000 in 1902 money for it. Then he tried to offer it to the Strauses for a mere $250,000 if they would sell him the unexpired lease on their old Fourteenth Street store and with it the custom of shoppers used to the location.

The Strauses are not ones to pay tribute. They instructed their architects to build around the little corner and used the $250,000 they had earmarked for its acquisition to acquire land to the west on which the twenty-story building was erected in 1924. The new land was first used to house the store's generating plant, which had been planned for the north side of Thirty-fifth Street on the site of the Pekin and the Tivoli, New York's famous brothels. As enthusiastically predicted, the Macy move uptown brought other stores to the area.

Over a half century of hard usage and architectural progress has not obsoleted the store the Strauses opened in 1902. It was first to install a vacuum-cleaner system for removing stale air, pneumatic

tubes for transporting cash, escalators with flat steps instead of in-
clined ones with cleats against which riders had to brace their feet.

The new building put Macy's in a position to compete on service
as well as on price. Instead, the Strauses sought new ways to dramatize Macy's low cash prices. As the twentieth century developed, the
policy led them into Alice and Wonderland projects. In order to
dramatize the advantages of cash, Macy's adopted the "6% cash
policy." As the years passed, it became more than an idle slogan.
Macy's virtually guaranteed to sell merchandise offered in charge
account stores at 6 per cent off. Socks that sold for $1 in other stores
became 94 cents on Macy counters in a clever adaptation of the
store's traditional off prices to accentuate the new policy. New
York's bargain-hungry crowds took Macy's at its word, calling lapses
of the price challenge to the attention of the management in such
numbers that it became necessary to hire a small army of clerks to
verify the claims. From this beginning was born the comparison
shopping department.

With the opening of the new store, Macy's launched its own answer to the inconvenience of carrying cash. Customers who traded
regularly at Macy's could deposit their money with the store and
draw against it as they made purchases. In order to encourage this
prepayment, Macy's paid a small bonus at Christmastime on the
average balance, which served to remind customers that someone
has to pay the interest on idle money and that this burden logically
fell on the customer when he bought on credit. To the surprise of
competing merchants, the Depositor's Account system worked.
Thousands of housewives transferred their secret savings out of the
grocery budget to Macy's, the store which was destined to get them
in the end anyway. Although the percentage of D. A. business never
grew to the 50 per cent proportions represented by charges in other
stores, it increased every year and has amounted to as much as 10
per cent of sales.

The next threat to the cash policy was the rise of installment selling, extended to finance refrigerators, ranges, washing machines and
the many other big ticket items priming the economic pump in the
twenties. Macy's knew its power. The store had once been forced to
discontinue the sale of pianos because of the small number of customers ready to pay cash for so large an expenditure. Finally, in

1939, the Strauses and Beardsley Ruml hit on a plan to serve installment customers abandoning their cash policy. Cash-Time, as it is called, permits customers to buy at cash prices plus a six per cent service charge for the privilege of paying in installments which brings the total cost to that charged by credit stores. Cash-Time proved an instant success, proving that credit customers are willing to pay interest and welcome the opportunity to know exactly how much it is costing them.

Macy's long and famous fight against fixed prices began early in the century when an association of book publishers sought to maintain retail prices and contended Macy's underselling process lowered the value of the copyright. Macy lawyers charged that the book publishers were a trust under the Sherman Act and sued for damages. Meanwhile, Macy's book department put in a lively decade keeping the company in the book business at all. Secret agents ranged the country to buy up popular titles and in one case at least secured copies from the author, who told his publisher he was buying the copies for his own use. In 1913, after nine actions in Federal and State courts, the Supreme Court of the United States vindicated the Macy contention. A photograph of the $140,000 damage check the publishers paid Macy's is one of the store's prized exhibits. A similar lengthy dispute with the Victor Talking Machine Company ended its attempt to control prices by licensing instead of selling the machine.

In lobbying, the Strauses proved no match for the big organizations of small retailers, especially in the drug field, which forced fair-trade measures through most state legislatures and eventually Congress. Macy's did devote part of its advertising budget to an attempt to mobilize consumers against the measures. Typical was a 1952 full page showing a snaky animal labeled "price fixing" under a headline "The Dragon Went Thataway."

The store continued to stock important trademarked items like Simmons mattresses and, except when a court decision provided a loophole for cutting, observed the new prices. But Macy's answered this challenge, also that of the discount houses, by increased emphasis on items manufactured to its specifications and sold under its own brands. Some of these dated from the days of Rowland Macy himself, who had the store make its own cigars and many other items. Housewives began to hear more and more about Supre-Macy towels,

Macy's own shirts, Lily White canned goods and Red Star articles of many kinds.

Rivals spread rumors that Macy's sold under its own name to make a higher profit margin, and in some cases this was true. Macy customers who continued to patronize Macy's were convinced that the store "made it up" on noncompetitive goods. A provocative little book *Barnum and Bunk* by E. C. Riegel described what he called Macy's "cash fallacy." Riegel contended that Macy's did not save by purchasing for cash; that cash handling was just as expensive as maintaining charge accounts, a cost Macy's in any case bore in providing D. A. service; and that credit losses amounted to less than one per cent.

In 1926, a Better Business Bureau investigation of Macy's 6 per cent less advertising claim uncovered many exceptions to it. Macy's resigned from the B.B.B. and changed its claim from "Lowest in the city prices and 6 per cent less than elsewhere" to "an endeavor to sell day by day for at least six per cent less than the marked prices of our competitors." In recent years the wording has been revised to conform with the current state of the fair-trade battle. In 1954, it read: "We endeavor, with reasonable exceptions which include goods price-controlled by the manufacturer, to save our customers at least 6 per cent for cash."

Macy's advertising department, now headed by Mrs. Frances Corey, has attracted many men and women of talent. Kenneth Collins, who first advertised the Macy Bureau of Standards, moved on to a series of executive posts. William H. Howard became executive vice president of the big store and joined Young & Rubicam, Inc. Mary Lewis, Estelle Hamburger, Margaret Fishback and Hildegarde Dolson all won fame as writers. Paul Hollister wrote some notable institutional copy. A 1948 Macy Christmas advertisement headlined "Oh, Darling—You Shouldn't Have!" and written by Barbara Collyer was chosen by Julian Watkins as one of the hundred greatest advertisements. Most remembered of all, perhaps, is Bernice Fitz-Gibbon, a forceful ex-teacher of English from Wisconsin. For Macy's, she coined "It's Smart to Be Thrifty," a slogan that is even painted on the store roof for the benefit of air travelers, and a few years later produced for its arch rival: "Nobody but nobody undersells Gimbels."

Price wars were the "circuses" which advertised the low-price policy, serving as entertainment in the days before television give-away shows. At first Hearn's was the main target: a tussle in 1902 on Japanese silk tumbled prices from 41 cents to a penny a yard in a single day and ended only when stocks were exhausted the next day at eleven yards for a cent amid scenes which a contemporary account records as "of the wildest excitement ever witnessed in a retail store." In later years the war has come to be regarded as a sort of public feud with Gimbels—a well-publicized war which has increased sales for both antagonists.

Relations opened amicably enough with a Macy advertisement welcoming the great Philadelphia store to its New York location just one block south of Macy's in 1910. They cooled almost immediately when Gimbels raided Macy's staff. During World War I and after, when salaries were rising and sales expanding, the Macy-Gimbel competition largely profited rising department-store executives, and even today, Macy's complains that it bears the training expenses for its biggest competitor.

Gimbels is less than half the size of Macy's, but is organized for merchandising scoops which can be aggressively promoted. Unlike Macy's, it has a bargain basement where price is frankly highlighted. Periodic price wars on specific items find comparison shoppers posted in the enemy store and when the cuts come thick and fast they complain of running out of change to phone back their reports. Since Macy's does a complete job of checking all stores, Gimbels can get by with a shopping force just large enough to check Macy prices. During the price war of 1951, Gimbels comparison-shopping department was headed by a woman appropriately trained in Macy's—a clear case of Macy's telling Gimbels. Both stores have on occasion bought peace at any price by buying out the other's complete supply of an item at issue.

During the war, the competition turned on availability of scarce merchandise. Macy's promised a brighter future with copy asking, "When will Macy's have it?" In reply, pugnacious Miss Fitz-Gibbon featured Gimbel exclusives under the headline "Gimbels HAS it!" The two stores occasionally vary the battle with friendly gestures. In 1946, they buried the hatchet long enough to adopt a well-publicized uniform outdoor decorating scheme for Christmas. In 1953,

Gimbels called attention to Macy's flower show with an advertisement which trumpeted, "Does Gimbels tell Macy's? No, Gimbels tells the world!" Macy's responded politely with a thank-you: "Nobody but nobody said it more prettily than Gimbels." Customers loved it as much as British sports fans love the way tennis contenders shake hands at the net.

The flower show, now an annual event, involves the collection of two million blooms in honor of Mother's Day. Half a million of them are flown by air express, with orchids coming from Hawaii and tulips arriving from Holland.

Macy's started its Thanksgiving Day parade in 1924 and it has been an annual event ever since, with the exception of two war years, heralding the arrival of Santa Claus in Herald Square. Norman Bel Geddes, Tony Sarg and Walt Disney have had a hand in creating the elaborate balloon figures made by the Goodyear Tire & Rubber Company and filled with helium. Special music has been composed some years for the event. The parade inspired the motion picture, *Miracle on 34th Street*.

During the twentieth century, Macy's growth has paralleled that of New York City. Sales climbed steadily from $10,800,000 in 1902 to $17,300,000 at the outbreak of World War I. Inflation as well as a war-detonated explosion in consumer expenditure pushed Macy's sales to $35,800,000 in 1919, the year the store was incorporated.

In the speculative years following World War I, the Strauses expanded horizontally, buying a controlling interest in Toledo's LaSalle & Koch's in 1923 and Atlanta's then ailing Davison-Paxon store in 1925. In 1929 they bought L. Bamberger of Newark, a store in 1925. In 1929 they bought L. Bamberger of Newark, a store notable for its pioneer radio broadcasting. In 1945, they bought O'Connor Moffatt & Co. of San Francisco and in 1947 the John Taylor Dry Goods Store in Kansas City.

Macy's Parkchester, built for the Metropolitan Life housing project in the Bronx was one of the first department-store experiments in decentralizing to follow the customers into the suburbs. Since then, Macy's New York has tried, with varying success, suburban stores in White Plains, Jamaica, Flatbush and Roosevelt Field. Every division of the corporation now has branches. Sales for all these units rose to a peak of $351,000,000 in the year ending July 31, 1951, which included the Korean buying boom. Less than half of this total represented sales at the big store on Thirty-fourth Street.

All Macy-owned stores are served by a Macy Corporate Buying Division, but the degree of their resemblance to the parent store varies. No attempt has been made to enforce a cash policy on LaSalle & Koch or L. Bamberger, which were bought as successful local institutions. Wheelock H. Bingham, now president of the New York store, quadrupled the sales of San Francisco's O'Connor Moffatt without destroying its endearing local characteristics. He did not change the name until public-opinion samples conducted over a two-year period proved San Franciscans wanted to have a Macy store in their town. Failure of a Macy store in Syracuse, New York, featuring the fastest-selling items in the New York store illustrated that what works in one community cannot necessarily be transplanted to another.

In 1922, Macy stock was offered to the public, but the Straus family retains control through a declining stock interest which now amounts to less than 20 per cent. Allocation of control within the family seems to have followed the law of primogeniture. Isidor, the eldest son of Lazarus, was the head of Macy's until he refused to enter a lifeboat of the sinking *Titanic* ahead of women and children in 1912 and his wife chose to die with him. A bronze plaque in the store pays tribute to their memory.

His sons, "Mr. Jesse" and "Mr. Percy" had already taken over running the store, and their younger brother Herbert and the two sons of Nathan Strass, while they contributed in other ways, never overcame the head start of the legendary pair. Whenever the slightest disagreement arose in public, Jesse and Percy would retire behind locked doors until one of them could emerge with the traditional pronouncement, "My brother and I have decided." A disagreement between Isidor's sons and uncle Nathan Straus led to a friendly sale of Nathan's interests to Jesse, Percy and Herbert. All three of the younger Strauses had sons, but the leadership descended on Jesse's eldest son Jack, the fourth eldest son in a row to take prime responsibility for the family business. Percy took over the store in time to allow his brother to accept the ambassadorship to France under F. D. R. Great grandsons of Isidor Straus are now serving their apprenticeship in Macy's.

Executives from outside the family fill important posts in both the stores and parent company. Vice president and treasurer of the latter is Edwin F. Chinlund, formerly president of the Postal Telegraph Company. Q. Forrest Walker has been the firm's economist and investment adviser since 1924. Notables as varied as Dean Donald K. David of the Harvard Graduate School of Business Administration and Robert Montgomery, the actor, have represented the public on Macy's board of directors. Wall Street, incidentally, considers the report of the proceedings which Macy's mails its twenty-three thousand stockholders after each annual meeting something other corporations should emulate.

How big can Macy's grow? Its horizontal expansion by the addition of other stores is no problem, for R. H. Macy & Co. is much smaller in total volume than several department-store chains. The frequently asked question refers to the size to which the New York store might go. Richard Weil, quixotic grandson of Isidor, who suggested the employment of Mortimer Adler, the philosopher, as vice president in charge of thinking, when Weil was president of Macy's New York, once set an annual sales volume of $350,000,000 as the goal for the Thirty-fourth Street miracle. All observers agree that the mechanical limitations are not insoluble. Pneumatic tubes replaced cash girls. Electric trucks extended Macy's delivery system until it was consolidated with United Parcel in 1946. The Thirty-fourth Street store couldn't have been better located and the Strauses have not had, as have some of their competitors, to move into new buildings to adopt new methods. The ceiling, President Wheelock Bingham believes, is now the store's ability to organize people.

Macy management has addressed itself to this problem for more than a generation. The first move occurred in 1914, when a member of a New York welfare group, the Committee of Fourteen, interested Percy Straus in an investigation of the suggested relationship between low wages for girl store clerks and immorality. Three women investigators were given free run at Macy's, and while their report turned up no spicy stories, they did uncover a degree of apathy and inefficiency among the working force which shocked the Strauses into organizing one of the first personnel departments concerned with store morale rather than the mechanics of hiring and firing, and paternalistic largess such as the turkey went to every married employee at Thanksgiving until 1950.

Over the years, Macy's has experimented with aptitude testing for new recruits and has learned that teamwork rather than the schoolroom discipline of earlier days is the key to smooth operations. Employee benefits in the form of a lunchroom, recreational activities, paid vacations and pensions, medical services and the privilege of buying in the store at a discount have helped make attractive the grueling pace of work in Macy's.

A real contribution to store management was made when the early Macy managers started to recruit clerks of high academic and cultural background and train them in Macy's methods on the payroll. Between the world wars, this policy was extended to the very real problem of executive recruitment. The Strauses early recognized that the family itself could hardly grow the fifteen hundred executives now required to administer the world's biggest store. For more than a generation, Macy scouts have been visiting colleges to interest the brightest students in retailing and Macy's famous training squad has been enrolling them. The training is essentially an organized rotation through the store's operations similar to that which junior members of the family have experienced.

Boston-born President Bingham, head of Macy's New York since 1951, joined the firm by way of the training squad after studying at Harvard. Vice Presidents Murray Graham and David L. Yunich started the same way. John C. Williams, chairman of L. Bamberger & Co.; Charles H. Jagels, president of the Davison-Paxon Company; also Michael Yamin, Ernest L. Molloy and Alex G. Lewi, heads of Macy's divisions in Toledo, San Francisco and Kansas City, are all products of Macy training. Those who have moved on to key jobs elsewhere include Walter J. Brunmark of the May Department Stores; Walter Hoving, president of Bonwit Teller; and Joseph Eckhouse, executive head of Gimbels New York.

Like other giant business organizations, Macy's has discovered that it is necessary to keep a rising proportion of staff specialists working on policy formation. Stylists, consumer researchers, personnel experts, traffic engineers, economic analysts and tax advisers take their places beside the famous chute rider and such personalities as William Titon, the food taster, in supplying trained eyes, ears and brains for the giant organism. Recently, experiments in communication among these staff and operating executives have taken the form of discussion sessions among small groups chosen so that no executive is placed with another directly in his chain of command.

Some say the department store is doomed. Its costs have risen. Its plushy services are no longer attractive to the new middle classes who have accustomed themselves to the super market and the vending-machine shortcuts to shopping. The suburban matrons who were its mainstay a generation ago are no longer so important a market as working girls and servantless housewives bound to their housing projects by their contribution to the post World War II baby boom. Newer distribution channels, the critics say, have made many of the department store's lines unprofitable, notably large pieces of electrical equipment which in the New York area seem to be the province of the discount houses.

President Bingham of Macy's New York disagrees. "Nobody," he says, "need think that the department store is going to go out of business. It is a unique institution—the only place where the customer can find everything under one roof." He opposes, as a traditional Macy merchandiser, the suggestion that the store drop unprofitable lines. He has presided over experiments in self-service for certain types of merchandise (the store calls it "simplified selling"). He is going after the vital girl behind the counter with bigger and better training programs, intended to restore personal selling to the floor. He has even gone so far as to say that "the way the customer is treated in the store is surely as important as the merchandise it sells. The retailer by tradition has been interested in things. He must continue to be interested in things but he should become more interested in people." And if the customers no longer want to come to town, Macy's is studying the best way of following them to their native housing projects.

One symbol of Macy's faith in the future is its Red Star trademark derived from a tattoo on the hand of seafaring Rowland H. Macy. In recent decades it also has been adopted as the symbol of the Soviet Army and the name of its newspaper. Because of this many have urged Macy's to quit using it as a label and a cable address. Macy's feeling is this isn't necessary, the great store had the mark first and it intends to have it last.

XI. The Great A & P

World's Largest Food Retailer

THE A & P, as shoppers know the Great Atlantic & Pacific Tea Company, is the world's largest food retailer, the greatest exponent of chain-store operation, and also the biggest retailer. Its little postcard annual statement, perhaps the most laconic of any company that makes a report, in 1954 revealed profits the previous year of $30,395,806, a little less than one cent on the dollar on sales of $3,989,103,161.

In all American business only General Motors, American Telephone & Telegraph and Standard Oil of New Jersey reported greater figures. In the chain and self-service food field, its closest rivals were Safeway Stores with sales of $1,751,820,000 and the Kroger Company with $1,058,609,000.

What is the A & P? To Americans who visit them at the rate of six million a shopping day, it is 4,180 unpretentious stores, 2,200 of them super markets, so devoid of frills that they are simply machines for selling food. Though the stores are few in the West, and not to be found at all in ten states, into their cash registers go between 9 and 10 cents of every dollar of retail food sales in the country.

The A & P is also the largest food-processing plant in the country at Terre Haute, Indiana, and the world's largest cheese warehouse at Green Bay, Wisconsin. It is thirty-six big bakeries turning out bread and cakes, twelve coffee-roasting plants, four salmon canneries in Alaska, buying organizations in South America and the Far East, four laundries for washing uniforms and a print shop just for the printing of its private labels. Around three hundred of these are registered with the Patent Office.

The A & P is also research which has developed the big-breasted "chicken of tomorrow" and which may improve turkeys and hogs. It is also a meat-purchasing empire which buys around a billion pounds a year. It is also the biggest retailer of eggs, 100 million dozen a year as eggs and as ingredients in its cakes.

The A & P is a slick-paper women's service magazine, *Woman's Day,* which has a multimillion circulation without subscriptions or sale anywhere except at checkout counters of the A & P stores.

The A & P is 130,000 employees, clerks who mark every package in every store, managers who keep account of every paper bag, traveling auditors who descend in pairs to report on each store to headquarters in New York's Graybar Building where statisticians analyze and chart the figures.

The A & P finally is George Ludlum Hartford, patriarch of the family that created and owns the gargantuan food company. Though more than ninety, he still appears daily at the Graybar offices and each afternoon, as he has for seventy years, tastes the latest samples of Eight O'Clock, Red Circle and Bokar coffees, which are the company's pride.

For several decades, the A & P was also his dapper younger brother, John Augustine Hartford, who led the company's great expansion. Lean, silver-haired and dressed in gray, he visited the stores constantly and was known to thousands of employees. Active until the last, he died at seventy-nine of a heart attack in an elevator on September 20, 1951, leaving an estate of $55,695,290, most of it to a foundation bearing his name, which now owns 20 per cent of the A & P and probably eventually will control it.

The huge business was started by the father of Mr. George and Mr. John, as the brothers have been known. He was George Huntington Hartford, a shrewd Yankee from Augusta, Maine, who in 1859, when he was twenty-six, was employed by George F. Gilman, also from Maine, in a New York hide and leather business.

Tea then retailed in New York at $1 a pound. Hartford convinced Gilman this could be reduced to 30 cents by eliminating middlemen. Gilman abandoned hides and leather and the two formed The Great American Tea Company, a partnership which promised "to do away with various profits and brokerages, cartages, storages, cooperage and waste, with the exception of a small commission paid for purchasing to our correspondents in Japan and China, one cartage, and a small profit to ourselves which, on our large sales, will amply repay us."

Their first shop at 31 Vesey Street in New York resembled something from the Arabian Nights. A gigantic capital T, blazing with gas lights, illuminated the store's vermilion-red and gold front. Strings of red, white and blue globes festooned the windows. Inside the store, tea bins were painted red and gold, the cashiers' cages were built in the shape of Chinese pagodas and a green parrot stood on a stand in the center of the main floor. A band played on Saturdays, often far into the night.

To advertise the store eight dapple-gray horses pulled a tremendous red wagon through the city streets. A prize of $20,000 was offered to anyone who could guess the combined weight of team and wagon. All kinds of premiums were given away—dishpans, china, crockery, and chromos of babies. "This is the day they give babies away" was one of the song slogans used to attract customers.

New Yorkers swarmed to the store. Hartford and Gilman gradually added spices, coffee, soap, flavoring extracts, condensed milk, baking powder and other staples. Wherever possible they applied the same middleman-eliminating purchasing they inaugurated with tea.

They added more stores. There were five by 1865. There were eleven in 1869 and the partners adopted the more grandiloquent name The Great Atlantic & Pacific Tea Company. Hartford envisioned a chain of stores that would reach from coast to coast as the just completed Union Pacific Railroad linked the two seaboards. The older name was preserved in a subsidiary which still operates tea and coffee truck routes in forty-nine cities.

There were store chains, of course, before the A & P. President Andrew Jackson had been a partner in Jackson and Hutchings, which operated a chain of small stores in Tennessee. The Hudson's Bay Company and the makers of Singer sewing machines also had chain operations. The Fugger family had an important chain business in Europe earlier and a merchant had a chain of stores in China two hundred years before Christ. But the A & P by its size has come to be the symbol of chain operation.

By 1876, there were 67 A & P stores, all with the familiar red and gold façade, all conventional grocery stores with charge accounts and delivery service. They were operating as far south as Baltimore, as far north as St. Paul and as far west as St. Louis. A comic advertising card a little later listed twenty-five stores in New York and five in Brooklyn.

Gilman retired in 1878 to a life of luxury in Bridgeport, Connecticut, and left Hartford to run the stores. He was soon joined by two of his five children. These were his sons, George and John. A third son, Edward, became an inventor and did not enter the business. George, the eldest, born November 7, 1864, and named for his father, started to work at fifteen. Plump and short, he was first employed in 1880 as an office boy. After two weeks, he took the place of a cashier who quit, strangely enough because he thought the business might fail. There were then 110 stores and George counted and banked the cash from all of them. This came in by express, sometimes as much as $55,000 a day.

Keeping tab on the money aroused his interest in economy. Hearing that baking powder was only alum and sodium bicarbonate, George set a chemist mixing the ingredients behind a screen in the Vesey Street store. This brought down the price of baking powder and was the start of the company's own manufacturing operations.

John Augustine Hartford, eight years younger than his brother, went to work cleaning inkwells and sweeping floors in the Vesey Street store in 1888. His salary was $5 a week, and his mother, as frugal as his father, charged him $1 for board and made him bank another $1. When he received a $2 raise, his mother increased his board bill. Soon he was clerking, and also buying and handing out premiums, then an important part of the business.

In the panic of 1907, John's gift for strategy was credited with literally saving the business. He was sent to withdraw the company funds from a bank on which there was a run. Finding many depositors already in line, he asked the first, a little man who had been there all night, how much money he had in the bank.

"Four hundred and forty-seven dollars and ninety cents," he replied. "All I have in the world."

"I'll give you $450 for your place," John said. "Get back in line and maybe you'll get your deposit, too."

As it turned out, John Hartford salvaged the A & P thousands and the little man who had been at the head of the line also collected his deposit in full, becoming probably the only man actually to double his money in a panic that caused even J. P. Morgan some trouble.

At this time, A & P headquarters were moved to Jersey City, New Jersey, not far from Orange, where the Hartford brothers grew up and their father was mayor for twelve years without salary.

Cash and carry, one of the biggest innovations in A & P history, was introduced in 1912 by John Hartford. At this time there were four hundred stores, but charge account paper work, thousands of delivery horses and wagons and premiums limited profits. The success of a New Jersey grocer named Henry Cole with some cash stores caused John Hartford to think along this line. He proposed to his father and brother that they open "economy" stores to be staffed by one man and to sell at lowest possible profit but aim for large volume. They thought it a crackpot idea.

John persisted, however, until he persuaded them to let him open just one to prove his point. They invested $3,000, and to really test it, John opened his store on West End Avenue in Jersey City around the corner from the company's biggest money-making store. The economy store didn't even have a name but the customers rushed in when they saw its bargains. In six months the regular A & P store was out of business, and the economy store was in to stay.

For the next two years John opened economy stores at the rate of one every three days. By the end of 1915, there were one thousand A & P stores and each establishment was laid out exactly alike so customers could find things in the same location in any store. John often remarked he could go blindfold into any store and find a can of pork and beans. Salaries of managers averaged $18.08 a week.

The company borrowed $5,000,000 to finance the new stores but they more than doubled the sales volume to $75,000,000 in 1916. The father then turned the business over to George and John to run as a trust for themselves, their two sisters and their brother Edward, and, as they died, the heirs of these. In 1917, the founder died at eighty-four.

"Our one desire," the sons wrote later in an instruction book for store managers, "is to perpetuate A & P as a great public service, to have it stand forever as a monument to the integrity, perseverance and human understanding of the man who founded it, George Huntington Hartford." When the Chicago Merchandise Mart years later established its Hall of Fame of Retailing, the father of the A & P was among the first four elected, along with Marshall Field, Frank Woolworth and John Wanamaker.

Under the sons, the A & P became an even bigger integrated business empire. Among the new subsidiaries organized were the Quaker Maid Company, processing and packing more than forty products, many bearing the Ann Page label; the White House Milk Company, with milk-processing plants in Wisconsin; and the Nakat Packing Corporation, America's largest canner of Alaskan salmon and operator of an Alaskan fishing fleet. Meanwhile, the American Coffee Corporation set up thirty coffee-purchasing offices in Colombia and Brazil, and the company's agents attended tea auctions in India and Ceylon.

Departments for the sale of meat, now the most important single item in A & P volume, were added in 1925. That year also saw the company expand into Canada, buy group insurance for its employees, and decentralize its operations into geographical divisions, of which there eventually were seven, all with headquarters in the Northeast except the Southern at Jacksonville, Florida. The Pacific coast, which the company reached only after World War I despite its name, was made part of the Eastern division with headquarters in New York. Under the divisions were unit offices and the stores.

Each division was given a president, treasurer, director of sales, director of purchases and director of operations. Each unit had a similar group of specialists. Except in finances, each unit and store manager was free to run his business as he wished within overall company policy. New York continued to keep directly in touch with stores and units through traveling auditors who inspected stores and their records and reported directly to headquarters. In 1925, stores increased from 11,421 to 14,034 and sales were close to half a billion dollars.

Sales passed the billion-dollar mark for the first time in the fiscal year ending February 28, 1930. The number of red-fronted stores reached an all-time peak the next year with a total of 15,737, a figure attained without mergers or the purchase of any important properties. Earnings were $30,742,776, a record that stood for the next sixteen years.

The A & P was big but not beloved. Because of its bigness and success, it was one of the most unpopular of companies. In part, this was the result of the temper of the times. In part, it was disregard for public opinion on the part of the management. Like Macy's, Sears, Roebuck, and all mass buyers, the A & P drove hard bargains with its suppliers through allowances and discounts which then were legal. Competitors who were hurt by this, middlemen who were by-passed and others complained to the government. Bills having the principal aim of hampering or destroying the A & P were introduced in Congress and in state legislatures.

While all chains, as well as Montgomery Ward and Sears, Roebuck, had expanded, the A & P growth had been the most phenomenal. At the same time, the A & P had done nothing to explain itself to the communities in which it operated. While the "A & P Gypsies" were on the radio and the company's advertising appropriation had been increased from $2,000,000 to $6,000,000, this amounted to less than $8 a week per store.

Expansion had been so rapid that all sorts of men were A & P managers. "We went so fast," Mr. John once explained, "that hobos hopping off freight trains got hired as managers." While instructions from headquarters insisted that the stores give sixteen ounces to a pound and to mark and sell goods at correct prices, there were complaints of short change, short weight and "selling the broom." In the last, a broom was leaned against the checkout stand and its price added to each check as if the patron had purchased it. If noticed, the checker would simply apologize. It was an accusation against every chain food store.

The company left its gathering troubles to its lawyers. They succeeded in having an early North Carolina anti-chain store tax declared unconstitutional in 1928 but several setbacks followed. One came in 1931 when the United States Supreme Court, in upholding an Indiana chain-store tax, ruled that chain stores could lawfully be taxed differently from independent stores. Another came in 1936 when John Hartford sat in a Washington, D.C., courtroom and saw A & P store managers convicted of short weighing chickens in 48 out of 50 cases.

A stickler for complete honesty with customers, he spent the next six weeks personally signing 46,000 letters to A & P employees warning against any recurrence of this. At least one executive was fired for tolerating stock gains in his stores. In a case of a different sort, Mr. John heard of a New York City manager helping a butler cheat the woman for whom he worked. Mr. John required complete restitution and sent an apology and his personal check to the customer who until that time had not known that she was being cheated.

After hearings during which the A & P revealed it received $4,000,000 in advertising allowances and $2,000,000 in lieu of brokerage from its suppliers in 1934, Congress passed the Robinson-Patman Act. Becoming law in 1936, this permitted quantity discounts only to the extent of actual savings to vendors and prohibited advertising allowances and similar payments except on proportionately equal terms to all. Encouraged by passage of this bill, which had been drafted by counsel for the U.S. Wholesale Grocers Association, its sponsor, Representative Wright Patman proposed heavy federal taxes on chain stores.

This was his famous "death sentence" bill introduced in 1938 with the names of seventy other Congressmen as co-sponsors. This would have imposed a tax of $50 on the tenth to the fifteenth store of a chain and increased progressively until all over five hundred would pay $1,000 each a year. Then the tax would be multiplied by the number of states in which the chain operated. The A & P, which had just reported earnings of $9,119,114, the lowest in many years, for the fiscal year ending February 28, 1938, would have been required to pay the stupendous sum of $471,620,000!

The A & P decided to take its case to the public and employed at $100,000 a year plus expenses Carl Byoir and Associates, one of the largest public-relations firms. The feasibility of this had been demonstrated in California, where the California Chain Stores Association, of which the A & P was not a member, had induced voters to repeal an anti-chain store state tax by a popular vote of 1,369,778 to 1,067,443. Don Francisco, then a vice president of Lord & Thomas and later of the J. Walter Thompson advertising agency, directed the California campaign and advised all chains to look to their public relations. "Business cannot proceed on the assumption that customers are friends," he said. "They may go out of their way to save a few pennies at your chain store and then denounce you for paying low wages. . . . Without friends, without enlightened public opinion based upon self-interest, a business with a million customers can be crucified by a militant minority."

The A & P opened its campaign with a display advertisement over the signatures of George and John Hartford in fifteen hundred newspapers. In a candid statement of its position, the company announced the employment of Byoir, pointed out the importance of chain stores to farmers, workers and consumers.

While Byoir, who at times sat in presidents' meetings, rallied groups of all kinds to oppose the Patman bill, the A & P began to put its own house in order. Customers were encouraged to write their complaints to headquarters. John Hartford personally investigated many of these. A letter from a mother about the hours her son worked in an A & P store in Virginia, for example, led to the discharge of a store manager. Stores were forbidden to sell anything below cost. While the A & P continued its lone-wolf policy of not joining trade associations, it began to make contributions to some and eventually joined various state chain-store councils.

An important development in the company's promotion program was the conversion in 1937 of a giveaway "menu sheet" to a full-fledged women's service magazine. In a contest, two customers received $1,000 each for naming it *Woman's Day*. While Macy's and other retailers had attempted and abandoned magazines, *Woman's Day* was a success from the start. It expanded from the thirty-two pages of the initial issue to as much as 200 pages. The price has risen from 2 to 7 cents. Without subscriptions or newsstand sales, the circulation has reached nearly four million, and *Woman's Day* ranks seventh among all magazines carrying advertising. The bulk of the advertising is naturally from A & P suppliers but makers of sewing machines and similar items also advertise. Editorial space is given to child care, home decorating and sewing as well as cooking. The magazine's fiction, edited by Betty Finnin, is notable in literary circles. A *Woman's Day* story, "Pale Green Fishes," by Kressmann Taylor, for example, was chosen as one of the best American short stories of the year.

THE GREAT A & P

Most important was the tardy adoption of the self-service super market. Self-service had been the principal feature of the Piggly Wiggly stores, started in 1916 by Clarence Saunders of Memphis, Tennessee. Combined with the "drive-in" market idea, these evolved in California in the twenties into the super markets. Michael King Cullen, who quit the A & P to go into business for himself, started a Long Island chain of super markets in 1930. After two years he had eight and a sales volume of $6,000,000. His chain grew to twenty-seven "King Kullen" markets.

The super market had several advantages for the A & P. Consolidation of a number of small stores into one super market cut handling costs and enabled the company to escape some of the new state taxes levied on a per-store basis. Initially fewer employees were required and the management took advantage of the change to get rid of its incompetents and bad actors. But the super markets grew so rapidly that total A & P employment went up as the number of stores came down.

While the A & P was slow to have super markets, it contributed greatly to their development. New A & P markets, of which more than one hundred have been built by George W. Prassas & Company of Chicago, are airy, spacious structures usually with ample parking. The A & P pioneered the self-service sale of cellophane-wrapped meat with an experimental operation as early as 1940 at Uniontown, Pennsylvania. It also has been a proponent of packaged produce. While definitions vary, a super market, incidentally, has come to mean a self-service store with grocery, meat, produce and dairy departments and a sales volume of $500,000 or more a year. Those with a smaller volume are termed superettes.

To keep up its super-market traffic, the A & P increased its advertising appropriation to more than $12,000,000. While the Byoir organization prepared institutional copy for *Editor & Publisher* and other magazines directed at opinion makers, the company's advertising agency, Paris & Peart, began to turn out important campaigns for national magazines, acres of weekly newspaper copy and eventually television commercials. The A & P became the biggest newspaper food advertiser in New York City, Pittsburgh and many other cities. In some cities, A & P stores employed the Welcome Wagon service to greet newcomers and invite them into the stores to receive gifts.

The A & P and other chains produced such a distinguished array of witnesses against Representative Patman's death-sentence bill that the measure itself died in 1940 when a Congressional subcommittee refused to report it. Of the twenty-eight states which enacted anti-chain store taxes, fourteen have since ended them and no new ones have been enacted. The troubles of the A & P with the government, however, were not at an end.

Provisions of the Robinson-Patman Act were far from clear and the A & P's fresh fruit and vegetable purchasing organization, the Atlantic Commission Company, which then undertook to sell for some producers as well as to buy for the A & P, promptly ran afoul of the new law. One issue was the old brokerage allowances. Though forbidden by the new law, the Federal Trade Commission charged the company with collecting their equivalent from some suppliers. When courts upheld the F.T.C., the company in a 1940 instruction booklet for its buyers announced a policy of obeying the law "both in letter and spirit."

In 1942, the Department of Justice, nevertheless, started a criminal action under the antitrust laws against the A & P, charging conspiracy to restrain trade. Federal Judge W. H. Atwell at Dallas, Texas, threw the case out of court but Judge Walter C. Lindley of the U.S. District Court at Danville, Illinois, heard it. The government case centered around price preferences given the company by sixteen of its twenty-five thousand suppliers and the advantages the A & P had over competitors in the buying and selling roles of the Atlantic Commission Company. After two hundred witnesses and thirty thousand pages of testimony, Judge Lindley found the A & P guilty. When higher courts upheld the verdict, the company paid $175,000 in fines in 1949 and restricted the Atlantic Commission Company to buying for the chain.

Further action was demanded against the A & P, however, by the National Association of Retail Grocers, representing the independents. A few months later the Department of Justice filed a civil anti-trust suit in New York asking that the company's manufacturing and retail operations be separated, that the latter be split into seven different companies, and the Atlantic Commission Company be abolished. The A & P replied with a series of advertisements in two thousand newspapers and posted in the company's stores. These pointed out that the A & P share of the nation's food business was less in 1948 than it had been in 1933 when it had been 11.6 per cent. Statements of farmers, leaders of labor unions to which A & P employees belong, and even some small competitors were published in support of the company's position. A Gallup poll found public opinion in favor of the A & P two to one.

The case never came to trial. Following the change of administration in Washington, it was ended in 1954 by a compromise consent decree accepted by the company. Under this the A & P remained intact. The Atlantic Commission Company was dissolved and a new National Produce Division was set up to buy fruit and produce. The A & P agreed not to buy food for competitors nor to sell food to competitors except products made or processed by the A & P and then only on terms as favorable as to the company itself.

Head of the vast A & P operation is Ralph W. Burger, a pleasant white-haired executive who has risen from the ranks. He shares the Hartfords' aversion to personal notice and doesn't bother to fill out his *Who's Who in America* blank. Son of a long-time A & P employee, Burger was born in Kingston, N.Y., in 1889. He attended Wesleyan College but when twenty-one went to work part time for $7 a week in the A & P store at Glen Falls, New York.

A few months later, he became a full-time helper on one of the black, red and gold A & P wagons. At night, he and the driver would load the wagon with tea, coffee, baking powder and extracts. The A & P carried little canned goods in 1910 and fresh produce was in the future. At 5 A.M., they would set out and by 7 A.M. would reach their first customer, perhaps in Lake George.

The next year, Burger was promoted to the Jersey City headquarters as a bookkeeper and came under the eye of the Hartfords. He became increasingly the confidant and trouble shooter for Mr. John and in 1925 was named secretary of several of the A & P companies. In 1950, he succeeded the late David T. Bofinger as president of the New Jersey A & P, the principal operating company. After the death of Mr. John the next year, Burger became president of the Maryland A & P, the holding company over all the fourteen operating companies and subsidiaries. To complete the organizational pyramid, this holding company in turn is owned by the New

York A & P, which functions solely as an investment company for the Hartford family.

Boards of directors of the A & P companies are composed of Chairman George Hartford, President Burger, Treasurer J. D. Ehrgott and the heads of the seven divisions of the firm. William M. Byrnes is chairman and E. L. Reynolds is president of the largest of these, the Eastern. This has 710 stores, 400 of them super markets, in the New York, Los Angeles and Seattle areas. A super market of this division at Ninth Avenue and Fifty-fifth Street in New York does a world business. Crews of ships docked in the nearby Hudson River shop there and take the food abroad.

L. M. Cazayoux is president of the New England division at Boston. This includes 685 stores, 300 of them super markets. In these totals are the company's 133 Canadian stores, 69 of them super markets, directed through a unit at Toronto. The Canadian sales amounted to $90,000,000 in 1953. Joseph P. Smith is president of the central division at Pittsburgh. This has 600 stores, 325 of them super markets.

Dwight Bertram Austin, an Iowan who joined the A & P in 1919 as a warehouse superintendent, is president of the Middlewestern division at Chicago, with 620 stores, 266 of them super markets. Robert M. Smith, a Georgian who has been an A & P man since 1911, heads the 615-store Southern division at Jacksonville and John M. Toolin the 455-store Central Western division at Detroit. These have 210 and 218 super markets respectively. William F. Leach is president of the Atlantic division at Philadelphia. It has 495 stores, 240 of them super markets. O. C. Adams, an A & P veteran, is chairman of both the Atlantic and Southern divisions.

Among the headquarters executives are Francis M. Kurtz, director of subsidiaries, who came up by way of coffee, working for years in South America; Melvin B. Kling, an A & P man since 1917, who is president and general manager of the Quaker Maid Company, the manufacturing subsidiary; Frank W. Buxton is president of the important American Coffee Corporation subsidiary; J. A. Stuhmer, who rose from a display man in Cleveland to president of the coffee division; and Howard W. Gilb, who began in the Detroit bakery and is now president of the National Bakery Division.

Why has the A & P succeeded so fabulously? Mass buying and

mass selling, shrewd, hard bargaining and chain operation are not entirely the answer. There are more than thirty-one hundred grocery and super-market chains. What is now the big Grand Union Company dates from 1872, Kroger Company from 1882, the American Stores Company from 1883, H. C. Bohack Company, 1887. All operate similarly and successfully but none has approached the huge A & P volume.

Among factors in the A & P success must also be listed family ownership, its sticking to the grocery business, the firm's excellent accounting system, elimination of waste, good merchandising, decentralization, alert and loyal personnel. Some men who know the company intimately feel that these are as much responsible for the A & P growth as its low markup, of around three per cent, and its quick turnover.

The Hartfords have been content with a lower profit margin than companies owned by usual investors. Thanks to the family ownership, decisions at times have been reached and carried out more rapidly than might have been possible if many interests had to be consulted and convinced. The company has stuck closely to the grocery business it knows best. Non-food items have been added very slowly in A & P super markets.

The A & P has kept out of the real-estate business. George Hartford's short-term lease with many options is still the pattern for store sites. Though temptations have been great, the company keeps only a few weeks' inventory in its supply lines and has avoided speculation in commodities. "If we are in the grocery business," Mr. John often said, "let's stay there. If we want to speculate, let's sell out and go on the stock exchange."

A remarkable feature of A & P operation is its accounting system, one of the best in the world. Every item stocked is numbered and recorded. Costs are calculated to tenths and hundredths of a cent. Even electric-light bills are figured to the last cent. Percentage profits are worked out regularly. A unit manager knows at any moment exactly how much stock each of his stores has on hand, what percentage of profit, loss and wastage each is making. Store returns are analyzed and compared. Economies discovered in one store are immediately passed on to others.

Weekly figures reach division headquarters on the following Tuesday. There they are consolidated and sent to New York. Headquarters in the Graybar Building on each Thursday knows the condition of the company as of the preceding Saturday in some detail.

If clerks use large paper sacks when small ones would do, the accountants can detect it in the added costs. The A & P attempts to sell 100 per cent of everything it buys. Shipments are planned to prevent spoilage and loss. Handling is swift and painstaking. In the stores, every empty carton is salvaged and wooden boxes are saved for reuse or return.

"Our company," explains President Burger, "pioneered in bringing wages up and food costs down by concentrating on the food business, cutting out frills and giveaways, and eliminating unnecessary costs and handling operations. We found we could render the greatest public service by providing the most good food for the least possible cost. We dispensed with extraneous merchandise in order to use more efficiently our store areas." He credits this with enabling the average American to eat more and better food than he did before World War II.

A & P managers and executives are remarkable for their alertness and loyalty. Their achievements in emergencies have been notable. When the Kaw River in 1951 flooded the company's warehouse in Kansas City, Kansas, food trucked overnight from Chicago and St. Louis enabled the sixty A & P stores in the area to stay open and feed the flood refugees. To attract and keep the type of man it likes, the A & P has a national personnel department, training courses of many kinds and employee benefits as generous as any in the retail food field. This includes better than average wages, Christmas bonuses, hospitalization, group insurance and a contributory pension plan. Many managers of A & P super markets earn $7,500 to $10,-000 a year.

Some A & P men have established businesses of their own and many hold important posts with other chains. Lansing P. Shield, who rose from clerk to general auditor with A & P, became president of the big Grand Union chain. Roger M. Laverty rose to president and general manager of the big Fitzsimmons super-market chain in California. Sherwin (Bucky) Harris became president of the Mary Lee Candy Company of Cleveland. W. A. Coleman headed the Humpty-Dumpty chain in Oklahoma.

All look back at their A & P experience with nostalgic pride. One says: "The most profitable thing I ever did was work for them, not in money but in education."

A final factor that has worked for the A & P has been the increasingly nomadic character of American life. Families move about over the country more than in the past and the old loyalties to neighborhood and home-town institutions have become tenuous. Government workers, army people and employees of big corporations, some of which are as big as the A & P, are being constantly shifted from city to city. For families like these, the familiar A & P is a friend, sometimes the only friend, in a new and alien community. They cash their pay checks at the A & P and start their shopping there.

XII. Rich's

"The Store That Married a City"

RICH'S INC. OF ATLANTA for many years has been the biggest department store, both in sales volume and physical size, south of Philadelphia and east of the Mississippi River. It sells everything imaginable for the adornment of a person or the furnishing of a home, and is actually four stores in two buildings, each occupying an entire city block.

One building houses a fashion store for women and children and a store for men. Connected with this building by a four-story glass-enclosed Kublai Khanlike bridge over Forsyth Street, is a huge store for homes, beneath both a basement store. Each of the four stores has its own restaurants, entrances, restrooms, and escalators or elevators. Half a block away is a Rich's parking garage.

"Do you go by Rich's?" a woman once asked an Atlanta bus driver. He thought for a moment of the ramification of the store's twenty-nine acres of floor space.

"Madam," he replied, "I go by Rich's, under Rich's, through Rich's, and around Rich's."

This huge and unique construction is just one of the distinctions of Rich's. Its more than $50,000,000 a year in sales amounts to $140 for every resident of Atlanta, a very high per capita figure among metropolitan stores. In the face of able competition it sold $108 worth of goods for every square foot of its vast selling space in a year when the National Retail Dry Goods Association's average for stores of its type and size was less than $100.

Headed during the years of its greatest growth by an engineer, a rarity in retailing, Rich's has made notable advances in stock control and the mechanics of storekeeping. At the same time, in the tradition of the Rich family, it has achieved even greater advances in human relations with its employees, customers and the community. The store literally is married to Atlanta.

The business was founded by Morris Rich, one of four brothers who immigrated as youths to the United States from Kaschau, Hungary, just before and during the Civil War. In America all of the brothers speedily became clerks, peddlers and store owners. Only twenty years old but with six years of work as a clerk and peddler behind him, Morris rode a bay horse from Albany, Georgia, to Atlanta, where his brother William in 1865 had started a whole-sale-retail dry-goods business. From William, who soon moved his own business to Nashville, Tennessee, Morris borrowed $500 and established a tiny dry-goods store on Whitehall Street. It opened on May 28, 1867. His brothers, Emanuel and Daniel, joined him as partners a few years later.

His first move to make his store attractive was a simple one. Whitehall Street, this little more than a country lane, was always ankle-deep in dust or mud. Young Rich laid down a row of planks which permitted ladies to alight from their carriages and enter the store without spotting their high button shoes or ruffled skirts. Inside, a salesman rushed forward to take the shopper's parasol or umbrella. This was in the tradition of Southern hospitality and customers liked it.

In a day of haggling, he began with fixed prices. This did not deter him from granting liberal credit nor from trading calico and candles for sorghum, cotton and shelled corn. Another early adopted policy was that of permitting customers to return goods without question. It is now publicized as "You make your own adjustment at Rich's."

This is interpreted so liberally that several million dollars' worth of goods are returned each year. Adjustments are made in the departments involved and it is not necessary for customers to seek out a bureau of adjustment or complaint department.

An analysis of a year's returns once revealed that the store had refunded the price of an unused pair of women's button shoes thirty years old, an unworn man's shirt ten years old and a dead canary!

Also included was a suit inaccurately altered by the wife of the sad but resigned gentleman who returned it, who explained that his wife had not liked the work of the alterations tailor and had unhappily sought to improve upon it.

In addition, some fifteen customers presented goods for credit or exchange which were not even bought at Rich's. In such cases Rich's customarily points out that the store does not carry these lines. Invariably the customers brightly reply, "But I never shop anywhere but here." Facing such a delicate impasse, Rich's clerks accept even these items and requested adjustments are made.

There also was a lady who dropped in to explain that the wedding cake she had ordered had been yellow inside, and not white, as specified, a fact which caused her some sorrow, even though the cake had been excellent, the wedding party had eaten of it heartily and the bridesmaids had taken away the traditional slices to put beneath their pillows. The lady received another cake, white inside, and went away unaware that she had made history by becoming the first person ever to eat her cake and have it too.

The customers expect nothing else, and Rich's treasures the fact that, having sowed such policy seeds, it has reaped an invaluable customer-produced slogan: "You never have any trouble at Rich's." Consequently, Rich's executives greet the annual figures which show their returns for credit and exchange to be about 12 per cent each year—while the national average is nearer 6—with something of the spirit with which Harvard greets a 12-to-6 football victory over Yale. Experience has taught them their policy causes the returnees to break into a warm glow of good will and to stay around and shop, sometimes extensively.

So at Rich's there are no restrictions as to days or years about returning merchandise which has not been used or is unsatisfactory. This reputation is spread over the South, and Rich's esteems it as a pearl of great price in public-relations value.

Rich's declares that all its customers are honest, and annually is surprised and gratified to find them almost so. Very few abuse the trust. Occasionally there is a minor crisis. There was, for example, the character who was buying expensive, nationally advertised fountain pens, also carried by Rich's, at a jewelry-store going-out-of-business sale. He was buying them at about $2.75 below the regular price prevailing at Rich's. Each day for six days he brought in a pen and asked to have his money back, saying he had got a number of the pens for his birthday—all bought at Rich's—and did not need them all. On the sixth day, as he presented his sixth pen, a clerk said plaintively, not wishing unduly to strain the finer traditions of the store, "Don't you think you are being a bit unfair to us?"

The chiseler pondered this appeal to his sporting blood for a moment, and said, "Yes, I believe I am." He put pen in pocket and departed, accompanied by gusty sighs of relief from the fountain-pen department.

Rich's, known in Atlanta as The Saturday Banker, one year cashed $18,000,000 in checks exclusive of those presented for partial payments on accounts. Most of this "business" was done on Saturdays when Atlanta's banks are closed. For identification Rich's requires no more than a driver's license, one of their own Charga-Plates or some sort of identification issued by the person's employer. This service is open to all callers—customers and noncustomers. The bad check loss on $18,000,000 was about $5,000.

With men like Lucian W. York, David H. Strauss and members of the Rich family as executives, the store grew steadily through the years with the addition of department after department. York was a colorful figure who rose from bundle wrapper to general manager. As a boy, he had been ticket taker in an Atlanta theater and all his life collected autographs of stage folk who became his friends. Any parade of minstrels or show people was likely to turn into Rich's and wind up in York's office. Long before a cow named Elsie became an attraction, York filled Rich's with living Georgia animals, including possums and goats, to advertise a harvest sale. For another occasion, the store became a Chinese palace. He inaugurated an annual sale on the anniversary of Whitney's cotton gin and on this day for years Rich's sold more cotton goods than any other store in the world.

Emanuel Rich died in 1897 and Daniel Rich in 1920. The founder, Morris Rich, lived until 1928 but some years previously yielded his responsibilities to his nephew, Walter Henry Rich, a shy and kindly man who visited each department of the store daily for forty-five years and was one of Atlanta's best-loved citizens.

In 1901, the partnership was converted into a corporation with the stockholders gradually increasing to more than fifteen hundred.

In 1907, construction of a new building on Whitehall Street made Rich's the largest store in Atlanta. An expanded mail-order trade and an economy basement opened in 1910 further increased volume. But Rich's was placed on the defensive in 1918, when its carriage trade rival, the Chamberlin-Johnson-DuBose Co., moved into a new and bigger building.

Rich's answered the challenge with a still bigger building completed in 1924 a few blocks west at Broad and Alabama Streets. Other important stores moved from Whitehall Street at this time but instead of following Rich's to the west moved north to create a new shopping center along historic Peachtree Street. There were many who said that Rich's new location was a mistake and the first year's operation seemed to confirm this.

With greater space, larger stocks, more help and increased expense, the store did only one-tenth more business and was left with a burdensome inventory. At this time, York, the general manager, died of a heart attack. As a final ominous note, Macy's was buying the rival Davison-Paxon store and Sears, Roebuck and Company was building a $3,000,000 branch in Atlanta.

In this crisis, Walter Rich turned for help to Frank H. Neely, a mechanical engineer without retail experience but who at forty already had a remarkable background.

Neely was born at Augusta, Georgia, into a family which for generations had run largely to preachers and teachers. His grandfather had been the former and his father the latter. The father had served with great distinction and success throughout the four years of the Civil War with the Confederate intelligence service, spending much of his time behind the Federal lines and in Federal-held cities. A superb linguist, he turned to teaching after the war and established the public-school system in Richmond (Augusta) County and later in Floyd (Rome) County. In both places he demanded as a condition of employment that he be allowed to build equal school facilities for Negroes and to teach in both schools. The high school at Rome, where he went when son Frank was an infant, is named Neely School.

Neely was not quite five years old when his school-superintendent father died, leaving nine children, of whom the future engineer was the youngest. He had a rough time of it, being farmed out to various relatives, who were deeply chagrined because the young orphan had no liking for school. He was generally regarded as a sweet but backward child by all except a doting sister at Cedartown, Georgia, who kept urging him into regular school attendance. The arrival of some new farm machinery at a nearby farm brought the boy, along with others, to view it. Fascinated, he went home and said, "I am going to Georgia Tech to be an engineer."

A relative in Atlanta took him in and sent him to summer school to cram for entrance examinations. With no Latin to trouble him, young Neely sailed right through and at sixteen was entered as a freshman at the Georgia School of Technology. He graduated at twenty with highest honors and the mathematics medal.

Neely was one of the first Southern graduates to be hired by the Westinghouse Electric Company. The starting wage was forty dollars a month. After three successful years in its Pittsburgh shops, he reversed the flow of Southern technical graduates and came home, setting himself up in a small office as consultant on scientific management.

About the same time he married his childhood sweetheart, Rae Schlesinger, and she began to apply the sort of scientific management which an intelligent and doting wife can provide. She kept him on an even keel and directed his enormous store of energy and ability. Once she insisted he spend the rent money to pay his membership fee in the American Society of Mechanical Engineers and to attend its annual meeting. His articles were published in the association's journal. One of them, explaining a system he had worked out to increase candy production by a new conveyor-belt arrangement for wrappers, attracted the admiring attention of the late Frederick W. Taylor and Henry Laurence Gantt, who pioneered scientific management in American industry. The three became friends, and Gantt was a frequent house guest in the Neely home until the time of his death. Neely developed a passion for Gantt's charts and invented many of his own, applying them to the reorganization of the Fulton Bag and Cotton Mills, which had seven large plants in the South. He had been in charge of these for a decade when Walter Rich offered him the vacant post of general manager.

"I've never worked a day in a store," Neely objected. "I'm too old to learn a new business. Besides you can't pay me enough."

Thinking to end the matter, he asked for a salary roughly equivalent to that then paid the President of the United States.

"When can you come to work?" countered Rich. Thus Rich's in 1924 gained the distinction of becoming the first department store ever to be run by a mechanical engineer. For that year, the store had net sales of $5,450,000 and sales more than a million greater the next year. Neely's impact was felt almost immediately.

One of his first moves was to eliminate mechanical time clocks and have workers simply sign in for a record of being at work. He urged executives to worry less about this sort of thing and to spend more time training and encouraging their employees. "Habits of industry," he quoted Gantt, "are far more valuable than any kind of knowledge or skill, for with such habits as a basis, the problem of acquiring the knowledge and skill is much simplified. . . . The general policy of the past has been to drive; but the era of force must give way to that of knowledge, and the policy of the future will be to teach and to lead, to the advantage of all concerned. . . ."

Looking about for executive help, Neely found in the store a young man, a graduate of the University of Pennsylvania's Wharton School of Commerce who had worked at Bamberger's in Newark. He was Richard H. Rich, a grandson of the founder. A son of a daughter of Morris Rich, he had adopted his mother's surname legally after a family discussion at the suggestion of his uncle, Walter Rich, to insure preservation of the name into the third generation. Born and bred in the department-store brier patch, so to speak, he demonstrated intelligence and ambition. Neely early began to let him carry extra weight.

About this time an eager young man from Georgia Tech presented himself at Neely's office and sought an interview. Always a patsy for anybody from his old alma mater, Neely saw him. The young man said he was writing a thesis on the subject of department stores and was interested in whether a store in Rich's location could succeed. He wanted a little information. This caused Neely—also a seeker in the same market—to quiver in his chair and to peer intently at the young face before him, seeking some hint of leg-pulling. There was none, and Neely went on to sweat out the study, leaning on it as a sort of augury. When thesis writer Ben Gordon graduated with an A-plus on a thesis which proved that management could make Rich's location much more desirable than any other, Neely hired him fast.

These two young men were also Gantt disciples. The three began to exchange problems of management the way others swap stamps. Their system relates buying, sales and inventory by departments and reaches down to the smallest category in each department.

Following the death of Walter Rich in 1947, Neely became president and two years later chairman of the board of directors. At that time, Dick Rich became president and Gordon executive vice president. They continued as a three-man executive team.

To meet the challenge of Macy's mass buying opportunities, Rich's joined the Associated Merchandising Corporation. This linked the store's buying with more than a score of big stores in other cities but left untouched the Rich slogan: "Atlanta-born, Atlanta-owned, Atlanta-managed."

Rich's refers to itself as a Southern institution and manages to create in its customers a feeling that they are privileged, dues-paying members. For many years a large share of its advertising has been institutional, identifying the store with the history of the state, its historical figures, colleges, artists, singers, musicians, the PTA, motherhood and so on.

When a hotel fire took 121 lives in Atlanta one weekend in 1946, the copy about a Georgia industry that had been prepared for the store's Monday morning institutional advertisement struck Neely as inappropriate for the grief-stricken city. He undertook to write something else.

After watching him crumple and throw away several drafts, Mrs. Neely, who is the author of a book of poetry, made a suggestion.

"Why not," she said, "just print the Twenty-third Psalm?"

This was done with the comforting phrases set within a black border. Only Rich's, Inc., in small italic type in a lower corner identified it with the store. When Atlantans recall the fire, they also recall this advertisement.

One of the stories told in the trade relates that an Atlanta competitor, attending a retail convention in New York, was asked the secret of Rich's success. "All they do," he said, with a wry face, "is stand on the corner and wave that blankety-blank Confederate flag."

But there is more to it than that. Bernard F. Gimbel, merchant prince of New York, spent some days in Atlanta as the guest of Robert W. Woodruff, head of the Coca-Cola Company. Gimbel cased the town thoroughly. A small dinner in Gimbel's honor was attended by Dick Rich, who suffered through seven courses with courage comparable to that of the Spartan youth whose vitals were being gnawed by a fox. The report was around that Gimbel would there announce that he was moving into Atlanta. After dinner, in an off-the-record talk, Gimbel praised Rich's highly and restored Dick Rich to a normal blood pressure by saying, "We don't care to come into Atlanta and buck competition as efficient and thorough as Rich's."

The addition of the Store for Homes and complete interior remaking of the older building gave Neely an opportunity to make an efficient building of the one he entered in 1924. The bold concept of a separate, bridge-connected Store for Homes was Dick Rich's, dreamed up while on duty with the Army in Brazil during the war.

Neely, Rich and Gordon, old-tie boys of Gantt's, beam happily at the system of underground conveyor belts which deliver boxes, crates and bundles from railway cars to the marking rooms while still another arrangement sends outgoing packages to delivery trucks. Customers may also turn in their parking tickets after making purchases and find their packages in their cars when they depart from the store's shoppers' garage.

Neely long ago junked the conventional display counter and went in heavily for special fixtures and decorations for various departments. He fetched decorators and designers from New York and had display technicians process ideas developed by his own staff. Atlanta came to expect of Rich's that each time a designer or decorator redid a floor or department in modern design and colors the town would be asked in to see a special fashion show and to greet the artist. This happy custom was suspended, maybe for all time, when the new basement and sub-basements, approximately a square block each in size, were thrown open to the public in a special night showing. Crowds jammed the streets all about the building, stopping all traffic and presenting a volume of humanity which simply could not be shoe-horned into the store. Management was much upset. Harassed executives went around wringing their hands until the crowd, unable to enter, was appeased via hastily set-up amplifiers and invited back on the morrow.

Rich's painstakingly identifies the store with the life of the city and state, for richer, for poorer, in sickness and in health. In the twenties cotton plunged. Rich's offered to take up to five thousand bales from Georgia farmers at a price well above the market, and did take what came in—a few hundred bales.

In 1930, Walter Rich picked up his morning paper and read that the city council had failed to find the money to meet the teachers' payroll. He telephoned the mayor and suggested that the administration issue scrip to the teachers, which Rich's would cash at full value with no obligation that they spend any of it with them. The city accepted with an alacrity exceeded only by the joyous pedagogues'. Rich's paid out $645,000 to teachers and held the scrip on faith until the city repaid it. The teachers and their families naturally think of Rich's as being more than just a commercial institution.

The Sunday before Labor Day in 1945, Dick Rich had the store's safe opened to provide nearby Fort McPherson with money to pay off a large detachment of troops which had arrived on Saturday afternoon to be discharged on Sunday morning. The fort's funds were in vaults time-locked until Tuesday.

While all executives serve in civic campaigns, Neely and Rich have led by heading up major campaigns for Red Cross, the Community Fund, Chamber of Commerce and other organizations. Neely has sponsored and fought through many of the city's physical reforms. He is a persistent man, and a succession of mayors, while respecting him, have had moments when they wished he had learned Latin and entered the Floyd County school system. The marriage of Rich's and Atlanta has not been altogether without the stresses and strains of the average alliance.

Long before Britain's Sir William Beveridge was advancing his idea of service that commentators facetiously described as "from the cradle to the grave," Rich's had it in effect. Every hospital-born Georgian is greeted with a card from Rich's which contains space for a record of the statistics of birth, such as hour, weight, doctor, hospital, and so on. When the youngsters are old enough to be brought along on shopping tours, Rich's has a nursery—soundproofed, air-conditioned and decorated—waiting for them, with a registered nurse and staff. Germicidal lamps, which glare witheringly at all germs, are a part of the equipment. This department was one of Engineer Neely's first constructions.

Nor does Rich's neglect the infants as they progress into school. Having tagged them at birth and nursed them while in infancy, the store uses radio stations in Atlanta and other cities to broadcast programs for the various age groups on music, art, Georgia history and other educational subjects. There are no commercials, but the children call them "Rich's program," a mysterious development which naturally pleases Rich's.

The Rich family gave a fully licensed radio station to the Atlanta public-school system. The schools use it daily for instruction, musical programs, lectures and announcements for which it is not possible to assemble the entire student body or class groups. There is no commercial here, but there is no secret about who gave this station and subsidizes it.

In addition to these ties with future wage earners and customers, the store awards about $3,000 annually in prizes to 4-H Club boys and girls, and offers trophies for the best grades in English in the Atlanta schools.

The college group is by no means forgotten. The Rich family gave a building to Young Harris College, in North Georgia, and set up a foundation, through which a $250,000 building was erected at Emory University for a school of business administration, a laboratory was furnished at Georgia Tech, $100,000 was given to Georgia Baptist Hospital, and many other gifts made. Neely has an almost sophomoric affection for Georgia Tech, and he has aided the school enormously, both in personal gifts and in heading up alumni drives to obtain funds, faculty members, buildings and equipment. He and his wife are devoted admirers of the Georgia Tech football team, regarding it as composed of Saint Georges constantly engaged against the dragons of evil.

For the out-of-college set, Rich's maintains Garden Center offices, which are used gratis by 201 organizations devoted to flowers. The traffic to Rich's is heavy. Fashion shows, many of them benefits for schools for mountain children; a carefully organized program of book reviews; lectures on homemaking, beauty and interior decorating lure adults. Periodic supershows called "Fashionatas" have a budget of about $75,000 and a New York cast of models and scenery. The customer and his contacts with the store come in for as much research as an orchid grower lavishes on his plants.

A shopping service was organized thirty years ago. It does more than remind citizens of anniversaries, birthdays and special dates. The housewife of a family moving to Atlanta is pretty sure to look up from unpacking the barrel of china to be greeted by a young lady who welcomes her to the city, presents her with a card good for two lunches in Rich's tearoom and an invitation to open an account.

The young ladies on the staff assist with weddings, help plan entertainments and offer suggestions on how to dress and how to decorate tables, rooms or lawns for these occasions. Their file is filled with human-interest items, such as one about the mother from a rural town whose son was marrying a Boston girl he met during the war. The provincial mother had an idea the girl's family consisted entirely of characters out of one of Mr. Marquand's novels, and poured out her story to the shopping service. They provided the proper wardrobes, made the right suggestions, and the affair came off beautifully. Each year hundreds of weddings in Georgia are planned by Rich's, down to the wedding cake out of the store's really fine bakery.

The store has never neglected the people who attend the department-store "machine tools," as envisioned by the chief engineer. As much attention and research are lavished on them as on customers. A forty-hour week was in force long before federal laws required it. So was the five-day work week. Rich's was the first Southern department store to install them. There has long been a clinic, primarily for employees, where a registered nurse and staff furnish medical attention in the event of injury or illness, as well as advice on matters of family health. Executives are supposed to visit the clinic at least once a week for a rubdown and sunlamp treatment. All employees for years have been protected by a hospitalization and sick-benefits plan. An employee recreation area features a snack bar, shuffleboard courts and sun deck. This is located on the roof of the Store for Homes. A credit union, three employee cafeterias and a Christmas-bonus plan which includes every regular employee are a part of the program. The city auditorium, seating five thousand, is rented for the Christmas-bonus party, and every seat is filled.

The voices of elevator operators are recorded and those who require it receive diction instruction. New sales employees receive six days' instruction before meeting the public and wear green training badges when they begin to sell. All are coached as to their appearance, manners and attitude. The store has a "resource squad" of young men and women, some from school graduating classes and others selected from the store, constantly in training for executive jobs. Several deaf and dumb persons, also a number of Lawson Hospital veteran amputees, work in the store bakery, the business-machines room and in various clerical posts.

The store has about two hundred people who have worked there more than twenty years. About thirty-five of these have been there more than thirty years, and several into the forties. One man—A. D. McCain in the rug department—will celebrate his fiftieth anniversary in 1955.

As the anniversaries of these employees roll around, an orchid is pinned on the ladies and the men are given ties. Dick Rich also has a little personal custom of opening a small bank account for each baby born into the Rich "store family."

The late Walter Rich wanted a store without any fear or awareness of big brass, and the store has none. "We can't expect our employees to be friendly to customers unless we lead a friendly existence ourselves," says Neely. The result of an absence of the big-brass atmosphere is a feeling, on the part of the employees of the store, of "belonging" and pride in their job and work. They are not nervous or worried.

Now and then visiting department-store executives—puzzled by the unusual policy of merchandising which allows the customer to make her own adjustment, noting the evident enthusiasm and loyalty of the employees, and examining the elaborate system of merchandising checks and balances which allows buyers to purchase efficiently and accurately—ask wistfully if Georgia Tech is likely to turn out another Frank Neely.

Dick Rich and Ben Gordon have the answer.

"Frank Neely is an engineer, and a great one," they say. "But he could not have succeeded in the department-store business had he not had something else—namely, the ability to apply the coldly scientific methods in such a way that they required happy and interested human beings to make them work best. Neely has always been more of a teacher than an engineer anyhow. Teaching ran in his family blood, and he has never stopped holding classes."

Perhaps the greatest tribute to Rich's was expressed in an address by Preston S. Arkwright, a president of the Georgia Power Company. After recalling that of twenty-three dry-goods stores in Atlanta in 1867, only Rich's survives, he said: "In all Atlanta, there is not a single human being who speaks ill of Rich's."

Rich's was strictly an Atlanta enterprise until 1954 when the firm purchased the fifty-year-old department store of S. H. George & Sons, Inc., in Knoxville, Tennessee, and renamed it George's-Rich's. A $7,000,000 expansion and modernization program is converting it into a landscaped suburban-type store in the geographic heart of the city. A tunnel connects the store with a garage and service building across the street.

XIII. The J. L. Hudson Company

Detroit's Colossal Store

A YOUNG merchant named Joseph Lothian Hudson was one of thousands of retailers to whom the panic of 1873 was a cruel blow. He was then twenty-seven years old and, in partnership with his father, was running a small men's clothing store in the lumber town of Ionia, Michigan. Soon after the failure of the Jay Cooke banking house in New York, the sawmills stopped in Ionia and Hudson's customers could not pay their bills.

The father died that year, partly from worry, but young Hudson struggled on until 1876. He went bankrupt, losing a flour mill and some timber land as well as the store that year to pay his creditors sixty cents on the dollar. He then started all over as an employee in another store.

Twelve years later, by remarkable enterprise, he owned a bigger store in Detroit. Even more remarkable, he looked up all the creditors whose claims had been erased by the bankruptcy proceedings and paid them in full with compound interest. Such action is rare enough at the present time. In 1888 it astounded the business world. The amazed creditors showered him with gifts and praise.

"We sent today by American Express two cases containing a clock and mantel ornament which we ask you to accept as indicating in some small degree our sincere respect and esteem," wrote David T. Leahy of E. H. Van Ingen & Co., New York. "Especially we have wished to make known to you our appreciation of your high sense of commercial honor as shown by your payment—in a quiet and unostentatious way—of principal and interest of debts forgiven to you by your creditors many years ago and indeed almost forgotten by them. Your failure was an honest one that left no stain upon your reputation. You could have found plenty of plausible reasons for not paying when you became able to. You chose the high and manly course. . . . Our best wishes for a merry Christmas and a happy and prosperous New Year."

This letter is cherished today in the great Detroit department store of The J. L. Hudson Company, and the integrity which it memorializes is one of the reasons Hudson's has forty-nine acres of floor space and in 1953 had sales of more than $155,000,000. Its twenty-five stories make it the tallest department store in the world. In space under one roof it is second only to Macy's. When the furnaces flare along the River Rouge and Ford and General Motors work extra shifts, as in 1952, automobile and industrial payroll dollars pour into Hudson's as fast as $1,500,000 a day. For months at a time, the volume exceeds Macy's main store in New York and makes Hudson's, as far as sales are concerned, "the biggest store in the world."

Hudson's and Macy's, incidentally, have the largest switchboards among telephone business customers. On trunklines, Hudson's leads 553 to 536. Macy's is ahead on extensions, 2,500 to 1,341. Only boards of the telephone company and the Pentagon are bigger.

Hudson's closest retail competitor in Michigan is its own basement store. This four-acre, two-level operation in turn boasts the largest basement volume in the world. When opened in 1954, Hudson's remarkable Northland development was the largest suburban shopping center in the world. Hudson's is the largest store in the big Associated Merchandising Corporation buying group.

One reason for Hudson's success is the completeness of its assortment of merchandise. In an institutional advertisement, it once boasted carrying 553,921 items "A to Z—from antimacassars to zippers, aspirin to zwieback. An African mask to Zeurcher cheese." Detroit's biggest bookstore, biggest drugstore and biggest toy store are all Hudson departments. Even a tiny department for dog owners offers canine candy, deodorants, dog books, leashes trimmed in gold, traveling boxes and supersonic whistles.

The drug department, which employs twenty-one registered pharmacists, offers fifty thousand items. To serve Detroit's polyglot population, clerks in the department speak fourteen languages and its stock includes ancient and exotic remedies as well as the sulfas and antibiotics. On the shelves are camomile flowers from Hungary, agar-agar from Japan, orrisroot from Spain, Biblical myrrh and manna, the latter now classed as a mild laxative; dragon's blood, balsam of Peru, Gilead's seed, and oils from everywhere, including Turkish rose oil that sells for $1 a few drops or $500 a pound.

In addition, the store sells hospital beds, screens, commodes, wheelchairs, canes, crutches, back rests, bed trays, sun and heat lamps, surgical garments, hearing aids and almost any sickroom article.

There is heavy emphasis on related selling. Hudson's is the No. 1 outlet for items like Simmons mattresses. But along with a mattress, Hudson's likes to sell everything related to it such as bedroom furniture, bedding, pajamas, nightgowns, bedroom slippers and even an alarm clock. Hudson's encourages home building with a planning center and often sells every item that goes into the home when it is built. Numerous weddings are outfitted completely at Hudson's even to the bride's flowers and tickets for a honeymoon trip. There are whole floors for boys and girls and also a barbershop for children where the small fry of automobiledom ride lions, tigers or reindeer while having their hair cut.

Also a factor in Hudson's success is the care with which it recruits, trains and keeps happy its 14,000 employees. The store has pioneered importantly in the development of buying and inventory controls and the use of business machines. It also lures 100,000 customers a day with year-around promotions which range from a Thanksgiving Day Santa Claus parade, which is several years older than Macy's, to a fashion show aboard an air liner in flight. It keeps its customers' confidence with a liberal returned-goods policy.

Most important of all in the growth of the big store has been a continuity of able, civic-minded management. This has been provided by the five publicity-shy Webbers. Despite their years, they are still termed, perhaps in tribute to their alertness, "the Webber boys." When J. L. Hudson, the founder, died unmarried in 1912, he left the store to his four nephews. Richard H. Webber, who had been his uncle's companion since the Ionia days and who had risen to vice president in the store, then became president. He is now chairman of the board. Oscar Webber, who started in the store as cash boy, is president. He is a Phi Beta Kappa graduate of the University of Michigan. James B. Webber and his twin brother, Joseph L. Webber, are vice presidents and directors of merchandise. James B. Webber, Jr., a great-nephew of the founder, joined the firm in 1936 and is now executive vice president. The store is family owned as well as family managed.

The story of the enterprise begins naturally with Joseph Lothian Hudson. He was born, the third of seven children, on October 17, 1846, in Newcastle-on-Tyne, England, where his father, Richard Hudson, ran a small tea and coffee business. In 1853, the father migrated to Canada and found a job with the Grand Trunk Railroad at Hamilton, Ontario. Two years later the family followed. At thirteen young Joseph got his first job as a telegraph messenger. He also worked as a grocery boy of all work at $5 a month in Hamilton. In 1860, the family moved to Grand Rapids, Michigan, where the father had another railroad job. Young Joseph worked on a fruit farm and managed to finish eight years of school. In 1861, the family moved again to Pontiac, Michigan.

There Joseph Hudson, now fifteen, met and went to work for Christopher R. Mabley, who was then running a small men's clothing store with sales of about $25,000 a year. The first month he paid young Hudson $4; this was doubled the next month and the youth showed such an aptitude for the business that, after five years, he was drawing $500 a year and board. The Mabley store volume rose to $100,000.

Mabley was a flamboyant personality who soon became one of the best-known merchants in the country. He was a pioneer in the then new field of men's ready-to-wear. This barely existed before the Civil War but when uniforms of Union soldiers began to be made by machine, it developed rapidly. Mabley was a big advertiser. He bought display space in newspapers and plastered fences and barns with his name. For a time, every fifth purchase made by a customer was free. He conducted pie-eating contests as publicity stunts and even raffled off horses, which he stabled in his show windows. Usually in partnership with somebody else, Mabley opened stores in Cincinnati, Baltimore, Toledo, Detroit, and elsewhere to become the largest retail clothing business up until that time. The Cincinnati store survives as Mabley & Carew.

In addition, one of Mabley's many ventures was a store in Ionia,

Michigan, in partnership with Hudson's father. In 1865, the elder Hudson bought out Mabley's interest and induced nineteen-year-old Joe to take over the management. It had attained a volume of $40,-000 a year when the panic of 1873 struck.

With this store bankrupt, young Hudson again became an employee of Mabley, this time as manager of his Detroit store while he went abroad for a vacation. Hudson did so well that he was rehired at $50 a week and given 10 per cent of the profits. These amounted to $2,500 at the end of six months. Mabley then gave him a quarter interest in the store and a guarantee of $7,500 a year for three years.

At the end of this time in 1881, Hudson went into business for himself. The first venture was in Toledo, Ohio, but within the year he opened a men's and boys' clothing business in Detroit on the ground floor of the old Detroit Opera House on the Campus Martius, not far from the present store site. Within a few years Hudson was prosperous enough to pay his old Ionia debts. He also opened branch stores in St. Paul, St. Louis, Grand Rapids, Cleveland, Sandusky and Buffalo. By 1891 he had eight stores doing a total volume of more than $2,000,000 a year and was the largest individual buyer and retailer of men's clothing in the country.

Business troubles following the depression of 1893 caused the sale or liquidation of all the stores except the main one in Detroit. This had been Hudson's favorite enterprise for some years. In 1884, he formed a partnership with Campbell Symington and took over additional space in another building to sell furniture, rugs and carpets, draperies and curtains. There was another expansion in 1887, and in 1891 he moved into a new eight-story building at Farmer and Gratiot Streets and added still more departments.

"He'll never make a go of it!" said Hudson's friends. The location was considered too far uptown and the fact that a Presbyterian church had occupied the site previously was deemed an ill omen for a commercial enterprise. But the store was successful and with Hudson giving it all his attention the business grew. In 1895, it was incorporated as The J. L. Hudson Company.

In 1905, he shortened store hours with the comment, "It has been shown we can produce with the same labor in eight hours what we used to produce in twelve." An addition was made to the Farmer Street building in 1907 and in 1911 a 10-story building was constructed on much of the Woodward Avenue side of the block. Though all of this frontage was not obtained until 1923, the store began to take on its present appearance.

As his nephews began to assume responsibilities in the store, Hudson gave more of his time to other activities. One of these was helping a relative, Roscoe B. Jackson, and his partners, Howard E. Coffin and Roy Chapin launch the Hudson Motor Car Company. Incorporated on February 24, 1909, the company was named for Hudson, who supplied most of the modest capital and became chairman of the board. The firm started with $15,000 in cash; models, patterns and dies valued at $25,000 and subscriptions later paid in cash aggregating $58,990. It proved incredibly successful. On the next July 3, the first Hudson car, an efficient four-cylinder 20-horsepower model priced at $900, rolled forth. Within a year, four thousand had been sold. There was a profit of $587,355 the next year. This increased to $822,000 in 1912 and after Hudson's death earnings were as much at $21,000,000 in a single year. The company survived as an independent until 1954 when it merged with Nash as a division of American Motors, Inc. Hudson also had another connection with the automobile industry. A daughter of his sister, Mrs. William Clay, married Edsel Ford.

Three times in his career, J. L. Hudson assumed large indebtedness when under no obligation to do so. The preservation of the Third National Bank of Detroit was one example. Following the panic of 1893, banks were shaky and closing their doors everywhere. The Third National Bank, of which Hudson was an officer, but not a large stockholder, was ordered to close in 1894. Such was J. L. Hudson's reputation that the Comptroller of Currency appointed him receiver. The appointment of an official of an involved bank was without precedent. Hudson called the stockholders together, and announced that if they raised as much as $1 among themselves, he personally would see that the $300,000 needed would be secured. He believed many of the depositors had put their money in that bank because he was an officer in it! In the final accounting, Hudson put up half the needed cash, helped pay off the depositors and re-established Detroit's confidence in all its banks.

Hudson was perhaps the foremost philanthropist of Detroit and gave to charitable and civic endeavors not only of his money but of his abundant energy and personal direction. He was a humanitarian of rare quality, not only in the sense that he aided hospitals, orphan asylums, churches, scientific research, Y.M.C.A. work and innumerable charities, but he went out of his way to aid unfortunates, to work for prison reform, to help those who were down.

A murderer who had served out his sentence came to Hudson with an idea with which to rehabilitate himself. Hudson said, "Your idea needs publicity. We'll go over to the newspaper editor and talk to him about it." Afterward, the editor asked Hudson why he walked over to the newspaper office with the felon, when he could just as well have called up or sent a note. Hudson answered: "I wanted to help the man regain his self-respect. I wanted to show that I was willing to walk with him and be seen with him publicly."

Hudson played an active role in his city's political affairs. Though he served in many appointive positions, he never accepted any salary. His own personal interests were of secondary importance. For instance, two rival lighting companies were fighting the city's attempt to establish a municipal lighting plant. Hudson held stock in both of the private companies—and operated, in addition, his own plant for his own use. Hudson turned over his own plant cost figures to Mayor Hazen S. Pingree, which were given much publicity at the time, and the city voted to establish its own lighting plant as a result. Hudson was later named Detroit's first public lighting commissioner.

He founded, directed, and for many years practically supported Detroit's Municipal League, a nonpartisan body devoted to the general public's interest and to inquiring into local government affairs.

The store had sales of about $2,000,000 a year when the founder died in 1912 on a vacation trip to England. This was considered remarkable but the spectacular growth of Detroit and the enterprise of the Webbers over four decades combined to multiply this seventy-five times. In doing this they had the help of selfless, devoted executives, many of whom have spent their entire careers in the service of the big store.

One of these was William T. Petzold, a parcel boy on the original staff. He rose to secretary and treasurer of the company and retired in 1951 after seventy years of continuous service. His son, Herman

G. Petzold, for many years basement-store manager, became a vice president and general manager in 1954.

Very important contributions were made by the late Carlos B. ("Pop") Clark, whose pride for thirty-three years was that he was "controller of The J. L. Hudson Co." Clark was a leader in formation of the Controllers' Congress of the National Retail Dry Goods Association and received this organization's first gold medal for distinguished service. As chairman for years of its taxation committee, he was the first to propose that individuals should be given credit for "earned" income on their tax returns and that corporations should be allowed reasonable deductions for contributions to charities. Congress adopted both. On Clark's retirement, in 1946, Lew Hahn, N.R.D.G.A. leader, termed him "one of the most interesting and valuable men" in retailing. He left his mark on the operating systems not only of Hudson's but of many other great stores.

Vice President Lewis B. Sappington, in charge of merchandising and publicity, and Vice President Walter E. Simmons, general merchandise manager of the upstairs store, are among the company's employees with more than twenty-five years' service. So are Frank J. Wilton, merchandise manager, and Harry Hogan, director of personnel.

Physical expansion continued. The store was rebuilt and enlarged in 1927 and 1928. Air conditioning was installed gradually. A regular cycle of interior modernization was adopted by the store's architectural staff with increasing emphasis on open displays and greater facilities for self-selection. In 1945 the old Sallan building at the corner of Woodward and Gratiot was demolished to make way for a twelve-story addition. Completion of this building in 1946 made the Hudson store a full block square. In 1946, two additional stories were added to the Grand River end of the building. In addition, the mezzanine floors in both the Woodward and Farmer buildings were enlarged considerably.

All of this gave the store a ground area of 420 by 220 feet and a building containing fifty-one passenger elevators seventeen more for freight and two escalator systems. The building contains five restaurants and an employees' cafeteria. There are 705 fitting rooms, believed the most of any store, scattered over ten floors. There is a store hospital, considered one of the finest industrial hospitals, with four doctors, four nurses, a laboratory technician, and six visiting nurses who make regular calls upon employees who are ill. The hospital also includes a silence room where employees may relax during their rest periods.

Suburban shopping centers naturally came under consideration at Hudson's as Detroit began to share the traffic congestion which its products have created in all cities. The Webbers decided to build three centers to be known respectively as Northland, Eastland and Westland after a survey by the Detroit *News* revealed that 50 per cent of the city's suburban residents did not come downtown to shop. After several years of planning, a subsidiary company was organized and the first of these, Northland, completed in 1954 at a cost of $25,000,000.

With 1,317,030 square feet of roofed space, this was 25 per cent larger than any previous suburban shopping development. Hudson's Northland branch store, managed by Dick Schroeter, a former University of Detroit football player, was located at the center of the big development and is adjoined by more than eighty other stores, shops and restaurants. Surrounding all the structures is the largest all-paved shoppers' parking lot in the world providing space for more than seventy-five hundred automobiles and offering all of the participating stores an equal chance at customer traffic.

Designed by Vienna-born Victor Gruen, Northland combines beauty and efficiency. All truck delivery is underground. A central plant supplies steam heat and air conditioning. The Kroger super market delivers by belts and chutes a customer's packages to a covered pickup station into which the shopper can drive her car. With the first purchase, the shopper is given a sheet of adhesive labels. One is affixed to each package. Carrying a load of parcels does not cut short shopping. Purchases in the Hudson store can be delivered similarly to a pickup station at the lower-level entrance or sent home by Hudson's regular delivery service.

Colonnades, malls, covered walkways, modern art and flowers make the center attractive. Planted were 1,500 shade trees, 625 flowering trees, 1,900 evergreens, 18,000 ground cover plants and 23,000 bulbs. Harold Gluckman and Alfonse Rapaczak of Hudson's display department painted a mural 500 feet long for the branch store. Fountains, statuary and other art objects by Gwen Lux, Lily

Saarinen, Marshall Fredericks, Richard Hall Jennings and others adorn the malls. Miss Lux's "Totem Pole," a dramatic abstraction inspired by Indian carvings, is a favorite meeting place for shoppers.

Hudson's Northland stocks about $7,000,000 worth of merchandise and offers all the lines of the downtown store though naturally not in such depth. It also has its own training department for converting neighborhood housewives into efficient salespeople. Many of the initial staff had not previously worked in a store. It is the largest department store branch. It has attracted visitors from afar and is rapidly becoming as much of a Detroit landmark as the downtown store.

Hudson's has the tallest flagpole in Detroit, rising 125 feet above the 25-story tower, to a height of 522 feet above the ground. The gold-leaf ball at its top is two feet in diameter. The flag flies every business day and downtown Detroiters watch it intently. Let it be a foot or two below the top of the pole, and several persons will telephone the store. Let it be ripped by a sudden gale and there will be more calls. A new flag goes up about every two months.

This interest in flags led the store to have "the largest flag in the world." The first big flag was made to order by Annin & Company of New York and unveiled on Armistice Day in 1923. It measured 90 by 230 feet and covered eight floors of the big Woodward Avenue side of the store. The flag was displayed at least every Flag Day, decorated the U.S. Capitol in Washington on Flag Day in 1929 and was shown at the New York World's Fair. It was replaced by one still larger in 1949. Made in Detroit by the George P. Johnson Company, this is of wool and measures 104 by 235 feet. The stars are 5½ feet high and the stripes are 8 feet wide. It weighs 1,500 pounds and 6,240 feet of nylon rope are required to suspend it.

In a long-remembered public-relations project, Hudson's designed a county flag for each of the eighty-three counties in Michigan. Then the store had the flags made up of fine material and presented them in individual ceremonies at county seats. Each ceremony was an important local event and it took the better part of two years to complete the task. Hudson's then published a book, distributed it free to libraries and other educational institutions, with pictures of each flag and a brief history of each county.

Probably no event of the holiday season other than Christmas itself is more keenly anticipated by youngsters within a hundred-mile radius of Detroit than Hudson's annual Thanksgiving Day Parade. Estimates of the throngs packing every curb space and window along the 2½-mile route each year range from 100,000 to 300,000 boys and girls and their parents.

Hudson's display staff, which creates and builds the huge and colorful floats, tries to visualize its work with the eyes of the youngsters it tries to please. Over twenty-five floats, one thousand marchers and more than a dozen bands take part in the huge spectacle, which has wound its way down Woodward Avenue every year since the 1920's with the exception of a brief lapse during World War II. It is a Detroit tradition; so much so that it is generally considered to be the official start of the holiday season in the Motor City.

Christmas at Hudson's means a Santa Claus awe-inspiring in his authenticity on a big golden throne in true North Pole surroundings. It also means ingenious animated windows and the world's tallest department-store building decked inside and out with trees, lights and decorations of a hundred different kinds. The Hudson Carolers, employees singing group, appears daily during December on the selling floors, and winds up the season with a Christmas Eve television show.

Art and music have always had a prominent place in Hudson's activities. School children have been entertained at symphony concerts and store musical organizations have made tours. Since the early days of radio, a daily hour of music has been sponsored on WWJ, Detroit's oldest station. The store's art department is the largest in any department store. Numerous exhibitions have been devoted to modern design and related subjects.

For a "Michigan on Canvas" art project, Hudson's in 1946 employed ten leading artists at a cost of $75,000 to paint, without restrictions, scenes about the state. The artists were Arnold Blanch, Aaron Bohrod, Adolf Dehn, John DeMartelly, David Fredenthal, Joe Jones, Doris Lee, Carolos Lopez, Ogden Pleissner and Zoltan Sepeshy. The ninety-six canvasses which they produced, depicting automobile making, lake freighting, mining, agriculture and similar subjects, were exhibited in thirty showings and won Hudson's notice in *Life* and many other publications. They are now displayed at Greenfield Village.

Hudson's advertising at times lashes out at discount houses with long lists of branded merchandise offered at competitive prices "plus the advantages of the many services offered by Hudson's . . . plus the security of knowing that Hudson's stands back of every piece of merchandise it sells." Most of the store's heavy volume of promotion, however, is of a dignified and an institutional character. Hudson's does not sell liquor and its copywriters refer to cocktail gowns as "after 5" dresses. Besides heavy newspaper space, as much as forty-eight pages come in an issue of the Detroit *Free Press*, Hudson's also uses a metropolitan shopping news, radio and television.

During Detroit's 250th anniversary celebrations in 1951, Hudson's bought newspaper space to publish twenty-five biographical sketches by Dr. Milo M. Quaife, local historian, saluting prominent Detroiters. The store also changed all of its Woodward Avenue windows to historical dioramas of the highlights in Detroit's history. When removed from the windows, they were presented to the Detroit Historical Museum, where they now circle the entrance hall. The store also has erected twenty-eight bronze tablets at points of historic interest about Detroit. Several Detroit guides and histories have been published by the store and distributed gratis.

In 1952, Hudson's joined the city's Get Out the Vote campaign by taking the glass out of its biggest Woodward Avenue window and turning the window into a vote registration booth. After the first day, the City Clerk doubled the number of registrars to four, and the window was the third most active registration point in the city.

Hudson's fame rests also on its meticulous service, its handling of telephone and mail orders, the faithfulness of its delivery men. Some of this is the reaction of well-trained and loyal employees. Mostly, it is the result of planning. Hudson's has a plan for nearly every contingency. Parcel-post shipments are speeded up by recording their addresses by Dictaphone. If it begins to rain, for example, a whole lot of things happen. The main-floor superintendent notifies the switchboard. The operators call several departments and tell appointed girls, "It's raining." By the time the first wet customers come in, extra umbrellas have been set out and there is extra help in the raincoat department.

The store has a charge account with Detroit's largest taxi company to provide a ride home for customers who become ill while shopping.

Through its personal shopping service the store serves many customers far from Detroit. Among these is the family of an American missionary in Bombay, India. For more than twenty years, the store has been outfitting the husband, wife and three children.

Hudson's has its own delivery trucks, mostly Internationals with Metro bodies painted a distinctive green. Large trucks shuttle goods from the Woodward Avenue store to the delivery center a quarter of a mile away to three substations. Others fan out daily from these for points as far away as forty-five miles. The 280 men who man these trucks drive 3,000,000 miles a year, deliver 11,000,000 packages, and are among Hudson's best salesmen.

Hudson drivers have started countless cars on cold mornings for ladies in distress, pulled cars out of mud with their trucks. They regularly find and return lost dogs and children. They've started the fire on a cold morning when grandmother was home alone, then stopped to check it later. They've been slugged, robbed. They've hidden their day's receipts from would-be robbers. One had his face pushed through the glass of his truck by a bandit.

A weeping but thankful mother once called the store. She was away when the driver arrived at the house, to be met by her young sons, one holding a revolver, the other some bullets, belonging to their dad. The driver took the pistol and got the next-door neighbor to step in and take over until mother returned.

A driver named Joe Krul had the most unusual adventure. It was just another busy pre-Christmas Saturday when he started on his package delivery route. Before completing his second stop, things happened. He heard a plane's motors close above. Then the thunder of a tremendous crash, just one street away. While his "jumper" ran to pull the fire alarm, Joe dashed to the scene. He stopped short. A big DC-3 cargo plane lay with its shattered nose buried in a home, a mass of smoke and flame. The women were yelling, "Save her! Save her!"

Joe looked up and saw a woman on the second floor of the shattered house, just staring, shocked. "The house was tilted over, so I ran up the side to the porch, grabbing onto the bricks that were shoved out," said Joe. He kicked the door in, dragged the woman out and passed her down to waiting arms. Then he leaped free of the collapsing porch. Wringing wet, dirty with smoke, his knees shaking, Joe called the store, headed home to change uniforms. Then he went back to work delivering his packages.

New Hudson employees, who are often chosen on the basis of aptitude tests, are indoctrinated with the store's ideals by tales of exploits like these and the Hudson Creed. This was formulated many years ago but is still kept before every worker. It reads:

I believe in Hudson's because into its makeup have gone the finest thoughts of those at its head.

I believe in Hudson's because back of every piece of merchandise which crosses the counter, there is something which says to the customer, "If not satisfactory, this may be returned and full value given therefor." Furthermore, each and every piece of merchandise is the best that can be produced at the price.

I believe in Hudson's because I am putting into it myself—the best that is in me.

My faith is not alone a faith in the store, the organization—it is a faith in the ideals of men, those who are responsible for this great house of industry.

And so I stand inspired with the blazing truth that I am taking an active part in building, through honest effort, one of the greatest institutions in this broad country—Hudson's, Detroit.

XIV. Sears, Roebuck and Company
The World's Biggest General Store

PRESIDENT FRANKLIN D. ROOSEVELT once suggested that the best way to convince the Kremlin of the superiority of the American way of life would be to bomb the Soviet Union with the Sears, Roebuck catalog. President Calvin Coolidge, an earlier chief executive known for his thrift, paid the company the compliment of becoming a customer. A lesser political figure, Governor Eugene Talmadge of Georgia, in addressing farmers, earnestly said: "Your only friends are Jesus Christ, Sears, Roebuck and Gene Talmadge." This helped him win election after election.

While a Georgia farmer's friends may be few, those of Sears, Roebuck and Company are numerous enough to give it a sales volume of $3,000,000,000 a year and to make it the world's greatest retailer of general merchandise. Of every $100 spent for this in the United States, $5 goes to Sears. One out of every seven and a half families in America is buying something from Sears on the installment plan. In an exact reversal of a quarter of a century ago, 30 per cent of this huge volume comes from the famous catalog and 70 per cent from the company's seven hundred retail stores. Since the opening of one at Casper, Wyoming, in 1953, these are to be found in every state, as well as in Hawaii, Latin America and, through Simpsons-Sears, Ltd., in Canada.

Chairman Theodore V. Houser, who became head of Sears in 1954, in the words of his predecessor, is "the greatest master of mass merchandising in the United States." While he is the first to point out that he is the heir to many years of statesmanlike management, the tribute has basis. There are forty-four Sears buying departments in Chicago and six more in New York for feminine apparel and accessories. These buy from some ten thousand sources and have branches in other cities and abroad. The smallest department handles a sales volume of $16,000,000, the largest $190,000,000, with the average around $60,000,000.

Sears strives to maintain its prices as low or lower than any competitor on its more than 100,000 items, which are as varied as diapers, diamonds and tombstones. At the same time, Sears' employees, who are one and a half per cent of all distributive workers in the country, earn an average of $11 more a week than retail workers generally. But on its big sales volume, Sears usually earns a larger percentage of profit than the average department store, specialty shop or food store. In 1952 and 1953, for example, Sears earned 3.76 and 3.95 per cent on sales as compared with 2.4 and 2.6 for department stores.

No other company is as close to the heart of rural America. No company has been more astute in forecasting future social trends and adapting its operations to capitalize them. It has been largely responsible for making American living standards uniform. It has brought city refinements to farms. It has helped create a great hemispheric market for manufacturers. No company has had to overcome more bitter prejudices in attaining success. No retail operation has about it a greater wealth of humor, lore and legend. Its success is a matter of "bargains, brains and ballyhoo."

These elements were supplied liberally by the founder, Richard Warren Sears. He was born December 7, 1863, at Stewartville, Minnesota. His father was a farmer-blacksmith who lost all his money in a stock farm and died when Richard was fourteen. To help support his mother and three sisters, the boy learned telegraphy and went to work for the Minneapolis and St. Louis Railroad.

The turning point in his life came in 1886 when he was twenty-three and earning $6 a week as agent for the railroad at its North Redwood station. This served Redwood Falls, Minnesota, a county seat town, two miles to the south. In an effort to increase its small freight business there, the line allowed its agent special rates and he dabbled in selling coal and lumber and also in buying and shipping meat and fruit.

Opportunity knocked when a local jeweler refused to accept a C.O.D express shipment of watches. It was then a common practice for wholesalers to send unordered goods to retailers and when the "mistake" was discovered to offer it at half price. But the Redwood Falls jeweler would have none of these watches. So Sears opened up the box, made a deal with the shipper to buy them at $12 each, and began to sell the flashy gold-filled timepieces himself.

While similar watches retailed for $25, Sears sold most of his for $14. He sold watches to his neighbors. He sold watches to the train crews. Finally, he sent sample watches to his brother agents up and down the railroad and they began to sell for him. In six months, he made about $5,000 in the watch business and left the railroad to start the R. W. Sears Watch Company first in Minneapolis and then in Chicago, where Montgomery Ward had been in the mail order business since 1872.

While the watches that Sears sold were attractive and low priced, some of them came back for repairs. He also found that he could cut his costs by buying movements and cases separately and assembling them. So on April 1, 1887, he advertised in the Chicago *Daily News* for a watchmaker who could furnish his own tools. The applicant who received the job was Alvah Curtis Roebuck. He had been born January 9, 1864, in Lafayette, Indiana. At twenty-three, he was earning $3.50 a week and his board running a watch-repair shop in a delicatessen store in Hammond, Indiana.

Thus began a famous alliance. Roebuck was a tall, unusually thin man, whose black suit and high collar caused some to think of him as a Methodist minister. He was gentle and unaggressive. Sears at the time was a handsome, mustached restless young man of ingratiating personality, boundless optimism and incredible energy. Of Sears, an admiring banker once said: "He could sell a breath of air!"

In addition to watches, the firm began to sell jewelry and diamonds, the last available on installment payments if desired. Every article was "warranted exactly as represented," some of the watch movements were guaranteed for six years, and anybody dissatisfied could have his money back. A small catalog was printed and the wares advertised in magazines. A branch was established in Toronto.

Sears had a momentary doubt early in 1889 as to the permanence of it all. At twenty-five, he sold the Chicago business for $72,000 to what became the Moore and Evans Company. For $2,950, he sold Roebuck and another employee a half interest in the Toronto branch and a little later for $5,190 the remaining half. Sears spoke vaguely of becoming an Iowa banker and, in his mother's name, did invest $60,000 in Iowa farm mortgages. But in a few months he returned restlessly to the mail-order jewelry business.

As he had agreed not to do business under the Sears name for three years, he reopened in Minneapolis under his middle name as The Warren Company. But in 1891, Sears invited Roebuck to rejoin him and on April 6, 1892, the business was incorporated as A. C. Roebuck, Inc. Of 750 shares, Roebuck held 250; Sears 499 and his sister, Eva Sears, 1. Sears was president; Roebuck secretary-treasurer, and the three made up the board of directors.

In addition to jewelry, silverware and pistols were sold. On September 16, 1893, the three-year ban on the name having expired, the firm became Sears, Roebuck and Company.

An enlarged catalog of 196 pages, nearly all of it written by Sears, appeared at this time. In addition to watches, jewelry and firearms, it offered sewing machines, furniture, dishes, wagons, harness, saddles, buggies, bicycles, shoes, baby carriages, musical instruments and a little clothing. Prices were guaranteed "below all others" for the same grade of goods and anybody unhappy with his purchase was assured his money back. For the next two years, the catalog was enlarged to 322 and 507 pages respectively, despite a serious business depression. To obtain better shipping facilities, the firm returned to Chicago.

Roebuck became worried by the chaotic nature of the business. There was little system in filling orders. Sears sometimes advertised items without adequate stocks. Net sales increased from $276,980 in 1892, to $388,464 in 1893 and $393,323 in 1894 but profits did not and the firm's debts grew. This was too much for Roebuck's stomach and nerves. He insisted on selling his interest. Sears paid him $25,000 and began to look for another partner.

Roebuck allowed the firm to use his name and continued for a time as the salaried head of the watch department. He then formed a company which made stereopticons, motion-picture projectors, and later typewriters for Sears, Roebuck and others. In 1925, he sold out for $150,000 and entered the real-estate business in Florida.

When this boom collapsed, he returned to Chicago and in 1933 again went to work for the company that bore his name.

He was employed in writing a history of the beginnings of the company in 1934 when a manager asked him to make an appearance at one of the company's retail stores. The event was a success, some customers traveled a hundred miles to shake his hand. The next year, he was made a Kentucky colonel. He continued happily to greet visitors in Chicago and to visit stores until his death at eighty-four in 1948. His contemporaries amassed great fortunes, but poor Roebuck outlived them all.

The partner that Sears sought, meanwhile, walked in the door in the person of Aaron E. Nusbaum. He had made $150,000 from an ice-cream concession at the Chicago World's Fair in 1893 and had invested some of it in a firm making pneumatic tube systems. He hoped to sell Sears one of these, and the firm eventually installed an elaborate one, but he first found himself talked into investing in the company. More important, Nusbaum brought in his brother-in-law, Julius Rosenwald, who had been supplying some of its men's clothing.

The son of a Jewish peddler from Westphalia who established a clothing business in Springfield, Illinois, Rosenwald learned the business from the bottom up. He served an apprenticeship with his uncles who ran Hammerslough Brothers in New York. In 1885, he and a cousin had started the manufacture of men's suits in Chicago, and in 1890 he married Nusbaum's sister Augusta. In 1891, their first son, Lessing, was born.

When the firm was reincorporated under Illinois law on August 23, 1894, with a capital of $150,000, Sears held 800 shares representing $80,000. He was still president. Nusbaum and Rosenwald each held 350 shares worth $35,000. Nusbaum was treasurer and general manager. Rosenwald was vice president. But Sears sold more of his shares to the two until on April 12, 1898, each of the three partners owned 500 of the firm's 1,500 shares.

With his partners expertly handling phases of administration that bored him, Sears had more time for the advertising and selling for which he had an extraordinary talent. The addition of rural free delivery to the mail service beginning in 1896 helped the firm. Sales soared from $800,000 in 1895 to $11,000,000, a volume greater than Montgomery Ward, for the first time, in 1900. But it was not a happy partnership. Sears and Nusbaum were different types. Sears, for example, issued suggestions rather than orders and believed in praising employees. Nusbaum was a fault finder and thought criticism more effective than praise with employees. He also refused to commit himself on important matters.

The crisis came in 1901. Sears demanded of Rosenwald either that he join him in buying out Nusbaum or that the two brothers-in-law buy the Sears shares. It was an agonizing decision for Rosenwald. He was bound to Nusbaum by many ties. His wife was Nusbaum's sister. It was Nusbaum who had brought him into the firm. On the other hand, the business had been built largely on Sears' understanding of the American farmer, his needs, his hopes, his suspicions. Neither of the other partners had this understanding.

Rosenwald sided with Sears. Nusbaum agreed to sell his third interest for a million dollars and at the last minute demanded a million and a quarter. Sears and Rosenwald were furious but agreed. By 1903, the full amount had been paid and Sears and Rosenwald were free to deal with other problems.

The country storekeepers and their friends opposed the growing mail-order business with a barrage of slander and calumny as bitter as any in the history of commerce. The goods were denounced as shoddy. They were said to arrive damaged and late. In the race-conscious South, it was rumored that both Sears and Roebuck were colored. When Rosenwald included Negroes in his philanthropy, the rumors began anew. Under the pressure of local merchants, many newspapers not only refused to sell advertising to the big mail-order houses but joined in the derision directed at their operations and their customers.

There were many printed gibes at "Monkey Ward," "Shears and Rawbuck" and "Rears and Soreback." One rural journal, for example, reported a local resident buying from Rears and Soreback a watch that was not only "half price but ran twice as fast" as any watch purchased from the local jeweler. Kansas editors like Ed Howe of the Atchison *Globe* suggested that mail-order buying was a greater sin than adultery and really treason to the community.

Where a storekeeper also was the postmaster, it took courage to accept the delivery of a Sears catalog, but money orders in the firm's name and later pick up the merchandise all under his scornful eye. A man ran for mayor in Warsaw, Iowa, on the pledge that he would discharge any municipal employee buying from a mail-order house. In some small towns, children were given ten cents each or admission to movie theaters for every mail-order catalog that they produced. The catalogs thus collected sometimes were burned publicly, the only authentic "book burnings" in American history.

The net effect may have been to advertise the mail-order houses, to move the curious who might not have thought of it surreptitiously to send off their orders. In the 1903 catalog, the firm offered to send goods without the name of the shipper appearing and promised to keep "every transaction with us strictly confidential." It countered the charges that its executives were colored by publishing their photographs.

There was also persuasive propaganda, both planned and fortuitous, in behalf of the company. Customers were invited to visit the firm when they came to Chicago. In the course of a tour, a visitor lost a $5 bill. Richard Sears gave him another. A village committee seeking funds to build a new church were told by a local merchant to write to "Rears and Soreback." They did and to the merchant's chagrin received $10.

An Ohio customer complained that the brake on a Sears bicycle ridden by his son had failed to work. In a pile-up into a tree, the boy's leg had been broken, a local doctor had set it improperly, and the boy seemed destined to become a cripple. Richard Sears had the boy brought to Chicago at company expense. A famous surgeon reset the leg and the boy recovered.

As a conductor helped a woman off a streetcar, his watch fell to the pavement and was smashed. Sears was aboard the car and asked him where he had bought the watch. He replied: "Sears, Roebuck." Sears unhesitatingly gave him another, announcing: "We guarantee our watches not to fall out of people's pockets and break." This story won good will for Sears, Roebuck throughout the country.

As the company's operations became more systematic and the goods of better quality under Rosenwald's influence, there were more satisfied customers. In 1905, these were encouraged to make customers of their neighbors. It was one of Dick Sears' most successful promotion ideas. In return for premiums in proportion to the resulting purchases, customers were asked to distribute personally catalogs to twenty-four friends most likely to buy. This was first tried in Iowa and produced such a flood of orders that the whole country later was "Iowaized."

That winter saw the firm move into a new $5,600,000 plant constructed for it by the Thompson-Starrett Company on a forty-acre site at Homan Avenue and Arthington Street on Chicago's West Side. Railroad sidings eliminated much of the trucking previously required. In the new quarters, order gradually came out of chaos. Unfilled orders no longer lay around for weeks.

A remarkable "schedule" system of handling orders was worked out by Otto C. Doering, operations superintendent, and others. The mail was weighed as it came from the post office in the morning and hourly during the day to give the departments an idea of the work ahead of them. The first automatic mail openers ever devised slit letters at the rate of twenty-seven thousand an hour. Girls removed remittances, checked catalog numbers, typed out order forms, stamped a scheduled shipping time, and shot them by pneumatic tube to stockrooms. From these, items moved by conveyor belts and gravity chutes to assembly points. There they were packed and dispatched by mail, express or freight. Some heavy items were sent direct from the factories where they were made. Though filling and shipping an order involved twenty-seven steps, orders for a single item began to be filled in one day and mixed orders, involving goods from several departments, moved out in two days. As there was a different-colored form for each day of the week, delayed orders were detected quickly. Henry Ford studied the Sears operation before setting up his famous assembly line for automobile making in Detroit.

All of this required money. At the suggestion of one of Rosenwald's boyhood friends, Henry Goldman of Goldman, Sachs and Company, the firm was incorporated in New York on June 16, 1906. Lehman Brothers and Goldman, Sachs and Company underwrote the sale of $10,000,000 in 7 per cent preferred stock and $30,000,000 in common stock of the new corporation in return for $500,000 cash and $5,000,000 in common stock. The preferred was marketed at $97.50 a share and the common at $50 a share.

Sears and Rosenwald received $4,500,000 each in cash in exchange for their previous stock. The latter advanced $90,000 to some senior employees to enable them to buy stock. The preferred, eventually all retired by 1924, was listed at once on the New York Stock Exchange and the common was traded there beginning in 1910.

Timing of the recapitalization was fortunate. The year 1906 was one of prosperity. Sales of Sears, Roebuck for the calendar year were more than $50,000,000, an increase of a third over the previous year. But in the fall of 1907, the Knickerbocker Trust Company closed its doors in New York and a national business panic followed. Sales of Sears, Roebuck for the fiscal year ending June 30, 1908, dropped nearly $10,000,000 to $40,843,866 and profits dropped 37 per cent to $2,034,796.

Dick Sears, who had been traveling in Europe with his ailing wife, returned and urged increased advertising and promotion as a means of meeting the crisis. In earlier years, he had spent 9 to 13 per cent of sales profitably on advertising. For the fall of 1908, he suggested going as high as 17 per cent. Rosenwald opposed increasing advertising or any other expense on the ground that customers simply didn't have the money to buy more goods. When two of Sears' own appointees, Louis Asher, the general manager, and J. Fletcher Skinner, the merchandise manager, reluctantly agreed with Rosenwald, the founder resigned as president on November 21, 1908.

He took no further part in the company's affairs though he was elected board chairman for a time and continued as a director until November 26, 1913. He had worked such long hours and at such a furious pace for so many years that his health, as well as that of his wife, was impaired. He spent his last years at Waukesha, Wisconsin, and died there in his fifty-first year on September 28, 1914, leaving an estate of $25,000,000 and an unmatched record as a "Barnum of merchandising."

Under Rosenwald, who became president and later chairman of the board, the company entered a period of calm growth. Prosperity returned. Farm income increased. The start of parcel post service in 1913 proved a great boon. A branch house opened at Dallas was continued and others opened at Seattle and Philadelphia. Dubious patent medicines and electric belts vanished from the catalog. This became bigger but less flamboyant. It began to include automobile and electrical items, including telephones. A thirteen-year-old boy named Charles Franklin Kettering bought one of the latter to dismantle and started his inventive career. For a time, a Sears automobile was made and sold but it was not a success.

More attention was paid to the development of reliable sources of supply. A testing laboratory was started to insure the quality of materials. One of the early laboratory men, Donald M. Nelson, later rose to executive vice precident of the company, and during World War II headed the War Production Board. While on a hunting trip, Dick Sears had noticed a $150 cream separator in a farm kitchen. He thought one could be made to sell at $50 and found a manufacturer able to do so. Thousands of separators were sold. This became the pattern for many other ventures. When what was desired could not be bought, Sears invested in manufacturing facilities. This happened in the case of farm implements, pianos, stoves and many other items.

Rosenwald bombarded his executives with maxims like these: "Treat people fairly and generously and their response will be fair and honest and generous. Sell honest merchandise for less money and many people will buy. Sell for less by buying for less. Sell for less by cutting the cost of sales. Make less profit on each individual item and increase your aggregate profit by selling more items. But maintain the quality." The formula worked. In addition to regular cash dividends of at least 7 per cent, Sears declared stock dividends of 33⅓ per cent in 1911, 50 per cent in 1915 and 25 per cent in 1917.

During World War I, Rosenwald became a $1-a-year man for the government and left Sears, Roebuck in the able hands of Vice President Albert Loeb, as *de facto* president. This gentle and able lawyer had been with the company since drawing the documents for Rosenwald's purchase of an interest in the firm and contributed greatly to its success. While serving as chairman of the committee for the purchase of noncombat supplies, Rosenwald drew no salary from the company and allowed it to sell articles to the government only at cost. But he took along some Sears, Roebuck catalogs when he made a tour of American camps and hospitals in France as a representative of Secretary of War Baker and the Young Men's Christian Association. Farmboys in hospitals found the catalogs a voice from home. As the only civilian in a party of generals in the course of this trip, Rosenwald once introduced himself as "General Merchandise."

The most dramatic service of Rosenwald to the firm came in 1921. In the fiscal year ending June 30, 1919, Sears sales reached a record $234,242,337 with profits of $18,890,125. A 40 per cent stock dividend was declared. The next year, sales rose to $245,373,-418 but profits dropped to $11,746,671. Prices of farm products began to tumble. Corn fell from $2.17 to 59 cents a bushel. Other prices followed and Sears was caught with millions of dollars' worth of merchandise bought at high prices. Many small mail-order houses failed. Lehman Brothers, Goldman, Sachs and Company and four Chicago banks loaned Sears, Roebuck $50,000,000 on notes but this was not enough. Despite a reduction in the number of employees from 21,652 in 1920 to 18,144 in 1921 and other economies, the firm operated in the latter year at a loss of $16,435,469.

On December 29, Rosenwald pledged $20,000,000 of his personal fortune, $4,000,000 in cash, to aid the company. He gave the firm fifty thousand shares of its stock and paid the cash as down payment toward purchasing its Chicago real estate for $16,000,000 if necessary. The cash enabled Sears to meet its bank debts. The stock rose eight points on the news. John D. Rockefeller, Jr., telegraphed his praise to Rosenwald and C. W. Barron, the publisher, wrote: "I do not know of anybody in the United States in the mercantile line who today is held in higher esteem or sounder regard than you and your great enterprise." Business improved, profits the next year were $5,435,168, the debts gradually were paid and common stock dividends were resumed in 1924.

Two important new executives joined Sears that year. To become president, Rosenwald brought in Charles M. Kittle, executive vice president of the Illinois Central Railroad. While working in Washington, Rosenwald had been impressed by the ability of rail executives to handle large affairs. Before settling on Kittle, Rosenwald had asked an employment agency to compile a list of the ten most outstanding railroad vice presidents under fifty years of age. At the same time, he added a new vice president, Robert Elkington Wood, a retired Army general with whom he had become acquainted in Washington but who lately had been working for Montgomery Ward. Both were elected on October 28, 1924.

Kittle's tenure was brief but important. He was without previous experience in merchandising but did not shrink from bold decisions. He supported the building of additional mail-order plants in Kansas City, Alanta, Memphis and Los Angeles. More important, he and General Wood in 1925 took the company into the retail-store business a few months after Montgomery Ward moved in that direction. In that year, Sears' sales of $258,318,000 came 95.5 per cent from mail order and 4.5 per cent from retail stores. The latter figure grew steadily and from 1931 onward accounted for more than half of the firm's volume. Kittle did not live to see this. He died January 2, 1928. In his short regime, the last preferred stock had been retired and four new mail-order plants and twenty-seven retail stores had been paid for out of earnings.

General Wood was then picked as president by Rosenwald, still the largest stockholder despite huge gifts to philanthropy. Two older vice presidents, who may have expected the post, then resigned. They were Otto C. Doering, operations, and Max Adler, merchandising. The latter became interested in planetariums and built the Adler Planetarium on the Chicago lakefront in 1930 at a cost of some $600,000. Adler was succeeded by Donald M. Nelson and Doering by the chairman's son, Lessing Rosenwald. In 1932 on the death of his father (who left $17,415,500 after giving away $63,-000,000) the latter became chairman and on his retirement in 1939 was succeeded by General Wood. Replacing him as president were Thomas J. Carney, who died in 1942; Arthur Barrows, who retired four years later, and Fowler B. McConnell, who thirty years earlier had started to work as a Sears stock boy. But until his own retirement in 1954 in favor of Vice Chairman Theodore V. Houser, a veteran merchandiser, it was General Wood who led Sears into new fields.

He brought to Sears a background of colorful military experience. Born in Kansas City, Missouri, on June 13, 1879, he studied engineering at West Point, where he was graduated in 1900. After service as lieutenant of cavalry during the Philippine insurrection, he worked for a decade on the Panama Canal, handling supplies both for the Canal and the Panama Railroad. He retired in 1915 but returned to active service during World War I, became a brigadier general under his old Panama chief, Major General George W.

Goethals who was quartermaster general, and earned the Distinguished Service Medal as well as British and French decorations.

In 1919, Wood became vice president in charge of merchandising at Montgomery Ward. One of the first to see clearly the changes in American life heralded by completion of the Lincoln Highway and the increasing number of automobiles, he urged the establishment of retail stores to which farmers could drive. He also interested himself in the sale of automobile tires and put Ward far ahead of Sears in these though the general volume of the latter was greater than Ward's. But differences with the president of Ward sent Wood to Sears in 1924. Four years later, incidentally, T. V. Houser, who was Wood's eventual successor as chairman, joined the Sears organization after spending ten years at Ward's. He entered merchandising after studying electrical engineering at Iowa State College.

When Wood joined Sears, the best direction for its development was by no means clear. Some believed that it should merge with Montgomery Ward and pointed out that millions would be saved in catalog printing. But the engineering firm of Sanderson and Porter, employed to determine the advisability of this, reported adversely. In 1929, Wood undertook to work out a merger with the J. C. Penney chain, concluding a letter with "our position is that we are ready, if you are, on any fair basis." But negotiations failed.

While a retail organization was built, new lines of merchandise were added and old ones improved. What Wood and Houser had done for automobile tires at Ward's, they also did at Sears. In 1925, the Sears product was inferior and Ward outsold Sears in tires, 2,000,000 to 700,000. Wood drew specifications for a greatly improved tire and contracted with Goodyear, the leading tire manufacturer, to make it. Cash prizes totaling $25,000 were offered in a contest to name the new tire. One of the 937,886 entrants, Hans Simonson, an art student of Bismarck, North Dakota, won $5,000 for the name "Allstate." In 1929, Sears sold 4,300,000 Allstate tires, 3,000,000 of them in retail stores, and was far ahead of Ward. Goodyear gave Sears such favorable terms that the contract drew a Federal Trade Commission complaint and was a factor in the passage of the Robinson-Patman Act. The complaint came to nothing but the law caused Goodyear to cancel the contract and Sears returned again to smaller tire makers.

The Allstate brand was applied also to automobile supplies and accessories and in 1931 to automobile insurance. Though far removed from its usual field, the last proved one of the most successful Sears ventures. Carl Odell, a Chicago insurance broker who handled some of General Wood's policies, suggested to him that the cost of automobile insurance could be cut by selling it by mail. With Odell as an officer, the Allstate Insurance Company was organized with $700,000 from Sears. Within a year, it was operating profitably. A companion firm, the Allstate Fire Insurance Company, was then added and likewise proved highly profitable. From 1934 to 1938, Sears also owned a life-insurance company. Though named Hercules this did not thrive and was sold. In addition to selling policies through the catalog and booths in Sears stores, the Allstate companies now have branches and agents throughout the country. In 1953, they collected $173,613,000 in premiums.

Another Sears success was the Coldspot electric refrigerator. The great electric manufacturers were not interested in making a refrigerator for Sears. Undaunted, Sears turned to an idle factory in Evansville, Indiana, which had made locomotive headlights. There General W. I. Westervelt, who joined Sears in 1929 as director of technical services, and others developed a trouble-free electric regrigerator which could be sold in a six-cubic-foot size at the price being asked by competitors for four-cubic-foot boxes. The final design was the work of Raymond Loewy, the well-known industrial designer. It soon became one of the most popular refrigerators.

Everything, of course, was not a success even though usually nothing was listed in the catalog until it had attained a degree of acceptance. A notable failure was a line of high-fashion gowns styled by Lady Duff-Gordon. She gave each a name and one was called "I'll Come Back to You." This was prophetic, for every dress sold of that style was returned to Sears. The sale of groceries, a catalog item for many years, was abandoned in 1929 in the face of A & P competition.

Then there was the *Encyclopedia Britannica*. Because Julius Rosenwald golfed with Horace Everett Hooper, one of the proprietors who brought the venerable reference work to America, Sears first marketed a "handy volume" edition and then in 1920 bought the enterprise. When Sears needed money after the 1921 depression, it was sold back to Hooper with a loss to Sears of $1,848,000. But in 1928, Sears purchased control of the *Britannica* and attempted to make a success of it until 1943 when it was given to the University of Chicago. The *Britannica* was too costly and sophisticated for Sears' customers. Five years later it began to publish a simpler and less expensive work, the *American People's Encyclopedia*. It also launched the Sears Readers Club which offers best-selling volumes in special low-cost editions.

The firm committed some egregious errors in establishing its retail stores but mistakes were corrected rapidly. While as many as three new stores a week were opened at the height of the expansion, most were well located at the edge of cities where real estate was less costly and easily accessible. At first, sites were purchased but later, to free capital for further expansion, most were sold to insurance companies or institutions and leased back under long and favorable terms. With their excellent lines of hard goods, the Sears stores attracted men from the first, and as the soft goods line was made more attractive and fashionable, they lured the entire family. Retail stores presented problems of display, merchandise selection, store layout and personnel that did not exist in mail order but with the aid of outside experts, like Alvin E. Dodd, these were gradually solved.

Retail-store managers at first reported to branch mail-order plant managers who often had little understanding of the problems involved. A committee of Sears executives, composed of T. V. Houser, J. M. Barker and E. J. Pollock, and an outside firm of consultants in 1930, worked out a more workable form of organization. While preserving central buying and fiscal authority in Chicago, this called for both retail and mail-order plants to report to territorial executives. The depression delayed adoption of this but under Vice President Barker, formerly an assistant professor of civil engineering at Massachusetts Institute of Technology, it eventually was carried out. A store planning and display department headed by Les Janes was set up in 1932. Every fixture was especially designed for a new windowless air-conditioned Englewood store opened in Chicago two years later. A Pico Boulevard store in Los Angeles, featuring rooftop parking, later attracted wide attention in architectural circles.

The stores proved so profitable and inventories were so well controlled that Sears came through the depression thirties, when general business was far worse than in 1921, with a loss only in the year 1932 when the company was in the red to the tune of $2,543,-641. Salaries were cut 20 per cent. The next year there was a profit of $11,249,295 on mail-order sales of $120,334,000 and retail business of $167,860,000. Totals for both rose steadily, with the exception of 1938, but the retail grew at a greater rate until the present time when the ratio is approximately 70 per cent retail and 30 per cent mail order.

World War II, which saw many Sears factories converted to war work and some of its hard goods available on priorities, slowed Sears growth only a little. Sales soared past the billion-dollar mark in 1946 and two billions in 1948. By then, Sears had eight thousand suppliers turning out goods to its specifications and one thousand of them had been doing so for more than twenty years. The company owned 22 factories outright and had financial interests in companies operating 109 more plants.

With the 1942 opening of a retail store in Havana, Sears started a retail expansion into Latin America. As a young army officer in the Canal Zone, General Wood had invested profitably in a Panama City hardware store back in 1905 and realized the possibilities. From the Dallas branch, Elmer Scott had dispatched a carload of sewing machines to Mexico back in 1909 but outbreak of the Madero Revolution prevented anything further at that time.

World War II interrupted the expansion program and it was not until 1947 that a big store was opened in Mexico City and others have again followed in Guadalajara, Monterrey, Tampico, San Luis Potosí, Mérida and Puebla. Stores were opened two years later in São Paulo and Rio de Janeiro, Brazil. A crowd of 120,000 persons, including Papal Nuncio Carlo Chiarlo, who blessed the establishment, attended the opening of the latter. The first of six stores in Venezuela was opened in Caracas in 1950. Four more units followed in Colombia and one in Lima, Peru.

All Latin American stores of the company are staffed almost entirely with nationals of the country and the bulk of their merchandise is manufactured locally to specifications from Chicago. Local customs are respected to the extend of closing some units from 2 to 4 P.M. for the traditional afternoon siesta. Sears is the largest advertiser in Mexico.

Sears moved into Canada in 1952 as a partner of the eighty-year-old Robert Simpson Company, Ltd., the second largest retailer in Canada. Each invested $20,000,000 in a new company, Simpsons-Sears Limited, formed to sell by mail in Canada and through retail stores to be located at least twenty-five miles distant from the five big Simpson department stores. The new firm paid $48,000,000 for the existing Simpson mail-order business and facilities. The first Simpsons-Sears catalog, a book of 556 pages, appeared in 1953. New stores were built at Ottawa, Vancouver, Hamilton, Moose Jaw and elsewhere.

Without counting Simpsons-Sears establishments, Sears in 1954 had 694 retail stores, 11 mail-order plants, 570 catalog sales offices and 43 telephone sales offices. Of the stores, 94 in 68 cities were of the "A" type, a Sears designation for a complete department store with at least 100,000 square feet of selling space. Next are "B-1" stores, slightly smaller but carrying most lines; "B-2" selling furniture, appliances and hard lines; "B-3" selling hardware and electric appliances; and "C" stores with special emphasis on farm equipment and a catalog sales department. There are more than 600 "B" and "C" stores.

While Sears stores receive an increasing amount of the merchandise from nearby sources, store managers can buy only from a Chicago-approved list of items. On the other hand, no buyer can require a Sears manager to stock anything. Sears stores in Florida will not be asked to sell snow shovels, something that is supposed to have happened in the early days. Bonuses, determined by success, are an important part of the earnings of store managers. They can adjust prices to meet local competition. They have considerable freedom in hiring and advertising. Some, for example, employ the Welcome Wagon service to invite newcomers to the community to the store. Credit usually is limited to installment contracts; 6,759,-000 of these accounted for 38 per cent of Sears' 1953 business. But in Tulsa, Shreveport and New Orleans, where Sears took over stores which did so, thirty-day charge accounts are offered.

Public relations, advertising and employee relations became vital as the business grew gargantuan. Though not the primary target of the anti-chain store and fair-trade-law agitation of the thirties, Sears operations were affected by both. The fair-trade measures caused the company to emphasize its own brands even more. Except for a few popular and well-advertised items, such as General Electric small appliances and Johnson & Johnson bandages, all fair-trade items were eliminated from the Sears catalog. The anti-chain-store pressure impelled the company to systematize its public-relations activities in a department headed by Edward J. Condon, later a vice president, and to identify itself more strongly with the communities in which it operated.

"Business must account for its stewardship not only on the balance sheet," said General Wood, "but also in matters of social responsibility." Sears' first community activities naturally were in agriculture. As early as 1912, Julius Rosenwald gave $1,000 to each of the first hundred counties to employ a professional farm advisor. Learning that many of its farmer customers were part-time trappers who had trouble marketing their furs, Sears in 1924 started a raw marketing service without profit to the firm. Trappers sent in their furs and received money or merchandise as they wished. More than seven million copies of *Tips to Trappers,* a booklet by "Johnny Muskrat," were distributed. Annual fur shows with cash prizes for the best lot of pelts were started in 1929. Much of the $50,000,000 paid for furs through this service has come back to Sears in payment for traps and other catalog items.

A great variety of nonprofit activities are handled by The Sears Roebuck Foundation, first formed in 1923 and rechartered in 1941. The initial objective was to help the farmer "farm better, sell better, and live better." Early projects showed farmers how to do a better job of marketing their products and, in some cases, Sears provided market facilities. In recent years, the foundation has worked largely with institutions and organizations. Motion pictures produced by the foundation, for example, included *Under the 4-H Flag,* about the 4-H Clubs; *The Green Hand,* about the Future Farmers of America; *A Stitch in Time,* about safety on the farm and made in co-operation with the National Safety Council and Kansas State College.

Projects have included a great "cow-hog-hen" program, prizes for the best seed corn, cotton and home decoration, clubhouses for youth groups, a lending library boat in Alaska. Efforts to improve and diversify agriculture have involved turkey raising in Texas, grape growing in the Ozarks, forest conservation in Mississippi, strawberry growing in Kentucky, rodent control and dairy projects throughout the nation. College scholarships have been given farm boys and girls by the foundation since 1936. Boys are selected on the basis of interest in agriculture, leadership, grades and financial need. Girls are aided through scholarships in home-economics courses. About 900 agricultural and 150 home economics scholarships are given each year.

An annual Community Service Contest, administered by the National Grange, has been sponsored since 1948. Top award of $15,-000 is given by the foundation to the local chapter which has done the most to improve its community. This has encouraged the Grange members to work on soil improvement, park development, the rehabilitation of churches, schools, hospitals and similar projects. A national 4-H Club home improvement contest also is sponsored. A Town and Country Church Development program was launched in 1952. This provides cash awards in recognition of progress by churches in communities of less than four thousand in Southern states. It embraces all faiths and aims "Toward a Better Church; Toward a Better Community; and Toward a Better World."

Newspaper advertising, which amounted to but $480,000 in 1925, was increased greatly. By 1945, this had grown to $11,130,000. In 1953, it reached $36,340,500. This bought 251,646,500 lines of space in 1,020 daily and weekly newspapers. In addition, Sears spent $8,318,000 for other media. In the space, often with colored ink, Sears advertised not only its retail store offerings but often its purchasing in the locality. A page in the Dallas *Morning News,* for example, pointed out Sears had four thousand employees in Dallas, and Sears merchandise sources included more than one hundred Texas factories in thirty cities and towns of the state. Space in the Rochester *Times-Union* explained Sears spends $11,000,000 a year for "fine merchandise produced in the Rochester area by Rochester craftsmen" and listed twenty-four local suppliers.

The ubiquitous catalog, which is really two large and five small catalogs a year, now appears in eleven regional editions specially edited to appeal to sectional interests. Covers may show activity or scenery peculiar to the section. Contents as well as the covers are different. Some prices are different because of freight rates. Because of differences in climate, some items given many pages in one edition may be barely mentioned or omitted entirely in another. Items like diamonds and corsets appear in all, but heavy woolen union suits and maple-syrup equipment are found only in the Northern editions and cotton-picking costumes are shown only in the Southern versions. Women in the South buy frillier underthings and prefer nightgowns to the pajamas favored by their northern sisters, but in the main, movies, magazines and television have made American tastes the same in all parts of the country.

Biggest of the catalogs are the two general catalogs issued for the spring and fall seasons. Each contains about thirteen hundred pages, weighs around five pounds, and lists over 100,000 items. A poll of customers found that the most popular cover ever to grace the big book was a landscape by George Inness. For the 1934 edition, Edgar A. Guest, the famous Detroit poet, wrote a poem especially for the company titled "The Catalog." There also are two midseason catalogs of about four hundred pages each, supplements to the general catalog in spring and fall, two "sale books" approximately the same size as the supplements, and a Christmas gift book of around five hundred pages which appears in October. The catalogs cost from 40 cents to $1.40 each and 4,000,000 to 7,500,000 copies of each are distributed.

The expense of printing and mailing some 50,000,000 catalogs a year is so great that much thought has been given to cutting their cost and increasing their attractiveness. In the early days, customers were asked to pay postage on the catalog and it was even sold briefly at $1. Free but judicious distribution proved the most effective. The firm once toyed with the idea of letting noncompeting outsiders share costs. In 1931, Chevrolet and the Curtis Publishing Company were allowed to buy catalog pages at $23,000 each in a short-lived experiment. From 1903 to 1923, Sears did its own catalog printing. It then found an outside plant more economical. In recent years, R. R. Donnelley and Sons and the W. F. Hall Printing Company have done the printing and binding under conditions of great secrecy with prices set into type only at the last minute.

Color printing, lightweight but improved paper and high-quality photography have improved the attractiveness of the catalog. From modeling for its pages, beauties like Joan Caulfield, Norma Shearer,

Susan Hayward, Gloria Swanson, Elyse Knox and Anita Louise moved to Hollywood. Some seven hundred persons, mostly in Chicago and New York, produce the catalog, art and copy. This must comply with the frequently revised two-hundred-page *Advertising Guide* and is a model of accuracy, simplicity, taste and forceful salesmanship in print. Exaggerated claims and unrestrained superlatives are forbidden. "Sweat" is preferred to "perspiration." For hard work, the word is "pants." For dress, it is "trousers." The catalog itself explains: "Our descriptions are simple, honest, straightforward statements of facts." There is always the line: "Satisfaction Guaranteed or Your Money Back." When Julian Lewis Watkins, an authority on the subject, in 1949 chose "The 100 Greatest Advertisements," one was the Sears, Roebuck Catalog.

The catalog moves customers to send orders by the thousands, as many as 100,000 a day to the Chicago mail-order plant before Christmas. Each one hundred pounds of mail contains approximately thirty-five hundred orders for about $12 each, or $42,000 in business for each one hundred pounds of mail. Most letters contain only order blanks but some are chatty missives informing the firm of the customer's health and activities, asking for advice on all sorts of problems, or even ordering a mate. There is a legend that at least one such order was filled satisfactorily. A plea from a Montana rancher fell into the hands of a spirited girl clerk who was weary of Chicago. They were married and continued to buy from Sears, Roebuck. The catalog of "Shears Robust and Company" figured pleasantly in the hit musical show *Finian's Rainbow*.

Good employee relations began with Richard Sears, the founder. He was chary of using first names but was as considerate of his associates as of his customers. He made suggestions rather than issued orders. He did not summon men to his office but went to their desks. His approach was "What do you think?" or "Will you?" and he was quick to praise good work. The company began to publish an employee house organ, *The Skylight*, in 1901.

Elmer Scott, who rose from Sears' office boy to general manager, eliminated night and Sunday work, common in the early days, and began systematic employee training around 1904. Scott opened and managed the Dallas branch until 1913. After differences with Rosenwald, he then resigned and devoted the remainder of his long life to welfare work, adult education and civic cultural activities. He was one of Dallas' most beloved citizens at his death there in 1954.

Rosenwald also was concerned with employee welfare. Some of his activity was on the negative side. Of the sixty-two pages in a manual for new employees, twenty-eight were taken up with the evils of drink, the futility of smoking, the desirability of morality, diligence and thrift. He chased saloons from the neighborhood and the nearest put up a sign "first chance."

But The Savings and Profit Sharing Pension Fund of Sears, Roebuck and Co. Employes, one of the company's greatest distinctions, was set up by Rosenwald on July 16, 1916. A stockholder, Mrs. Joseph T. Bowen, had suggested something of the sort to him in a letter a year earlier and he had been impressed by a plan started by the Harris Trust and Savings Bank of Chicago. It has since grown to be the largest fund of the sort not only in retailing but in all industry. Changes in it through the years have only increased benefits for the employees.

To this fund, Sears employees of a year or more can contribute 5 per cent of their annual salary but no more than $500. Each fiscal year the company contributes to the fund a fixed percentage of its net profits before taxes. This money is split among the employee members of the fund. For employees of less than five years' service, the company deposits an equal amount from net income if the year is normally prosperous. For those of five to ten years' service (but excluding those over fifty years of age with more than fifteen years' service), the firm trebles the amount. Finally, for those who have fifteen years or more service and are over fifty years of age, the company quadruples their deposit.

The market value of the fund by 1954 was $501,391,000 and at the start of the year 120,558 employees were members. While enough government bonds are purchased to cover the employee contribution, most of the fund is invested in Sears stock. The block controlled by the fund, currently 26 per cent of the outstanding shares, is the largest holding.

Withdrawals can be made at any time for grave emergencies and senior employees are encouraged to invest in annuities. An employee, upon completing five years of service, who leaves the company for any reason receives his share of the fund. In 1954, the average value of the holdings of fifteen-year employees more than fifty years old in the fund was $32,047 per depositor. Many oldsters pile up sizable amounts. A woman clerk who never earned more than $3,900 a year and who in thirty-five years contributed only $3,400 to the fund, for example, retired with $117,580 in cash and securities. A man who had deposited $7,900 received $208,000.

From inception of the fund until the end of 1953, the company contributed $278,469,000. Employees deposited $168,825,000 and withdrew $305,998,000. So that employees prevented by the $500 limitation from depositing the full 5 per cent of their salaries may receive additional benefits upon retirement, the company in 1944 set up a supplemental contributory retirement plan for employees earning more than $10,000. In the next decade the company contributed $20,500,000 to this supplementary plan.

Meanwhile, in 1931 a central personnel department was established in Chicago and it was decreed that no employee of five years standing could be fired without its approval. Under Clarence B. Caldwell, a former store manager who rose to vice president in charge of personnel, systematic training programs, involving manuals, films and job rotation, were evolved. Promising college graduates, sometimes six hundred a year, began to be hired systematically. A monthly picture house organ, the *News-Graphic,* was started in 1936 for employees. A group hospitalization plan was added.

Beginning in 1939, an independent research organization was employed to ask employees, in anonymous questionnaires and interviews on company time, to express frankly their feelings about Sears, their job, their boss, their working conditions, their pay, and their fellow employees. These attitude surveys, covering more than 800 units and 150,000 employees, revealed many points of unsuspected irritation but 95 per cent of the employees said they would rather work for Sears than any other company.

Psychological tests help Sears select and develop executives. With the aid of the University of Chicago experts and others, a variety of tests were given executives and prospective executives beginning in 1942. As a result, the "standard executive battery," a commercially available test designed to reveal mental ability, personality, sense of values and vocational interests, was given more than 18 thousand candidates for executive positions. "Though no man has ever been promoted or assigned on the basis of tests alone," explains Vice President Caldwall, "the tests have served to affirm or deny opinions previously arrived at and to insure that the important decisions regarding executive placement were made objectively—on the basis of scientific facts."

With an expanding organization and an almost mandatory rule that those earning $10,000 must retire at sixty-three, promotions are frequent at Sears. Regular estimates are made of future requirements. For senior assignments, these are made as much as five years in advance. In 1953, there were 916 promotions into executive positions and 1,146 who were already executives advanced to higher jobs. The retirement of one senior supervisor resulted in the promotion of fourteen persons.

"Which is more important," asks Chairman Houser, "to continue longer with one man, no matter how well qualified, or to let fourteen others move upward and spread the growing reputation and the attraction to Sears for young people?"

XV. Lane Bryant

Maternity and Special Size Fashion Pioneer

"MATERNITY DRESS, size 32, Amerika," wrote a young woman in Poland on an envelope. With only this address, her letter reached New York and was delivered promptly as the writer intended to the Lane Bryant store on Fifth Avenue at Fortieth Street, opposite the stone lions of the Public Library.

Most of the company's business is now something else but Lane Bryant is such a synonym for maternity that the post office could hardly have done otherwise. No other company in the world does as much business in layettes and maternity wear or does it so widely.

The story of the enterprise starts with the birth of an indomitable girl named Lena Himmelstein in Lithuania, then part of Czarist Russia, in 1879. Her mother died ten days after her birth. As a child in the home of her grandparents, she witnessed cruel Russian persecutions. At sixteen, she gladly accepted the invitation of some distant relatives to accompany them via steerage to America.

They delayed telling her that they were bringing her along as a prospective bride for their son. When she met the young man for the first time in New York, Lena wept. Rather than marry somebody she did not love, she joined her sister Anna, who had preceded her, and went to work at $1 a week in a "sweat shop."

This was in Lispenard Street where negligee and lingerie manufacturing was just beginning. "We made beautiful lingerie for fast women," the immigrant girl later recalled. Within four years, she learned to speak English, learned machine sewing, and advanced to the then high wage of $15 a week.

She gave this up to marry a man she did love. He was David Bryant, a young Brooklyn jeweler. Evenings she helped him in his store and they made brave plans for the future. But soon after their son Raphael was born on February 3, 1900, the husband became ill. Six months later he was dead of tuberculosis.

As the expenses of his illness wiped out the store, his twenty-year-old widow was left with only a pair of earrings set with small diamonds, his wedding gift, with which to face the future. She pawned the diamond earrings for enough money to make a down payment on a Singer sewing machine and turned again to sewing as the only possibility of keeping her son with her and at the same time earning a living.

In a small apartment on West 112th Street, which she shared with her sister Anna, the young widow set up working quarters. Her modest venture went unnoticed in the news of the day. The 3,437,-202 New Yorkers who had just been enumerated in the 1900 census were engrossed with the excavation of the city's first subway. Mayor R. A. Van Wyck and other charitable folk extended their sympathies to the victims of the Galveston flood and the sufferers of a great fire in Hoboken. America's first automobile show was held in the old Madison Square Garden. The Floradora Sextette sang "Tell Me, Pretty Maiden" to enraptured audiences at the old Casino.

It was the bicycle and shirtwaist era. The feminine ideal was the hippy and busty Gibson girl drawn by Charles Dana Gibson for best-selling novels and magazines. Her waist was so tightly corseted that bosom and hips were accented. To achieve the popular hourglass figure many women wore bustles.

The Gibson girl could buy blouses and skirts in stores of the day but her dresses had to be made for her. If she were wealthy, they were made in Paris and imported. If she were in modest circumstances, she made them herself. If she were in between, she had her clothes made by seamstresses working either in her home or theirs.

In addition to the ubiquitous blouses and skirts, three dresses and a suit composed the average woman's wardrobe. These were carefully repaired and were worn for years. Collars came to the chin and hems of dresses literally swept the ground. Shoes and stockings were concealed and fewer than one American woman in a thousand possessed a pair of silk stockings. Big stores principally sold yard goods which dressmakers, chosen by customer or store, made into clothing.

Mrs. Bryant's skill and instinctive love for fine things attracted an increasing number of customers. Women came in carriages for her negligees and tea gowns made from delicate laces and fine silks. But there were difficult days. She delivered the finished articles herself and sometimes had to spend hours waiting for customers to pay. The diamond earrings had to be pawned more than once for the purchase of materials and supplies. She worked with her young son on her knee. One day while her attention was distracted he pushed his finger beneath the swiftly moving machine needle. For a time it was feared that the finger might have to be amputated.

In 1904, the year that New York opened its first subway, young Mrs. Bryant moved to 1489 Fifth Avenue. This was between 119th and 120th Streets and only a short walk from Mount Morris Park, where there was a playground for her son. For $12.50 a month, the household of three rented the first floor of a new six-story building. They lived in the rear and used the front room as a shop, hanging garments from the gas fixtures.

Enough trousseau finery was made to cause the place to be known as a bridal shop. An early sign misspelled it "bridle." But Mrs. Bryant soon earned more than a neighborhood reputation for fine work of all kinds, especially for women of unusual proportions. She estimated lengths by eye, ignored tape measures and patterns, kept few records but turned out better-fitting garments than many of her customers had previously worn. More carriages began to arrive at the door and the earrings made fewer trips to the pawnshop.

Into the modest shop one day walked an attractive young woman for whom Mrs. Bryant had previously done some sewing. After exchanging greetings, the customer announced: "I am going to have a baby, Mrs. Bryant. What shall I do?"

For an instant the young widow thought that her visitor was asking medical advice but this was not the case.

"You make all kinds of things," continued the visitor; "can't you make me something that will be both pretty and practical and in which I can entertain at home?"

While the Empress Eugénie had been recorded as having worn a maternity dress in Europe, such a garment was unknown in New

York in 1904, but Mrs. Bryant met the challenge. She created a comfortable and attractively concealing tea gown by the simple device of an elastic band attaching an accordion pleated skirt to a bodice. The result was the famous No. 5 maternity gown, so called because it was given this number when the business grew large enough for a price list.

The first purchaser was grateful and enthusiastic. She was happy to pay $18 for the gown and praised it continually to her friends. She volubly told them about the ingenious little widow who made it. More expectant mothers ordered the tea gowns.

Word of Mrs. Bryant's talent and popularity reached the big downtown stores and two of them offered her jobs. But she preferred independence and the opportunity to rear her son. Her sister had married, and her new brother-in-law offered to lend the young widow $300 with which to open a bank account and to use as working capital for the purchase of fabrics.

Formalities required that Mrs. Bryant appear in the ornate quarters of the old Oriental Bank at 182 Broadway. She was so unaccustomed to the grandeur of the surroundings and the awe of having so much money that she filled out the deposit slip not as Lena Bryant, but as *Lane* Bryant.

Thus was born Lane Bryant. The young widow was at first too timid to rectify the mistake and later grew to like the euphonious name. She used it when she opened a new shop in a loft at 19 West Thirty-eighth Street, a few yards off Fifth Avenue. There she employed a dozen girls and began to serve a more numerous clientele.

Mrs. Bryant, however, was still not entirely free from financial worries. She increased her balance in the Oriental Bank to $400 just in time to see the institution close its doors in the financial panic of 1907. She eventually recovered the money. In the meantime the diamond earrings again served as collateral. But despite the unbusinesslike methods, the little business grew.

Romance flowered again for Mrs. Lane Bryant soon after her move to Thirty-eighth Street. Through mutual friends, the twenty-seven-year-old dress creator had met a handsome young engineer named Albert Malsin. He had also been born in Lithuania and they had many common interests. After being graduated as a mechanical engineer by the Polytechnic Institute at Gothen, Anhalt, Germany,

Malsin immigrated to America and became associated with an engineering firm that constructed amusement parks all over the world.

Albert Malsin and Mrs. Bryant were married in 1909 and he adopted her young son, who henceforth was known as Raphael Malsin. For a time, the engineer continued his work. Mrs. Malsin, however, soon began to wear her own maternity clothes. Three children, a daughter and two sons, were born to the couple within the next four years.

At first of necessity, and later because he saw great possibilities, Malsin took an increasing role in his wife's unique enterprise. While she continued to design the dresses, he took charge of the business and began systematically to develop and expand it. Where his wife had worked without patterns and measurements, he instituted engineering exactness. Where she had set prices at sometimes the first figure that came into her head, he installed modern cost accounting.

To handle the financial end of the Lane Bryant business, which had grown to more than $50,000 annually, Malsin in 1910 enlisted the services of an astute friend of the family, Harry Liverman. For his task, Liverman had a remarkable background. As a youth he had sailed from England to Australia to seek his fortune in the gold mines. There he took part in civic affairs and served as both city counselor and acting mayor of Leonora, Western Australia. En route there after a vacation in England, he stopped off in New York and decided to remain. His varied business experience and calm judgment proved invaluable to the Malsins.

One day Malsin and Liverman went walking and chanced to pass Crocker's, a store devoted entirely to the sale of mourning goods. This was possible because of the then rigid observance of mourning and a death rate that would now be considered high.

"This is a country of specialization," said Malsin, calling Liverman's attention to the mourning-goods store. Liverman agreed. They decided that Lane Bryant should specialize; that the company should choose certain fields of retailing and concentrate on them. The obvious first choice was maternity wear to which the business already owed most of what success it possessed. Bridal finery was dropped.

The firm took the revolutionary step of designing maternity dresses for street wear. Up until this time expectant mothers had nothing appropriate to wear outside of their homes and few ventured abroad in the daylight.

At the same time the earlier maternity gowns and dresses for indoor wear were varied and improved in construction. In addition to the original elastic, drawstrings, snaps, hooks, buttons and other devices were employed to adjust the garments to the changing figures of the wearers.

To obtain maternity dresses in quantity, Lane Bryant abandoned on-the-premises manufacturing and began to creat a unique phase of New York's remarkable women's clothing industry. By mechanically cutting dozens of identical dresses at once and employing high-speed sewing methods, this industry began to produce dresses at lower costs than ever before. By 1910, it was large enough to support a newspaper and *Women's Wear Daily* was founded. Since then the manufacture of women's clothing has become the biggest industry of the biggest city and its products have made American women the best-dressed women in the world.

At a time when any kind of ready-to-wear dress was a novelty, the manufacture of maternity dresses presented more problems than the average contractor cared to face. More material and more work were required for a maternity dress than for an ordinary dress. Some also believed the maternity business would never be great.

Lane Bryant overcame these objections by supplying designs, patterns, materials and, in practically all cases, actually financing the contractors. Only then did the unique maternity wear begin to flow from the factory to the store. Once educated to the merits of the dresses, the suppliers became interested and helped the store to work out still more improvements.

One stumbling block remained. This was the refusal of newspapers, in keeping with the prudery that then existed, to accept advertisements for any kind of maternity clothing.

It was not until a memorable day in 1911 that the New York *Herald,* a forerunner of the present *Herald Tribune,* accepted a Lane Bryant advertisement for maternity dresses. The forthright copy read:

Maternity wardrobes that do not attract attention. It is no longer the fashion nor the practice for expectant mothers to stay in seclusion. Doctors, nurses and psychologists agree that at this time a woman should think and live as normally as possible. To do this, she must go about among other people, she must look like other people.

Lane Bryant has originated maternity apparel in which the expectant mother may feel as other women feel because she looks as other women look.

Response to the advertisement was astonishing. More customers appeared than ever before. Malsin, Liverman and a boy working in receiving and packing had to help the two saleswomen wait on the eager throngs. By closing time, the store's entire stock of maternity dresses for street wear had been sold for $2,800. Mrs. Malsin, who was at home with her children, could hardly believe the figures when they were relayed to her.

Lane Bryant's fame for maternity wear and also its regular advertising date from this day. The business doubled within a year and was moved to still larger quarters in the same block at 25 West Thirty-eighth Street.

As expectant mothers were still shy and embarrassed customers, the side-street location was actually an advantage to the store. Some sensitive women even took pains to leave their carriages a block away and to hold veils over their faces as they entered the premises. Mail-order customers often insisted that their maternity dresses be sent in plain wrappings, and some still do. "Honest, mister, it's for my sister," explained a Miss Jane Smith in a letter.

Mail business even in 1910 was large enough for publication of price lists illustrated by simple line drawings. A 1911–1912 winter catalog of thirty-two pages was the first bound publication distributed.

Though other garments were made, maternity wear accounted for the bulk of the business and a 1916 advertisement announced: "Society should not be abandoned by the mother-to-be. She needs the stimulus of the Opera, the Theatre, and other social functions."

The year 1916, which saw a woman elected to Congress for the first time, also saw the business incorporated as Lane Bryant, Inc. Employees of the store subscribed to 25 per cent of the capital stock. The company expanded its advertising from New York newspapers to *Vogue, Woman's Home Companion* and the *Ladies' Home Journal.*

World War I, like other wars, increased the birth rate. Young men marching the "long, long trail" of a popular song of the day and their wives wanted heirs. Lane Bryant's maternity business soared and the company's sales passed $1,000,000 for the first time in 1917.

As a natural expansion of maternity activity, Lane Bryant early developed and has continued a large business in simple and elaborate layettes. When twins or triplets arrive, the additional layettes are free.

Maternity dresses for street wear were no sooner established than restless Albert Malsin, who always kept a T-square and a drawing board on his desk, turned his engineering talents to another specialty. Maternity clothing was a fine thing but its possibilities were limited. Not all women became mothers and those who did so required maternity clothes only at a few intervals in a comparatively brief period of their lives.

Engineer Malsin began to study women's figures and found, as Shakespeare had observed four centuries earlier, that they came in an infinite variety. He began to chart feminine curves with the same thoroughness with which he earlier had planned the curves of scenic railways in amusement parks all over the world.

As a research tool, he invented a flexible yardstick for figure measurement. This device was of soft metal alloy which could be bent and twisted by slight pressure to conform precisely to the curves and angles of the human body. Springs held the metal in place while a tracing or other record was made. Release of the springs straightened the metal.

With this yardstick, Malsin measured the figures of 4,500 Lane Bryant customers. In addition, he obtained from a large insurance company the body measurements of more than 200,000 women policy holders. He also studied population figures as to sex and age.

Malsin found that nearly 40 per cent of all women were larger in some or all of their dimensions than the perfect thirty-six figure idealized by designers and artists. They were entirely healthy, normal and attractive women. Nature and inheritance simply had chanced to endow them with more flesh than their slenderer sisters.

Here were both the challenge and the opportunity that Malsin was seeking. Stouts were stout all of their lives and many became stouter as they became older. At the time, there was no ready-made clothing for women of larger sizes and most made-to-order clothing actually seemed to accent the size of the wearers. Some had even written letters to Lane Bryant begging that clothing be designed for them.

"Won't some ingenious man please take pity on us poor stout women?" read a typical appeal. "It seems as if some way should be found for us to walk into a store and buy comfortable and also stylish clothes as easily as our slimmer sisters do."

Malsin recognized the need and Mrs. Malsin began to design clothing especially for women requiring larger sizes. Dresses began to be made in a wide range of sizes to meet the needs of the three general types of stoutness that Malsin's research charted. These were the stout over-all type, the full-busted but normal-hipped type, and the flat-busted but large-hipped type.

As a crowning psychological stroke, a size system was adopted which allowed a woman who requires a 42 elsewhere to fit comfortably into a Lane Bryant 40. More important, colors and lines were chosen which minimized the wearer's silhouette. Lane Bryant's designs for larger women borrowed both from the "height, slenderness and airy grace" of Gothic cathedrals and the camouflage innovations of World War I.

Camouflage is not the exclusive property of war [explained a company catalog], but has been used for years in architecture, in landscape gardening, in house furnishings and in the making of clothes. In camouflaging ships, for example, the idea was not to make the ships invisible, as many supposed, but to deceive the eye of the submarine observers as to the ship's size, its course and its speed.

Likewise, broad eaves are used to make a narrow house appear wider, and a striped wallpaper is used to make a ceiling seem higher. By the same principle, if correctly applied to the designing of one's clothes, the wearer may be made to appear smaller or larger, taller or shorter, as may be desired. Lane Bryant stout garments are not merely large sizes; instead, they are especially made with lines that create the optical illusion of slenderness.

So novel was the idea of styles for fuller figures when introduced by Lane Bryant that both manufacturers and customers were at first incredulous. The store had to finance its initial orders. Some of the customers thought that "stretched" maternity garments were being offered. Many 1916 advertisements headed "Appearing Stout Is Merely a Matter of Clothes" were required to convince shoppers that a distinct new line was being created.

Half sizes were first developed to eliminate excessive alterations for the average woman—this means the average American woman who is actually five feet five or under. The half sizes are distinguished by the fact that the shoulders are cut narrower, waistlines are shorter, hips fuller, and skirts shorter. The sleeves are fuller through the upper arm. They are generally young styles and close in fashion and styling to regular misses-size dresses.

In addition to negligees and dresses, Lane Bryant gradually added extra sizes in foundation garments, suits, blouses, sweaters, skirts, shoes, hosiery, both cloth and fur coats, gloves, sportswear and bathing suits until literally everything for the larger woman came to be stocked. Gloves are available in sizes up to 9½. Shoes are offered in sizes to 11, and in width to EEE. Even tent-size umbrellas are offered.

A salesman once attempted to sell a Lane Bryant executive a stock of reducing pills for sale to the store's stout customers.

"If these women reduced," objected the executive, "they wouldn't need our clothes."

"Don't worry," answered the salesman. "These pills don't work." Whereupon he was shown the door.

But even without pills, Lane Bryant records indicate that larger American women are becoming more slender. Of the company's 38 to 60 sizes, 46 was long the largest seller. By 1950, it was 44 with 42 and 40 close seconds. Diet and activity have been responsible.

The introduction of each of these articles in special sizes presented all the difficulties that had been overcome in maternity wear. Manufacturers were reluctant to manufacture them. Large-size coats and dresses demanded a great deal more material and work than the same articles in usual sizes. The knitting of extra-size hosiery and the making of large shoes actually required expensive additional machinery. In the case of almost all of these items, it was necessary for Lane Bryant to create an industry.

When fashion and artists like John Held emphasized the slender, flat flapper figure in the twenties, Lane Bryant's service to fuller figures became doubly welcome. By the time of Albert Malsin's death in 1923 the store's larger-size sales had passed its maternity business in volume, despite steady increases also in the latter, and accounted for more than half of the $5,000,000 annual business at that time.

With such a background of success with the special-figure problems, it was only logical for Lane Bryant later to turn its ingenuity to two other important feminine groups with challenging figure problems of a different sort. These are tall women and chubby girls.

The average height of women in the United States is 5 feet 3 1/6 inches. Thirty-six per cent, however, are taller than 5 feet 4 inches; 20 per cent are more than 5 feet 7 inches; and there are enough six-footers to compose several tall-girl clubs.

Women of the latter groups are taller than most of the men with whom they come in contact and must dress carefully not to appear too towering. Dresses and accessories expressly designed to solve their problems are stocked by the Lane Bryant "Over Five Seven Shops," under George T. Palley, son-in-law of the founder. These operate individually as well as in Lane Bryant stores. For the tall customers there are even suitably long necklaces, earrings and umbrellas.

The chubby customers are young girls and teenagers who are plumper than their companions. The plumpness is usually a temporary condition but while it lasts may be a grave problem to sensitive youngsters.

For these Lane Bryant established the first special department in which sizes were determined not by age but by measurements. Here attractive dresses and coats designed to minimize weight are available, along with underwear and other articles in special chubby sizes. These range from 8½ to 14½ for girls and 10½ to 16½ for teens. Manufacturing problems similar to those encountered earlier were overcome in producing these.

A Chubby Club is also sponsored by Lane Bryant. The members have a newspaper, style shows of their own, and meet at intervals for special events. The discovery that other youngsters have the same problems gives members confidence and poise. The newspaper carries encouraging accounts of famous actresses and singers who outgrew their girlhood chubbiness to become glamorous figures.

The Lane Bryant special-size business has increased so amazingly through the years that it and the subsequently developed related departments account for 95 per cent, and maternity garments for only 5 per cent of the company's annual sales of more than $60,000,000. Another indication of the shifting emphasis is the company's mail-order business.

In 1919, the stout catalog had fifty-two pages and the maternity catalog seventy-six pages. By 1950 the stout catalog had grown to one hundred pages while the maternity had dropped to thirty-six pages. Each issue of the latter goes on request to 175,000 prospects while each issue of the catalog of stout apparel is sent to 1,850,000 regular mail customers. Norma Shearer of motion-picture fame, incidentally, was once a model for the Lane Bryant catalogs.

As business increased and the modern wholesome attitude toward maternity developed, the Lane Bryant stores gradually emerged from side-street upstairs operations to Main Street locations in the hearts of shopping districts.

When Harry Liverman succeeded Mr. Malsin as president after his death in 1923, Lane Bryant had stores in Manhattan, Brooklyn, Chicago and Detroit. Customers elsewhere were served by mail. Stores were established in Philadelphia and St. Louis in 1925 and in Baltimore in 1926.

Lane Bryant, in 1928, purchased two Midwest groups of stores, Newman Cloak & Suit Company and Benton's Coat & Cloak Company. These were combined as the Newman-Benton Stores and integrated by opening in them Lane Bryant departments selling maternity and special-size clothing. From time to time other stores of this type have been added until now there are eleven.

A new Lane Bryant store was opened in Pittsburgh in 1949. Since then stores have been added in Cleveland, Miami Beach, Manhasset, Minneapolis, Miami, Beverly Hills, Oak Park, Trenton, Milwaukee and Houston.

Mail-order operations were shifted in 1941 from New York to Indianapolis, where modern quarters provide four acres of floor space. There six hundred workers handle the mailing of some 8,500,-000 catalogs a year and fill an average of eight thousand orders a day. The fronts and backs of the order blank are printed in reverse to enable workers to read both sides with one turning. For maximum speed, only right-handed girls are employed for this work. Lane Bryant's $13,000,000-a-year mail business is the sixth-largest in the country.

Under the imaginative leadership now of Raphael Malsin, whose birth was a factor in the start of the business, the Lane Bryant company has recognized increasingly its obligation not only to its customers, but to its employees, to its stockholders and to the general public.

President Malsin is probably the only head of a retail company in America who is a member of both Phi Beta Kappa and Sigma XI, honor society distinctions which he earned at Yale. He was a secretary of the late Arthur Brisbane, famous Hearst journalist, and worked as a newspaper reporter on the New York *Mail* and *Evening Journal* before joining Lane Bryant in the merchandising office. He later became advertising manager and then general manager. He served with the Lend Lease administration in North Africa during World War II, is trustee of a hospital and is active in numerous civic organizations.

The four thousand employees of Lane Bryant for years have participated in a profit-sharing plan. This involves the annual distribution of a share of the company's profits before taxes. Employees share on the basis of length of service.

After one year, all employees receive life insurance and Blue Cross hospitalization, all costs of which are borne by the company. Veteran employees also participate in a company-financed pension plan. The Pension Fund, with assets of almost $1,500,000, guarantees a minimum of $400 a year to retired workers in addition to their Social Security benefits. Employees of stores acquired by Lane Bryant are given pension credit for half of their previous service. An advisory committee of employees assists management on profit-sharing and retirement matters.

Employees may continue their education under the Albert Malsin Scholarships. These are administered by the company's Twenty-Five Year Club. The company contributes $100 to the club as each member joins and the organization raises additional funds by contests and benefits.

During World War II, the company paid to the families of employees in the Armed Forces approximately a third of the difference between their service pay and previous earnings at Lane Bryant. Those who returned to the company went to work at an average salary increase of 39.6 per cent over their prewar earnings.

After World War II, all Lane Bryant stores served as collection stations for maternity and other clothing for the devastated areas of Europe. Tons of clothing were collected and forwarded through various organizations to grateful women in a dozen countries.

Many Americans have vivid memories of aid from Lane Bryant in time of disaster. When explosion and fire devastated Texas City in 1947, the fifty-eight mail-order customers of Lane Bryant there received direct and through the Red Cross an offer to supply free new clothing to any whose wardrobes had been destroyed. The same offer was made to customers in Danville, Indiana, and Coatesville, Indiana, when tornadoes struck those communities in 1948. Some customers accepted in each area and scores wrote warm letters of thanks.

The company has done much to assure its customers that parenthood is a normal and even an amusing experience. There is a lounge for "expectant fathers" in the New York store. The firm's public-relations department, headed since 1946 by Jerome Klein, has given prizes for the most novel birth announcements.

Scientific prenatal care has been publicized by Lane Bryant since 1914. The company now mails free in plain wrappers to expectant mothers a series of seven letters prepared by the Maternal Center Association and titled *Stork Facts*. Each explains the necessary care from the third month onward. The letters are used in more than seven hundred schools, hospitals, health centers and clinics. All county health officers in the state of Mississippi use the data.

Two awards of $1,000 each, known as the Lane Bryant Annual Awards are now given annually by the company to individuals and organizations for outstanding unpaid community service. A committee of distinguished civic leaders chooses the recipients. The initial award for 1948 was presented to the Citizens' Schools Committee of Chicago for its successful efforts to improve the school system of that city.

Senator Paul H. Douglas of Illinois, in an address at the award presentation, praised the company for "going back into the communities to search out and to recognize the groups of men and women who struggle unselfishly and without hope of reward to make our life better. . . . These awards may inspire others to start and to carry on similar works of unselfish citizenship." The awards earned an American Public Relations Association award for the firm.

Such activities combined with half a century of conscientious service to customers have made Lane Bryant a world-famous institution and have increased the company's business far beyond the dreams of its founder.

Mrs. Malsin, a modest, gray-haired grandmother too small in stature to wear any Lane Bryant garment, lived to see her modest venture become a great enterprise. Though her sons had directed the business for years, she still had an office in the New York store when she died at seventy-two of a heart attack on September 26, 1951. After bequests to her sister and twenty-one charitable and educational institutions, her will divided her $1,909,648 estate, $1,795,034 of it in Lane Bryant stock, equally among her four children.

XVI. J. C. Penney Company
A Main Street Chain Built on Partnerships

JAMES CASH PENNEY, twenty-seven-year-old son of a minister, and two partners on April 14, 1902, opened a tiny cash dry goods store in Kemmerer, a frontier town in the southwest corner of Wyoming. For his third, Penney, who ran the store, invested his $500 savings and a borrowed $1,500. His partners offered to lend him this at 8 per cent but Penney found his home-town bank in Missouri would let him have it at 6 per cent. Thriftily and characteristically he obtained the money there.

He named the store the Golden Rule, and remembering his Baptist father's admonitions undertook to deal with the local coal miners and sheepherders in accordance with the Biblical injunction: "Therefore all things whatsoever ye would that men should do to you, do ye even so to them."

Nearly all local trade was on credit at stores of the mining companies. Failure was predicted for Penney's store. It was only one room, twenty-five by forty-five feet, and off the main street. Penney and his young wife lived in the attic overhead. Their furniture was made from packing cases. Water had to be carried from a Chinese restaurant a few doors down the street.

With his wife as his only clerk at first, Penney went ahead undaunted. Thanks to a liberal distribution of handbills and staying open from sunrise to midnight, first-day sales were $466.59. Thereafter, the store opened at 7 A.M. on weekdays and 8 A.M. on Sundays,

255

and stayed open as long as there was a miner or sheepherder on the street. Sales for the first year amounted to $28,898.11.

From this small beginning grew the great J. C. Penney store chain which in 1953 had profits of $38,472,932 on record sales of $1,109,-507,674. The company now has 1,650 stores. These range in space from 2,500 to 250,000 square feet and in dollar volume from $150,-000 to $10,000,000. The average for all Penney stores in 1953 was $680,511 each. There are now Penney stores in all states. The company is the biggest seller of soft goods in the world and in all retailing only A & P, Sears, Roebuck and Safeway are larger.

The chain is by far the biggest in the specialty or apparel field both in units and in sales. It has earned profits every year of its existence. In 1953, its sales were more than double and its profits more than treble those of the Allied Stores Corporation, biggest of the department-store chains. A few of the largest Penney stores, such as in Cincinnati and Seattle, rank as department stores, but the bulk of the huge business is in men's, women's and children's apparel, shoes, blankets, draperies, yard goods and work clothes.

In the last field, Penney's is regarded by Sears, Roebuck as its greatest competitor. Penney's work clothing has such fame that even movie stars like Clark Gable, a customer at the Van Nuys, California, store, buy it for ranch wear.

The Penney Company is famous for the large-scale sharing of its profits with its managers and its employees, who are called associates. There is a $10,000 ceiling on salaries but the Securities and Exchange Commission records reveal that in 1953 this, plus their earnings under the "general office compensation plan," amounted to $103,446 for each of eight executives.

A Penney store manager earns from $5,000 to $50,000 or more a year and may receive a third of the profits of his unit. Prior to revision of the profit-sharing plan, in recognition of the fact that big operations are more than a one-man job, two store managers earned as much as $125,000, more than any officer at the New York headquarters. The incentive system extends to all of the company's fifty-five thousand regular and thirty thousand seasonal employees. Sales clerks receive from 2½ to 6 per cent commission on sales above quotas and there are year-end bonuses.

Penney woos the public with the slogan "Live Better for Less."

Half a century of selling reliable goods at low prices has made its public relations as excellent as its employee relations. Customers sometimes actually petition the company to locate a store in their neighborhood. A new unit in National City, California, for example, was opened in 1954 in response to a petition circulated by Mrs. H. A. Bolen, who had been a customer before moving there. About this time a rancher drove fifty miles to the Penney store in Buffalo, Wyoming, and spent $910 outfitting his family of ten children.

Ultra-simple procedures plus the loyalty of its employees and decentralization of authority enable the company to operate its vast retail network with a minimum of staff and expense. It is to everybody's advantage to get things done as efficiently and as economically as possible.

A zone and regional staff of twenty-five persons, seven of them secretaries, directs the company's big Eastern zone. This does 28 per cent of the company's business and includes four hundred stores in an area extending from St. Louis to the Atlantic Ocean, and from Canada to Paducah, Kentucky. This economy of personnel extends to headquarters in New York, where the president, his assistant and a publicity man all share one secretary.

Most of the company policies, also its thrift and habits of hard work, trace back to the founder and his early associates in the little store that he opened in Wyoming in 1902. At that time James Cash Penney had a variety of experience behind him.

He was born the seventh of twelve children on September 16, 1875, near Hamilton, Missouri, on the mortgaged farm of his father, an unsalaried Primitive Baptist minister. While keeping the farm, called Bluegrass for the Kentucky the parents had left, the father also bought and mortgaged a house in Hamilton to let the children go to school.

The family was poor. From eight onward, Jim ran errands for money to buy his clothes. A number of childhood incidents made indelible impressions. Jim learned a lesson in thoroughness one Sunday when he shined his self-bought $1 pair of shoes only in front and a neighbor named MacDonald called attention to them. Five boys of the MacDonald family later worked for the Penney stores, two of them becoming directors.

At ten Jim was in the pig business and learned a lesson in public relations when neighbors protested the odor. His father made him sell them at once, before they were fat enough for full value, but Jim collected $60 and deposited it in two banks, lest one fail.

On graduation from high school, Jim began to grow watermelons on part of the family farm. When the county fair opened, he took a wagonload of them to a spot just outside the entrance. He was doing a brisk business when his father appeared and sternly ordered him home.

"You're disgracing the Penneys," said the minister. "Folks selling inside the fair pay for the privilege."

"But I wasn't inside the fair," Jim protested. "I was on the outside."

"Exactly," his father told him. "You were getting trade away from others without paying for the privilege." Jim never forgot this.

The boy's enterprise convinced his father that he had the makings of a merchant and he obtained a job for him at the J. M. Hale & Brother General Store in Hamilton. Mr. Hale didn't need anyone at the time but he took Jim on as a favor to the father.

Jim, then twenty, went to work for Hale in 1895 for $2.27 a month. Though timid at first, he soon became a good salesman. In addition he swept floors and sidewalks, sorted, dusted and kept the stock in order. He studied the latter so thoroughly that he could close his eyes and tell the grade, weight and price by the feel.

Jim's success in the store was a comfort to his father in the last days of his life. Shortly before he died some weeks later he said: "Jim will make it. I like the way he's started out."

Jim worked so hard at the Hale store that in three years' time he was raised to $300 a year. But he was also wrecking his health and a doctor warned him to get outdoors and out of Missouri. "Go to Denver at once," advised the doctor. "Otherwise you'll become a consumptive."

Jim did so. He worked briefly for two Denver stores, then went north to the small town of Longmont where, with his entire savings of $300, he bought a butcher shop.

Longmont's leading hotel was his best customer. One day Jim's meat cutter told him the hotel cook threatened to stop buying from them because Penney had neglected to send him a bottle of whiskey each week.

Penney bought the whiskey, sent it over, then thought about it. He remembered that, in Kentucky tradition, his grandfather and great-grandfather, although preachers, had each kept whiskey in their cellars. But his father had broken with the tradition, and the more Jim thought about it, the more convinced he became that it was wrong to bribe the hotel cook. The following week he told the cook as much and promptly lost the hotel business. Not long after the shop failed.

Flat broke, Jim looked for another job. He found one at $50 a month with T. M. Callahan, who with a partner, Guy Johnson, owned several stores in and around Longmont. On the strength of his $50 salary, the most he had earned until that time, Penney on August 24, 1899, married Berta Hess, who also had been sent to Colorado by a doctor.

It was with the backing of Callahan and Johnson that Penney opened in Kemmerer. He did so well there that when his partners decided to end the partnership in 1907 he was able to buy the Kemmerer store and two others for $30,000.

By this time Penney was the father of two sons and hoped to have a chain of six stores. He thought he could do it with $75,000. "It's shooting at the moon," he told his wife. Berta assured him he could do it. Penney agreed. "If I can find the right men for partners," he said. "Men who are capable of assuming responsibility, men with indestructible loyalty rooted in confidence in one another."

After interviewing fifty candidates, he found such a man that same year in Earl Corder Sams, a restless man from Simpson, Kansas. Sams worked first as Penney's clerk in Kemmerer, then managed a store for him in Cumberland and, in his third year, became a partner in a new store opened in Eureka, Utah. From then on, Sams became increasingly important in the company.

Penney's goal increased to a chain of twenty-five stores. He then had fourteen, and his working plan was this: To enable a store manager to accumulate enough capital out of his earnings to buy one-third partnership in a new store, provided he had trained a new man to open and manage a new link in the chain.

Penney believed he had no right to be in business unless he could save his customers money on everything they bought. He confined his stores to small communities, refrained from expensive locations, had no fancy fixtures, and handled only merchandise for which there was a common demand. This merchandise was piled on tables where customers could see and touch it, there was one price for all, cash was paid and purchases carried home. If customers were not satisfied they could return the merchandise and get their money back.

Penney prices in 1910 were unbelievably low. Children's underwear sold for 7 cents up, ladies' fancy cloth coats $2.98, men's heavy cassimere suits, $4.98 to $6.90, men's ties, 15 cents.

In 1910 the fourteen Penney stores had gross sales of $662,331.16. Penney then had eight partners, all of them small-town men who started at the bottom. He had given up management of the Kemmerer store and set up headquarters in Salt Lake City, Utah.

Soon after this move, Penney and his wife planned a long-postponed wedding trip to Europe. But before they could leave, Mrs. Penney developed pneumonia and died.

Penney plunged into work and opened twenty additional stores in rapid succession. In all, thirty-four Golden Rule stores dotted eight Western states. Finally, still beset with grief, Penney went to Europe alone. When he returned he changed the name on the stores from the Golden Rule to J. C. Penney.

Another change was made in 1913, when the J. C. Penney Stores Company was incorporated under the laws of the State of Utah. Ten thousand shares of stock with a face value of $10 each were issued. These were nonassessable, carried no dividends and were all issued to Penney as trustee.

The company owned no stock. Preferred stock was issued to the partners in proportion to their store interests. Dividends were paid against the earnings of each store and distributed according to individual holdings in each store.

By 1914, the chain had extended to 48 stores, and that year had sales of $3,650,293.75. A central buying office was established in New York that year, and Penney visualized a national chain with perhaps as many as 500 stores. Two years later there were 127, doing an annual business of $8,428,144. When Penney went to the annual convention of partners in Salt Lake City in 1916, he nominated Earl Corder Sams as his successor, and on January 1, 1917, Sams became president while Penney was elevated to chairman. Sams vastly expanded the company.

During World War I, during which headquarters were moved to New York, the government had imposed heavy taxes and one of the first things President Sams had to do was find new sources for borrowing to finance the rapidly expanding business. New York bankers did not like the Utah articles of incorporation and to win them over Sams and Penney agreed to change the preferred stock to common. A board of directors was authorized to issue a limited amount of this for public sale for meeting tax burdens. The common stock, issued only to partners, was to be used for expansion purposes. Actual earnings controlled the issuance of common stock and if a partner wished to dispose of any or all of his holdings he had first to offer them to the board of directors. The book value of the stock was then computed after which the directors could offer such stock for sale to other common shareholders. If stock so offered was not disposed of within thirty days, its owner was permitted to sell wherever he chose.

These changes satisfied the bankers and expansion went on with tremendous strides. Hundreds of new stores opened. In 1923, Penney bought the store of his first employer, J. M. Hale & Brother in Hamilton, Missouri. It was reopened as the five hundredth store in the Penney chain.

The company expanded further in 1927–1929 with the purchase of 54 stores from F. S. Jones and Company, 20 stores from Johnson-Stevens Company and 113 stores from the J. B. Byars Company and the J. N. McCracken Company. All of these were in the West and Middle West. Their acquisition pushed the number of Penney stores past one thousand. At the end of 1929, there were 1,395 stores and the company had record sales of $209,000,000 that year and more than $12,000,000 in profits. Penney stock was listed on the New York Stock Exchange beginning October 23, 1929, just six days before the market crashed, heralding the depression.

Sales dropped to a low of $155,271,981 for 1932 during the depression but even then there were earnings of $5,082,672. This was the only year that the company failed to pay a dividend. Recovery began for the company the next year. With 1,466 stores, seven fewer than 1932, sales soared to $178,773,965 and profits more than doubled to total $14,235,638.

Florida bank failures and the temporary decline in the value of

Penney stock at this time were a blow to founder Penney's personal fortune, then more than $40,000,000. He successfully met the crisis by again drawing a salary from the company for a time and by borrowing $7,000,000 from five New York City banks.

The Penney Company was one of the first to recognize the strength of the anti-chain-store movement. From 1927 onward, the company directly and through trade associations fought anti-chain measures in courts, before legislative committees and in public forums. In 1935, Penney joined the California Chain Store Association which employed the public-relations firm of Braun & Company to defend the chains. This activity was redoubled when Representative Wright Patman of Texas introduced his "death sentence" anti-chain bill.

This would have imposed additional taxes of $63,912,000 on the J. C. Penney Company at a time when its earnings were $13,739,-160 a year. Only the A & P, Woolworth and Kroger Company chains would have been harder hit by the measure.

As the first opposition witness at 1940 hearings of a Congressional subcommittee considering the bill, President Sams traced the history of the J. C. Penney Company and asked defeat of the measure for these reasons:

1. It would destroy the Penney Company or any other similar company.

2. It would destroy the finest field of opportunity that has ever existed in retailing for the young ambitious man born without family means.

3. It would add to the cost of living for every American family of limited means and would lower the American standard of living.

4. It would deal a staggering blow to the entire economic life of this country and would be especially destructive of the smaller cities and towns for the benefit of the larger cities.

5. It would hurt and tax this entire nation for the protection and enrichment of a small minority group of self-interested middlemen and of another small minority group of ill-advised marginal retailers.

In addition Mr. Sams told the committee:

If the national chains were wiped out, it would remove the most substantial bulwark which these small trading centers have against the pull of the big cities. It has been said that chain stores were ruining the smaller communities. Chain stores didn't ruin them. The automobile and the good roads naturally caused the people to turn to larger centers to do their trading. No law, no human mandate can breathe life back in the very small trading center which formerly supported a couple of general stores. Those stores existed only because without automobiles or good roads the customer couldn't get to the city. Because of horse-and-buggy transportation and because of mud roads the customer bought what the general store offered at its own price or she ordered by mail.

In behalf of all the chains, President Sams presented a brief, *Keep Main Street Open,* summarizing the arguments in favor of chain stores and refuting, in some cases with the same statistics used by the opposition, the charges then raised against them.

Salient arguments of the document were these: Chain stores raise the standard of living. Chain stores keep business and purchasing power in the towns. They developed as the product of local enterprise. Ownership of chain-store stocks is widely dispersed. Chain headquarters are distributed all over the nation. Chains have no interlocking directorate. Chain stores pay better wages, higher rents, and bring capital into town. Chain stores widen markets and improve farm income. Chain stores invest in community welfare. Chain stores respond to disaster needs. Chain stores pay more taxes, set high standards for all retailing and offer equality of opportunity to the consumer.

Scores of witnesses, including spokesmen for farm, labor and consumer groups as well as the chains, followed Sams in condemning the bill. It was killed in committee.* No more states have enacted anti-chain legislation, and some of the earlier measures, in California and Utah, for example, have been repealed.

Proposals for a merger of Penney with, first, Montgomery Ward & Company and then Sears, Roebuck and Company were considered seriously when the mail-order giants moved into the retail-store field but negotiations came to nothing. There seemed no way to transfer good will and trained personnel.

To handle its land and building matters, the company has a wholly owned subsidiary, the J. C. Penney Building & Realty Cor-

---

* Godfrey M. Lebhar, *Chain Stores in America 1859–1950,* Chain Store Publishing Corporation, New York, 1952, pages 240–276.

poration. This is headed by Vice President John F. Brown, who first joined Penney's as a salesman at Denison, Texas, in 1921. He has been in charge of real estate and construction since 1947.

The company prefers to lease rather than own store properties. In an expansion, it will sometimes buy, sell and lease back property. Only about 50 stores are owned outright. This avoids tying up capital and keeps operations flexible. Changes are always under way. In 1953, 8 new stores were added, 6 were closed, 17 were relocated and 176 were renovated or enlarged.

New stores are planned to fit their communities. The company designs both its buildings and its fittings with a view to cleanliness and low-cost maintenance as well as low initial cost and attractiveness. The practice of having the name against a yellow panel on every store has been abandoned in favor of individual treatment. Typical of Penney architectural policy is the beautiful five-story early American store in Alexandria, Virginia.

Automobile parking has been a prime consideration in locating new stores in recent years. Penney has more than 200 stores in suburban shopping centers and 24 of 32 new stores built in 1954 were in such locations. An interesting Penney store in Phoenix, Arizona, occupies a new $3,000,000 building with a separately operated 500-car parking garage in the basement. As a sample of Penney lease arrangements, the store pays three per cent of its gross or a minimum of $110,000 a year for this 109,000 square feet of high traffic space and has a twenty-five-year renewable lease.

California has the most Penney stores, a total of 144, and Texas is second with 124. Next come Iowa, Ohio, Minnesota, Washington and Pennsylvania. The 58th Penney store in Pennsylvania was opened in 1954 as the largest of 30 stores in the big Levittown Shopping Center. There also are new Penney Stores at Levittown, New York, and at Lake Success, also on Long Island. The New York City store is run chiefly for the 1,850 Penney office employees and does not advertise.

While Penney buildings vary greatly, Penney men and women are the same everywhere, rarely flashy but always hard-working and trustworthy individuals who are assets to their stores and communities. The company trusts them. The more than a billion dollars that flows into its cash registers each year is all cash or the equivalent. Managers bank it locally. But no Penney employee is bonded. While a Penney man goes wrong now and then the loss is much less than the cost would be to bond all who handle the money.

Everybody starts at the bottom with Penney. This is true whether newcomers walk in the door or are recruited from colleges. The nearest store manager recruits the college graduate. Before hiring him the manager may visit his home and, if the prospect is married, talk to his wife. The company believes the right home background is important. Once hired, a promising man receives training and coaching from his store manager and also the district manager.

A "Penney type" man, besides liking retailing, must know how to be helpful to people and treat them fairly. He must know how to make money and build a business. He must know how to make a place for himself in any community to which he may be sent.

An example of the sort of managers Penney likes to have is Emery E. Freeman, who as manager of its store in Mount Pleasant, Michigan, won the top Community Builder Award from *Chain Store Age* in 1938. To enumerate only a few of his activities at that time, Freeman was president of the Chamber of Commerce, chairman of the local Red Cross chapter and had increased its membership by a third, had helped raise money for a new Methodist church, the Parent-Teacher Association, the Boy Scouts, and other causes, had provided part-time work in his store for fourteen college students, had promoted a city-wide Santa Claus sales event to increase Christmas shopping and had provided free movies.

All top Penney executives have started at the bottom. Earl C. Sams, as noted, began as a clerk in the original Kemmerer store. After managing several other stores, he served as president from 1917 to 1946. He then served as board chairman until 1950, when he died at sixty-six, leaving an estate of $9,340,468.

The next president, Albert H. Hughes, a native of Skaneateles, New York, as a young man tutored Mr. Penney's sons in Latin, and decided that retailing would be more exciting than teaching a dead language. He also started at the bottom in a store at Moberly, Missouri. He later managed stores in Utah and Georgia, joined and became head of the personnel department in New York, and was elected vice president in 1937 and president in 1946. He served beyond the usual retirement age. Under President Hughes, the company's sales passed the billion-dollar mark.

William M. Batten, top vice president, first worked for Penney while attending high school in Parkersburg, West Virginia, his birthplace. He washed windows, worked in a stockroom and then sold shoes. After graduation from Ohio State University, he joined Penney in Lansing, Michigan, as a shoe salesman. He became assistant manager of the store and then joined the personnel training department in New York. He was promoted to assistant to the president, then became vice president.

Executive Vice President George Mack, whose schooling ended at thirteen, joined Penney in 1921 in Everett, Washington, and came up through the ranks. Vice President Fred A. Bantz, in charge of merchandising, joined Penney in 1922 as a buyer of hosiery and knitwear. Vice President Herbert H. Schwamb, in charge of personnel, began in 1923, as a salesman in Bakersfield, California. Secretary August J. Raskopf joined as a secretary in 1919. Comptroller Robert C. Weiderman, born in Brooklyn, began as an accountant in 1916.

Authority naturally stems from the board of directors, composed entirely of active or retired executives. All of the latter, including Chairman Penney, the founder, serve without pay.

An operating committee of eight executives, including all department heads, passes on all matters of importance. President Hughes and his assistant are not members of this committee but sit in on its twice-a-week sessions. The committee acts on new store and real-estate proposals, also promotions, transfers and discharges of store managers. A manager cannot be discharged without approval of the committee and one objection is enough to save him.

Linking headquarters and the store managers are five zone and thirty-three district managers. These spend most of their time visiting stores to "counsel" with managers on problems of all kinds, to detect new customer tastes, and to help train store personnel. Zone and district men meet for a fortnight in New York each December. There are quarterly district meetings for managers. These in turn meet frequently with their department heads and clerks. There is free discussion at all levels and executives regard this as a great source of company strength.

The store manager is the key man. He hires and trains his help. If he runs a store in the Southwest, this may include Spanish lessons. He decides what to do about advertising and local causes. He orders most of his merchandise from lists and samples sent him by head-quarters but is not required to accept anything he thinks unsuited to his climate or customers' tastes. He can choose which central office training, promotion and advertising aids best fit his needs. Ninety per cent of the advertising expenditure, usually $3\frac{1}{2}$ per cent or less of sales, is usually in newspapers but store managers can use other media if they like. An average Penney store with annual sales of around $600,000 will have a basic staff of a manager, an assistant manager, a girl cashier, a girl bookkeeper, two department heads, eight full-time salespeople, some of whom act as department heads, an alteration woman, a display person, and a stockroom man. Reports go to New York three times a month and a budget is submitted twice a year but paper work is held to a minimum. Everybody sells in rush periods.

Simple two-part sales checks are used, one half going to the customer. In addition to selling, clerks wrap purchases and have stockkeeping duties. Open displays permit customers largely to serve themselves and one clerk can serve a wide area.

Economies in operation are reflected in prices and a Penney store is supposed to turn its merchandise five or six times a year. The annual inventory usually finds less than one-tenth of one per cent of the merchandise a year old. Seasonal articles like bathing suits are supposed to be cleared within the season. There are automatic markdowns, similar to those in Filene's basement, on Penney dresses. An $8.90 number, for example, which doesn't move in thirty days will be cut to $5, then to $3 and finally to $1. Most items move, however, at an average markon of about 35 per cent.

Like Sears, Roebuck, Penney has a Thrift Fund into which employees can deposit up to 5 per cent of their salaries. The company adds several times this amount, and something, even if the employee deposits nothing, if he qualifies under the profit-sharing plan. The money can be drawn out in time of need or when the worker retires or leaves the company.

Fashion as well as value is now stressed in Penney apparel. Cashmere sweaters and other quality items are now offered as part of a general trading-up policy. A semiannual publication, *Fashions and Fabrics,* reports fashion news and forecasts trends for the home sewer. Fifty thousand copies of this are given away to home-economics teachers and others as part of the company's public-relations program. This program also includes the circulation of motion-picture films on Penney operations to schools and colleges.

Most Penney buying is done in New York, where Vice President Bantz, 14 merchandise executives, and 180 buyers deal with 9,000 vendors. Buying offices in Dallas and Los Angeles cover the dress industries in those areas. While the company once owned its own corset and brassière factory, everything is now purchased, partly in the open market, but very largely from manufacturers with whom buyers work closely to plan articles of definite quality to sell at predetermined prices. The International Silver Company, for example, created silverware of a special pattern for both the Penney twenty-fifth and fiftieth anniversaries.

When founder Penney in company with his original partners, made his first buying trip to New York, he astounded them by washing samples in the washbasin of his hotel room to determine for himself if they were as washable and color fast as the manufacturers promised.

Since 1929, the company has had a sizable research laboratory in its eighteen-story building on West Thirty-fourth Street in New York for this sort of testing and also for the development of new and desirable products. Organized and directed by Charles W. Dorn, a Kentuckian who once taught chemistry at Penn State College, a staff of fourteen uses machines, microscopes and devices with descriptive names such as the Fadeometer, Perspirometer, Launderometer, Flammability Tester, Rain Tester and Stoll Abrader, to test all kinds of merchandise. The Fadeometer evaluates materials as to color-fastness in sunlight. To be acceptable for draperies, materials must withstand eighty hours of continuous exposure in the device without appreciable change in color; materials for suits, overcoats and other outerwear must withstand forty hours.

Raincoat materials are tested by three methods. Coated fabrics (as in rubberized coats) and plastic films (again plastic raincoats), are tested on a hydrostatic pressure tester. Water-repellent fabrics are given a spray test in their original condition, then tested again *after* washing and dry cleaning to determine how well the material actually repels moisture. The third test, made by the Rain Tester, an instrument that simulates light showers, heavier rain and actual rainstorm conditions, determines whether the construction of the fabric, plus the finish, is suitable for rainwear.

Shoes and other items subject to destruction from bacteria and molds go through a Sanitized process used extensively by the Penney Company. The method used prolongs the life of shoe linings, keeps insoles from becoming hard and brittle, and from shrinking. The fungus that causes athlete's foot will not grow in Sanitized material. The process also retards the development of odors from absorbed perspiration and is used on foundation garments for women, socks and hose, jacket linings and all areas where perspiration is likely to become concentrated. Perspiration, incidentally, has no odor until attacked by bacteria.

The laboratory studies the resistance of woolen blankets to moth damage. Dorn raises his own moths, chiefly the buffalo moth, which is the most destructive, and, to test moth-resistant compounds, feeds the larvae on wool blanket samples, ten worms to the square inch. This is equivalent to 270,000 moths per blanket, and if a sample withstands this onslaught, the compound is considered effective. Penney gives a five-year guarantee on treated blankets.

Director Dorn is an authority on textile standards and has headed and served on numerous industry and government committees concerned with problems of color, shrinkage and flammability. European retailers often list a visit to the Penney laboratory as high spot of a tour of the United States.

Though approaching eighty, founder Penney continues to work a full day, often through the lunch hour, in the New York office. He refuses a salary and now has only a small stock interest in the company. In 1953, he received the Tobé award for his contributions to retailing and an honorary degree from the University of Missouri in recognition of his aid to agriculture. Among his gifts to the university have been an experimental farm and a herd of 225 prize Guernsey cattle worth $750,000.

In memory of his parents he built the Home Community in

Florida for retired Protestant ministers and their families. He made large donations to the Bowery Mission in New York, the Montlawn Vacation Center in Nyack for underprivileged children, the Industrial School, the National Youth Radio Conferences, and to orphanages in China.

The white-haired founder now spends at least half of each year visiting Penney stores and lecturing to Rotary Clubs (he joined in 1942) and other groups, and assuring them America is still the land of opportunity. Whenever asked what made the Penney Company such a success, he replies: "Unquestionably the emphasis we have laid on human relationships, toward the public on one hand by careful service and in giving the utmost values; and toward our associates on the other hand."

He assures audiences that "chain and variety stores are only on the threshold of their development."

There is still a Penney store in Kemmerer, Wyoming. It is better located, more attractive and bigger than the one in which everything began and it now does about five times the business of the founder in his remarkable first year.

XVII. Bullock's and I. Magnin
Glamour Pioneers of the West

Boastful Californians spend their increasing wealth in all manner of stores, but take the greatest pride in the spacious and beautiful establishments of Bullock's, Inc. and I. Magnin & Co. The latter became a subsidiary of the former in 1944. Since that year, additional branches, and increased business, have roughly trebled the combined sales volume. This passed $118,000,000 in 1954.

The warmth of Bullock's relationship with its customers is, perhaps, best illustrated by the grade-school composition of a little Los Angeles girl named Janice McCoslar. When she and her schoolmates were asked to list what they liked best, Janice wrote: "1. Birthdays. 2. Bullock's. 3. Home. 4. School." The store heard about it and sent Janice a doll. Her mother acknowledged this with a note ending: "Anything I buy from now on until the year 2000 will be from Bullock's."

Both the Bullock and Magnin stores are noted for dignity and taste. Both sell world-famous lines. There are sales only once a year in August. Volume then is as much as $1,000,000 a day. Advertising is restrained and often entirely institutional. The store buildings are famous in architectual circles for their adaptation to the sunny climate, the luxury of their interiors and the prescience with which they made provision for automobile traffic in a state which now leads all others in automobile registrations.

Both companies have grown with the West and their executives have had leading roles in civic affairs. One of them, for example, was largely responsible for Southern California obtaining its vital irrigation water from the Colorado River by a 392-mile aqueduct over mountains and deserts.

To students of store organization, Bullock's is notable for its decentralization of authority and its "unitization" of merchandise. The latter is the division of usual merchandise sections into separate units according to type, use, proportion or price line. It is also the assembling in one location of all the related merchandise of interest to a particular type of customer. Each unit is the responsibility of a buyer, who has the responsibility for selecting and training its salespeople. To keep abreast of customer desires, each buyer is required to spend at least two hours a day on the floor actually selling merchandise. Other stores do something in this direction but Bullock's carries it further than most.

Unitization encourages impulse buying and also has the merit of making shopping more pleasant by saving time and energy for the customers. The system is credited with helping make Bullock's Downtown one of the biggest stores in the highly competitive area and to enable it to maintain an unbroken record of profitable operation, including the depression thirties, for more than forty years.

The company is named for John Gillespie Bullock, a Canadian of Scotch ancestry who brought to business all the Scotch virtues of energy, frugality and integrity. He was born January 14, 1871, in Paris, Ontario. His father, a railroad employee, died two years later. When he was eleven, the boy went to work at $2 a week delivering groceries for Munn & Co., a tiny local store.

"We kept open until midnight Saturdays," he recalled years later, "so Mother used to come down and fetch me, so I wouldn't be afraid of walking home in the dark." All of his life he treasured a picture of the little store and a penny notebook in which he wrote orders.

He moved on to Rheder's, a dry-goods store that was the largest in town, but at twenty-five he was not earning enough to marry. So when two uncles, who were mining in the West, wrote back about the wonders of California, his widowed mother staked him to a railroad ticket to Los Angeles and loaned him $150.

His sister packed him some food and he reached Los Angeles in January of 1896 with all of the $150. He deposited this in the

Citizens National Bank and drew it out $1 or $2 a week while he read newspaper advertisements and looked for work.

"It was a time of unemployment and I walked the streets in vain until late in February," Bullock recalled later. "Then I read in a newspaper that a bankrupt stock was to be sold the next day in a store at Broadway and Fourth. I was there early but the man in charge said he needed no more help. Still I waited around with the crowd for the store to open. It was soon filled and the front door had to be locked until some of those inside left by a rear door. I went in that way and told the man it looked like he could use me. I was hired—at $12 a week."

Bullock's employer in the busy little forty-foot store proved to be Arthur Letts who had purchased a bankrupt stock for $8,167 with borrowed money. In September, by which time Bullock was beginning to do some of the men's wear buying, Letts hired as cash boy another Canadian. He was fifteen-year-old Percy Glen Winnett, a short youth in short pants who had come to California from Winnipeg with his parents. By then, there were twenty-six employees and the place showed signs of growing into the great Broadway department store which it became.

Letts pioneered odd-cent prices in Los Angeles and it was the job of the new $2-a-week cash boy to handle the pennies. He was short a penny one day and was scolded, an experience that he never forgot, but the growing store usually was a pleasant and exciting place for all. Bullock spurned offers of jobs with a bakery and another store. He was soon making $75 a month and married his Canadian sweetheart. Winnett advanced from errand boy to wrapper in the men's furnishing department for which Bullock became the buyer. Between packages, Winnett worked behind the counter and learned what he could from Bullock. Both learned from Letts.

Born in Holdenby, a village in Northamptonshire, England, in 1862, Letts had been apprenticed at fourteen to the dry-goods, or drapery business, as it was known in England. He worked in London long enough to pay his passage to Canada and informed his parents of his departure only when he was aboard ship. He arrived in Quebec in 1883 and went to work at $7 a week for Robert Walker & Sons in Ontario. He married in Toronto in 1886 and moved to Seattle, Washington, just before fire destroyed the business district there in 1889. After this he opened his first store in a tent on Second Avenue and stocked it with wearing apparel and men's furnishings. This went bankrupt in the panic of 1893 and, after paying his creditors thirty-five cents on the dollar, Letts moved to Los Angeles.

As soon as the Broadway venture began really to prosper in 1902, Letts, like J. L. Hudson back in Michigan, looked up the creditors in his bankruptcy and by 1905 had paid them in full. When some of them were hard hit by the San Francisco fire the next year, he sent these additional checks for 6 per cent interest on his debts for twelve years.

As the Broadway store grew, Letts made Bullock superintendent and gave him the responsibility for all hiring. After five older men had failed in the spot, young Winnett succeeded him as men's furnishings buyer. He later bought women's and children knit underwear and hosiery. As the salespeople disliked bothering with the complicated sizes, he found the children's end neglected and returns high. He established a children's section and placed a woman in charge with firm instructions not to leave to sell any women's garments. Her attention and specialized knowledge made the section a great success and convinced Winnett of the merit of what became known as "unitization."

Opportunity came for all in 1906. Eastern merchants planned a department store at the northwest corner of Seventh and Broadway. With the steel framework for seven stories erected, the death of one stopped the venture and E. T. Earl, the builder, offered the unfinished structure to Letts. It was outside the shopping area of the time but, being only three blocks away, appealed to Letts as an alternative site for the Broadway department store if he could not renew his leases on favorable terms. He signed a fifty-year lease with Earl who completed the building.

To utilize the new structure until the time that it might be required for the Broadway store, Letts intrusted Bullock with $250,000 and the task of establishing an additional store. Winnett, who at twenty-six held an important merchandising job, asked to be allowed to join the new venture and Letts somewhat reluctantly consented. A third executive from the Broadway, William A. Holt, the advertising manager, also went along. They planned to call the new store Bullock's Department Store but Winnett argued for a shorter name like

Macy's and it was shortened to Bullock's. Bullock was president and Winnett vice president and general manager of the new company. Letts gave them complete freedom.

They set up an office in the Lankershim Hotel across the street and hired a staff of four hundred who sat on beds as they were interviewed. H. M. Bigelow, who had just sold his general store in Grundy City, Iowa, walked in and was employed as floor manager. Buyers were sent to market. At last everything was in place and on the night of March 2, 1907, Letts and the public saw the new store at a nonselling preview. Thousands crowded through the brightly lighted buildings to listen to bands play on the lower floors and to see a pony show in the roof garden. In later years, employees conducted Easter services in this roof garden.

But rain, something of a rarity in Los Angeles, fell when the store opened for business on March 4 and customers were few. "You could shoot a cannon through the aisles without hitting anyone," recalls Winnett. Those who came found a beautiful store, singing canaries and violets. Bullock's has given away violets every March 4 since then. Customers unable to get downtown that day sometimes ask for and receive the free flowers by mail.

Unexpectedly, the finer-quality merchandise sold more rapidly than the inexpensive. Buyers replaced their stocks with better goods and the "mistakes" were cleared in the first of the August sales. Bullock's was opened as a strictly cash store but within a few months established charge accounts and devised a coat of arms marked *suprema regnat qualitas,* Latin for "Quality reigns supreme."

But there were troubles. The panic of 1907, started by failure of a bank in New York, hit in October. Two other Los Angeles stores started at the same time as Bullock's failed. Bullock's struggled ahead. Whether there were packages in them or not, Barney C. Slavin bravely sent out the store's six immaculate horse-drawn delivery wagons. Some shelves were filled with empty cartons and one floor was closed off.

Nevertheless, Bullock and Winnett counted sales of $1,309,141 for 1907, $1,509,832 in 1908, and operations became profitable. Letts, meanwhile, renewed the Broadway store leases and decided to continue both stores. Bullock's sales reached $2,029,034 in 1909 and $3,746,024 in 1912. In that year began expansions which eventually spread the big store over the entire Broadway, Hill, Sixth and Seventh Street block. A street dividing the block, called St. Vincent's Court after a college once on the site, was bridged.

Bullock's also grew in character and prestige. While other stores were advertising $25 men suits for $15, Bullock's startled the community by offering $15 suits for $15. Thousands laughed and bought the suits. The store's policy of continual but dignified advertising was born. A citation accompanying one of many awards won by Bullock's advertising once described it as "unique and original art technique and wise use of white space, copy that is brief, succinct and restrained, the best type of copy exemplifying freedom from price exaggeration." Bullock's was one of the first stores to use color in newspaper advertising and boasts the distinction of publishing the first "three-dimensional" store advertisements, a series in the Los Angeles *Times* that had to be read with colored glasses.

A customer was so moved by one of Bullock's annual Christmas institutional pages that she decided to embroider a sampler of it. So the store obligingly had the engraver make proofs of it on nylon, rayon and cotton and sent all three to the lady.

Bullock kept on his office wall the motto: "The ideals of this business must not be sacrificed to gain." Like many another executive, he gave every employee a copy of Elbert Hubbard's "Message to Garcia." In executive offices, Bullock posted: "A man's worth is measured by the degree of supervision he requires. The more a man has to be told what to do, checked up and guided, the less he is worth. The employee who burdens his superiors most is worth the least." A reminder from Winnett said: "Nothing much counts in the retail game until somebody sells somebody something."

The aspirations of Bullock and Winnett were best expressed, however, in "The Bullock Ideal," written by William A. Holt, the first advertising and publicity director, a talented graduate of Leland Stanford. Reprinted thousands of times in employee manuals, annual reports and elsewhere since its first appearance as an institutional advertisement in 1912, this reads:

> To build a business that will never know completion but that will advance continually to meet advancing conditions
> To develop stocks and service to a notable degree

To create a personality that will be known for its strength and friendliness

To arrange and co-ordinate activities to the end of winning confidence by meriting it

To strive always to secure the satisfaction of every customer.

These words were backed by deeds. There was little that Bullock's would not do for a customer. Anything wanted would be obtained. In his usual wing collar, Mr. Bullock was once at the door bidding customers good-by the evening before St. Patrick's Day, when one expressed her regret she had found no clay pipes for an Irish party planned next day in Santa Monica. He noted her address, had the city scoured for clay pipes that night and had them delivered to the amazed customer in Santa Monica.

One Saturday at 11:30 P.M., a night watchman answered the phone in Bullock's. A customer complained tearfully that a set of chinaware, purchased as a golden wedding gift, had not arrived and that the anniversary was the next day. The watchman called an executive who called a packer. The executive delivered the china himself on Sunday morning in time for the celebration.

One holiday season, a Bullock's employee overheard a conversation about how a doll and a toy truck which a widowed mother, who worked as a waitress, had purchased to come from Santa Claus had been delivered too early and had fallen into the hands of the children. Without charge, the store sent some more toys as coming from Santa Claus.

A motorcycle messenger was dispatched once 150 miles to Trona with an evening dress required by night. A special trunk required by a customer was delivered to him, also by messenger, in Paris, France. Southern California's growing population, especially the segment connected with the movie industry, appreciated such service.

Sales reached $7,000,000 in 1918 and Bullock's increased its buying facilities by becoming a charter member of the Associated Merchandising Corporation. Volume passed $10,000,000 the next year and by the time Arthur Letts died in 1927 was running more than $22,000,000 a year.

To finance purchase of the store from the Letts estate, the bank in which Bullock had deposited his mother's $150 when he first arrived in Los Angeles was happy to extend him a credit of $6,000,-

000. A new corporation, Bullock's, Inc., was organized and $4,000,-000 in bonds and $4,500,000 in preferred stock was subscribed in an hour in the first public store financing in California.

On September 26, 1929, Bullock's Wilshire was opened in a beautiful new building fronting three hundred feet on Wilshire Boulevard at Wilshire Place. Uniformed attendants parked customers' cars. It quickly became a high-fashion showplace and established a new shopping area. In later years, its parking area was doubled by the construction of an additional deck. One of many features of this store is a children's barbershop patronized by the sons and daughters of Bob Hope, Jeanne Crain, Hal Roach and many other Hollywood notables.

Investors in the new company received dividends from the start. Though sales dropped from a peak of $27,000,000 in 1931 to a low of $18,000,000 in 1933, Bullock's earned profits all through the depression. Bullock's Palm Springs was opened in the famous desert resort in 1930 and Bullock's Westwood shop in 1932.

John G. Bullock had a happy and triumphant life. He lived to see his store successful beyond his dreams and Los Angeles grow into a great metropolis. He was married happily twice. He served twelve years as president of the Retail Merchants Credit Association of Los Angeles, a trustee of the California Institute of Technology, and was active in countless civic organizations. As a director of the Metropolitan Water Board, he helped arrange a $220,000,000 bond issue for construction of the Colorado River Aqueduct and led a delegation to Washington to obtain a $40,000,000 Reconstruction Finance Corporation loan to start the great project.

One of the happiest days of his life came in 1930 when he returned with his daughter to his birthplace of Paris, Ontario. Henry Rheder, the merchant for whom he worked as a boy, and the Board of Trade gave a dinner in his honor. Mayor Stewart, once a schoolmate of Bullock, presided. Present even was Mr. Penman, the big mill owner whom Bullock as a boy never hoped to know socially. A scroll was presented to the local boy who had made good. Solemn toasts were drunk: "His Majesty the King," "The President of the United States," and "John G. Bullock."

He died of a heart attack on September 15, 1933, leaving an estate of $2,587,559, mostly in stock of the store. Mrs. Bullock presented two sets of bells to the Little Country Church of Hollywood in his memory. A bronze bust of the founder, the work of Helen and Holger Jensen, stands in Bullock's Downtown with a plaque: "This memorial testifies to our love for a friend and our loyalty to a leader whose spirit still lives and to whose ideals this business remains dedicated and devoted."

His successor both as president of Bullock's and as a civic leader naturally was the tireless P. G. Winnett who had shared the responsibility for the store from the first. Bullock's famous Collegienne shops, where women young in years or ideas find everything conveniently gathered, incidentally, were started because of the interest of his daughters in such merchandise. During World War II, he worked out the merger with I. Magnin & Co., headed the great Los Angeles War Chest campaigns. In recognition of these services, Occidental College gave him an honorary Doctor of Laws degree and the Welfare Federation of Los Angeles voted him its first medal for outstanding community service.

To finance modernization and expansion of both the parent and subsidiary stores, Bullock's increased its capital in 1945. The common stock was split three for one and 237,775 additional shares sold. Eighty thousand shares of a new issue of 4 per cent preferred stock also was sold at $103. Bullock's received $13,515,334, used $6,640,-757 to pay bank loans and retire the previous 5 per cent preferred, and had new capital of $6,874,577 for additional facilities.

Six millions of this went into a new Bullock's Pasadena branch, widely acclaimed for its beauty and revolutionary architecture. Six of the eight acres in the site between Lake and Hudson Avenues at Del Mar Street were devoted to automobile parking. A roof deck provided space for employees' cars. Planned by architects Wurdeman & Becket, the building is a merchandising machine specially designed for the best functioning under Bullock's "unitization" of the sixty individual shops of the branch. "Inside and out," commented *Architectural Forum* after opening of the show place on September 10, 1947, "it looks more like a club than a store—and a rather expensive club, at that."

On the topmost of the three levels is a terrace café called the Coral Room. It provides a fine view of the mountains and is the scene of a daily fashion show. The middle level contains a series of men's shops which can be reached without passing through the lingerie and other feminine areas on the same floor. On the bottom level are twenty-three home-furnishing shops and service facilities. These include two motor-court lobbies with "will call" desks to which packages are dispatched by chute and conveyor belts from wrapping stations in the building. The place is so much the domain of the motorist that there is only a single entrance for pedestrians.

President Winnett became chairman of Bullock's in 1950 and was succeeded as president by his son-in-law, Walter W. Candy, Jr. With the exception of war service as a commander in the Navy, Candy, a native of St. Louis and a graduate of Princeton, had been with the firm since joining Bullock's Wilshire as a merchandiser in 1935.

Other executives who came to the fore at this time included Philip Corrin, Mahlon E. Arnett, Ann Hodge and William F. Ashton, most of whom had spent their entire careers with Bullock's. After World War I army service, Corrin, a native of the Isle of Man and a *cum laude* graduate of the University of Southern California, joined the store as a copywriter. He succeeded Mr. Holt as publicity director, and became general manager first of Bullock's Wilshire, then the downtown store and a vice president.

Miss Hodge, a soft-spoken Ohio girl who came to Bullock's in 1912 after graduation from Mount St. Mary's College in Cincinnati, succeeded him as general manager of Bullock's Wilshire. As boss of one thousand employees there she is one of the most outstanding women in retailing. Arnett joined the firm in 1929 and rose to vice president and treasurer. Ashton was promoted to secretary and comptroller.

Hector Escobosa, a well-known fashion expert of Spanish descent, was chosen to head I. Magnin & Co. on the retirement of Grover Magnin at the end of 1950. Though a native of San Francisco, Escobosa for some years had been executive vice president and general manager of Frederick & Nelson, the Seattle department store of Marshall Field & Co. In this period, Magnin's in San Francisco moved into a new ten-story building with lavish fitting rooms and salons of baroque elegance. The Magnin units in Santa Barbara, Beverly Hills, and Pasadena also moved into finer quarters. New Magnin shops were opened in Sacramento's Hotel Senator and in La Jolla.

With the Magnin merger, Bullock's acquired one of the most famous women's specialty store organizations in the world. It was founded by Mrs. Mary Ann Magnin, a tiny energetic woman of unerring taste in high fashion. Born in Scheveningen, Holland, she married Isaac Magnin, a Dutch wood carver, in London, and together they migrated to San Francisco. There Magnin became a decorator and, fearing that he might be hurt at his work, Mrs. Magnin in 1876 opened a shop.

She began by making and selling fancy baby clothing. Later she made trousseaus. She moved her business from shop to shop as the fashionable retail trade centers shifted and acquired an exclusive clientele who relied on her for the latest and finest gowns and accessories from Paris. The business became a corporation with beautiful stores in San Francisco, Los Angeles, Beverly Hills, Pasadena, Hollywood, Santa Barbara, Coronado, Oakland, Del Monte and Seattle. Pink beige Rose de Brignoles marble was imported from France for the $3,000,000 Los Angeles shop opened in 1939 on Wilshire Boulevard.

The name Magnin became a synonym for elegance and its showings of new models by designers like Christian Dior, Pierre Balmain, Jacques Fath, Molyneaux, Balenciaga, Jean Patou and Marcelle Chaumont, important events for California society. As the business grew with California, Magnin's became the largest buyer in the high-priced wholesale dress market and acquired exclusive West Coast representation of some of the greatest names in fashion. It earned profits continually except in 1906, when earthquake and fire destroyed the San Francisco store, and 1932.

"People want more than 'thank you' in this world," said Mrs. Magnin as she explained her quest for the finest in apparel. She yielded management of the business to her sons beginning in 1903 but continued to interest herself in its affairs. A remarkable personality, she lived on in the St. Francis Hotel, celebrating her birthday each April with a big party, until she died there December 15, 1943, at the age of 95.

A few weeks later, President Winnett of Bullock's and two of Mrs. Magnin's sons, E. John Magnin and Grover Magnin, quickly worked out the merger. Magnin stockholders received one Bullock's share in exchange for three and a half shares of the stock of the other company.

While you can pay $350 in Bullock's for seven pounds of Blum's candy in a box covered with hand-sewn sequins and some Magnin salons consider any dress under $125 "popular priced," both groups of stores recognize the importance of average working women as customers. Nearly all of the stores are open at least one night a week for the convenience of employed people. The Los Angeles Magnin shop stages weekly evening fashion shows for special employee groups in the area and uses some of the selected group as fashion models. Girls so selected are rewarded with merchandise bonds, hosiery and receive a Charles of the Ritz make-up. The audience votes for the best models on blanks which become a mailing list for the store. Winning models return for a runoff or mass show for all the employee groups which have previously been invited singly. One of Bullock's overtures to employed women was the sending of orchid corsages to the two hundred maids employed by the Los Angeles Statler Hotel when opened.

When Bullock's was founded, the California apparel industry consisted of little more than the Levi-Strauss production of work shirts and tight-fitting overalls for cowboys. While continuing to draw on all the fashion centers of the world, both Bullock's and Magnin's have been important factors in encouraging the growth of California's great sportswear industry with products appropriately designed for a state that has more swimming pools than any other as well as hundreds of miles of beaches. The West Coast leads the world in bathing-suit production and Magnin prides itself on selling each August bathing suits which will not be sold in other parts of the country until the next year.

XVIII. Neiman-Marcus
The Pride of Texas

A T THE Inaugural Ball celebrating the advent of President Dwight
Eisenhower's administration, the new First Lady wore a remarkable gown of pink ribbed silk embroidered with four thousand
sparkling jewels encrusted on the bodice and scattered across the
wide skirt. It was described as pale Renoir-pink "peau de soie" but
it was not a dress from France, though the Eisenhowers had spent
years there. The gown was the handiwork of the American dressmaker, Nettie Rosenstein, whose creations are sold by many great
stores in the North and East, but it came from none of these.

Neiman-Marcus of Dallas, as everybody who read a newspaper or
news magazine that week discovered, had sold Mamie Eisenhower
her gown for the ball and also a Hattie Carnegie suit for the parade
and inauguration itself. The enterprise, care and resulting fame involved in these transactions do much to explain the success of this
remarkable specialty shop and how it has become probably the best-
known store of its size in the world.

The story of the gown and the suit began three years earlier.
While on a European buying trip, Stanley Marcus, the eldest of four
brothers who now run the store, was introduced to General Eisenhower at Supreme Headquarters in Paris. Marcus expressed his ad-
miration for General Eisenhower and recalled the latter's residence
in Texas.

"I hope you win the nomination," said the merchant as he departed. "If you are nominated, I hope you win the election. As you
were born in Texas and served in Texas, I hope you'll remember

there's a store in Texas that would like to dress Mrs. Eisenhower for the inauguration."

General Eisenhower laughed and nodded. When the votes were counted, and the Eisenhowers were deluged with proposals of all kinds, Marcus reminded the general of the conversation in Paris and submitted a number of sketches. Mrs. Eisenhower chose the Rosenstein number. While Neiman-Marcus issues amber-inked releases to the press almost daily, it said nothing about this news. Others announced it more than adequately.

To Miss Kay Kerr of Neiman-Marcus' New York office, Mrs. Eisenhower the next week wrote: "I have so many things for which to thank you—your patience, your courtesies, your helpfulness, your excellent opinions and judgment. . . . I can imagine what difficulties were imposed upon you where fittings were concerned by my nasty cold. . . . That you accomplished so much under handicaps is a tribute to your patience and efficiency. . . ."

One reason Neiman-Marcus does a business of more than $26,-000,000 a year from comparatively small quarters in Texas is its talent for showmanship. It has an ability to get aboard and even to create news that earns word-of-mouth and printed notice that is the exasperated envy of competitors. For example, when a fortnight's strike of pilots threw American Airlines' hostesses out of work, the store hired forty of them as models and salespeople. They earned their money and spent much of it in the store. Neiman-Marcus garnered two pages in *Life* and newspaper notice throughout the country.

Behind this sort of thing, the Marcus family has built a foundation of solid merchandising, extraordinary service and day-to-day promotion appropriate to the warm climate, easy living and chauvinism of the Southwest. This appeals alike to the Texans of legendary wealth and also to their less rich sisters who like to have the same label in their coats. Neiman-Marcus has thirty-five hundred charge customers who spend more than $2,000 a year with the store, but the average of all its 100,000 charge accounts is only about $250 a year and it has been the average accounts that have accounted for most of the store's increased sales in recent years.

The store was founded by three remarkable individuals, Herbert Marcus, his sister, Carrie, and her husband, A. L. Neiman. Herbert and Carrie had been born in Louisville, Kentucky, and had moved to Hillsboro, Texas, where a brother had a grocery, and thence fifty miles north to Dallas. There Herbert sold women's shoes and was promoted to boys' department buyer for Sanger Brothers. Carrie followed him and became an assistant buyer at A. Harris & Co. When Al Neiman, a promoter of department store sales from Cleveland, conducted a sale at the latter store in 1905, he met Carrie and they were married.

At this time, Herbert Marcus, married and the father of a newly born son named Stanley, demanded a raise at Sanger Brothers, then the largest as well as the oldest of Dallas stores. The raise was granted but only for $1.87 a week. He quit and joined Neiman in opening an advertising and sales-promotion agency in Atlanta, Georgia.

They succeeded so well with this that two years later they had the choice of selling it for $25,000 cash or trading it for Coca-Cola stock and a Missouri franchise for the soft drink. They spurned the latter, which quickly became worth millions, took the $25,000, returned to Dallas and started Neiman-Marcus. This once caused son Stanley to remark that the store was founded "on bad business judgment."

The actual capital was $22,000 from Neiman and $8,000 from the Marcuses. Herbert was then twenty-nine and Carrie twenty-three. The trio rented at $9,000 a year a two-story building at Elm and Murphy Streets and spent $12,000 on red mahogany fixtures and luxurious carpeting. Each contributed valuable talents and experience to the enterprise. Neiman was an able financial man. Marcus was a born merchant who even in his last blind years could accurately judge the quality of leather by its feel. Carrie Neiman's contribution was the most important of all—unerring taste and a shrewd judgment of style.

To avoid merely duplicating existing Dallas retail operations, they undertook from the first to make Neiman-Marcus a specialty store of style and quality for customers who did not need to haggle over pennies. Carrie Neiman spent $17,000 in New York for an initial stock and in the fall of 1907 with a page of the Dallas *News,* the new firm announced:

On September Tenth will take place the formal opening of Neiman-Marcus Co., the South's finest and only exclusive women's ready-to-wear shop, the most elegantly equipped storeroom in the South. . . . It shall be the policy of Neiman-Marcus to be at all times leaders in their lines and to give buyers in Texas something out of the common-place. . . . With these aims in view, exclusive lines of high-class garments have been secured, lines which have never been offered before to the buyer of Dallas. . . . We will miss a sale rather than have a garment leave the establishment which is not a perfect fit. . . .

Carrie Neiman and Herbert Marcus were ill on opening day, the latter with typhoid fever, and failure of the Knickerbocker Trust Company in New York precipitated a national business panic the next month. Nevertheless, within a few weeks the stock of "demi-costumes, modish waists, dress and walking skirts, better coats and millinery" was sold. There was money from cotton and also from oil in Texas even in 1907. Within three years, Carrie Neiman was making buying trips to Paris. In addition to women's clothes, the store began to sell accessories, infants' wear, girls' clothing and eventually men's wear and many other items.

In 1913, the firm had a $20,000 profit on a $380,000 sales volume despite a fire which destroyed the store. Neiman-Marcus then moved east to its present site at Main and Ervay Streets but not without difficulty. The owner declined to sell but was agreeable to a ninety-nine-year lease on condition that a building costing at least $100,000 be erected. As the firm's capital amounted only to $80,-000, Al Neiman sold five blocks of stock at $10,000 each to New York manufacturers. One of these has held its stock through the years and seen it increase to $700,000 in value. With additional funds borrowed, the firm built a $192,000 structure.

By 1916, Neiman-Marcus customers were becoming familiar with names like Callot Soeurs, Lanvin, Revillon Frères and Martial and Armand. Sales reached $1,260,046 in 1918 and $2,191,911 in 1919 as more oil fields were discovered in Texas. The Neimans and the Marcuses began to take larger roles in civic affairs.

Herbert Marcus, whose formal schooling ended at fifteen, helped raise money to launch Southern Methodist University. He gave Miss Hockaday's School for Girls $100,000 for a fine-arts building and served as a trustee. He helped found the Southwestern Medical Center. He helped bring grand opera to Dallas. He owned canvases by artists as noted as Renoir and Sir Thomas Lawrence. He encouraged his sons in similar tastes.

The store continued on its luxurious way during the twenties and sales reached a peak of $3,600,000 in 1929 but the firm went through a crisis the previous year. After twenty-three years of married life, Al and Carrie Neiman were divorced. Marcus bought the former's interest in the firm and he moved to New York. There he remarried, founded his own merchandising firm, Neiman Associates, and outlived both his former partners. Though he became blind in 1946, Herbert Marcus continued active in the store almost until his death at seventy-two from hypertension in 1950. His sister, by then "Aunt Carrie" to many, died three years later.

Stanley Marcus, Herbert's eldest son, who joined the store as a floor man in 1926 after earning a master's degree in business administration at Harvard, stepped into many of Neiman's duties. In 1928, he became secretary, treasurer and a director, also merchandise manager of the sports shop. The next year he was promoted to merchandise manager of all apparel divisions. In this role, he met Mary Cantrell, a pretty buyer in the store's sportswear shop. In 1932, he married and retired her. "Mr. Stanley," as he was soon known in the store, became executive vice president in 1935, and, after the death of his father, president.

As they grew up, his three brothers also joined the store, Edward becoming executive vice president; Herbert, Jr., taking charge of men's wear; and Lawrence, in charge of the expensive second-floor women's shop with the title of vice president and secretary. As of 1954, executives also included Joe Ross, formerly of Macy's, as vice president in charge of merchandising operations; Robert A. Ross, vice president and store manager; Nicholas Parker, vice president; Norman W. Bramley, formerly of Brooks Brothers, treasurer; Mary Lloyd, vice president in charge of personnel; Jane Trahey, director of advertising and sales promotion; and F. William Johnson, director of customer relations.

According to the organization chart, "Mr. Stanley" is supposed to deal only with the executive vice president, and the public-relations director, Marihelen McDuff, a soft-spoken former Dallas newspaperwoman; but actually he deals at times with everything and everybody. It was "Mr. Stanley" who first believed the store could attain national stature. In his first year at work, he started weekly fashion shows. He began to advertise Neiman-Marcus in national fashion magazines when such advertising was almost unknown. Many of the store's dramatic promotions have been his ideas. In addition to everything else, he personally has sold more than $5,000,000 worth of fur coats.

The two sides of Stanley Marcus' personality make him both an intellectual and a hard-driving merchant. His library includes works on art, china, brass, silver. He is both a collector of primitive sculpture and a serious student of typography. The time-consuming business of retailing has not prevented him from serving as president of the Dallas Art Association, as a trustee of the Dallas Museum of Fine Arts, and as president of the Dallas Symphony Orchestra. He is also a fellow of the Pierpont Morgan Library.

In the role of merchant, Stanley himself admits he has difficulty in delegating authority. During the day, he's all over the store, looking into everything, even running his finger along a counter in search of dust. He works himself and his staff hard. Wherever there's a customer who might be interested in Neiman-Marcus merchandise, Stanley believes in going to the customer. He even sends fashion shows to Fort Worth, bitter rival of Dallas, which is somewhat like having the Hatfields invade the home grounds of the McCoys. Women in Detroit have also been subjected to the temptations of a Neiman-Marcus fashion show, and when Stanley once heard of a woman in St. Louis who wanted a fur coat, he took the coat to her. The Neiman-Marcus fur staff now travels eighty thousand miles a year and shows its collection in forty-two cities. This bold seeking of business, even in the back yards of other stores, has helped to nourish the national reputation of Neiman-Marcus.

During the depression, the store lost money for two years. Though it was in 1930 that the great East Texas oil field, biggest the world has ever known, was brought in, there still weren't enough big spenders even in Texas for Neiman-Marcus to grow large with just the expensive lines of its early years. Some of this "new" oil went for as low as ten cents a barrel, and while it served to cushion the money panic that was about to paralyze the rest of the country, the store could no longer depend exclusively on high-priced merchandise.

It was during these depression years that Neiman-Marcus decided to split its personality and cater to the moderate income as well as to the wealthy. New lines of lower-priced, though well-edited, merchandise began to appear back to back with glamour apparel. When the Prudential Insurance Company later balked at Stanley's request for a loan, on the basis that Neiman-Marcus was too "frothy" and catered too much to the big spender, Stanley was able to prove that there were two sides to the argument—that a new chapter had been added to the legend of the fabulous Neiman-Marcus. He showed Prudential that the bulk of the store's sales actually were made to the "upper masses" rather than to the "upper classes."

In 1942 the store went after the under $20,000 income group in earnest. This policy increased sales between 1942 and 1953 almost five times. Not even the store's 1946 fire, which destroyed much valuable merchandise scheduled for pre-Christmas sale, slowed up Neiman-Marcus' progress. It continued to expand. With the dedication of the new Neiman-Marcus downtown store in October, 1953, a $9,000,000 expansion program which had begun ten years ago was completed. The Preston Center branch store was opened in 1951, and next year a new service building, with vaults designed for 20,000 fur coats, was completed.

As the store expanded, so did its customer service. It began opening at Preston Center on Monday nights, the downtown store on Thursday nights. Additional fashion shows were staged, with the emphasis on less expensive merchandise. Credit plans designed for lower incomes were instituted.

But President Stanley had no intention of dimming the gilded aura that had always surrounded the Neiman-Marcus premises. Continued was the rigorous inspection of incoming goods for size as well as quality which sometimes rejects half a million dollars' worth of merchandise a year. Continued was the search for beautiful clothes. New designers were introduced as they appeared, often before their work was acclaimed generally. On more than one occasion, the store has pointed the way in fashion. In 1948, Neiman-Marcus' early acclaim of Dior's New Look did much to establish it.

Some of Neiman-Marcus' glamorous labels can be duplicated no closer to Dallas than stores in Los Angeles and New York. Not even these stores provide the fabulous vicuña coats in the Neiman-Marcus manner. Probably no instance of Stanley's astute merchandising has made such retailing history as his promotion of vicuña. He has publicly had to deny that the store invented the precious fleece—that it was traditional garb of ancient Inca royalty. However, it was Stanley who brought vicuña from Peru, realizing that the expensive little cousin of the camel was an ideal article for a store whose customers are both wealthy and residing in a warm climate. Now even Peruvians buy their vicuña coats in Dallas. According to one South American customer, the Neiman-Marcus tailoring is infinitely superior.

The store also continues to win, hands down, in offering other glitter merchandise. In a year when Tiffany's Christmas catalog listed a $20,000 bauble as its most expensive item, Neiman-Marcus advertised an emerald and diamond ring at $30,000. This lavish sort of advertising is based confidently on past customer performance. A 1953 Christmas advertisement portrayed Marilyn Monroe wrapped in yards of mink, wearing a diamond bracelet and a satin and black lace nightie. Gift-hunting husbands were advised to "send $21,-173.75" and the merchandise shown would be wrapped and delivered—minus Marilyn. The items were sold, though it took three different husbands, in New York, Colorado and Chicago, to foot the bill.

Neiman-Marcus' reputation was built by the free-spending customer. Perhaps the most famous was Electra Waggoner Wharton Bailey Gilmore, heiress to land and cattle fortunes, who bought as much as $20,000 worth of merchandise in a single day—and returned the next day for another $20,000 she'd forgotten. This was in the early years of the store, but even today Neiman-Marcus' roster of customers includes such substantial spenders as the Dallas man who regularly sends $11,000 every month on account. His wife, daughter and mistress all have excellent taste in clothes.

Neiman-Marcus has found a ready market for ladies' jeweled pipes and a Dior gown tagged at $2,250 is no occasion for special comment on the store's expensive second floor.

Service of a de luxe kind is as much a tradition of the store's operations as is expensive merchandise. Neiman-Marcus' training program has produced, according to author George Sessions Perry, salespeople who "are to ordinary clerks as statesmen to politicians." When the store began to solicit the patronage of the defense worker's wife and that of the clerk and the schoolteacher, who might buy no more than a single dress a year at Neiman-Marcus, the salespeople took this new clientele in their poised stride.

Stanley Marcus takes great pride in his sales personnel and fashion models. He was furious when their morals were aspersed by Jack Lait and Lee Mortimer in *U.S.A. Confidential,* a book published in 1952. Suit for $7,500,000 was instituted against authors, publishers and printers of the book. The publishers and printers made public apologies in coast-to-coast newspaper advertising, and in letters to more than fifteen hundred Neiman-Marcus employees. The offending material was removed from future printings. Like everything else about the store, the libel suit itself is exceptional. In fact, it is unprecedented in the field of libel law, in that in a single suit it incorporates three types of charge of damage: damage against the individual, damage against an entire class, and damage against a corporation.

While Neiman-Marcus resorts to many ways of publicizing the store, Stanley Marcus believes in the use of newspaper advertising for pure hard selling. He has seen to it that the store's newspaper advertising, like its merchandise, is outstanding. Zula McCauley, Neiman-Marcus' first advertising director, set the pace for the distinctive copy and layout that has characterized its advertising ever since. Today Stanley and Jane Trahey, present advertising director of the store, check advertising proofs for typography and color printing. However, no store buyer sees copy or art until the advertisement appears in the paper. "That way," says Director Trahey, "you can have personality in your ads."

Stanley is convinced color advertising in newspapers is here to stay, and the store uses a great deal of it. Neiman-Marcus will introduce a new fashion color theme by means of such advertisements as a huge black cat sipping a dish of golden cream against a honey-colored background. Stanley's interest in typography, acquired at Harvard, has led him to take a special interest in the appearance as well as the message contained in any advertisement the store runs.

For some years Neiman-Marcus has used an editorial-type column captioned "Point of View" as an effective part of its advertising. Written by Warren Leslie, a former newspaperman with a novel to his credit, this column is signed simply "Wales." It appears several times a week as part of the daily Neiman-Marcus advertising in the Dallas *Morning News,* and often fails to mention any merchandise in the store. Instead it may discuss a new movie or devote itself to personality sketches, humor or anything else that strikes Wales' fancy. This was Stanley's brain child, and is reminiscent of the personally written advertising of John Wanamaker fifty years ago.

After years of seeking ideas and fashion-minded customers all over this country and abroad, Neiman-Marcus is now in the enviable position of having the fashion world come to it. The store's elaborate fashion shows, press parties, and special events gather notables from all directions.

Neiman-Marcus was chosen by Australian industrialists and businessmen to present American fashions to Australia in 1950, in anticipation of Australia's return to the dollar market. The store sent models and clothes nearly ten thousand miles, to Melbourne, Sydney and Adelaide, and brought them home by way of Europe, a junket entirely around the world.

George Antheil, the composer, created a special musical suite, "The Carnival of the Beautiful Dresses," for one of the store's anniversary fashion shows.

One of the store's more unusual fashion shows opened a swank flying dude ranch near Bandera, Texas. DC-3's were chartered to fly in the guests, who came from coast to coast, and every detail of the lavish menus and two-day entertainment was arranged by Neiman-Marcus. Stanley used the occasion to bring the East and West sportswear markets together for the first time. Over the barbecue, he persuaded them to schedule their seasonal wholesale showings on different dates, so that store buyers could attend both without splitting their ranks.

An unusual promotion was the Neiman-Marcus cookbook, *A Taste of Texas,* produced by Marihelen McDuff and Jane Trahey in 1949. They asked notables to contribute their "favorite or most tantalizing" recipes. E. L. De Golyer, Ilka Chase, J. Frank Dobie and many others did so. Paul Gallico, the writer, retorted with a letter saying he was planning to start a store and would like Neiman-Marcus to send him free "your favorite or most successful pieces of merchandise" and particularly "a fur evening wrap for a small blonde woman, about size 14, solid gold cuff links, a fine rod and reel for deep sea fishing, a pair of diamond and sapphire clips. . . ." The editors published his letter as a recipe for "Specialty Store à la Gallico." Six printings of the book have been sold.

Men's Night, a regular part of the Neiman-Marcus pre-Christmas promotion, is an elegantly staged affair for the benefit of tired though prominent business and professional leaders. Gift merchandise is displayed amid balloons, floating angels and hundreds of glowing Christmas trees. Nontransferable invitations written on pink perfumed paper begin "Dearest," and urge the recipient to come and do his shopping in comfort.

Greatest of all the Neiman-Marcus achievements, from a promotional point of view, is the annual presentation of the Neiman-Marcus Awards—the fashion "Oscars" for "distinguished service in the field of fashion." Instituted in 1938, the presentation is the climax of a five-day celebration which includes two fashion shows, lively Western-style parties and a Champagne Ball. The store also takes this opportunity to present what it deems The Ten Most Prophetic Fashions of the Year.

Awardees have included internationally famous personalities. Madame Henri Bonnet, wife of the French ambassador to the U.S., General Julius Ochs Adler of the *New York Times,* and Dr. Francis Taylor, director of the Metropolitan Museum of Art, have shared honors with Norman Hartnell of London, dressmaker to the British Royal Family; Hattie Carnegie, Christian Dior, Elsa Schiaparelli, Lilly Daché, Nettie Rosenstein, Adrian, Anne Fogarty, John Frederics, Jacques Fath, Emilio Pucci and others. The editors of *Vogue* and *Harper's Bazaar* have journeyed to Dallas to receive the silver and ebony plaque from the hands of Stanley Marcus.

Some years ago the store added a Consumer Award for Personal Fashion Discrimination, the first being presented to Mrs. Leland Hayward. It also has gone to Gloria Swanson and Dolores del Rio.

The Marcus brothers spare neither pains nor money in dramatizing these fashion expositions. One year $60,000 worth of modern sculpture was imported for display, to emphasize that year's fashion theme—New Shape, New Form. It was said to be the most comprehensive collection of contemporary sculpture in America outside of a museum or gallery.

XIX. L. L. Bean, Inc.

Sporting Goods by Mail from Maine

MOTORISTS following U.S. Highway 1 through the "Down East" section of Maine come eighteen miles north of Portland to the old village of Freeport. It is a pleasant tree-shaded community of less than twenty-five hundred which was famous in early Maine history as the place at which documents were signed giving the state its independence from Massachusetts.

Freeport is now famous as the home of L. L. Bean, Inc. This unique firm sells annually more than $2,000,000 worth of sporting goods to hunting and fishing enthusiasts all over the Western hemisphere. To it have been delivered promptly letters addressed merely "Bean, Maine" and "Mail order sporting goods house in a small town in Maine." Signs encountered five miles out on the highway lead the traveler to a store and offices over the Freeport post office and huge frame buildings to the rear which house workrooms, warehouses and a printing establishment.

Regardless of the day or hour, you will find the place open and somebody on hand to sell you a hunting or fishing license, a package of waterproof matches or any of several hundred items for the sport, dress or comfort of hunters and fishermen. This twenty-four-hour service is an example of the consideration of customer needs that has enabled Leon Leonwood Bean, now in his eighties, to build this remarkable business deep in Maine and to stamp his colorful personality on it.

"We have thrown away the key to the place," the bronzed, booming-voiced founder explains. "A lot of our customers drive up from

New York and Boston. Many leave right after work and are so eager to start hunting or fishing that they drive all night. This often brings them through Freeport in the middle of the night or even on Sunday. Where else can you get a hunting or fishing license on Sunday?"

Hundreds of places offer Maine hunting and fishing licenses but the $95,000 worth sold each year at Bean's is the largest total written at any one place and accounts for about a fourth of all issued. The firm collects the usual twenty-five-cent fee on each, but more important is the traffic that it brings to the store.

"Only about one person in twenty-five who comes in for a license goes out without buying something else," says Bean. "When they leave home, they don't worry about being short something. They say: 'We can always get it at Bean's.' " And they can.

The store stocks all the four hundred items offered in the famous Bean mail-order catalog, plus several hundred more that are being tested to see whether they merit space in it, and finally items like ammunition and waterproof matches which cannot be sent through the mails.

Bean is ecstatic about waterproof matches. "A city fellow can't appreciate them," he says, "but if you have been tramping through the woods in the rain and come in with everything you have soaked, there's nothing like waterproof matches. Shed water like a duck. Will light after being submerged in water four hours." He has sold thousands of cartons.

The merchandise ranges from twenty-cent cartons of matches to $340 aluminum canoes. The firm is the largest outlet in the United States for the famous Hudson's Bay Company's woolen blankets. There are scores of sporting accessories. But the backbone of the Bean business is in its own boots and shoes. These are stitched by Singer machines or made by hand in Freeport. In fact, the enterprise grew out of a special hunting shoe devised and made by Bean on a financial shoestring.

Bean was born in 1872 on a farm at Greenwood, Maine, the fourth of six children, five boys and a girl. The family is of Scottish descent. "My father lived on a farm," the merchant recalls, "but he was really more of a hunter and trader." Lennie, or L. L., as he became known, inherited both of these interests. When he was eleven, and the family moved to Milton Plantation, his father gave him the choice of going to a fair at Norway, Maine, or using the money to buy five muskrat traps the boy had been wanting. Young Bean settled for the traps. When he was thirteen, both parents died. He grew up with relatives at South Paris. His first big business deal was transacted at sixteen. L. L. went hunting and shot a good-sized buck. An empty-handed hunter offered him twelve dollars for it. With the money Bean bought some bread and salt pork and a pair of mittens, returned to the woods and went trapping in earnest. When he came out three weeks later, he was carrying five sables, plus a wildcat and most of the twelve dollars.

In 1912, after many jobs and ventures, L. L. became a partner of his brother Guy in a small clothing store in Freeport. It was just across Main Street from the present location of the firm. Some old newspaper advertisements attest that they sold overalls and shirts at thirty-nine cents each and some handkerchiefs at one cent apiece and ten cents a dozen. They once attracted a big crowd by closing the place up mysteriously for some days and having a big sale.

Bean eventually bought out his late brother and the latter, who was one of the few Democrats in Maine, became Freeport postmaster. This facilitated the arrangement of the store over and adjoining the post office. In consequence, Bean's merely drops packages down a chute to mail them, an arrangement also enjoyed by the big mail-order houses in Chicago, but exceptional in a village the size of Freeport.

L. L. was so much more interested in hunting and fishing than in shopkeeping that the clothing store kept going only through the tolerance of his creditors and customers. Then in his forties, Bean was considered an easy-going failure until he began to discover business opportunities as well as personal happiness in his sport.

His success began when he came home with sore feet one day from a hunting trip. Woodsmen's shoes were then heavy and stiff. After being wet, they dried into torturing shapes. Bean sought something more comfortable. Next time out, he tried wearing rubber overshoes and three pairs of wool socks.

He found this comfortable but at the end of a day's hiking had a "flat-footed" feeling. The wool socks also were not substantial enough for tops. He remedied the first by contriving an inner sole with a steel arch. Instead of the socks, he had Ted Goldrup and

Dennis Bibber, local cobblers, cut and sew leather tops to the rubbers. He tested the new hybrid shoes in the woods and found them light, waterproof and comfortable. Thus was born Bean's famous "Maine Hunting Shoe."

When some of his friends also liked the shoes, Bean borrowed $400 from the local bank and began to have them made in the basement of his store. By way of advertising he sent holders of hunting licenses a single blue sheet circular showing the shoe and describing it as "designed by a hunter who has tramped the Maine woods for the past eighteen years." Orders came in and a pair of these shoes were in the first parcel-post package mailed from Freeport when the service began in 1913. A tag on each guaranteed absolute satisfaction. Ninety of the first hundred pairs came back. The rubber had been too light and had torn away from the uppers. Bean made good on all and the shoe was improved.

By 1915, he moved the business across the street. The clothing store faded out and on stationery resplendent with ducks and fish in color, Bean became a manufacturer of "leather and canvas specialties." As he sold more and more shoes, he began to add related items, of similar quality and utility, starting with socks. While his formal education had included only grammar school and a short commercial course, he described his goods with such persuasive simplicity that the business grew steadily.

With some patented improvements more than a million pairs of the Maine Hunting Shoe have been sold. General Matthew Ridgway, a regular Bean customer, wore them in Korea. Rear Admiral Donald Macmillan, a native of Freeport, outfitted an Arctic expedition with them. Big-game hunters like Richard Sutton have worn them all over the world. U.S. Marines took them to Iceland.

Fame of the shoe led the government to employ Bean as a consultant and contractor during World War II. By inducing the Army to use boots with twelve-inch instead of sixteen-inch tops he lightened the burden of many a soldier and saved millions in costs. He also designed for the Navy a nonskid boot for wear on aircraft carrier decks that could be removed quickly if the wearer fell into the sea.

"For hunters who go just before the first snow," explains a recent catalog note on the Maine Hunting Shoe, "it is next to impossible to find footwear that is adaptable to both bare ground and snow hunting. For bare ground, its lightweight cushion inner-sole keeps it from drawing feet, while the crepe rubber sole keeps it from slipping. Outside of your gun, nothing is so important to your outfit as your footwear. You cannot expect success hunting big game if your feet are not properly dressed. The average hunting shoe weighs about four ounces more than ours. As big game hunters walk about seven miles (or 18,480 steps) a day they lift 2310 pounds more than necessary."

Bean's sales passed the $100,000-a-year mark in the early twenties and attained $1,000,000 for the first time as the business celebrated its twenty-fifth anniversary in 1937. Spurred by important notice in national magazines and the spread of the shorter work week which gave more men leisure for hunting and fishing, the business doubled again in less than a decade.

With growth came an increase in employees to more than one hundred, and incorporation. L. L. became president with his sons, Carl and Warren, vice president and treasurer. John Gorman, a son-in-law, is a director and one of the buyers. But L. L. continued to buy the hardware and any entirely new items. Adding machines, cash registers and a teletype were added to the office, and the factory expanded crazily on many levels.

The friendly informality that charmed customers like President Calvin Coolidge and Franklin D. Roosevelt, Babe Ruth and many other notables, was preserved. Bean's twice-a-year catalog has grown to 104 pages, many of them in full color. The printing requires 154 tons of paper a year and the more than 400,000 copies of each adds up to the biggest circulation of any Maine publication. But it is still the strangely indexed, fascinating hodgepodge of early days.

When Bean says in his catalog that the hook disgorger on Bean's Pocket Fish Knife "is the best I have ever tried," fishermen know Mr. Bean himself has given it a workout. Even when Mr. Bean appears to have been out of town when the catalog was put together, and Bean's Improved Double L Fly Rod Outfit is described as one with which "Mr. Bean landed an 18-lb. Atlantic salmon while fishing on the Tobique River," the customer is convinced Mr. Bean personally left this message for him before he departed.

The effectiveness of low-pressure selling is well understood by the astute Down Easter. Typical is this catalog statement: "While it is impossible to find any knife that is 100 per cent perfect for all purposes, we think this knife comes nearest to anything on the market."

A big-game hunter, under the influence of a recent edition, wrote Mr. Bean: "Your catalog is a dangerous book. A sportsman can no more pass it up than a drunkard can pass up a saloon."

The sportsman must also weave his way along from item to item, for Bean puts his catalog together in the manner of a general store displaying its merchandise. Ladies' Scarlet Underwear and Bean's ten-inch Ranger Boot are displayed on facing pages, while Shoes are scattered from one end of the catalog to the other, listed under twenty-two different categories and separately from Oxfords. Succinct listings in the index include Dehydrated and Legs—the former referring to potatoes, the latter to plastic trouser protectors. No detail of the sportman's equipment is too minor for Bean to take seriously. Bean's Maine-Made Clothespins "proved so useful both at home and at camp that we decided to list them."

Bean's "Toter and Deer Carrier," a stretcherlike contraption with a single bicycle wheel suspended from its center, is one of the products of L. L.'s fertile brain. Bean's New Field Coat, with a game pocket that lets down to serve as a waterproof seat is another— described by gunners who previously had to sit on a frosty log as one of the greatest inventions since the wheel. Bean's vest with sleeves and Bean's coat without sleeves were evolved in the same laboratory as Bean's hunting coat with the built-in match-scratching device— out in the Maine woods. Whatever Mr. Bean can't test in action himself, he turns over to friends or employees to test for him.

Almost every item offered is presented as "Bean's." Despite the fact that some of the merchandise is clearly identified in print as having been made or conceived by other manufacturers, it is still labeled "Bean's" as long as Bean approves of it and sells it. This has never seemed in any way inconsistent to L. L. nor to his customers. The Hudson's Bay blanket is one of the very few items allowed to fly strictly under its own flag.

Bean fosters a sense of neighborliness between his customers and himself, whether by mail or in direct conversation. An impressive number of celebrities have sat down in the store over the post office to chat. Mrs. Roosevelt, Ted Williams, Jack Dempsey, Lauritz Melchior and Kenneth Roberts are among the many who have stopped by on vacation trips to Maine. Famous autographs are to be found in Bean's letter files. But they remain in their alphabetical niches. Bean makes no capital of names in selling his merchandise.

"They're just customers," he says, "just customers. Sportsmen are more interested in the product than who uses it."

Sportsmen who climb the stairs to Bean's factory salesroom are exposed to the same temptations and organized chaos the catalog reader undergoes. In spite of the sales staff, it's often necessary in a rush season for customers to wait on themselves. They're encouraged to prowl around, write out their own sales slips, and bring the load to one of the girl cashiers. When a cashier checked over one sportsman's order, she noted that the red hunting cap for which he'd written a sales slip was missing. The man pointed to his head. The girl glanced up and said: "That one's soiled. Let me find another one for you."

"No," replied the customer. "I got this one here last year and somehow forgot to pay for it. So I just included it in this batch."

Bean says only one customer has ever tried to gyp him—and then for only $3. "But the man wasn't a sportsman," he adds quickly. "He was a cook in a logging camp."

The customers are happy with Bean's privately stocked testing pond, where they're invited to try out a rod or a pair of wading boots. Once Bean even coached a tearful "trout widow" in the art of fly casting for three days, and let her catch a few in the pond before he sent her home.

Largely to save himself time in answering questions, Bean in 1942 wrote and published a small book, *Hunting-Fishing and Camping;* into 106 pages, he packed a world of practical advice based on his own game bag. This has included, incidentally, thirty-six deer, two moose, one bear and a caribou, as well as all sorts of small game and fish ranging from brook trout to tuna.

"To my mind," he wrote, "hunting and fishing is the big lure that takes us into the great open spaces and teaches us to forget the mean and petty things in life." He advised on what to wear, what to carry, where to go in Maine and how many to include. "A perfect trip," he warned, "may be ruined by one person who does not fit. I recommend small parties, not over four. Two make a good party."

"No one should enter the big woods without being posted on Chapters 3, 13, 14, 15, 16," warns Bean. These, respectively, are How to Dress a Deer, Safety Rules, Signals for Hunters, How to Use a Compass and How to Find a Lost Hunter. He also included advice on bobcat hunting and camp cooking recipes. The initial printing sold out promptly at $1 a copy. Since then twelve additional editions have been published, each revised to map the previous year's kill of deer and bear in Maine, and more than 100,000 copies sold.

Bean's prescription for success is: "Sell good merchandise at a reasonable profit, treat your customers like human beings, and they'll always come back for more."

Just how much more they come back for is evidenced by an order received from a man in St. Mary's, Pennsylvania. The sportsman wrote that it would take "too damn long to fill out the list he wanted," and instructed Bean to send him every item in the catalog on pages 8 through 64 inclusive!

Customers like to trade ideas with the receptive Bean, and frequently send him suggestions for improving one product or another. Some of the ideas he has adopted include a fur-lined bottle holder that enables a bottle to be tossed about without breakage, and a decoy with a removable head which permits more lifelike attitudes.

The philosophical cement which binds Bean to his customers is expressed by Bean himself on a page in his catalog. Entitled "What Is a Customer?" the often-quoted definition reads:

A Customer is the most important person ever in this office . . . in person or by mail.

A Customer is not dependent on us . . . we are dependent on him.

A Customer is not an interruption of our work . . . he is the purpose of it. We are not doing a favor by serving him . . . he is doing us a favor by giving us the opportunity to do so.

A Customer is not someone to argue or match wits with. Nobody ever won an argument with a customer.

A Customer is a person who brings us his wants. It is our job to handle them profitably to him and to ourselves.

Bean's Yankee honesty and frugality are persuasive factors in his phenomenally successful business. He reminds customers that the price of leather is high, and that he can repair worn hunting shoes at a fraction of the cost of a new pair. He also urges impulsive fishermen to trim down their shopping list.

"Nine flies are all anybody needs for brook trout, six for Atlantic salmon, six for bass," Bean says flatly. Of these latter he adds: "If bass won't take one of these, they aren't rising."

However, not all his customers take this sage advice. A man in Baltimore still insisted on buying $236.50 worth of flies.

The wife of a sportsman also once came in to see Bean, saying she had a complaint. "Mr. Bean," she announced, "you are keeping my husband poor!"

As a final word of caution, Bean reminds customers that "We think it best to state that C.O.D. charges are high and are paid by the customer. (A $2 C.O.D. has a 30 cent postal fee.)"

The 65,000 square feet of the place is spread through a maze of annexes and different floor levels. One mailing-room employee is also a member of the volunteer fire department. "I've got to change levels eight times and go through five corridors, nine doors and two flights of stairs when the siren blows," he says. However, he adds, he still gets there faster than the butcher up the street who's about the same distance away. Customers aren't always so agile. In the small hours of the morning, a sportsman somewhat under the influence lost his way. He was found next day peacefully asleep under an over-turned stack of hunting pants. The arrangement is actually not as inefficient as it seems at first glance and the hillside location permits trucks to deliver to the upper as well as lower floors.

Behind the apparent chaos in the office is also a systematic and highly profitable operation. Prices are arrived at by a simple 50 per cent markup on the cost. As the firm makes a large portion of its wares this results in prices that are competitive with any retailer offering the same merchandise. With a few exceptions everything is shipped postpaid. As the business, 90 per cent mail order and 10 per cent in the store, is for cash, there is little bookkeeping.

The catalog is printed on the premises but the presses are owned by Walter F. Dumser, the printer. When not busy with Bean work, he cuts down the overhead with printing for others. Bean sends a catalog to anybody who asks for it, but unless an order results within a year, a second request must be made to obtain another. If something is ordered, the name is kept on the mailing list for two and a half years, or four more catalogs.

Incoming orders are handled somewhat as at Sears, Roebuck and Company, with whose executives Bean has several times exchanged ideas. With a single typing, a girl fills out an address label for the shipment, three copies of the order (one to go to the customer), and a name and address card to be checked against the mailing list. Mrs. Mabel Hall, Bean's assistant, directs a staff of girls who work full time correcting the mailing list.

One winter day when the New York Telephone Company needed forty pairs of snowshoes for its repairmen in an upstate emergency, Bean's got them off within an hour. Nearly all orders are shipped the day that they are received. The around-the-clock operation and the over-the-post-office location facilitate this.

The government once threatened to build a new $85,000 post office for Freeport and move it to another site. Bean stopped this by spending $25,000 himself to enlarge the existing space. This made his late brother, Guy Bean, famous in postal circles as "the only postmaster ever to refuse an appropriation."

Since increases in parcel-post rates and enforcement of the rules against large and heavy packages, Bean has attempted to shift more of his mail-order trade to over-the-counter business. He thinks, incidentally, the postal rule that big parcel-post packages can be sent to small post offices, but not to large first-class offices, one of the most absurd things in government.

A women's department, opened in the Freeport store on Memorial Day of 1954, is one move in this direction. While the catalog already contained some feminine items, including ladies' long underwear, the fall issue that year was sprinkled with ladies' sweaters, boots, stockings, shoes and coats. Bean's wife is an expert at fishing and he has observed more and more women, especially young wives, accompanying their men on hunting and fishing expeditions. Men encourage this because they can get away oftener. He thinks this is a very fine thing both for domestic happiness and the Bean business.

"A man isn't fussy about what he looks like when he goes fishing," says Bean. "He cares about comfort, not appearance. A woman is different. When she goes to the beach, she wants to dress for the beach. When she goes dancing, she wants to be dressed for dancing. When she goes fishing, she wants to be dressed for fishing. There is a great future in this for us and something that the style people will give more attention to if they are smart."

XX. Ohrbach's, Inc.

"A Business in Millions, a Profit in Pennies"

HIGH style at low prices has been the announced goal of countless retailers of women's wear, but none has achieved it more convincingly than Ohrbach's, Inc. Its slogan, "A business in millions, a profit in pennies," is a literal succinct statement of its success. By faithful adherence to an economical, low-markup operation devoid of frills, the firm has expanded from small beginnings on New York's Fourteenth Street, to Newark, to both Wilshire Boulevard and downtown Los Angeles, and in 1954 challenged both the greatest and the finest Manhattan stores by taking over the eleven-story structure occupied for decades by venerable McCreery's in the heart of the Thirty-Fourth Street shopping area.

The firm was founded by Nathan M. Ohrbach, a cheerful, early-rising, self-made merchant who for decades personally opened the doors of his store each morning. He doesn't smoke and drinks only rarely. For years he has worked at an ultra-modern kidney-shaped desk in a glamorous book-lined office with paintings by Thomas Gainsborough, John Constable and Thomas Benton nearby. His appearance is that of a college professor or a leader of Boy Scouts, the latter in fact a civic activity that he has pursued so devotedly that it has earned him the Silver Buffalo Award as well as the acquaintance of President Dwight Eisenhower, the late Sir Robert Baden-Powell and other scouting enthusiasts.

Ohrbach was born far from such surroundings in Vienna, Austria, on August 31, 1885. The Strauss waltzes were being composed there at the time, but the pleasures of the Hapsburg capital were not for

305

the Ohrbachs. When Nathan was two, his parents took their share of the family's few kronen, derived from a toll gate and a small salt mine thirty kilometers from the city, and migrated to America without improving their fortunes.

Nathan and his three brothers grew up in Brooklyn. He attended the New York City public schools and the DeWitt Clinton High School. At fourteen, he went to work at $3.50 a week "running errands and sweeping out" for J. M. Tobias, a wholesale coat and suit house. At seventeen, he was traveling for the firm. He was briefly a Coney Island lifeguard and a delivery boy for Macy's.

At twenty, he became a buyer and "assistant to the president" of the First Co. of Jersey City at $25 a week. He later bought for Berlin's, a Brooklyn store, Erich Brothers, on Sixth Avenue in Manhattan, and Brager's of Baltimore. By 1907 his prospects were bright enough for him to marry Miss Matilda Kane of Brooklyn, a sister of two of his business acquaintances.

In 1911, he opened a small specialty shop, Bon Marché, Inc., on Fulton Street in Brooklyn and later one in Manhattan on teeming Fourteenth Street between University and Fifth Avenue. He also acquired some small stores in Pennsylvanian towns. All sold low-priced ready-to-wear clothing in small quarters but managed to attract crowds with a table of fast-moving merchandise just inside the door. This became a basic Ohrbach sales tactic.

By 1923, he had saved some money and had spent eighteen of his thirty-eight years in retailing. This experience convinced him that success for a retailer lay in two different directions. One was in providing customers with every imaginable attention and service and charging them accordingly. The other was in cutting expenses and services to bare essentials and sharing the savings thus effected with the customers. Like several other famous merchants, he chose the latter course.

He then interested Max Wiesen, a dress manufacturer, in financing a new store to sell ready-to-wear in large volume at low prices. Each invested $62,500 in a partnership and Ohrbach made a careful search for a high-traffic location accessible both by subway and surface transportation.

After considering many possibilities he settled on a narrow fire-gutted structure on Fourteenth Street not far from his own small shop. Across the street to the north was Union Square, where long-haired orators voiced their world-saving dreams. A few yards to the east and across the street was "S. Klein, On The Square," Sam Klein's famous cash store then small but within a few years to claim to be the largest women's wear shop in the world. To the west were several big stores. Some regarded it as "the toughest retail market in the world."

The site chosen by Ohrbach was historic ground. In the nineteenth century it had been the home of General Bronson Winthrop, law partner of Henry L. Stimson. On March 4, 1903, Adolph Zukor had opened there a penny arcade at which the first motion pictures were shown in penny machines. The pennies rolled in so fast that a small car mounted on a track was required to haul them to the basement where a shooting gallery also contributed to the profits. On the second floor, Zukor built the world's first nickelodeon. To entice New Yorkers upstairs, he made the steps of glass, installed an electric-lighted waterfall underneath them and called the place Crystal Hall.

It continued in business for two decades until badly damaged by fire a few months before Ohrbach decided to make a store of it. The partners spent $70,000, more than half their capital, repairing the place. Many weeks were required. The metal around the old shooting gallery and the railroad track to the basement defied removal until a giant Negro gave them attention. "I can't build, boss," he said, "but I sure can destruct!"

The two floors and basement were stocked with dresses to sell at $1 and coats at $5. Nathan Ohrbach, incidentally, then and later contended that there was nothing wrong with pricing items in round figures. "In the early days of the cash register," he once explained, "the odd price was developed by retailers as a method of compelling clerks to ring up sales. If an item sold for $1, and the customer gave the salesperson a dollar bill, the clerk might hand over the merchandise and put the dollar bill elsewhere than in the register. But if the item sold for 95 cents and the customer presented a dollar bill, the salesperson would be much more likely to ring up the sale on the register in order to get the necessary change. In certain lines, women's gloves, for example, the odd price has become firmly estabished in customer's minds, but I unhesitatingly brand the general worship of the odd price as rank foolishness.

"I believe strongly that every retailer should experiment in this matter of odd prices. Profits in retailing are made in pennies, and the difference between profit and loss in more than one store might be found by refraining from throwing away profits in the form of smaller markups due to the fanatical worship of odd prices."

A "grand opening" was scheduled October 4, 1923, for the new store. A huge sign announced "Ohrbach's, a bonded word for savings. . . . More for Less or Your Money Back." Ohrbach and his brother-in-law, Jack Kane, were at work in the store the evening before when the latter recognized Sam Klein, the patriarch of the "On The Square" store, peering through the door.

They invited him inside for what proved to be the only meeting of Ohrbach and Klein who were destined to be rivals until the latter's death many years later. Klein, a poor Russian immigrant who had made a fortune with pushcart methods, shook hands and looked around with amusement. "Such long counters," he said. "Such high ceilings! It's a joke!" He took his leave and announced: "I'll give them just seven months!"

Sam Klein proved completely wrong about Ohrbach's. The opening-day crowds overwhelmed the store's fifty employees. A score of persons were cut and bruised. The police were summoned. Additional merchandise had to be rushed in that night to fill the denuded racks. The store was a success from then on and the 1924 sales amounted to $1,600,000 and gave the partners profits of $119,000. As business grew, the original frontage of twenty-seven feet was expanded by taking over adjoining buildings.

A "Miracle Day" sale, a duplicate of the opening-day event, was held at the end of every month for three years with coats, suits and dresses that were not moving drastically reduced in price. An internal crisis then threatened the store. Wiesen, the investor, and Ohrbach disagreed over how the business should be run. When the former refused for a time to sell out, Ohrbach leased quarters nearby and announced plans for a second store (all earlier Ohrbach stores by then had been sold, one of them to his brothers). The move brought Wiesen to terms and in January, 1928, he accepted $650,-

000 for the interest which had cost him $62,500 less than five years earlier.

At this time Ohrbach abandoned special sales or, looking at it another way, undertook to make every day a sale day. He then personally coined the slogan, "A business in millions . . . a profit in pennies." He also added men's and children's furnishings and accessories. Most important, he began to "trade up" his women's merchandise and to offer garments of a higher style and higher quality than had been previously available regularly in the neighborhood. This caused some to call the store "the fancy pants of Fourteenth Street."

At this time, he also formalized the policies which enabled the store to open a branch at Market and Halsey Streets in Newark, in 1930, and to pass triumphantly through the depression, even earning 16 per cent on invested capital in 1932, and in the late thirties to wrest the Fourteenth Street sales leadership from S. Klein by a margin of many millions. Considered individually, these policies are not unique. Each is pursued by many stores, but the cumulative effect, supported by distinctive advertising and showmanship, has created a retailing institution of definite and unique personality that has been able to make good its boast "that the prices of our merchandise are lower than the prices of similar or comparable merchandise sold anywhere in the city."

"A customer," says Ohrbach's manual for its employees, "may state that she has seen an article like ours for less in a competitive store. When this happens, call your department manager at once. Someone from our comparison department will shop the article to determine whether the quality and workmanship are equal to ours. If the customer is proven right, our item is marked down. If the customer has paid the higher price, a rebate for the difference is given to her. . . ." It is the custom to return not only the difference but 10 per cent of the other store's price in addition.

Some of Ohrbach's low markup is made possible by the firm's buying methods. As most ready-to-wear, however, is produced on the same Singer machines by members of the same union, the possibilities in this direction are limited. Nevertheless, the store has developed special resources and often induces manufacturers to make additional runs at trimmed prices of their products without labels or under an Ohrbach label. Odd lots of manufacturers' close-outs are sometimes purchased for cash. As the firm is family owned, it can act more swiftly than some rivals in situations of this kind.

The real economies, however, are in the store's selling operations. Fair-trade merchandise is avoided entirely. All sales are for cash. "The more billing, the less cooing," has been Nathan Ohrbach's explanation for no charge accounts. Selling is semi-self-service. This enables Ohrbach clerks to cover more counters and racks than clerks in stores where the merchandise is less open.

There is no alteration service. If garments don't fit, customers must alter them or find a seamstress to do it. There is no delivery service but packages will be wrapped for mailing if the customer desires. Employees, who in other stores receive discounts of as much as 25 per cent, pay the same prices as customers for merchandise at Ohrbach's.

Ohrbach's low markup policy is a firm one. An executive of the Newark store, who telephoned with the suggestion that the price of umbrellas be increased because it was raining, once received a severe lecture from Nathan Ohrbach. Any change in price is supposed to be downward but, unlike in the vast majority of stores, there is no calling attention to this when it occurs.

"Promotion is like taking dope," asserts the founder. "You use one dose of it and you have to have another, and another, and another. The only price that matters on an item is the price for which it can be bought. The people who advertise $89 values for $19.95 simply insult the customer's intelligence. If you advertise dresses at $12.95 formerly $16.95, you are simply saying to women: 'Dear customer, we thought we could sell these garments to you at $16.95, but you were too smart for us. You have decided they are worth no more than $12.95, and that's what we are pricing them.' "

No sales slips are written. Each item bears a single price ticket. Half of this is torn off when it is paid for and, put through an International Business Machine at the end of the day, helps to provide an up-to-the-minute inventory. If an item is marked down, an entirely new tag is affixed. As the firm attempts to turn over its merchandise fifteen times a year, twice as often as some stores of its class, markdowns come fast if merchandise fails to move.

Style, adroitly advertised and publicized, as well as price, has figured in Ohrbach's success. In a book, *Getting Ahead in Retailing*, first published in 1935, Nathan Ohrbach wrote: "It is essential that the retail novitiate recognize the utter and absolutely autocratic sway of Dame Fashion and her satellites, style and design over the world of merchandise." In this work, since reprinted half a dozen times,* the store founder classified women shoppers in relation to fashion as follows:

A. The woman who is highly style conscious and whose purse is able to withstand the onslaughts of high style. Price is no consideration to her. She wants to be among the first to sport the new. . . .

B. The woman who likes style but not to the exclusion of price. Her desire for fashion first may be as keen as that of the other woman. But she must, perforce, keep a weather eye on her purse. She will not buy at the very start of a season. First she must assure herself that the fashion trend is set—she cannot afford to buy a fashion flivver. Second, she must assure herself that the price is not exorbitant. . . .

C. The frugal woman, who is style conscious but who, through habit or necessity, must bide her time. . . . She is quite eager to be up to the fashion. But she must watch her dollars carefully, and therefore she waits until the season is well on before starting to shop. She, also, represents an important group—and an individual pricing problem.

D. Our final type is the woman who buys only when clearances are featured. Women in this group may or may not be fashion conscious—the fact is that few women, these days, do not know the basic style trends. But for economic or other reasons, these women buy only when prices are at bedrock.

Women of the last three classes are Ohrbach's regular customers and, in recent years, the store even aspires to the "Class A" women with some original creations by French, Italian and American designers. Nathan Ohrbach was made a Chevalier of the Legion of Honor in recognition of his merchandising of French imports. Originals of French and Italian designers as famous as Jacques Heim, Madeleine de Rauch, Balenciaga, Gres, Fabiani, Simonetta, and Capucci as well as Charles James of America have been purchased by Ohrbach's and low-priced copies promptly made for mass sale. The firm had the good luck to contract with Charles James for a line of gowns labeled "derived from Charles James" just before he won the 1950 American Fashion Critics' Award.

* By McGraw-Hill Book Company.

Adroit publicity and advertising keep its customers aware of Ohrbach's fashion achievements. In 1946, the store's publicity director, Mark Klauser, a former *New York Times* sports writer, arranged a fashion show for a record Ladies' Day crowd of 65,000 attending a Yankee-Red Sox baseball game at Yankee Stadium. Fifteen jeeps carried models wearing sun suits, bathing garb and other summer wear about the field. Ray Bolger, the dancer-comedian, was master of ceremonies and five hundred pairs of then scarce nylons were given away. The stunt helped push the store's sales above $30,000,000 a year and its profits over the $1,000,000 mark for the first time.

In addition to general and sports-page publicity, the event earned Ohrbach's a picture feature spread over four pages in *Life*. The store was in the magazine prominently again the next year when Sally Kirkland, formerly of *Vogue,* became fashion editor and produced a feature on how a young career girl in New York could buy "The New Look for $100." While five stores were represented and credited in the $99.97 wardrobe, seven of the twelve items, including the girl's evening dress and coat, came from Ohrbach's. *Life* later devoted a cover story to the store itself. The firm's tie-up with Charles James and some other style ventures also earned national notice.

Advertising and high fashion have been a particular interest of Jerome Kane Ohrbach, son of the founder. Following graduation in 1929 from Cornell University where he was an athlete, he worked in the firm's advertising agency before joining his father to form one of the most successful father-son teams in retailing. He was successively assistant buyer, buyer, merchandise manager, general manager, vice president and in 1946, after war service as a colonel in the Army Air Forces procurement operations, succeeded his father as president when the latter became chairman of the board of the firm.

While many stores, at least on Christmas Day and New Year's, advertise themselves as institutions, all of Ohrbach's advertising as developed by Jerry Ohrbach has been institutional. As specific prices and items are not advertised, there is no need for turning out news of bargains under the pressure of newspaper deadlines. In fact the firm has no advertising department in the usual sense. An advertising agency and a publicity firm have been employed for many years. Preparation of advertising was entrusted to the Grey Advertising Agency in 1928 and when William Bernbach and others handling the account there formed their own agency, Doyle Dane Bernbach, Inc., in 1949, Ohrbach's continued with them.

Unusual, gay illustrations, ample white space and short, often humorous copy have characterized Ohrbach's distinctive advertising. Many early advertisements of the store were one-panel cartoons depicting the adventures of a big-eyed, curvaceous young lady called Melisse who always snared her man and otherwise asserted that "the girl in the Ohrbach dress" was irresistible in all situations. This series attracted national attention and the original Melisse, Mildred Oppenheim, the artist who created the character, went into business for herself.

Several paintings from a notable collection of New York scenes commissioned by the elder Ohrbach were used in the store's advertising. This collection of sixty paintings, by ten artists working without restrictions, also was exhibited at the Museum of the City of New York and attracted attention in art circles. The artists included Thomas Hart Benton, Aaron Bohrod, Adolf Dehn, George Grosz, Peter Hurd, Fletcher Martin, Paul Sample, Georges Schreiber, Lawrence Beall Smith and Frederic Taubes. Later some abstract illustrations by Erik Nietsche were used in Ohrbach advertising and proved so abstract that it was suggested that they be repeated upside down.

Humorous drawings by Peter Arno and Paul Rand followed and gave way to equally amusing photographs, sometimes published awry or in fragments. Though copyrighted, one captioned "Don't walk your legs off," and showing a young lady apparently doing so, was copied widely. Another showing bearded men dueling was captioned: "I'd rather die, sir, than give up a woman who shops at Ohrbach's." The firm's advertising has been praised by rival merchants like Walter Hoving and has received awards from the National Retail Dry Goods Association, the American Institute of Graphic Arts, the Art Directors Club of New York and others. In addition to sizable newspaper space, the store has sponsored a New York breakfast radio program and used subway posters, but total advertising expenditures in most years have been held to 1 per cent of sales, less than half the ratio for many specialty-store operations of comparable size.

Some idea of the originality and effectiveness of Ohrbach's advertising was revealed by a classroom survey in the Julia Richmond High School of New York in 1951. With names and addresses deleted, twenty full-page advertisements of big Manhattan and Brooklyn stores from Sunday editions of the *New York Times* and New York *Herald Tribune,* were shown to students. Eighty per cent of them remembered and identified the Ohrbach's advertisement. Only one other advertisement was recognized by as many as 50 per cent. The pages of three stores were identified by 25 per cent, eight had a smaller score and the remaining seven pages were entirely unrecognized.

The firm's expansion to California was initiated by Jerome Ohrbach, who was first attracted there by the growing Coast fashion industry. The firm employed the services of a buying office in Los Angeles as early as 1939 and in 1945 opened one of its own there. Three years later it leased three floors and the mezzanine in a wing of the glittering new Prudential Insurance Company building on fashionable Wilshire Boulevard's "Miracle Mile." Into the 150,000 square feet of floor space went fixtures and decorations, including some mural paintings, costing $2,500,000 and merchandise valued at the same amount. Kermit Claster, formerly merchandise manager of main-floor departments of the New York Store, was placed in charge.

Lured by newspaper and radio advertising of the same institutional type that had proved successful in New York, thousands were on hand for the initial day's business. Nine minutes after the doors were opened, they had to be closed and, as in the case of the Manhattan opening back in 1923, police had to keep order. By afternoon, spot announcements on local radio stations were saying: "Please don't come to Ohrbach's today; come tomorrow, or next week." Customers buying bargain nylons, handbags and similar items overwhelmed the store staff and twenty-five additional cashiers were flown from New York to handle the rush which continued for days.

So well received was the firm in the West that in 1953 it purchased Milliron's, a downtown Los Angeles store dating from 1905, and spent $1,000,000 modernizing its eleven-story quarters at Broadway and Fifth. Using golden scissors, Mrs. Nathan M. Ohrbach cut a ribbon to open formally the refurbished store. A crowd of seventy-five thousand rushed in for opening-day bargains. So crowded was the store at midday that newcomers were admitted only as those inside departed. While Milliron's had previously been a store with credit, charge accounts and deliveries, these services were discontinued by Ohrbach's without loss of sales. In fact, the opening day's business under the new management was greater than during the entire last month under the previous regime.

Many famous and glamorous shoppers became customers in Los Angeles. These, however, were not unknown in the New York store. Two women once arrived there from Philadelphia in a chauffeur-driven automobile and ecstatically spent $2,000 in one day. Ignorant of Ohrbach's sources, some visiting merchants from Latin America have at times purchased a few stylish numbers for resale abroad. Professional photographic models have been frequent customers. Joan Crawford, Jane Russell, Merle Oberon, and Jeanne Crain of the movies shopped there occasionally.

This sort of patronage greatly increased in California. Present at a 1951 Ohrbach fashion show there, for example, were Baroness d'Erlanger, Gene Tierney, Lady Lawford, Mrs. Gregory Peck, Mrs. Oliver Echols, Mrs. Ira Eaker, Mrs. Noah Dietrich, Princess Pignatelli and many others. Linda Christian told the store how she paid $10 for a coat at Ohrbach's, wore it awhile and then sold it to a thrift shop for $15.

When the Wilshire Boulevard store sold the bankrupt Merry Hull stock of costly children's clothing at a 70 per cent markdown, Mrs. Alfred Vanderbilt bought $600 worth of the garments and Lauren Bacall $500 worth and later $300 worth more. The store has outfitted many famous network television shows.

With the California stores functioning smoothly, the Ohrbachs next undertook a bold expansion in the heart of New York on West Thirty-fourth Street off Fifth Avenue, just across the street from the Empire State Building, the world's tallest skyscraper. The opportunity came when the venerable James McCreery and Sons store, immortalized in *Life with Father,* closed its door after becoming unprofitable. Undaunted by the fact that any store in this location must compete with Macy's, Gimbels and Saks 34th Street to the west, and such famous fashion stores as Lord & Taylor, B. Altman, Russeks, Arnold Constable and Franklin Simon nearby on Fifth Avenue, the Ohrbachs, father and son, decided to take over the site. A ninety-year lease was arranged through William Zeckendorf, president of Webb and Knapp, Inc., the realtor famous for assembling the United Nations site, and Ohrbach's took possession of the property early in 1954. At a cost of $2,000,000, all eleven floors of the old building were rebuilt and remodeled under the direction of Raymond Loewy, noted industrial designer.

Around 100,000 persons crowded into the store on opening day, August 26, 1954, and spent $500,000. "If you live through this, you are ready for Macy's," said the latter in an advertisement welcoming its new neighbor.

Morale is high among Ohrbach's more than four thousand employees. Practically all executives have risen from the ranks. The Ohrbach Mutual Association, Inc., operates dining rooms and cafeterias which serve good food at low prices. It also conducts social affairs and athletic activities, which have included notable basketball and swimming teams, one girl diver even competing for America in the Olympic Games. There are also sick benefits, life insurance, pension plans, and for top executives, stock option purchase plans. All regular employees after five years receive a week's winter vacation in addition to a summer's fortnight vacation. The company has a revolving loan fund on which employees can draw in financial emergencies.

Ohrbach clerks are given careful instruction in courtesy and grooming but are allowed more latitude in dress than in many stores. In the summer, for example, girls are permitted "leg makeup properly applied" in lieu of stockings. An Ohrbach girl is supposed to look "crisp, clean and well-put-together." She is supposed to start each day with a bath, brush her teeth thoroughly at least twice a day and see her dentist every six months. She is instructed: "Don't go in for slouching, or slinking, walk naturally—don't rumba."

Employees are invited to make suggestions for the improvement of the store and its operations and a "Suggestion Committee" distributes cash prizes for those accepted. Employees also are rewarded for the detection of shoplifters.

"A customer owes you nothing," the store tells its employees. "You owe her courtesy by the very fact that she is in your store. . . . It is our aim to make every Ohrbach customer a satisfied one —satisfied not only with any merchandise that she might purchase here but also with the friendly, courteous treatment she receives from each and every employee whom she chances to contact in the store. A customer should never be made to feel that she must buy; she should know that she is perfectly welcome to shop."

Nathan Ohrbach believes that the retail leaders of the future will be college graduates. In addition to the Boy Scouts, he has been interested for many years in the New York University School of Retailing, the Fashion Institute of Technology and Design, and the Central High School of Needle Trades as well as other institutions. At New York University, a Nathan Ohrbach prize is awarded annually for the highest scholarship in the Fashion Apparel course. He also has chairmaned an advisory committee which has arranged part-time jobs for retailing students at the College of the City of New York.

He has found that college-trained men and women grasp important facts better and advance quicker. But by college graduates, he does not mean shy bookworms who consider selling "undignified." To succeed in retailing, a person must enjoy meeting people, have a feeling for merchandise and enjoy competition. "Retailing," he has written, "when stripped of all its details, is found to be the art of pleasing people. . . . Brains, imagination, courage and all the other attributes of youth are demanded by retailing as by no other single industry."

XXI. Webb's City

"The World's Most Unusual Drugstore"

THE modern drugstore, one of the most amazing of American institutions, is the heir both of the itinerant "medicine man" and the ancient apothecary's shop. Physicians of Greece and Rome compounded their own prescriptions but in A.D. 754, an Arab named Abu Coreisch Isa el Szandalani, at the instance of the Caliph of Baghdad, opened in that city probably the world's first apothecary shop. Developments followed in England, Germany and France. Immigrants brought the pharmaceutical traditions of these countries to America.

Elias Durand, a pharmacist with Napoleon's Grand Army, for example, opened a shop in Philadelphia in 1825. It was the first to boast a soda fountain. As early as that date, it is interesting to note, pharmacists of both Philadelphia and Boston were attempting to stabilize retail drug prices. "One evil where there is a difference in price," one of the latter noted, "is that the purchaser either thinks that the one who charged high wronged him as to price, or that the one who charged low wronged him as to quality." It is not surprising that like-minded merchants in the twentieth century, through the National Association of Retail Druggists, advocate state and national fair trade legislation.

Other drugstore owners believe it more profitable to cut prices. There also are differences of opinion as to what a drugstore should sell. Lascoff's in New York, Sam Porter Jones of Louisville, Kentucky, and at least four hundred others carry on in the apothecary tradition, selling only drugs and, in many cases, only drugs prescribed by physicians. A great many more sell many other items as well and may be notable for their customers. One such is Schwab's in Hollywood where film folk gather at the soda fountain. Sanborn's of Mexico City, now a Walgreen property, is a remarkable institution. Housed in an old palace, it is one of the best eating places in the city and does a big gift and silverware business.

But it is in St. Petersburg, Florida, a pleasant city so largely inhabited by aged pensioners that the curbs are sloped for wheelchairs, that the world's largest and most extraordinary drugstore is located. By bargains and ballyhoo, it has attained a sales volume of more than $22,000,000 a year and does the largest retail cash business in the South. For years this establishment has advertised itself widely as "Webb's City, The World's Most Unusual Drug Store." Nobody has objected.

In fact, it might also be called "The World's Most Unusual Meat Store," "The World's Most Unusual Barber Shop," or several other distinctions with equal validity. For the store that sprawls over four city blocks has fifty-eight busy departments, including one selling women's ready-to-wear. There are five restaurants, a beauty shop, a gasoline station, a super market and on the roof even an Arthur Murray dance studio. Seven parking lots provide space for 1,500 automobiles. All of this attracts around 45,000 customers a day in a city where the 1950 census counted only 96,738 permanent residents.

But the heart of the operation is the drug department and the drugstore designation permits the place to do business from 7 A.M. to 11 P.M. seven days a week. Thirty registered pharmacists, possibly a record number, compound more than seven hundred prescriptions a day in immaculate quarters. Two-thirds of the main floor space is a super drugstore and despite the growth of other departments, the management asserts that drugs, the huge soda fountain, cosmetics, and related sundries account for more than half of Webb's huge volume. Everything is sold for cash and only for drug items is their free delivery service.

The site is between two railroads, and the main building is four stories high, with a basement cafeteria. Nearby is the Trading Post, essentially a super service station, which also houses sporting goods, paint and hardware stores. Also nearby, but not between the tracks, is the feed and fertilizer store. And some six miles away, outside the

city limits on Gandy Boulevard leading to Tampa, under a five-story
electric sign, is Webb's Outpost, a gift, sandwich and souvenir shop
which gives tourists information about St. Petersburg and Webb's.
Road signs, some of them 750 miles away, also direct motorists to
the place.

Responsible for it all is James Earl "Doc" Webb, whose portrait
painted handsomely in oil hangs in the store over the ascending
track of the escalator. Of slight stature but immense energy and with
a great flair for showmanship, he is a cocky bantam who has found
fun and fortune in running a store like a circus. He was born August
31, 1899, in Nashville, Tennessee, of Scotch, Irish and English descent. His formal education ended after the seventh grade but his
business education already had begun at that time.

"I began making money when I was nine years old, selling lemon-
ade, orangeade and sherbet, and later peddling both morning and
afternoon papers," Doc recalls. In his teens he worked around drugstores and had such an affinity for this type of business that "I was
manager of a retail drugstore with twelve adults working under me
by the time I was twenty," he says.

He was in Knoxville by this time and here earned his informal
title of "Doc" by developing a compound which was known through
Tennessee and Kentucky as "Webb's 608." This was a venereal dis-
ease remedy widely distributed in colored areas. Profits from it enabled Webb to buy an expensive Rickenbacker automobile.

"I have always made money and liked making it," Webb says.
"By the time I was twenty I had bought a great variety of stocks,
but now I own just one kind—Webb's."

After seven years in Tennessee drugstores, where he learned a lot
but never bothered to qualify as a registered pharmacist, Webb at
twenty-six decided to go into business for himself. Because he liked
the climate and there was a real-estate boom there, he chose the
west coast of Florida. But just as he arrived in St. Petersburg with
$5,000 and a partner, the boom collapsed and stores began to close
on the main streets.

Undaunted, he opened a tiny cut-rate drugstore with four employees in rented space seventeen by twenty-eight feet. It was in an
old building at the south end of the business area adjoining the
Negro district, and between the Seaboard and Atlantic Coast Line

railroad tracks. The exact spot is now more than occupied by Webb's cigar and magazine department but a museum replica of the original store is to be found on the fourth floor, labeled "Doc's Original Drug Store."

The first year's receipts amounted to $38,990.45. With $6,000 in bills unpaid, Webb and his partner then parted and the latter eventually received $18,000 for his interest. Webb says his partner was "too conservative." The next year sales reached $90,000 and Webb started the expansion that eventually took all the space between the tracks. By shrewd purchasing, ruthless price cutting and spectacular promotions, he began to lure crowds to the out-of-the-way location. Sales passed $1,000,000 in 1936 and $2,000,000 in 1939.

One of Webb's most spectacular loss leaders was the three-cent breakfast with which he introduced his basement cafeteria. For this price, you received one egg, two strips of bacon, three slices of toast, grits and ham gravy. After six months, during which the cafeteria became well known, the price was advanced to fourteen cents. During sales this later was cut to nine cents!

Webb once cut up "the world's largest cheese," a 2,480-pound chunk of Wisconsin cheddar, and sold it in a few hours. He sold a freight car of cantaloupes for two cents each, moved a carload of canned peaches in a day and even staged a carload sale of cigars. With sidings on two railroads, it is easy to handle such shipments. When butter was at seventy-nine cents, Webb's sold some at nineteen cents a pound and once marketed $17 automobile tires for $9.95. A cigarette "war" with a rival store ended with Webb's giving away two packs to a customer.

At times, Webb's has posted the sale advertisements of rival drugstores with an additional line: "10 per cent off these prices at Webb's." But the height of this sort of thing probably was the sale of two thousand $1 bills at ninety-five cents each, later the sale of twenty-five hundred more at eighty-nine cents each, and the repurchase a few days later of the "cheap" money at $1.35 per greenback. Mobs jammed the store for each event.

"Any merchant," Webb believes, "should have the right to sell any item in his store at whatever price he decides." His tactics natturally brought him into conflict with the fair-trade laws and at one time he had six law firms employed defending him in various actions. In several of these, he was successful in having Florida statutes invalidated, the Florida Supreme Court once ruling that inflexible price arrangements "are not in line with our traditional concepts of free competition."

The "Florida Poster Girls," one of Doc Webb's most durable publicity ventures, date from 1939. Each year eight Florida girls are chosen from several hundred on the basis of "beauty, character, talent and charm." Clad in bathing suits and other Florida fashion products, they present fashion shows about the country and otherwise publicize Florida, St. Petersburg and Webb's. Some years, they even invade Hollywood in a Florida versus California beauty competition.

Doc Webb's markups have been so low and his promotion expenses so great that at times he has been short of cash when expansion was required. In 1940, he needed $200,000. When local banks couldn't accommodate him and underwriters wanted 10 per cent for selling a stock issue, Webb decided to sell $100 preferred shares over the counter. He filed the proper papers, obtained a broker's license and put a big advertisement in the Sunday paper. It concluded "You have 7 days to buy these securities. . . . Come now! See J. E. Webb." A Monday page said "Today is the Day."

On Tuesday morning, he advertised "$73,400 of stock sold and paid for," on Wednesday, "$126,600 sold and paid for." On Thursday, a horrified representative of the Securities and Exchange Commission arrived to explain that securities could not be advertised like drugstore bargains. But the advertisement that morning simply said "Thank You." All the stock had been sold.

"At that time," recalls Doc Webb, "I found that we need never fear to be in the hands of the people."

This preferred stock subsequently was retired. Doc Webb owns a majority of the company's common stock and with his officers controls 70 per cent of it. The other 30 per cent is owned by some seven hundred persons, many of them employees or customers. The brief annual reports reveal a steady increase in volume and unbroken but varying earnings.

Sales increased from $3,693,946 in 1941 to $12,305,000 in 1947; $18,218,837 in 1951 and $22,000,000 in 1954. Earnings during these years ranged from $66,311 on sales of $5,675,000 in 1943 to

$333,092 on sales of $16,421,788 for the fiscal year ending August 31, 1950. Though it is common for heads of retail enterprises of this volume to earn more, Doc Webb pays himself a salary of only $30,000 a year.

The name, Webb's City, denotes the operation conducted by Webb and his associates. The business is citylike in the sense that more than fifty separate operations are carried on principally under one roof, and that most of the necessities and many of the luxuries of life can be procured in the various "stores." Each store has its own manager who is responsible for purchasing goods and selling them quickly at a modest profit which Doc Webb says nets between 1 and 2 per cent in an average year. The discount for paying cash is sometimes the only profit on an item. Over the fifty-eight store managers are five division heads, and over everybody are Doc Webb and his right hand, James Horace Willis, executive vice president and general manager. T. P. Johnson and B. H. Willis are also vice president and W. A. Willis is secretary-treasurer.

"This is not a department store operation at all, though one of the fifty-eight stores is a department store," Doc Webb points out. "Every manager is in charge of his own store and has the responsibility for its operation with help as needed from his division head or from Mr. Willis and me. Before World War II this was essentially a one-man operation—I had the ideas, planned the remodeling, made the rules and regulations. Now we have more of a team system."

The fifty-eight store managers are almost independent operators, for they hire and fire their own help, act as purchasing agents and are everything that their title implies. Seasonally, the number of employees varies between twelve and fifteen hundred. Turnover is low, morale is high, and many employees are stockholders. A bonus is paid each April, and there is incentive pay in the form of weekly commissions to augment salaries. There are paid vacations, sick leave and an insurance participation plan. Webb is proud of his employees and has announced that one of these days he is going to build a country club and swimming pool for them "and my customers." There are many ten-, fifteen- and twenty-year men in the organization and the attentiveness of clerks gives backing to an observation by General Manager Willis that "the employees feel they own the store."

Willis, a few years younger and a lot bigger than his boss, came to St. Petersburg from South Carolina and has been with Webb since 1934. He was in the food retailing business in South Carolina and set up the grocery store which now is Webb's biggest single operation. Willis has a crowded office just big enough for two desks, and from this vantage spot on the mezzanine a sweeping view of the main floor can be had. One of the desks belongs to Doc Webb.

"Most businesses start with one man and I started Webb's," Doc says, "but somewhere along the line you have to have help, and I am lucky to have Willis. We think alike, we breathe alike and we talk alike. We bring five or six men into this little office of his and we talk together and work out our plans. That's all you need an office for.

"You can't build a business staying in an office. The greatest failure in the world came when America's banks closed right and left back in the early thirties. If those bankers had been out in front meeting people and talking to them, the depositors wouldn't have taken out their money. But the bankers were back in their offices and look what happened. . . ."

Doc Webb usually doesn't get to the store and "out in front" until the afternoon but he has not been idle. The home which he and his attractive wife, Aretta, a businesswoman in her own right, share is equipped with seven telephone lines, three direct to Webb's City, and there are telephone outlets in every room. Doc does most of his business by telephone. When he does arrive at the "office," he probably will breeze in wearing a white suit, one of 150 that he owns in the jaunty manner of Jimmy Walker or Adolphe Menjou.

After an hour or sometimes less, Webb usually darts restlessly out of the office to do something more exciting. He may grab a microphone and over the public-address system announce a sudden bargain as if he were back selling medicine in the Tennessee mountains.

"Hear this, hear this!" he'll chant. "For the next thirty minutes, the next thirty minutes only, we will sell in the appliance department $25 electric toasters for $9.95 apiece. Hurry, hurry, *hurry!*" From all parts of the area, a mob will converge on the appliance department and in thirty minutes all the toasters may be sold.

If there are circus acrobats performing about the place, as sometimes is the case, Webb may strip to the waist and get into the act. He likes to jump up and down on mattresses. Though now a grandfather, he is a wiry and active athlete. With a tennis partner, he once won the veteran doubles championship of Florida and had no difficulty a couple of years ago obtaining a $500,000 insurance policy on his life for the benefit of the store.

Doc Webb also likes to stop at his free "park-a-baby" service for shopping mothers. If he sees one he knows, he'll stop, praise him extravagantly and maybe toss him aloft to the delight of baby and mother. This supervised fourth-floor department is one of the most popular.

Another feature which attracts thousands of potential customers is Webb's free check-cashing service. At any time in the day, there will be a line at the check window on the main floor. Checks totaling more than $25,000,000 a year are cashed—an amount greater than the store's yearly sales volume. This service costs Doc Webb $20,000 or more a year, but it is cheap advertising. Bankers' hours are unheard of at Webb's, and check cashing goes on day and night. Losses from bad checks are infinitesimal—and the few persons who try to impose on the system with bad checks are relentlessly pursued. "We cash more checks than most banks," Doc Webb claims proudly —and he doesn't have to add that a lot of the cash he hands out is spent in the store.

Doc Webb says he doesn't believe in setting aside any fixed percentage of income for advertising. "There just isn't any yardstick you can apply—you just have to spend what is needed," he declares.

The advertising budget for 1953 was around $600,000 with a gross volume of approximately $20,000,000. And in 1947, when the advertising budget was close to a quarter of a million dollars, the gross volume was about $12,000,000. Everything possible in the way of discounts, "push money" and advertising allowances is obtained from suppliers.

Advertising to Doc Webb means several things. It means first a heavy schedule of full-page and double-spread ads in the local newspapers; it means five hundred roadside signs extending as far north as Knoxville, where Doc used to live; it means a cross-country tour for the beauteous Poster Girls in their specially designed bus; it means entertainment of many kinds at Webb's during business hours, either on the main floor, or on a parking lot. There are other things, too, such as radio and TV time, but Doc's major confidence is in black-and-white newspaper advertising with emphasis on the big black letters and figures that announce his bargains.

Many things are conceived by Doc Webb or his staff to keep traffic flowing. There is the "Feudin' N' Fightin' Sale" which is touched off annually by departure of General Manager Willis on vacation. Webb then takes big newspaper space to advise his customers that while the tightwad Willis is away, he, the generous Doc Webb, is going to provide some real bargains. And he does, with clerks in hillbilly attire, and with "mountain" entertainment on the stage set up in the drug department. Since Webb is from Tennessee and Willis from South Carolina, the hillbilly motif is a natural, and huge crowds throng the aisles. Of course when Willis comes back from his vacation, he starts writing ads which offer even better bargains than Webb, so the sale is extended to the advantage of both the store and the customers.

Another summer special is the managers' sale, in which the various store managers try to outdo each other in the matter of bargains. Entertainers perform five times daily during this period. Sometimes there is a topsy-turvy day, in which the drug department may sell avocados, the cosmetic department may feature gallon cans of motor oil, and the bakery may offer hardware items.

The big stage on the main floor near the fountain has been the scene of many an unusual event. A reptile expert has milked rattlesnakes of their venom for the entertainment of the patrons; aerial acts have been performed; boxing matches have been staged; magicians have done their stuff.

On the No. 1 parking lot, just outside, there have been free elephant rides; clowns have cavorted; people have been shot from cannons; lion acts have been staged. Here, too, Doc Webb has invited his customers to participate in a "Country Fair," with exhibits of hobbies, crafts and foods—and the exhibitors were invited to sell their cakes, their bedspreads or whatever, even when they were competing with merchandise in Doc Webb's own stores.

Doc has brought to St. Petersburg such attractions as the Scotch Kilties Band, Sam Snyder's Water Follies, the Oklahoma Wranglers, recording artists from the Eddie Arnold show, and numerous groups of internationally known circus entertainers. If he doesn't offer this entertainment free, he underwrites it to the extent that admission prices are a fraction of their normal size. For example, he charged off as advertising in 1954 the sum of $20,000 which it cost him to subsidize the Water Follies on his parking lot. Tickets were a dollar, compared to the usual $3.50 or more.

Webb does things in a big way, always. In October of 1953, on the occasion of the store's twenty-eighth anniversary, a twenty-eight-foot-long cake was proudly built up on tables in the thousand-seat roof garden, which was still under construction. The night before the public was to participate in the big party, gallons of icing were spread over the mammoth cake. Also that night, a tropical storm blew in and whipped roofing gravel onto the icing. "We had to get down early, scrape all the gravel and icing off that mile-long cake and pour on new icing while ten thousand people milled around waiting for their cake and orange juice," a veteran employee recalls with a slight shudder.

Webb says almost solemnly that two miracles have occurred at Webb's City in recent years "even though we may not be the best of Christians."

"Right after the war when we were expanding faster than we could borrow money, we just about came to the end of our rope. Our newest building program was well along, but we had stretched our finances too far. I told Willis that we had to have $40,000 if we were going to pull out of the hole, and we were actually praying for divine help when we went home from the store one night.

"In the next morning's mail was a check for almost exactly the amount we needed from the U.S. Treasury. We had been trying to get a refund on taxes and we thought that this $40,000 had been returned to us from the Internal Revenue people. Actually, it turned out that the check had been mailed to us by mistake, and we had to pay it back with interest. But we used the money at the time for our building and it was four years before we had to pay it back, and we could afford to do it then. That has always seemed like a miracle to me.

"The other was a different sort of miracle. Webb's ran a highly profitable liquor store for many years—in fact it grew to a place where it had a $2,000,000 gross volume and was providing about half of our gross profits a few years after the war.

"Then I got to thinking that we were having to fire some of our people because they were drinking, and yet we were tempting them to drink with our liquor store. I didn't think that was fair and I could tell our employees didn't think it was right, so I decided to eliminate the liquor store. We did cut it out and here's the miracle —we had a bigger volume of business in Webb's City the next year and our net profits were $75,000 greater than they were when we sold liquor.

"I have always had a feeling that gold shouldn't be the master in any business, and I thought we ought to get out of the liquor business before it got too strong a hold on us. Some of our people didn't agree at the time; they felt that sale of liquor was legal and that there was nothing wrong with our liquor store. But I couldn't hear and read about people getting in trouble because they had been drinking and still feel right about selling it. And we're better off today for being out of that business. A store's principles are just like a person's; they've got to be good or you'll go down. . . ."

Some analysts have tried to figure that Doc Webb's success hinges largely on the fact that St. Petersburg is populated by a bigger-than-average number of oldsters who are looking for an interesting place to spend their pension money. Doc scoffs at this idea, though he is proud that "a lot of people with small incomes are able to live well because they shop at Webb's."

"I just run a fundamentally sound business, and I could do it just as well in Egypt or Paris if the state would let me operate without interference [Webb declares]. The United States is the last country where there is free enterprise, and it's a battle to have it here because of the chain stores and the fair trade laws.

"But I've whipped 'em on prices and I've whipped 'em on this fair trade thing, though it has cost me a quarter of a million dollars in seventeen years of fighting. It's nobody's business what I sell an item for after I buy it, and I'm going to keep giving my customers the lowest prices they can find anywhere."

Webb says he would never be interested in adding another "drugstore" in another city. All his efforts have gone into the St. Petersburg operation and his goal is to keep it expanding.

"We definitely plan to be bigger every year than we were the year before [he says]. There has never been a day in twenty-nine years that the hammers haven't been ringing somewhere to improve Webb's or make it bigger. I'm sorry about just one thing, and that is that I didn't put our various stores on wheels so they could be rearranged easier. We are always moving around and expanding these units. . . ."

At the moment he was saying this, some of his supervisors were going over plans for a $50,000 fountain installation. Doc had decided that the old arrangement consisting of a 160-foot-long soda fountain (they call it the world's longest) was inefficient. It was built with stools, backed up by booths to which customers could take their plates and drinks. The new scalloped counter installation was designed to do away with the booths, and provide counter service for all customers.

"We just created a lot of sightseers with those old booths," Doc Webb observed. "We need to keep the traffic moving."

Index